MARSHALL McLUHAN AND NORTHROP FRYE

Apocalypse and Alchemy

Marshall McLuhan and Northrop Frye are two of Canada's central cultural figures – colleagues and rivals whose careers unfolded in curious harmony even as their intellectual engagement was antagonistic. Poet, novelist, essayist, and philosopher B.W. Powe, who studied with both of these formidable and influential intellectuals, presents an exploration of their lives and work in *Marshall McLuhan and Northrop Frye: Apocalypse and Alchemy.*

Powe considers the existence of a unique visionary tradition of Canadian humanism and argues that McLuhan and Frye represent fraught but complementary approaches to the study of literature and to the broader engagement with culture. Examining their eloquent but often acid responses to each other, Powe exposes the scholarly controversies and personal conflicts that erupted between them, and notably the great commonalities in their writing and biographies. Using interviews, letters, notebooks, and their published texts, Powe offers a new alchemy of their thought, in which he combines the philosophical hallmarks of McLuhan's "The medium is the message" and Frye's "the great code."

B.W. POWE is an associate professor and the Creative Writing Program coordinator in the Department of English at York University.

Marshall McLuhan and Northrop Frye

Apocalypse and Alchemy

B.W. POWE

UNIVERSITY OF TORONTO PRESS
Toronto Buffalo London

© University of Toronto Press 2014
Toronto Buffalo London
www.utppublishing.com

ISBN 978-1-4426-4811-1 (cloth)
ISBN 978-1-4426-1616-5 (paper)

Library and Archives Canada Cataloguing in Publication

Powe, B. W. (Bruce W.), 1955–, author
Marshall McLuhan and Northrop Frye : apocalypse and alchemy / B.W. Powe.

Includes bibliographical references and index.
ISBN 978-1-4426-4811-1 (bound).—ISBN 978-1-4426-1616-5 (pbk.)

1. McLuhan, Marshall, 1911–1980. 2. Frye, Northrop, 1912–1991. 3. McLuhan, Marshall, 1911–1980—Criticism and interpretation. 4. Frye, Northrop, 1912–1991—Criticism and interpretation. 5. Mass media specialists—Canada—Biography. 6. Critics—Canada—Biography. 7. Mass media and culture. 8. Criticism. 9. Humanism.
I. Title. II. Title: Apocalypse and alchemy.

P92.5.M3P69   2014 302.23092   C2013-908759-1

University of Toronto Press acknowledges the financial assistance to its publishing program of the Canada Council for the Arts and the Ontario Arts Council.

 Canada Council **Conseil des Arts**
for the Arts   du Canada

This book has been published with the help of a grant from the Canadian Federation for the Humanities and Social Sciences, through the Awards to Scholarly Publications Program, using funds provided by the Social Sciences and Humanities Research Council of Canada.

University of Toronto Press acknowledges the financial support of the Government of Canada through the Canada Book Fund for its publishing activities.

For Paul Francis Earley (1957–2010)
Because he loved ideas
For Jeremy Earley
Because he loves music
For Kathleen Powe-Earley
Because she is brave

Contents

Acknowledgments ix

Prologue: The Juncture of Marshall McLuhan
and Northrop Frye in 1946   3

1 Intentions and Overview: Apocalypse and Alchemy
in McLuhan and Frye   11

2 Presences and Signatures: These Figures in Their Ground   55

3 The Critical Conflict between McLuhan and Frye   110

4 The Harmonies in Two Seers: Orchestrations
and Complementarities   169

5 Alchemy: Synergy in the Thinking of McLuhan and Frye   230

6 The Lessons of Two Teachers: Guidance and Signs   276

Notes   287

Bibliography   315

Index   337

Acknowledgments

I wish to thank the following people for their advice and influence on this book: Professors Ian Balfour, Susan Warwick, and Marcus Boon; also David Staines, Janine Marchessault, and Mauro Buccheri. Many other colleagues contributed to my research into this material: I thank in particular Dr Eric McLuhan and Dr Robert D. Denham, who illuminated and confirmed many essential details and provided me with access to the archival sources that proved to be pivotal in my explorations into the complexities of the Marshall McLuhan and Northrop Frye matrix. My thanks too to Mrs Corinne McLuhan for the permission given years ago to interview her and to quote from her husband's books and letters. My thanks to the Frye Archives for the same permission. Thank you to Eric McLuhan, Robert Denham, Janine Marchessault, and Michael McLuhan for their assistance. The majority of quotations in this book are taken from works in the public domain. My editor at the University of Toronto Press, Siobhan McMenemy, saw this manuscript through the long process of readings and revisions. I am indebted to the notes and recommendations made by all those involved with the venerable press. I also appreciate the work of copyeditor Barbie Halaby and project manager Mae Lum.

Many others supported and encouraged the work. It is important to thank Julia Creet, Art Redding, Thomas Loebel, and Dean Robert Drummond. I am also deeply indebted to the advice of Peter Paolucci on computer technicalities and to Christopher Innes and Susan Swan, who listened while I expanded on some of the ideas contained herein. My students in the English department at York University inspired many of the ideas I have proposed in this book. Prominent among these students have been Karl Leschinsky, Monica Krawczyk, Sabrina Lightstone, Jason Buccheri, Pedro Jacobetty, Joseph Glover, Lai-Tze Fan, Lisa

Polivka, Adebe DeRango-Adem, Roxanne Mastromatteo, Joshua Moore, John Cronin, Oliver Jones, Tonya Del Sole, Ernest Reid, and especially Karim Wissa. The research, however, is mine; all misunderstandings and misreading (errors and oversights) are my own.

Other readers outside the York community, or outside academia, also contributed ideas and suggestions: these include Professor Elena Lamberti, Professor Derrick de Kerckhove, R. Murray Schafer, Dr Robert K. Logan, Cristina Miranda de Almeida, Matteo Ciastellardi, Raven Murphy, Charlene Jones, Carol Sill and James K-M, Edward Lemond, Frank Zingrone, Harold Bloom, and George Steiner. Doug Coupland and Philip Marchand made many useful observations which I've absorbed into the arguments and reflections here. The late Donald Theall provided important and stimulating insights. The following authors illuminated thoughts and provided sentences for me to sample and revise: J.S. Porter, Frances Yates, George Steiner (again), Oliver Sacks, Anne Carson, Joyce Carey, Simone Weil, Norman O. Brown, Richard Tarnas, and those from innumerable poems and works of fiction that I cannot hope to list here. If I referred to everyone and every text that influenced or shaped a sentence or thought, then my note pages would be longer than the arguments in this book.

My deepest thanks to the administrators at IN3, Universtat Oberta de Catalunya in Barcelona, Spain, where I worked on the final versions of this manuscript. Dr Josep Lladós Masllorens and Montserrat Mir Buxalleu were instrumental in giving me a quiet place to work. I owe much to the Bibliotecha Virtual, directed by Neus Milán Llorente, for tracking down works I needed for research purposes. Many doctoral students at IN3 were influences on the movements of my writing.

I owe a special debt to my family. My children, Kate and Tom, put up with the long hours it took to research and write. They certainly experienced much neglect during that time. For their love and support I offer my loving thanks. My father, Bruce Allen Powe, was generous with his time and comments. My partner, Maria Auxiliadora Sánchez Ledesma, gave good advice on the last stages of the manuscript. My sister Kathleen and my nephew Jeremy offered unwavering support and affection. My brother-in-law Paul Earley also made himself available for commentary. He died before he could see the finished work. Rest in peace, Paul.

Pages from this work were aired at different events in many locales. Excerpts have been published in journals. I spoke on the McLuhan-Frye matrix at the Vanier College Canadian Culture and History Speaking Series at York University in February 2010. I gave keynote lectures on the themes of this book at the Northrop Frye Festival in Moncton in April 2011 and then at the McLuhan Galaxy gathering in Barcelona, Spain, at the University of Catalunya in May of that year. I spoke on Marshall McLuhan at the Ottawa International Festival of Authors in October 2011. Portions of these studies were published in the following journals: "Magnetic City Alchemy" in *English Studies in Canada* 36, 2–3 (June/September 2010); "Apocalypse and Alchemy" in *International Journal of McLuhan Studies* 1 (2011); and "Presences: Signatures and Evocations" in *Ellipse* 87–88 (2012). I'm indebted to the organizers of the events and to the editors of the journals.

I have been tempted many times over the seven years it took to write this book to say enough of the homage to mentors. It seems I have done this too much in my life. (This book is about male teachers, but what about all the mothering figures? The female teachers?) Then it occurs to me again how it is right and true to appreciate and love these paths, while I move forward: other acknowledgments are to come.

The Wise Perceive Imminent Events

The gods perceive future events, mortals present ones, and
the wise perceive those that are imminent.
—Philostratus, *Life of Apollonius of Tyana VIII.7*

Men have knowledge of the present.
As for the future, the gods know it,
alone and fully enlightened.
But for matters on the verge of occurring, things that
are imminent,
these the wise perceive. Sometimes,

when they are deep in study, their hearing
is convulsed. The veiled hum of imminent events
approaches. And they listen rapt. Meanwhile,
out on the street, the people hear nothing.

—C.P. Cavafy

Whatever the soul does, it does through agents.

—Meister Eckhart

Prologue: The Juncture of Marshall McLuhan and Northrop Frye in 1946

They met in Toronto in 1946. H. Marshall McLuhan, fresh from Assumption College and Saint Louis University, had just been hired at the University of Toronto in the Department of English. H. Northrop Frye had been an associate professor in that department since the late 1930s. *Fearful Symmetry*, Frye's canon-changing study of William Blake, was about to be published. McLuhan's first book, *The Mechanical Bride: The Folklore of Industrial Man*, would be published in five years. Frye was about to become a public critic of impressive influence. McLuhan's stardom was to come in the 1960s. Their meeting took place at a faculty gathering in Victoria College on the campus of the University of Toronto. It was a moment of a rare convergence.

One came from Canada's western provinces (Edmonton, Alberta). One had come from the east coast (Moncton, New Brunswick). They encountered one another in the centre of Canada, in the city – of Toronto – the country's *omphalos*. An *omphalos* is the name philosophers give to an intellectual-spiritual centre, a site of sacred and turbulent power. They met one year after the end of the Second World War. It was almost the midpoint of the twentieth century. The Cold War was beginning.

They were introduced to one another (by whom?) at a social occasion, a welcoming to new faculty members. The two men shared spiritual pathways. McLuhan was a convert to Catholicism, but he had been born into a Methodist-Baptist family. Frye had been born into the Methodist heritage too, but he had left his fundamentalist-literalist background to become for a time an itinerant United Church minister. He was once asked what his religious vocation brought to his teaching: "I marry and bury students," he quipped.[1] But his sense that writing and teaching were about elevations of the soul never left him. McLuhan was asked what his spiritual hope might be: "Our only hope is apocalypse," he said;[2] by this he surely meant revelation and trust: new worlds will come. The two men would be colleagues in the Department of English at the University of Toronto for the next thirty-four years.

I like to imagine their first conversation. Was it about Blake? Perhaps it was about James Joyce. They shared a passion for these epoch-turning authors: Blake, an apogee figure of Romanticism; Joyce, a pioneer of Modernism. Perhaps McLuhan and Frye discussed their educational paths in the 1930s. Frye had gone to Oxford; his MA work was guided by Edmund Blunden. McLuhan went to Cambridge to be a candidate for a PhD; his doctorate was guided by Muriel C. Bradbrook, a noted Shakespearean scholar. Oxford, Cambridge (or "Oxbridge," so Virginia Woolf liked to call a conjunction of the two illustrious universities[3]): one was the royalist university of John Ruskin, Walter Pater, Oscar Wilde, and W.H. Auden, among many – a place sometimes called the school for aesthetes; the other was the revolutionary college, the school that sided with Oliver Cromwell during the Civil War. When McLuhan arrived at Cambridge, the university had on its faculty I.A. Richards, Q.D. and F.R. Leavis, and Ludwig Wittgenstein. McLuhan and Frye were mere kilometres away from one another in their years of learning, of being shaped by study and mentors.

They must have been amused – or mystified? – by their names. Mars Shall Clue; North Frye (his name had hot and cold in it). Each with the same first name initial: H. Frye's first name was Herman, McLuhan's – Herbert. "The name of a man is a numbing blow from which he never recovers," McLuhan would say later.[4] They were one year apart in their birthdates: 1911 for McLuhan, 1912 for Frye. Both were born in July; one week separated their birthdays (Frye on the fourteenth of the month, McLuhan on the twenty-first). Both Cancers, though I know this recognition would not have passed through their minds. They were wildly ambitious, English professors whose visionary gleam would take them far beyond their specialized domains.

In a fit of premonitory inspiration, the university hiring committees had summoned the two men who would become the most formidable and influential intellectual-seers that Canada had yet produced. Their offices would be close by. They attended departmental meetings, participated in curricula discussions, shared students, debated points of theory and observation, riffed in conversation, muttered diatribes in private talk and some lectures, in letters and notebooks. Above all they read and reread the other. They would absorb the other's genius and intensities and use them to fire up their probes and inquiries.

I like to think that at their first meeting the sparks of brilliance between them were palpable. They may have thought: here was someone in Toronto, in the tweedy halls of the university, who could match their inner fire, their proclamations to themselves of the original flame. Frye declared in his journal (circa the mid-1970s), "I had genius. No one else in the field known to me had quite that."[5] McLuhan wrote in two letters to his mother, Elsie, (on 12 April 1936 and on 28 June 1936) that "My life in Canada will be a continual discontent. My task as a teacher will be to shake others from their complacency" and that he wanted to "tear the hide right off Canada some day and rub salt in it."[6] Did each man size up the other? Both must have intuited: this is a worthy opponent. All reports of their first meeting are sketchy. The intimations are that the first encounter was cordial. Still they were good readers of atmospheres. Here was another person who had considerable presence.

McLuhan and Frye crossed one another's paths that day. They would do so again on the wooded campus pathways. They were to cross each other in their ideas and perceptions. When two such powerfully charismatic spirits converge, the moment is a crossroads – it is a juncture, an apocalyptic instant. Can I prove that they instantly recognized the presence of intellectual and spiritual fire in one another? No, but I can imagine what was happening: Frye spent a lifetime teaching that we recreate when we read and reread (all rereading is revisionary); McLuhan teaches that every moment thrives with influences and effects: all times are etched in the here and now.

Two souls had met. A story had begun. Henceforth what they lived would be what they had dreamed for themselves: epic quests of discovery, intellectual journeys that would alter the spirit of their age and the one to come. They would hunt for media laws and codes of the imagination. They would be obsessive in their need to find unities and patterns. At stake? Nothing less than whole vision. Nothing less than breakthroughs into conditions of intensified consciousness. They would be more than teachers or critics: they would be indispensable guides – to the new environment of electronic super-Nature, to the super-structure of our imaginations incarnated in literature.

At this first juncture McLuhan and Frye might have observed the other jot down an idea on a torn piece of paper. McLuhan was left-handed, Frye right-handed; complementary patterns again. Epiphanies came quickly to them. "These fragments I have shored against my ruins,"

T.S. Eliot wrote in "The Waste Land" (1922),[7] a poem in pieces, each jigsaw line like an epiphany: they would both place it on their course reading lists. (In 1946 Eliot was a cutting-edge poet, not yet canonic: his Nobel Prize would come in 1948.) Neither McLuhan nor Frye could affably offer a car lift home because neither had – nor would ever have – their driving licences. Their wives, Corinne and Helen, did most of the driving for them. (Were these two formidable women present that day? They would have instrumental roles in their husbands' lives; their stories need to be told too.) The two enjoyed witticisms and puns, though McLuhan's need to pun bordered on the compulsive. Did he troop out one of his innumerable jokes to see if the shy Frye would grin or laugh outright? McLuhan flourished in public gatherings: conversation was invariably a springboard for an improvisation on his latest ideas. His verbal riffing was known to provoke his colleagues into astonished or angry reactions or paralyse his listeners into confounded silence. Frye was sensitive to the jostle of crowds, tending towards a polite reserve. The mood in the college greeting room that day was no doubt smoky. McLuhan favoured cigars; Frye didn't smoke. Both liked to drink: Frye would share a beer with colleagues and students; McLuhan drank just about anything. They may have quoted lines of poetry. McLuhan and Frye had formidable memories and could reel off lines from Shakespeare, Milton, Blake, Coleridge, Pound, and Eliot.

Let me digress: I will propose – and quickly paraphrase – what McLuhan and Frye would have been bringing to this juncture of 1946 in the small city of Toronto, a sort of nowhere at that time in the North American grid. McLuhan and Frye had revelations early, enough to stock several lifetimes of perceptions and insights. These are the McLuhan epiphanies I will be engaging here: all things connect, and our inventions, like Nature herself, mould us. Every human artefact (technologies, or media) influence us in a perpetual mutuality. These glosses are part of the meaning of his most famous aphorism, "The medium is the message." Hence for McLuhan there is almost no need to invent anything in our imaginations: all we need do is reveal the world, in its extravagant metamorphoses. But we have decisively altered the cosmos with the advent of super-Nature, electric technology. There is no retreating from this. Yes, we shape our world with technology, but our technologies in turn reshape us. Bewilderingly, we are becoming post-alphabetic creatures in a phase of hyper-Darwinian acceleration. The results of this are massive; it will take generations to truly sense and appraise them. Thus the urgency of the seer: we must wake up or sleepwalk ourselves into auto-destructiveness.[8]

While McLuhan was years away from announcing these breakthrough thoughts, we know they were incubating in his fertile mind. His early essays and letters confirm that he was beginning to move towards the restless realization that the twentieth century was an apogee time, a breach time. His classroom lectures and improvisations to puzzled students had already skittered away from prescribed reading lists to the effects of radio and that startling new technology, television.

Frye had been working on *Fearful Symmetry* for a decade. His readings of Blake had led to epiphanies: the imagination has an order, and this order is best perceived through poetry. Humankind is a stranger in an alienated, corrosive universe; without the imagination, without art, we would perish in meaninglessness and deceit; fear and brutality would overpower our ideals. But once we begin the process of deep reading in literary texts, we begin to perceive unities, enduring patterns (types). All texts interpenetrate, forming one great text that is the way the human spirit fuses with the great Spirit of creation. Literature is the educated ground for the imagination itself. The sentences and poetic lines of literature are shaping us, reforming and clarifying our minds, impelling us towards an epic revision of our souls. In books there is the Great Code at work (the phrase, significantly, is Blake's), which is the story of our awakening identity, our rising to the singular question, "Who am I?" The code seeks to overcome a world that often appears ominously chaotic, satanically cruel. We are searching for identity when we read for the keys that will open the Great Code, inside the illuminating Book that literature forges. The dreamland of literary work is the dream that awakens us to our higher selves.

To both McLuhan and Frye, reading is a vocation – a calling forth. They wanted us to be inspired readers with the exalted mission to elevate ourselves to wider states of consciousness, concentrated awareness: the mind abuzz with possibility. They divided over what needed to be urgently read. To Frye, the alphabetic text was primary, the ground of all other recognitions. Train the mind, educate the imagination, and we would begin to see the pattern in books; then turn that radical attentiveness outward to transform the world. To McLuhan, there were two consequent and simultaneous texts: the Book of Nature (the first creation) and then the Hyper-Text of super-Nature (the extension of creation).

The alphabetic text was one of many inventions, not necessarily primary. There were codes in numbers, music, visual art, architecture, in cinema, radio, telephones, and TV.

At their first meeting at Victoria College, I doubt if their looming clash was apparent in any way. If they talked of Blake, or of Joyce, of *The Marriage of Heaven and Hell* or *Finnegans Wake*, it might have been simply to say they delighted in the pleasure of difficult works. But they must have communicated that for them the study of literature was not merely a career in a tenured security net or a quiet indulgence or a leisured contemplation of obscure works or an epicurean revelling in the sensuality of sentences. Reading (so I will amplify in these pages) was the return of a golden age, restoration of the original Adamic perception – vision, imagination, apocalypse, prophecy, in the garden of the mind and senses. They would provide codes for inspiration; and inspiration and influence are closely allied. Reading books, reading the world, would move us from waking up to awakenings; we would learn to rise to revelation.

Let us move ahead from 1946 to the 1960s and 1970s when McLuhan and Frye were at the height of their fame. McLuhan had become a joke on Rowan and Martin's frenetic TV show, *Laugh-In*: in 1968 Henry Gibson would say on that show, "Marshall McLuhan – what are ya doin'?" On the University of Toronto campus this piece of doggerel verse about Frye was published in a local student paper: "Norrie Frye – what a guy / He's read more books / Than you and I."

McLuhan and Frye would be at odds by then. The congenial first meeting in 1946 eventually gave way to a trenchant public conflict (agon). I posit that this clash is the central Canadian visionary dynamism. McLuhan opposed literary specialization – in fact, any fragmenting specialization whatsoever. "The specialist is one who never makes small mistakes while moving toward the grand fallacy," he announced in *The Book of Probes* (2003).[9] Frye dismissed media studies. "Global village my ass," he wrote in his *Notebooks*.[10] To McLuhan, Frye had become a solitary heretic whose grandiose theoretical archetypes were frozen in unusable pictorial stasis. Frye was the prototypical bookworm, unaware of the effects of the technological shifts in the world, periodically and predictably censorious about the electronic revolution. To Frye, McLuhan had become the media guru, the apostle of electric junk, avatar of corporate interests, betrayer of the printed word, a sacrificial figure to the combustions of celebrity.

But the initial cordiality, the welcome at that Victoria College gathering, would sometimes reappear in their public statements of those subsequent decades. In 1967, when McLuhan was giving the Marfleet Lectures at Convocation Hall on the University of Toronto campus, he digressed to call Frye "extraordinary, with his frontiersmanship between the world of literature and the unconscious." Frye had a "world position, and it is very much a frontier activity."[11] To be on the frontier means to be an explorer. Explorers do not take the map for the territory. Frontiers are stark places of identity-shifting originality. People on frontiers make a pact with revelation: whatever is hidden or overlooked, buried or forgotten must be disclosed. Frontiers can be badlands, harsh and unforgiving (under the wilderness stones, poisonous snakes curl up, waiting to strike); but these edge-sites have their codes and signs. In 1980 Frye called McLuhan a great "improviser," the best he ever heard.[12] (I note that Frye's praise came after McLuhan's death in 1980). In an extensive interview with David Cayley, published posthumously in 1992, Frye inextricably linked himself with Harold Innis and McLuhan in the Toronto School of Communication Theory.[13]

George Steiner commented on their entwined and yet complicated relationship over their thirty-four years of close proximity when he wittily described his first meeting with Frye and McLuhan in the early 1970s:

> Many years ago, one evening in Massey College, I sat with Robertson Davies, Norrie Frye, Kathleen Coburn (the world's greatest Coleridge scholar), when in walked a very much younger Marshall McLuhan. Astounded (I had not met him yet), and very much without thinking, I turned to Professor Frye, and said, "There's Marshall McLuhan." I cannot hope to reproduce the air of sardonic melancholy which immediately invaded Norrie's features. He had a long look, and said, "So the man alleges."[14]

In the same recollection, Steiner asserts how the University of Toronto was in part "the absolute centre for the study of Letters and Humanities, possibly in the world," in part because of the presences of McLuhan and Frye. Steiner refers here to the idealized form of the university that the two visionaries sought to initiate: the university could become a School of Being and Becoming. This would make a school more than a remote Kafkaesque castle or a bureaucratic and claustrophobic labyrinth: it meant that a centre like the University of Toronto could be a powerful vortex of prophetic knowledge – a *paideuma*, Alexandria reborn, where charges and streams of thought and poetics meld and ripple outwards, carrying illumination and transformation and vision and inspiration into our society and culture.

From their first meeting would come decades of proposals and controversies. Toronto was to become an intersection of their energies in the burgeoning global theatre. Contrary positions would enrich their visionary dynamism.

Years after their deaths (McLuhan on New Year's Eve, 1980, Frye in 1991), their meetings and engagements had been honoured in the geography and cultural symbolism of their city. Their names were encoded by Toronto city planners on the university campus. There is Marshall McLuhan Way, once just called Saint Joseph Street, a street running east and west (or west and east, depending on your entry point): there is Northrop Frye Hall, a building that straddles the north-south mapping of the city's circle at Queen's Park. This junction is our *axis mundi*, a meeting of two intellectual and spiritual streams, the crossing enshrined in raucous streets. Their conjunction – and their differences – are visible in the naming.

The naming of a street and a building can guide us and move us. It helps us to remember twin geniuses and their invaluable creation of a legacy of insight and vision. McLuhan and Frye are with us in spirit, when we walk or drive down these city streets. From 1946 on, after their first meeting, they entered the sphere of converging apocalyptic thought. They heard eternity's footsteps on Toronto's Philosopher's Walk. We need the two for our imaginations, for our perceptions: their conflict brings recognitions of how complementarities govern dynamism; they are central to the Canadian soul – and I will argue to the global theatre (which we should no doubt now call the global pulsing membrane) – in their bold originalities. Through their writings and teachings they transformed generations of students and readers. The two met and created an essential dialogue. Their debates persist, in often unacknowledged ways, suffusing twenty-first-century culture.

They continue to summon us and to mentor us.

They were my teachers.

The sparks of their meetings enflame us.

1
Intentions and Overview: Apocalypse and Alchemy in McLuhan and Frye

At the Edge of Intensified Consciousness

What brought Marshall McLuhan and Northrop Frye together in Toronto in 1946? What moved them into controversial engagements for the next decades? What drew them to this centre in the country? What inspired them to recognize that Toronto could be a Magnetic City, an epicentre for awareness? What made both of them wake up and stir to the ideas of apocalyptic understanding? What brought them to the threshold of the idea that we could reverse our fall into ignorance and destructiveness and rise into illumination and awakenings?

What happens if we view them together, with their destinies linked? Do we truly know their stories, their shared history? Can we see yet how they profoundly incited and influenced one another? What would be the result of melding their signature ideas of "the medium is the message" with the Great Code Story? Is there the possibility of a McLuhan-Frye alchemy, a mixing of their chemical traces and energies? What happens if we let the two together become catalysts for a new agency of thought, a code of inspiration and awareness?

I argue here that Marshall McLuhan and Northrop Frye initiated a visionary-apocalyptic tradition in Canadian letters. It is an original tradition, seminal to understanding the uniqueness of the Canadian spirit. Their range of thought, the depth of their perceptions and speculations, the complexity of their engagements, the impact of their writings, the drama of their ideas, the effects of their intensities of insight and foresight are still being attacked, absorbed, debated, and adapted by critics, philosophers, writers, and teachers. McLuhan and Frye form an exciting alternative visionary protocol to other (European-based) theoretical propositions, a distinct intellectual re-creative stance. They were an audacious pair. So compressed and allusive, provocative and inspirational is their work that I will say that they are our most necessary literary figures. Certainly, they continue to be among the most influential authors in what I call the Canadian sublime, the essential literary and intellectual tradition emerging through our writers and artists, thinkers and poet-philosophers.

I submit that McLuhan and Frye are primary because they are prophetic. The prophetic possibility means the charged capacity to make writings and thought perpetually relevant now, in a quickening of interpretation and re-creation. In ways I will explore, they are permanently controversial. There is a pressing, vital challenge at the core of their work that compels us to lift ourselves and respond. They knew controversy brings frictions; friction yields to more ideas, deeper perception.

Philosophers and critics (those who have come after deconstruction) often struggle to locate the two in a European or American context. I propose something more robust and radical for them and from them: they have authored themselves, creating a new line – subtly, insistently part of the new that is Canadian and yet (paradoxically) universal. They are their own tradition. While well-schooled in Western literary traditions and what I will call the ancient wisdom, they paid almost no heed to what was emerging in European intellectual circles in the 1960s on. One of their boldest acts is to put communications (media, literary studies), rather than ideology, at the heart of their thought. They initiate and ignite: their conjunction features a decisive turning away from an enslavement to others' systems of thought in order to seek their own sources of perceptions and ideas, in a championing of poetics.

Frye wanted to bring on an apocalypse of recognition through the cultivation of the educated imagination. His *Notebooks* reveal his gift for aphorism and maxims, and yet he preferred to write a prose known for its chastened eloquence. Frye was wary of media attention, choosing to keep mostly solitary, preserving the sometimes blasphemous complexities and ironies of his thought in literary texts. McLuhan wanted to bring on the apocalypse of perception through public performance and exaggerated pronouncements. He damned prudence in his thought and jammed onward into celebrity. His early essays reveal his talent for critical prose, but he preferred the quickness and dazzle of the aphorism. He gave us bursts of thinking, the exuberance of his iconoclasm. At crossroads ahead they appear, turning towards us. By being ahead of us they ask us to move forward.

I intend to recast McLuhan and Frye, these University of Toronto counterparts, as pivotal apocalyptics. Prophecy and apocalypse were part of their literary and educational mission: to awaken people's minds, to sharpen awareness, to make more meaning, to reveal structures and forms, to move us to higher states of concentration and consciousness, to bring epiphanies, to show us patterns and sources, to clear new paths of perception and knowledge, to seize us and solace us with inspirations and the company of their thoughts. By altering readers' minds, and students' minds, they entered their age and altered it. I find an unapologetic humanism in their work. In the electronic media saga that is our second Nature and second creation – when time/space have been collapsed and catapulted into a mesmerizing moment, where users of iPads and tablets have been granted access to storage and retrieval on a scale unrecognizable to previous generations, through the apparently incoherent jumble of literary texts and critical methods, when literature itself threatens to become the rarefied obsession of an indentured elite – McLuhan and Frye wrote and taught to show how we each have perceptive gifts, the radical genius, to recognize in ourselves an enlightened humanity. They embraced multiform aims that clashed at times and yet were implicitly harmonious in their grand visions of redemption and grace. McLuhan and Frye are memorable mythmakers at the centre of our literature and our imagination, larger and more daring than the majority of their contemporaries or their followers.

McLuhan and Frye are endlessly, sometimes bewilderingly, fascinating to me because of their intellectual gifts, their innumerable controversies, their own contradictory personalities, and the enormous, heroic ambitions they held for their ideas and propositions. Mostly conventional in their styles of living – hardly high Romantics in reckless adventuring or hot-headed shenanigans – they often stayed off the grid, as it were, in their private ways, devoted to family and to teaching. Nevertheless, they still scourge us with the urging to expand our minds. This is what I intend to show here. I say "scourge" because their accomplishments, in books, in propositions, are matchlessly fit for continuing contentions. There can be no resolution of the controversies they initiated. This is a good thing. You should be wary of being understood too easily. McLuhan and Frye hungered to leave lasting marks on their time and place. And their intellectual, perceptual marks on our minds and imaginations in Canada are indelible signatures of our culture. These signs and signatures reward attention. We are still learning how to read them. Thus the necessity of an appreciation of the two together.

Meditations on Breakdown and Breakthrough

One of my primary intentions is to reflect on the overt and sometimes cloaked conflict between McLuhan and Frye. This is their agon. An agon is strife, conflict, competition, antagonism. It is a way of struggling with ideas and accomplishments that must lead to both clash and breakthrough. Sometimes the visionary must break down the forms and conditioning of his or her antagonist to usher in the new for him- or herself. "Without Contraries is no progression," William Blake said in *The Marriage of Heaven and Hell* (1790).[1] An agon is a complementary struggle; it is pivotal to the antagonists, who recognize the other to be equal to their ideas and experience. An agon is a striving for understanding and for the comprehension of your destiny. We find in Luke 13:24 this vivid and admonishing description of that striving: "Strive to enter in at the strait gate: for many, I say unto you, will seek to enter in, and shall not be able." An agon, therefore, is a contest, a race. This is invoked in Hebrews 12:1: "... and let us run with patience the race that is set before us." The contestants, the contraries, are not polarized opposites; they are part of a yin and yang structure in which their energies are set in a resounding drama and pattern of echo and reflection. All contrarians need the other. Their wrangling requires faithful engagement, authentic struggle.

Contraries set up struggles towards awareness. Blake's aphorism on progression implies this is how humanity learns and evolves. His poetics obviously inform Frye's work, from Frye's canon-changing first critical book, *Fearful Symmetry* (1947), to the essay published just after his death, *The Double Vision* (1991; the title taken from Blake's 1802 letter to Thomas Butts). Blake also informs McLuhan's understanding of the role of states of mind, of perception, in shaping our awareness of volatile technological environments.

Conflicts and contraries are defined by the strain to differentiate and individualize. But an agon depends on the intensity of the rivalry and on a mutual recognition of the supreme value of the encounter. The breakdown of an argument may lead to a breakthrough in perception and the quixotic recognition of a unity in the striving: the contest finally links us, in our hunger to know destinies and truths.

Agons are about inspiration and imperatives. Antagonisms, even if amiable on the surface, extend intellectual reach, focus dialogue, extend interpretation, provoke polemics, compel attention and impel direction, start re-creations, make things new. Out of such clashes come followers and accusers. An agon is an allegoric narrative structure which implies a subtextual quest to define and refine a singular self. Agon is a romance form, an expression of the mystical quest for identity. Frye reflects on the quest-conflict structure in this supremely defining moment in the "Theory of Myths" essay of *Anatomy of Criticism* (1957):

The complete form of the romance is clearly the successful quest, and such a completed form has three main stages: the stage of the perilous journey and the preliminary minor adventures ... We may call these three stages respectively, using Greek terms, the *agon* or conflict, the *pathos* or death-struggle, and the *anagnoris* or discovery ... A quest involving conflict assumes two major characters, a protagonist or hero, and an antagonist or enemy ... The central form of romance is dialectical: everything is focused on a conflict between the hero and his enemy, and all the reader's values are bound up with hero ... The conflict however takes place in, or at any rate primarily concerns, *our* world, which is in the middle, and which is characterized by the cyclical movement of nature.[2]

I observe in this passage Frye's abiding concerns and stylistic shifts. I see, in microcosm, his thematic core and his artful, muted tonality: the quest for identity, which he will in later works state is the heart of Western literature, if not of art and theology; then the nature of the hero; the inference that there can be no quest without conflict; then the critic's, or the reader's, role in re-creation; and lastly the masking in his prose of his incendiary thinking. Frye's stylistic restraint in his published books of criticism is contrasted by the fiery aphoristic explosions, the furore, of his notebook entries.

I note how Frye crucially joins conflict with quest. The struggle with antagonists, with mentors, with traditions and texts, with thought, with observations, is itself a form of quest, an intellectual adventure, a turbulent movement towards self-definition, a jagged line of argument and story which leads to new grounds for reflection and spiritual autobiography. An agon is a striving that moves us towards recombination – alchemical unity, a mixing of energies.

Like all seers and prophetic figures, McLuhan and Frye impel crisis. They make us respond, making us rethink where and who we are, inviting us to recognitions, engulfing us with ideas; they issue an invitation to make journeys. Communing with the Spirit world is an act of a mantic (an inspired one), potentially an act of hubris. Inspiring others, communicating the élan vital, may lead to distemper (a radical unease). It is we who must also break our preconceptions, our conditioning, to let in the ideas, giving the new a chance to root itself in our minds and souls. But the strong missionary intentions of a seer must lead to clashes with others who are similarly driven. These conflicts can be of pride and ambition: a struggle between singularity (uniqueness of breath, the *pneuma* of being) and the masks of ego (expressions of extraordinary personality).

I will show how McLuhan and Frye were deeply aware of, and ardently conflicted by, the presence the other had in the theoretical terrain of literature. And yet their intensities of insight share the complementary impulse towards revelation. They were not, however, saying the same thing in a lively, contrasting rhetoric. McLuhan spoke of the orchestral analogies of things and forces; electricity was speedily altering identity. Electronica is creating a global interconnectivity that will displace all we have known. Frye wrote of the alphabet of literary forms; reading initiated entry into the deep structures of identity, the order of words slowly disclosing the Great Code of Being and Becoming, the liberating intentions of the Spirit. Both were obsessed with suggestions and significances. However, they grandly proposed ideas and perceptions over thirty years of writing and teaching, of re-vision and speculative reflection, that harmonize in a crucial way in their concerns, ambitions, backgrounds, implications, polemics, and (above all) in their demands and reach. Humanist scholar-writers and teachers whose goals were illumination and awakening, they called their perceptual and aesthetic intentions apocalyptic.

Doors in the Wall, the Practical Apocalypse

What do I mean when I say they are apocalyptics? "I am an apocalyptic only," McLuhan said.[3] He said, "We are on the verge of the apocalypse. In fact, we are living it." By apocalypse McLuhan did not mean Armageddon, the end of the world, the annihilation of being and the existential, historical advent of the kingdom of God. Apocalypse is heightened awareness, the moment of epiphany, where an individual sees into, or acutely apprehends, his or her time and place. An apocalypse could seem violent, a heart- and mind-wrenching experience. It can be dislocating, surely a subversion of the status quo for the one who experiences that shattering moment. Apocalypse spells the end of the ideas and opinions that we have so far held. The usurping moment proclaims: reality is not settled.

The word "apocalypse" means "revelation," the tearing of the curtain, the opening of the eye, the rift in the temple veil, the lifting of the mind to the blaze of brightened consciousness. This revelatory moment may lead to a new way of life (a conversion of sorts). Dante's *Vita Nuova* (1295) is a parabolic contemplation of a shift in consciousness, from afflicted lost soul to the vocation of poet and chronicler of the epic quest through a haunting and hallowing metaphysical cosmos. James Joyce's *A Portrait of the Artist as a Young Man* (1916) reinvents the Dantesque apocalyptic movement in the Modernist literary context through his evocation of the evolution of a poet's mind: Stephen Dedalus discovers his aesthetic vocation in Dublin through a series of epiphanies. McLuhan was immersed in Dante and Joyce and in the idea that art itself, allied with criticism, aphorism, eloquence, poetic metaphor, and quotation, could bring the user or reader to an edifying awareness of the structures and patterns at work in his or her surroundings.

What did the McLuhan apocalypse demand of us? What did he want us to apprehend? I believe this: we must see how we are wandering in the wilderness of electronica, that we are an addled and vexed mass humanity trekking in the global village or theatre, the wired-in planet, all of us experiencing its pulse and the externalizing nerve ends of electricity. His discontinuous aphorisms and probes were meant in a structure of "allatonceness" to both mime and satirize the tumultuous whirl of the electronic charge that floods and draws us. This second creation, the electronic big bang, is for McLuhan the new text of the communications' media, though the central texts are a screen (mini or flat), a billboard, an icon, or a technological invention, and not a handwritten or printed page.

His most memorable aphorism is "The medium is the message." It was first introduced in textual form in the *Report on Project in Understanding New Media*, prepared for the National Association of Educational Broadcasters, commissioned by the US Department of Health, Education and Welfare, in 1960.[4] This document remains unpublished. McLuhan had already uttered – or "outered," so he often said – the phrase in discussions, classrooms, interviews, and informal conversations. It is an aphorism much debated over the years. I say it points to the subliminal effects, the submerged drama of all human inventions. The aphorism highlights how our environments are constructed by massively influential artefacts. Specifically, it was meant to illuminate how electronic inventions – TV, radio, cinema, computers – affect us without our awareness of their effects. Electronic forms have succeeded mechanical ones. This is radically new. We are immersed in their oceanic beat. And we do not know what we are doing to ourselves by hooking up and ravishing ourselves. Any jarring into perception must be apocalyptic. "The new media are not bridges between man and nature – they are nature," he said in *The Book of Probes*, an arrangement of his most profound aphorisms and observations.[5] The deliberately hyperbolic "medium is the message" evokes a sense of how our context is quick, fluid, elusive, lustrous, dense (massed), here. We live in whirlpools of change, conditionings from wired and wireless technologies, in the rushing communications of global networking. Electricity is Dionysian flux, Orphic, immersing. But it is the source, the rechanneled energy of life.

The media are forms, in McLuhan's perception. But the forms are not (and never will be) static; they are metamorphic, perpetually shifting in their appearances, always changing in their effects. This is why all technological ground is unsteady, even apparitional. TVs are subject to radical alterations of appearance and function (from boxy tube sets to digital flat screens); ingenuity and markets drive the new into transforming mania: no one can truly keep pace. Mercurial super-Nature ramps up the shifts of Nature: a TV screen now experiences seasons of hyper-transformation in the way a maple tree experiences a spring breeze, summer storms, autumn's coaxing of the leaves into flaming colour, and the snow blankets of winter.

In an act that spurred breathtaking controversies, McLuhan transformed himself – and (or?) was transformed by the forces he was engulfed by – into the media guru. This was his attempt to turn the ecstasy and terror of the global village, "resonant with tribal drums," into a theatre of revelatory oratory and debate. The theatre could be a cathartic awakening from the narcosis of media; but the theatre of global communications is under constant surveillance by satellites. In the electronic cosmos we observe ourselves observing and expanding our technological reach and reconnaissance power; this power can be addictive and traumatizing in its sensory swarm. Thus the apocalyptic goal of awakening is a visionary pursuit. In the grip of this cosmopolitan operation we are trying to make sense, re-enacting the poetic process. "Truth is not matching," McLuhan said in *The Global Village: Transformations in World Life and Media in the 21st Century* (1989), the posthumously published collaborative work with Bruce R. Powers. "It is neither label nor mental reflection. It is something we make in the encounter with the world that is making us. We make sense not in cognition, but in replay. That is my definition of intellection, if not indeed, scholarship. Representation, not replica."[6] Representation and making for McLuhan are the original initiations of the poet-seer. I submit that "Making, not matching," will turn out to be his most audacious statement, because it implies that all our actions are expressions of our poetic souls.

McLuhan says in his *Report*, years before the publication of *The Gutenberg Galaxy* (1962) and *Understanding Media* (1964),

Personally, I feel quite helpless and panicky as I contemplate the range and new assumptions and frames and parameters which our new technology has imposed upon us. If the great culture of number was needed to keep the technology of letters in a precarious poised continuity these past centuries, where is the wisdom to manage human values in the post-number, post-literate magnetic age? Are we still not inclined to suppose that our former objectives are still valid even though all of our assumptions and parameters have changed? What are we to say of the hypnotic daze of such people? Educators present a uniform, homogeneous front of somnambulism.

(McLuhan, *ROPUNM*, 8)

I note how many of McLuhan's stylistic qualities and intellectual intentions are already alive here: the perception of a moulding and remoulding context, the questioning provocateur, the curt dismissal of ignorance, the emphasis on reporting (insight into the manifestations of the age), the latent concern for the overturning of values, the strenuous demand that we re-evaluate all views, the prophetic sense that technology's immanent presence has eclipsed our ability to understand it, the troubled urgency of a visionary who perceives a world burning up with new informational codes.

I turn to Janine Marchessault to confirm his apocalyptic strain in her wise study *Marshall McLuhan: Cosmic Media* (2005):

[H]is cyclical view of history ... is infused by the conjunction of electricity and spirit. This romantic and mystical association, not uncommon among the French artists and intellectuals who so influenced him (from Mallarmé to de Chardin) produces the kabalistic [*sic*] paradox, which is the relatedness of multiplicity and unity, of the one and the many. This simultaneous experience of unity and multiplicity enabled by the electronic media represents a kind of cosmic consciousness that McLuhan never defines.[7]

Now I ask, how does Frye articulate the apocalyptic? In *The Great Code: The Bible and Literature* (1982) he speaks of *kerygma* for the first time in a published book. This word roughly translates into apocalyptic proclamation.[8] Frye's work on the Bible appears in three primary texts: the aforementioned *Code*, its companion work *Words with Power: Being a Second Study of "The Bible and Literature"* (1990), and the posthumous *The Double Vision*. In these he writes his way towards what must be understood to be a heretical expression of the proclamation of the sacred and its mirror, "the secular scripture" that composes literature. By heretical I mean Gnostic and alternative: seeking inner light and truth outside dogma, beyond institutional guidance, aside from theoretical structures established by others. A brilliant and crucial narrative of being and becoming is proclaimed in the books that expand our re-creating imagination. It is the story of how the nightmare of history can be turned into the dream of compassion.

I recognize Frye's existential urgency in his perception of the questing core of literature. He hoped to overturn desolation and loneliness through acts of comprehensive, unifed reading: these place us in the dream-time of literature. The countering dream-time reveals through vital inwardness the contour of a developing inspired consciousness, embodied in the Great Code story. By "spiritual" Frye usually means peaks of consciousness, the mind operating at its apogee; but he does often mean contact with the imaginary, for him always a communing with the universal Spirit. This transformation is enabled in literature through the study of the techniques and archetypal patterns of certain pivotal books. I propose that we read Frye's texts, from *Fearful Symmetry* through *The Educated Imagination* (1963) to his last works on the Bible, in the terms of a bold annunciation of the DNA of identity, the code or romance-quest that illuminates a pathway through data chaos, towards the retrieved shape of edenic knowledge, the very roots of paradise, the soul itself wholly realized. Literature will show darkening, ironic modes, too. But these can be perceived in larger transforming patterns. Frye's apocalyptic intention is to find a harmony of being which transcends dislocation and dis-ease. *Kerygma* suggests abundance and overflow; it is the proclamation of the pleroma, the fullness or splendour that fills us, what Paul of Tarsus means when he speaks of pleroma ("the fulness") in Colossians 2:9, when he refers to the realm in which everything exists in a rich condition of light, wisdom, liberty and energy in harmony.

Literature reveals the pattern of prodigal communications, books in their verbal teeming and the cosmos attempting to break into eloquent speech. The Elysian state of mind developed through study emerges to overcome and finally redeem the ravening foolishness of factual time.

Frye said in his *Late Notebooks, 1982–1990* (2000), "Apocalypse is the hidden flame lit up, first setting the world on fire, then shining its own light of awakened consciousness *(omnia sunt lumina).*"[9] This cryptic comment should be set beside his often quoted statement in *The Educated Imagination*: "Literature is a human apocalypse, man's revelation to man, and criticism is not a body of adjudications, but the awareness of that revelation, the last judgment of mankind."

A.C. Hamilton confirms Frye's apocalyptic intentions when he describes the mode of the seer in his pioneering study, *Northrop Frye: Anatomy of His Criticism*. The venerable Hamilton says,

> Frye's dialectical method derives from an apocalyptic or revolutionary mode of thinking, which leads him to place literary works within some framework or diagram of binary poles, antitheses, or dichotomies, in agreement with Blake's dictum that "without Contraries is no progression" – forces which function as magnetic fields: the closer we come to one field, the stronger its influence, though both are always present, being contained rather than excluded. These forces are held in tension rather than in opposition, and are never reconciled or synthesized, for Frye is neither a pluralist nor a monist. His theory of criticism is essentially contestatory rather than harmonizing.[10]

It is the premise of my book that the intellectual energies of McLuhan and Frye continue to be "magnetic fields"; they attract and resist each other in the apocalyptic mode. I have disagreements with Hamilton's arguments: tensions require the potential of harmony, and the mystical promise of the one and the many (monism and pluralism) may be held in a paradox where seemingly disparate premises find moments of revelatory intersection. Moreover, the energy of the new comes in hybrids, crossings where we may glimpse other configurations: new synergies.

Frye and McLuhan knew that to use the word "apocalypse" inevitably invokes the title of a canonic book of the Christian Testament. Often called Revelation, it is the last disclosure of the biblical epic-narrative that begins in Genesis with the creation. Revelation ends the passage through myth and time – light and darkness – with an image of a closed book, in 22:18–19. McLuhan and Frye removed the word from this context to make a new frame, to suggest another beginning. *The book of life is still open, the book of life is still being extended.* Through this opening and extension comes their refiguring of the global theatre sublime, the prophetic line of thought and perception.

It important to note here that their thinking shares heresies: to open the book of revelation, when it is has been closed by the administering angel, is to risk spiritual wrath or (and?) the wrath of their contemporaries. Although both would downplay their intentions with humour and mutable positions (McLuhan) and with shy, often evasive statements (Frye), they were moving into the frontier of the Spirit, where inspired speech begins. Apocalypse only comes when your reality is broken up or broken down and you begin to perceive the new. The encouraging flux of ideas and impressions must propel the pilgrim, the adventurer of the new, into sensations and associations that are rich and strange. Inspired speech may lead the mantic one into controversies never expected and maladies hardly welcomed. If inspiration is not tempered by patience and compassion, and by good will and wisdom, then whirlwinds will descend.

Apocalypse is beyond revolution. It breaks the cycle of time that Blake called the Orc cycle of revolution and reaction. What Blake meant by this is that revolutionary surge – the attraction of the new vision – is followed by reactionary return to the status quo. Apocalypse cracks this cycle. It does so by drawing knowledge into myth, where the past, present, and future coexist. Exodus is an articulation of this mode of awareness because it is the story that represents *the venturing out into the wilderness to the promised land.* McLuhan recognized Frye on that frontier edge, and over the years, Frye came to see McLuhan in those vivid terms too, a fellow voyager in the now of communications, the here of poetic communion. The energy it takes to voyage out rekindles the senses. This is why when we reread McLuhan and Frye we encounter their perpetual youth, which is their enthusiasm.

Visionary enterprises, like theirs, are not quite wisdom work, unless (of course) you mean by wisdom the urging towards restoration of vigorous insight and the recovery of a sense of destiny (meaningful life). Michel de Montaigne and Blaise Pascal are avowedly wisdom writers. McLuhan and Frye are critics who sought vision; but in the visionary quest, wisdom surely comes. To McLuhan, media, the electronica, extend the nerves and wrench the senses: our hyper-culture barrages and uproots us. To Frye, innumerable books are published every month, but we must select our readings to know the code and role of the soul. The two herald a project, with brio and nuance, that recalls the magnum opus of the alchemic mind-soul mission: their books and aphorisms become sites for inspiration. Provocations can be inspirational too. I have immersed myself in their works and aspirations to understand them, finding my own inspirations and quests and my time for clashes and brooding.

They converge on the idea of apocalypse. To McLuhan, apocalypse is found in the forms and effects of new media, and our cultural and social conditions are inherently revelatory and devastating; to Frye, apocalypse can be found in literature and through the honed awareness that comes in critical comprehension. Although both will declare humanist intentions, we should not sidestep the metaphysical, even the mystical, implications of the word: apocalyptic implies the pressing awareness of who we are (Frye's identity quest) and where we are (McLuhan's perception of transfiguring contexts). The world has to be seen with new eyes to understand media; literary text has to be read with new eyes to see the vast links of the quest to know who we are.

Observe that in his "Polemical Introduction" to *Anatomy of Criticism* Frye states from the beginning how his work "consists of 'essays,' in the word's original sense of a trial or incomplete attempt" (8). I know that the emphases in Frye's sentence are on "trial" and "incomplete"; this advises humility and seems to ask for patience. Still we should recognize how the words point to agon and the quest for whole vision (summa). Agons are trials, structures for charge and counter-charge. Every agon is also an acknowledgment of a need for completion. The contrary pattern is set up to incite and inspire dialogues. These may occur with the reader and fellow critics, even with the author himself, and surely those authors from the past who represent complex positions of ingenuity and similar visionary aspirations. Without contrary visions and voices there can be no progression. Each illumines and irritates the other.

Do apocalyptic intentions require trauma? Shamans rebuke and hector their initiates in the ceremonial magic cultures of the First Nations' peoples: they are granted the privilege of speaking their mind, of shape-shifting into creatures which may lunge and soar, slap and torment. Zen masters often scold and strike their students. Plato's dialogues are melodramas where there is frequently a sly unseating or a blatant humiliation of the unwary questioner. Arthur Rimbaud and Charles Baudelaire, Nietzsche and Kierkegaard assail readers with aphorisms and ironies, shifting personae – sudden swerves into grand statement or subversive thought experiments. If the prophetic-apocalyptic tradition, in which we should see McLuhan and Frye, is one which draws on wells of inspiration, then we should understand that illumination and irritation are twins.

But critics (unfriendly to them) will mark out a decisive difference between apocalypse and aesthetics. McLuhan and Frye were, after all, literary critics, devoted to the beauties of poems and fictions. It would likely seem to some that the aesthetic appreciative side of their work – the side that admired symmetries and metaphors – would be at odds with their apocalyptic designs. I assert they are both paradoxically obsessed with disclosure and prophecy, a vision of the art forms of the new, and with the splendour in the unity of letters. This may seem an impossible yoking. (But they are Canadians; everything in Canada is impossible, including the notion of the country itself.) Still these twin urges in them – appreciation and revelation – are so powerful that they contribute to the complexities in their work that beguile us and frustrate many critical readers.

Their procreant urges and revelatory sweep are complexities that compel me. This compulsion has moved me for over thirty years since I first met them and engaged them when I was their student. (And I am still their awe-struck student.) Their designs were prophetic; and yet their designs on us include – and extol – the wonder of literary experience, the sheer power in the shaping of rhetoric. Simultaneously, they wished to elevate our souls, enlarge perception, into conditions of sublime, life-altering connection.

This is why I emphasize the words "apocalypse" and "alchemy." McLuhan and Frye disclosed patterns and structures in uncanny statements and reflections. And there is at times a presence of magic incantation and forceful rhetorical flight in their best passages and memorable aphorisms. All these give us shivers of recognition – realities appear, dimensions seem greater and more complex, synchronicities rhyme, what was hidden stands exposed, implied order becomes visible image, doors open wide enough to let in light and dark – and they give us the pleasures of reading or reflecting on a book or an image or a line or a thought or a citation or a quotation or a gnomic remark or an arrangement of words in an artful sentence.

My Teachers Here and Then

At this point I turn confessional. I am wrestling with two people who were my teachers in 1978 and 1979 at the University of Toronto. McLuhan and Frye are my elders. They are also my fearful angels of instruction who have remained with me, sometimes more like magnetic fields than guides. They rear up, called again in words. I have engaged McLuhan's perceptions and Frye's concepts so intimately over the years that I am not sure where their thoughts end and mine begin.

I continue to struggle with their purposes for literature. It is a struggle with their definitions of reality and with their Christian metaphysics. This book is part of my reconciliation with them, my attempt to find the point-counterpoint in their thinking. I found it important at times to resist them. My wrestling with them was at times like a war; at other times like necessary wariness, a pulling back. I have felt bruised by their demands to think deeply. I have felt that I was on the edge of letting my voice be subsumed into a mix of theirs (paragraphs and aphorisms in an uneasy chemistry).

Yet I have never stopped engaging the two. The passing-on continues, occasionally raging. Sometimes surrendering the will through openness allows for more acute impressions.

I needed their teachings for guidance. Never fully a McLuhanite or a Fryegian, I have often disliked the zealous insularities of their admiring circles. But is any master ready for the ardour or the breaches of their students? What do you acknowledge higher than yourself? "If the pupil is ready, the Master comes," the adage says. Passionately, I have had to understand them and then use – or apply – them.

I have also tried to resist the totalizing tendencies in their thinking. What is that tendency? They appear to absorb every word and every atom into their methods and myths and then to remark, whether implicitly or gnomically, on how very obvious it all is that everything fits into their networks of thought. Surely McLuhan left gaps; Frye sometimes stops in his tireless note-taking in what seems like a breathless pause. Yet their totalizing is impressive. They found and revealed much. Still I find myself getting lost and craving those feelings of being lost, starting over (and over) in my global village wandering. Openings mean finding where words end and where the new meanings are, which is the moment of radical unfamiliarity. Strangeness compels me into nights and days I do not understand, yet.

Nietzsche's Zarathustra tells his disciples, in chapter 3 of book 1, in the concluding passages of the existential sermon *Thus Spoke Zarathustra*, "Now I go alone, my disciples. You too go now, alone. Thus I want it ... One repays a teacher badly if one always remains nothing but a pupil ... Beware lest a statue slay you ... Now I bid you lose me and find yourselves; and only when you have all denied me will I return to you."[11] McLuhan and Frye admonished us, there should be no followers. I will explore this admonishment in a later chapter.

In Genesis 32:24–8, Jacob battles with the angel "until the break of day." Jacob would not release this nameless night figure until he blesses him. It is difficult to tell what sort of ethereal being it is that Jacob fights. The dark figure seems vampiric. He (or she) fears the dawn. But this is a being that comes to bid him rise to life, the conflict of being. After their combat goes on for hours in darkness, the angel mysteriously disappears. Yet the otherworldly spirit leaves Jacob lamed. Out of his wound come Israel and the promise of universal justice.[12] Biblical commentators go so far as to suggest that Jacob grapples with his supernatural twin. Jacob also had a (fraternal? identical?) twin brother, Esau.

Nevertheless, the blessing is a curse, a crack in the soul, a branding, a hieroglyphic mark open to interpretation, a spiritual tattoo, an acknowledgment of indebted lineage, an enigmatic coding on the body and soul. But the blessing means more life in all its glorious forms. The mark promises an abundance of meaning. The blessing signifies tradition, the handing on (the meaning of the word "Kabbalah"); it is the peace found in the mysterious promise that all shall be well. The lesson is clear: the spiritual traditions inspire and brutally scar.

It has taken years to understand the importance of turning away from my teachers and returning to struggle with them. Coming back to them has become an unexpected but solacing action in the moments when my feelings of isolation and anxiety desperately surge and resurge. The wrestling is my lesson.

And in a bewildering moment I have realized how my wrestling has gone on with two figures, not one. I suppose there is a dreadful irony in this, or a latent ambitious impulse verging on a megalomania that I am not wise or brave enough to understand. To see them in a complete way is at any rate beyond my capacity. (Their thought is endlessly fascinating, therefore endlessly open to interpretation.) But in my confession here I admit to seeing them at times like one figure – Janus-like, a singular force with many expressions.

McLuhan and Frye are thus to me signal figures whose bequest has marked the Canadian field. The mutable tensions between them, and within them, are those of the scholar-humanist and the experimental discoverer, the perpetual reader and annotator and the reimagining aphorist and poet. They are incarnate paradoxes. Frye writes in a scholarly style that can seem, on first reading, slow and cautious. This wisely covers his apostolic zeal for liberation; however, a lyrical exuberance sometimes shakes his prose into intoxicatingly ecstatic passages. McLuhan evolved a style and form that was satiric, intuitive, playful, quarrelsome, destabilizing, futurist, and alarming. The playfulness covers his cautionary concern. They wrestled with ideas and perceptions, the changing global communication environments and the structural content of all literature. We may never know their personal agons, how they struggled in themselves. The letters and notebooks offer inklings, and we can speculate. Clearly, they wrestled; part of the wrestling was with one another.

Here is how I express my encounter with them. It is in the rediscovery of their aims and in their pursuit of codes and laws, symmetries and breakages. What I write is revisionary. (One responsibility I have to my teachers is to remake them.) Immersed in and conflicted by their thought over decades, I have nevertheless been engulfed by their energies. I find renewal in their words, but I also find in my work a worrisome repetitions of their ideas. Still I know that when I rise to struggle with these angels of instruction and inspiration, what comes is a reinvention of the two through a recombination. I have learned to channel the flood of their powerful minds into a single source. This recombining is the alchemy I address in a later chapter. At hand is the necessity of clarifying what they meant by certain keywords. One is apocalypse, the other is visionary; there will be more words that need redefining, but these will do for a start.

Sacred Geometry

What is a visionary? What do I mean by the apocalyptic? I propose that visionary conditions for McLuhan and Frye were both voluntary and involuntary: the conditions were not dependent on apparitional encounters or occult manifestations. The apocalyptic mode can be a willed act, encouraged through the practical act of reading and the training of perception in the subliminal fields of electromagnetic energy. Yet visionary experience can be a moment (sudden in a shaft of sunlight) which illuminates signs and paths, leaving the imprint of awe. I will be arguing that they applied their illuminations to their probes and books, to teaching and the architectonics of their thought. While there is ample wit and irony in their texts, and they surely accepted the secular ground of their audiences, there is an implicit sense in their work that their intellectual impulses originated from sacred epiphanies which in turn led to the contemplative states and the practice of their critical methods. "Visionary," "apocalyptic," "seer," and "Pentecostal" are charged words. Let me explain how they apply to McLuhan and Frye.

I turn now to the role of the fours. The number four holds a special place in numerology and in biblical symbolism: there are four zones of the world (east, west, north, south), four winds, four Gospels, four quarters of the ancient cross (up, down, across, and the nexus of the centre), and four primordial forces (fruitful or barren earth, fertilizing or devastating water, inspiring or annihilating wind, warming or scorching fire); the cherubim of Psalm 80 – the figures that guard the gates of Eden – have four faces; there are four rivers in Eden; the Tetragrammaton is based on a pattern of fours, and this is why the unspeakable name of God is beheld in the four enigmatic letters JHVH. There are four seasons and four elements; and Blake writes in a quatrain in his 1802 letter to Thomas Butts,

> 'Tis fourfold in my supreme delight
> And threefold in soft Beulah's night
> And twofold Always. May God us keep
> From Single vision and Newton's sleep!

The number four is part of the sacred geometry of the Pythagorean tradition: it signifies symmetries. The soul, according to the wisdom traditions, is composed of body, mind, world, and spirit; we comprehend the soul primarily through symbol (religion and art), energy (life), psyche (consciousness), and transformations (experience). Then there is the sacred quartet of the emotions: compassion, wisdom, trust, and courage. McLuhan and Frye based much of the patterns of their thinking on fours: we find it in the structure of *Anatomy of Criticism* (four essays), and we find it in what appears to be McLuhan's last great obsession (in the late 1970s) with the tetrads he called Laws of Media. (McLuhan was also obsessed with the numbers three, five, nine, and twelve; he was deeply superstitious about the appearance of any of these; I can attest to this, in my experiences of him in class and in personal conversations in his office hours after class. I will return to McLuhan's numerology shortly.)

The gift of the Pentecost, when the dove descends on the shoulders of the disciples in Acts 2:1–26, is said to come in a fourfold way: the dove brings harmonic perception which is the gift of grace and inspired speech, the moment of healing, the time of prophecy, and the wisdom of understanding how the spiritual world and the material world interfuse with one another. The pursuit of, and the welcoming of, apocalyptic conditions moved McLuhan and Frye towards the polysemous: many meanings existing simultaneously. But how to clarify and outline, even describe and apply, this hunger to express multilevel possibility?

The two converge in their desire to articulate potent harmonies of meaning—vision and experience interpenetrating I find both immersed in the study of the four levels of exegesis: the literal, moral, allegoric, and anagogic. The concerns for this tetrad of verbal interpretation we find in Frye's *Anatomy of Criticism* and developed in his readings of the Bible in *The Great Code* (1982) and *Words with Power* (1990).[13] McLuhan explores the fourfold levels in his PhD dissertation, *The Classical Trivium: The Place of Thomas Nashe in the Learning of Time*, presented to Cambridge University in 1943 and truly his first book. He mines their depths again in his late collaborative texts, *Laws of Media: The New Science* (1988) and *The Global Village*. McLuhan's final literary essay is a largely unknown work he wrote for *New Literary History* (composed in 1978, published in 1979) called, without the usual McLuhan flamboyant titling, "Pound, Eliot, and the Rhetoric of *The Waste Land*." In his examination of Pound's editorial intervention into what was then Eliot's raw confessional manuscript, McLuhan revives the ancient tetradic structure of meditative speculation (the four keys of the Pentecostal gift are knowledge, inspiration, interpretation of tongues, and the tempered power to know how to use and communicate these gifts). He recognizes how Eliot's poem gained enormous power from Pound's decisive editing; and I note how Eliot absorbed into his epoch-shattering poem the five-part divisions of rhetoric that Pound recommended. Still Eliot loved the meditative fours and integrated this mystic numerology into the fours and fives of his elegaic *Four Quartets*. The retrieval of this metamorphic fourfold pattern is a field of complementarity in the thinking of McLuhan and Frye. They discovered the exegetical numerology in different sources: Dante, for Frye; Thomas Aquinas, Saint Bonaventure, and the alchemist-Hermetist Albertus Magnus, for McLuhan.

To Frye, the goal of literature is to put the Pentecostal dove on the reader's shoulders. The intention is to achieve an exciting condition of constant inspiration – artistic call, critical response; a new thought that is a moment of creation, the re-creation that comes in writing down that thought – a process that costs not less than everything. To McLuhan, the point of an aphorism is to ask the dove to descend so that we can ascend to sense and sensitivity. These intentions are part of their charisma, a word that unites charm (magic) and the gift of spiritedness.

The four levels of re-creative meaning and textual extension are a form of natural visionary experience which can be applied in any situation *without sectarian creed or the aid of occult ceremonies and initiating drugs.* Apocalyptic action becomes an act of concentrated will, energy, intuition, and imagination together. The method is open to anyone willing to engage the pattern behind patterns. I posit that when we become aware of this primordial tetrad, so the Kabbalah says, the vital intellectual spiritual channel is suddenly available. Learning itself becomes a guide to transcendence, tuning the brain to conditions of supra-consciousness. The word "spirited" beautifully describes this dynamism.

Let me outline the forms of the four parts. (I have tried to understand the forms of reading in depth over many years, often through sometimes vexed and baffled states. Writing about them before has led me to speculate: are they the alphabet of the soul that Rimbaud searched for? Are they the lost keys of the Orphic voice, therefore of the source of poetry itself? They haunt me because of their recurrence in poetics. And they resurface for me because I suspect they are the greatest lesson of the ancient wisdom traditions. Are the fours the keys to the mystery initiations, what was said to move a random universe into radiant cosmos? Once we are initiated into the power of the four levels, do we edge towards what wants to speak through us? Poets seek intensified experience; poetics teach us this intensity of intuitional power is within our reach, in part when activated by the inspiration of numbers. And so exegesis becomes a symbolic, transformative event. The four energies of the life force, according to esoteric wisdom, are configured in love, inspiration, time, and death. Walt Whitman gazes at a single blade of grass in the first lines of the 1855 edition of *Leaves of Grass*: then sensationally, through one trembling leaf comes ... everything.)

First, the literal: this is the sensual level of engagement with textual experience. For our purposes, it is the reader's initial encounter in poetry, drama, or fiction, with action, plot, character, and setting. This is the realm of becoming in geographical space, historical time. It is the horizontal plane, the east-west intersection across the existential grid. All stories, or poems, or dramas, or fables, if they are to be persuasive, must play in the theatre of laughter and tears. The literal level is always the entry point. (Opinion is a characteristic of the literal level, one of the reasons, no doubt, why many opinions are shallow.) Strong writers remake conventions – of genre, of thematic concern – to make their streams of association and apprehension thrillingly, compulsively immediate.

Second, the moral: the dimension of morality, politics and history, sexuality, and psychology. These are the stories of the horizontal plane. The moral dimension is supremely concerned with how we encounter the immediate appearances of fact and epoch. For Marxist and Freudian critics, existentialists, and empiricist biographers, the moral level is the one of psychological motive and power, of revolutionary action, the politics of Eros and Thanatos, of affirmation and negation. It is the domain of tragic suffering, heroic endurance. The literal and moral levels inform the existential historical. McLuhan and Frye turned away from a final emphasis on these two levels, and in so doing decisively turned away from the dominant concerns of postmodernism. (Ideologues of postmodernist criticism tend to stay on the first two levels, the historical and political, dismissively calling the next two levels "fictions" and "meta-narratives." I engage the responses of four significant representative postmodernist critical-theorists to McLuhan and Frye in another chapter.)

Third, the allegoric: this is the level of the subtextual story that exists in a shadowy course to the storylines and directives of the literal. These subtextual narratives may be parallel (a match); more often they are associative (a making). The shadowing dimension of allegory often has didactic purposes, say, in drawing a reference to the story of the mysterious birth and then the mission, miracles, parables, crucifixion, and resurrection of Christ.

According to Frye, the four narratives essential to the Western literary imagination are drawn from Homer, Virgil, Ovid, and the Bible. These are not homogenous. The Homeric tales are myriad. There are *The Iliad* and *The Odyssey*, then modifications and expansions of them in Sophocles and Euripides (among many). The Homeric myths are encyclopedic treasuries of characters in quests and agonizing tests; heroes are always challenged during their voyages, in their longing for home (*nostos*). Virgil revises Homer by dramatizing the eternal significance of Rome: Aeneas flees from Troy's falling towers and founds the Imperial City. Ovid invokes intersections of the supernatural and the natural in violent explosions of mythic retelling. The Bible – "the books" – is an assemblage of overlapping, often contradictory narratives, a mosaic of wisdom writings, proverbs, poems, parables, and prophecies. All four texts become sources to be re-envisioned by inspired poets and artists.

Fourth, the anagogic: the plane of eternal similitude, of analogy, association, correspondence, suggestion. On this level events and artefacts are understood to be metaphoric; the anagogic is the point of the symbolic vortex where meanings ignite and spin; it is the domain of the vertical, the north-south line of the intersected grid of the imagination. Vertical information is represented by the words we use to evoke and invoke being, consciousness, impalpable energies, invisible presence, mystery, dreams, intuition, the gods, the sacred, divinity. The fourth level encompasses the others: the moment when infinity bursts through the boundaries of the material, or literal. The breakthrough can be traumatic (or devotional), the moment when everything ordinary becomes extraordinary. Infinity floods us, and we swim, or drown, in meaning.

It is easier for me to show the fours at work than it is to explain them. So let me recall Bob Dylan's anthem "Like a Rolling Stone," voted by *Rolling Stone* magazine the most influential song of the mid- to late twentieth century. (The editors did not do this without self-interest: look at the name of their magazine.) In each successive refrain Dylan sings, "How does it feel / To be on your own / Like a rolling stone," and the word "it" takes on greater weight. The lyric begins in a personal reference to a failed love affair, then lifts into the quest for identity and the encounter with the cryptic IT that moves every quixotic trek. The song's generational impact comes from the breakthrough Dylan makes when he goes from the literal to the anagogic; the one becomes the many. The anagogic point is the intersection of the vertical and the horizontal where the personal and the mass meld. To the uninitiated eye, the movement from private biographical meaning to infinite possibility is the deluge; there seems no limit to the enthusiasms of pattern-making. Frye calls the fourth level "the centre of the beatific vision."[14] Why? It is the point where meaning vaults into a kind of beatitude; the spiritual life becomes more than a possibility, it becomes reality.

I offer a second example in Blake's quatrain to the "Auguries of Innocence":

> To see a World in a Grain of Sand
> And a Heaven in a Wild Flower,
> Hold Infinity in the palm of your hand
> And Eternity in an hour.[15]

The fours exist simultaneously here: on the poem's literal level there is the glance at a grain, at a flower; then comes the moral level in the political existential necessity for vision to crack prohibitions on perception; shimmering beneath is the allegory of the Mental Traveller, the poet-pilgrim who seizes Nature and shapes it into image and story; last, the charged soul-plane where grain and flower multiply in associations. On that plane, the flower becomes a Dantesque rose, the flowering of cognitive power, the receptive petal of being (a prophetic anticipation of Whitman's leaf of grass), an analogue for the soul's growth. The mind goes from a single sensuous moment to supra-consciousness. I see why Frye's critical quest began with Blake.

McLuhan retrieved the four levels of exegesis in *The Classical Trivium*. I argue that this is the turning point in his intellectual development. He soon transformed the awareness of the multidimensional meanings of alphabetic text into a technique for comprehending media's multiple effects. The ancient world knew poetics as myth, myth as poetry. There was no subject called "Literature." Students were braced with studies of grammar, rhetoric, logic: the trivium; then they were trained in music, astronomy, mathematics, and geometry: the quadrivium. This structure of learning is outlined in Ernst Robert Curtius's *European Literature and the Latin Middle Ages* (originally published in English in 1953).[16] Curtius shows how the trivium and quadrivium structure of learning was in place through the medieval and Renaissance traditions of schooling. The "triv" and "quad" are the origins of Joyce's punning reply to an interviewer who had asked him if his puns were "trivial." "Yes," Joyce said, "and some of them are quadrivial." The anecdote amused and impelled McLuhan. He used it to begin his 1953 essay "James Joyce: Trivial and Quadrivial."[17]

McLuhan's use of the four-level exegetical process is his version of the practical apocalypse. It is a learned method of apprehending many dimensions: the technological, cultural, personal, public, mythic, sensory, and spiritual exist in dynamic gestalt. He was, however, ambivalent about his insights into electronic second Nature: media confers connecting conditions and chaos. What was once the province of students of spirituality, of visionaries and seers, of prophets and mystics, of poets and mythmakers, is now in the reach of everyone with access to electric super-Nature, so McLuhan insisted – and I have proposed elsewhere (and will explain in subsequent pages). No need for LSD when you have a TV.

McLuhan and Frye are Ulyssean visionaries journeying into the maelstrom (the turbulence of mass media space) and the maze (the traps and ravages of history). If we use the exegetical fours to illuminate the odyssey analogy, this pattern appears. When Ulysses descends into the underworld in Book 11 of *The Odyssey*, the questing hero goes to consult the dead. On a literal level, the descent shows confused Ulysses requesting guidance from Tiresias, the blind seer. On the moral level the tale represents a call for help: to retrieve the wisdom vital for endurance. The dead prophesy, offering nutrition to the mind and inspiration for the living. On the allegoric level, the descent is archetypal; it recurs in poems with enough consistency to earn a decisive mythic place in our consciousness. It spells out the narrative fall and the hope for return to the light of the surface, after Hades's ghosts. On the soul-plane of infinite analogy the descent shows that at the eye of the whirlwind and the centre of the maze is death; but death's domain throngs with energies. The descent is what the searcher does to rise again when you find yourself desolately alone and there seems to be nothing you can do.

(I have elided the instance where Ulysses coolly slaughters a heifer and drains its blood into a sacrificial gutter. A bloody offering summons the hungry spirits. The hero's brutalization of the beast, and the vampiric overtones of the spirits' craving for blood, should be explored elsewhere. Ulysses's descent is prepared by violence. The avid dead swarm round to drink dripping warmth. Wisdom, in the *Nekuia*, is gained by sword and sacrifice. A twenty-first-century reading of this moment, through a revision of the ancient wisdom that McLuhan and Frye recast, would resist the bloodiness of the expiation and reshape it in a symbolic expression. Blood becomes wine. The command and call then is not for death but for life.)

In Frye's terms, the romance-quest structure of fall and rise is the enduring tale behind every tale. When we read books we enter the order of words and experience imaginative patterns that are the tongues of fire from the dead who revive in our engagements. In McLuhan's terms, in ever-rushing spirals we spin in the media maelstrom where communications and miscommunications swirl. However, when we thrive inside the vortex, the life-surge electric source becomes palpable. In *Understanding Media: The Extensions of Man*, McLuhan attributes an insight to Yeats and applies it to media: "The visible world is no longer a reality and the unseen is no longer a dream."[18] This aphorism evokes the McLuhan-Frye visionary conjunction at the core of my argument. Revelation and enlightenment can be brought on by immersion in practice and education. In a realization I find enthralling, and infinitely rewarding, this means visionary experience can be made democratic.

The word "Pentecostal" recurs in their writings. This is another word rich in unsettling, revelatory overtones. The following passage from Acts 2:17–18 is relevant to the apocalyptic traditions that McLuhan and Frye uphold and initiate in Canada: "And it shall come to pass in the last days, saith God, I will pour out of my Spirit upon all flesh: and your sons and your daughters shall prophesy, and your young men shall see visions, and your old men shall dream dreams ... And on my servants and on my handmaidens I will pour out, in those days, of my Spirit; and they shall prophesy." Essential to this I must add these enigmatic but stirring lines from First Corinthians 15:51: "Behold, I shew you a mystery; We shall not all sleep, but we shall all be changed." The outpouring of sense, the trembling of vision, the intimations of Spirit, the charismatic charge of inspiration, the hope of new dreams, sleeplessness, change: these are keywords and phrases to which I will be returning.

Living Encyclopedias

I have described how McLuhan and Frye met at the University of Toronto. While Frye was initially the more renowned of the two – he had published two major works of criticism by 1957; McLuhan's *The Mechanical Bride* (original title: "Guide to Chaos") was published to some critical recognition and almost no sales in 1951 – McLuhan's later celebrity was fractious in ways that mark him today. They were conscious of the other's presence on campus, in the English department for which they both taught, in the collegial conversations of university gatherings, in classrooms where they often shared students, and in the public domain of review and reputation.

But there is more to the phenomenon of their physical nearness. They were dramatically aware of the other's writings and ideas; their notebooks, letters, books, public pronouncements, and essays are charged with pointed exchanges. Although they never debated one another in person, they conducted conversations and arguments in these books and articles.

Agons can be stinging structures of influence. These critics of media and literary structure knew that there was another teacher close by who was similarly absorbed in a visionary-prophetic intention, searching for – and receiving – the patterns and codes of inspiration.

Further, McLuhan and Frye chose to remain in Canada and at the University of Toronto when they could have accepted long-term appointments at universities in the United States. Canadian identity – in its evasive amorphousness and elusive ambiguity – informs the positions in their work and their relations to one another. Put succinctly, I am arguing that their conflicts, their harmonies and complementarities and the possibilities of a synergy between them, are the crux of an indigenous apocalyptic tradition.

My agon proposal is indebted to Harold Bloom's theory of conflict and struggle in writers.[19] My propositions swerve antithetically – for me necessarily – away from Bloom's clawing vision of authors at war, battling to find supremacies of voicing in precise tracings of imaginative articulation. Newness, daring, negation, thematic and intellectual autonomy, and stylistic distinctiveness born of tragic mortality are the imperative virtues of his premises. Bloom deals primarily with poets and the crisis of renewal and vitality in the crushing wake of their over-burdening precursors in *The Anxiety of Influence* (1973), *A Map of Misreading* (1975), *The Breaking of the Vessels* (1982), and *Agon: Towards a Theory of Revisionism* (1982). Although in these books he examines his thesis from different angles, they are where he develops his critical discourse.

Bloom's paramount notion of agon is anxiety-ridden, rooted in the family romances of Freudian depth psychology. It also comes from the confrontational battles and existential codes that Nietzsche establishes between figures that represent both intellectual ingenuity and damaging paternal sway. According to Bloom, writers, philosophers, poets, and thinkers engage in extreme revisions of their chosen parent-precursors. While his premises point to the imaginary in this conflict, it remains an eternally bitter combat. There is no conciliatory harmony in the soul or imagination for titanic rivalries of mind and will.

My premise is a less aggressive (read: Canadian), arguably a more benign understanding of agon. The Canadian agon and convergence of McLuhan and Frye serve as light opposition to the ferocious, sometimes nihilistic American, Emersonian conflict that Bloom establishes. Frye and McLuhan were well aware of the other's value and stature, of the other's ambitions and provocations, and were able to absorb this awareness into acts of call and response, therefore of indirect collaboration and inspiration. They were transforming catalysts for one another. While their contentions were often truculent, rooted in critical and philosophical differences and in a pointed religious difference (Catholicism, Protestantism), they nevertheless were able to use the other's works as contrasting proposals. The other helped to catapult their thinking into greater orbits of comprehension. They willingly inherited an apocalyptic tradition, founding a variant of it in Canada, needing the other to help extend and refine their epiphanies.

McLuhan and Frye circle one another, creating new refractions and reflections. We gaze on, contemplating and engaging their cycling and recycling, their spheres of influence, absorbing differences so we may re-create and expand them and ourselves.

In person, they remained *mostly* polite with one another. They reserved fire for words and ideas. Still McLuhan's three biographers – Philip Marchand in *Marshall McLuhan: The Medium and the Messenger* (1989),

W. Terrence Gordon in *Marshall McLuhan: Escape into Understanding* (1997), and Douglas Coupland in *Marshall McLuhan* (2009) – paint a picture of an intense rivalry between the two. They imply a paranoid friction that was irreconcilable (or a matter of show business). John Ayre in *Northrop Frye: A Biography* (1989), the only detailed biographical work on Frye so far (which was written and published before Frye's death in 1991), hints at a dismaying discomfort between them.[20] The four biographies suggest that the McLuhan-Frye conflict erupted on the University of Toronto grounds like a geological fault.

However, my correspondence with Robert D. Denham, eminent Frye scholar, directed my premises towards these important observations by both himself and editor and critic Alvin Lee:

> [Denham writes,] Were they in fact rivals? ... What Frye criticizes are McLuhan's ideas and McLuhanism. It could be that the community at Toronto saw these two great Northern Lights as rivals. I don't think Frye saw McLuhan as a rival ... If Frye saw McLuhan as a rival it seems doubtful that he would have argued long and hard that McLuhan should get the governor general's award for *Understanding Media*.
>
> [Note: Frye in fact worked to get the Governor General's Award for *The Gutenberg Galaxy* in 1962. He was successful in his efforts.]
>
> [Alvin Lee writes,] The claim by Marchand ... and others, that Norrie and McLuhan "detested" each other is not sound, in my judgment. I personally observed them in social gatherings together and they were always amiable and collegial with each other. I also discussed the work of each with each of them separately and always came away with the sense that they respected each other though they were doing very different things and thinking in very unlike ways – and that they disagreed on some things. Norrie was more than willing to learn, and did, from his colleague Marshall, who worked with him setting exams and discussing curricula ... All kinds of people tried to stage an antithetical war but when these lively, brilliant men came together to articulate things there was always a good deal of mutual respect and learning from each other.[21]

Echoing these comments, I restate that Frye and McLuhan were amicable members of the same literary community in Toronto. But in their writings and lectures there is an awareness of what they took to be differing approaches to the visionary and apocalyptic. The differences create the essential nexus. Resentment and envy are extreme personal reactions and lead to estrangement. Debate and the absorption of ideas will come from resolute contrary spirits; that contrariness seeds evolution. Denham's and Lee's unpublished observations point to how the McLuhan-Frye clash was ironically Canadian (local) and cosmopolitan: courteous, cagey, contradictory, wholly absorbing and catalytic, frictive without being corrosive, iconoclastic without being nihilistic. I read their convergence of contraries in the way of lightness, hence of sympathetic resemblance. The gift of tongues, Paul counsels, in First Corinthians 12:29–31, 13:4–7, and 13:13, should be tempered by charity; it is love that subdues hubris.

I will turn Blakean: contraries are creative; animosities are (likely) corrosive. Contraries create contexts: animosities obliterate them.

Frye anticipates this recognition when he writes in his *Late Notebooks, 1982–1990*, "Critics, like words, discover their identity in disagreement; consensus is achieved in spite of themselves ... it leaks invisibly and is visible centuries later."[22] McLuhan liked to say, "A fish is never aware of water."[23] These observations allude to hidden influences, atmospheres, environments, and milieus, to states of mind. They suggest that patterns only become fully visible after time. The McLuhan-Frye conflict and convergence is one pattern. Under accelerated conditions – the culture of crank-up, at the speed of light, breakdown, and breakthrough[24] – time is compressed: the value of their dialogues and disagreements is becoming truly apparent now.

They share this: their work is more concerned with abundance than with annihilation; exploration was more important than enmity; insight and understanding were the sensible instrumentalities to be handed on, rather than the disabling territorialities of ego and protective specialization. McLuhan divined with eerie prescience the configurations of the post-literate media culture, the new grammars of TV, screen, hydro-based technologies, newspaper, radio, and computers; Frye, with prescient insight, understood that what is passing are the habits and contexts of critical reading and literary knowledge. Frye provides an encyclopedic overview of the nature of the literary tradition. McLuhan exposes in paradoxical perceptions the descent into the whirlpool of electronic waves. On the first page of the preface to his first major book, *The Mechanical Bride*, he provides the brilliant metaphor to which he will always return: Edgar Allen Poe's story "A Descent into the Maelstrom," where a sailor finds solace during a storm by studying the manifestations of its raging waves. The sailor-pilgrim finds an equipoise that allows him to find a way out.[25] At the conclusions of *Fearful Symmetry* and *Anatomy of Criticism*, Frye advocates auguring the mythic patterns in literature and what this patterning might portend for the practice of criticism – in what Coleridge calls the esemplastic power of the imagination. Frye reminds us, through his lifelong charting of symmetries in an essential array of poems, of the power of our verbal heritage to interpenetrate matter and spirit.

They differ in this way: McLuhan wrote a detailed history of the technological future; Frye offered up the content of our imaginations. However, each grasped, with unerring accuracy, that the products of our time (our artefacts and machines) require the shaping of the awareness of the possibilities and limitations of written words. McLuhan is our necessary perceiver of present technological forms and their impact on our senses; Frye is the persistent romancer of literary tradition, whose readings are part of the inward identity quest. To McLuhan, the world is layered with texts. We are still reading the Books of Nature, and now second Nature. To Frye, the alphabetic texts that compose the total vision of literature give us the counter-myth to history; this prime opus takes us into imagination's heart. That process in turn exalts the existential realm. In the directions of these concentrated visions we find their true, lasting differences.

McLuhan and Frye were brilliantly aware of their mutual participation in the representations and expansions of a Canadian sphere of intelligence and perception. We can see this brilliance in their sheer prodigiousness, the abundance of words they left us: over thirty books by Frye published in his lifetime, with the many volumes of notebooks, aphorisms, diary entries, prayers, and letters that have been published since his death; fourteen books by McLuhan in his lifetime, with the letters, collaborative works, unfinished manuscripts, lectures, and interviews that have been gathered up and published since his passing. Yet their literary devotions share a powerful receptivity in the rich, sometimes troubled, references to what speaks beyond words and books. What is beyond the printed word is a primary subject in the "Alchemy, Synergy" chapter of my book.

I submit that there are pivotal ideas and urgent metaphysical concerns to address in their antagonisms and harmonies, questions about what is hidden until revealed and what is visible but ignored. Are there inklings of cosmic consciousness present in their intentions? How did their differences and disagreements route through their writings and in their public and private statements? What point-counterpoint can we discern? How did McLuhan's instrumentalities of probe and percept, aphorism and mosaic contrast with Frye's theoretical architecture, scholarly prose styling, and identification of the Great Code thriving at the core of Western literature? What religious issues put them at odds with one another? How did spirituality unite them? If the two meet in intersections, then they must also divide and travel down separate paths. The contrasts between them come in decisive issues of method and sensibility: how to organize observations and recognitions, how to compel readers and audiences, how to continue explorations, how to offer the key to Pentecostal voices and grace.

Frye glimpsed the differences between their methods and intentions, what he calls the revisionary "anti-book," in this candid notebook entry:

> There is, then, if I'm right, a lesser & greater antibook ... The lesser is the Christian-Classical one ... [the greater] the Xn-Buddhist one ... one is personal, theistic, & voluntary & the other depersonalized, atheistic, & enlightened, I haven't a clue how to proceed. It would be strange if I turned out to be a Great Reconciler after all ... Of course, the foreground antibook, a very minor one, is the contrast represented by McLuhan & myself. I hold to the continuous, encyclopedic, linear-narrative Christian structure, and, of course, "discontinuous" is very much an in-word at present. There is no such thing as a discontinuous poem.[26]

Frye is modest about how "minor" the contrary patterns are – "*the foreground antibook*" (emphasis mine). Their visionary edge is the heart of our apocalyptic tradition. But Frye, with disarming honesty, recognizes how he prefers continuity, the careful comprehensive structures we find in *Anatomy of Criticism* especially. He means his preference is for the continuous prose of essays. The power to persuade comes from the (apparent) self-evidence of speculative connection and supporting documentation. This is what McLuhan, echoing Harold Innis,[27] would call Frye's bias. In contrast, McLuhan's perceptions about discontinuity and making, not matching, put him at odds with the conventional apparatus of scholarship. To McLuhan, discontinuity is the supreme Modernist method of juxtaposition without copula, of the ideogram or vortex of symbol and image, of the aphorism set in the gaping white space of typographical openness, of omitted information in order to generate reader engagement or outrage, of the enjambments that come from the use of mixed modes. The aphorism is a technique of hyperbole and confrontation.

It is an outsider form. The "continuity" versus "discontinuity" debate is central to my examination of their methods.

The visionary implications of their work compel a re-evaluation of their engagements. I can only touch on this vast aspect of their thinking and writing. Nevertheless, there are proposals in their texts and their public pronouncements, in notebooks and letters, which suggest radical illumination: their criticism becomes poetically charged metaphysics. If apocalypse means revelation, then they surely believed they were revealing something essential.

What can we show by implication and juxtaposition? Could there be a synergy in their words and metaphors, a recombination that yields to vistas of perception and recognition? Is there a crux where the aphorism "the medium is the message" joins with the Great Code? Is there a voice for the humanities spoken through their questing proposals that is relevant to thinking and curricula now?

I posit a reading of the synergy in their thinking that will reinstate them in the company of visionary Romantics and Modernists. I have said they resist the movements in postmodernism and deconstruction. They supply us with warning signs and literary symbols, metaphors for navigating through discouragement, implicit strategies for overturning meaninglessness. I believe their attempts to find laws and codes, to offer environmental awareness and systems of literary patterns as memory-triggers, were meant to insulate themselves against decay and death, and to quicken us, enlivening us into immediacies of visionary intensity.

It is no coincidence that of signal importance to their thinking were their later readings of Frances A. Yates's seminal study: *The Art of Memory* (1966). It confirmed the centrality of mnemonic devices. Art and criticism are essential retrievals of intelligible forms. Yates's work of reconstructing scholarship showed how through ancient times to the Renaissance period when Shakespeare lived, Nature and the universe were understood by poets and philosophers to be a book of life that could be decoded: there is a cosmos in a word, and words reflect and recompose the cosmos. Art and the art of reading make memory systems where everything can unfold to us.[28]

I witnessed how McLuhan's spiritual urgencies and Frye's subtle passions were apparent at the University of Toronto. McLuhan had a small handwritten sign hanging on the west wall of the Centre for Culture and Technology that said, "The important thing is to acquire perception, though it cost you all you have"; in a sermon preached in the Victoria College Chapel in 1968, Frye said, "The language of symbol is the language of love, and that, as Paul reminds us, will last longer than any other form of human communication."[29] These were words I often heard him say in class.

McLuhan's "the medium is the message" is koan-like, a mnemonic device. Frye wrote of how his theories of modes, symbols, myths, and genres, outlined in *Anatomy of Criticism*, composed a contemplative memory system in which the reader could retrieve the codes of literary structure. He called his system of fours "a mandala."[30] A mandala is simultaneously an ideogram that helps to concentrate the mind on an idea and a talisman of reflection that unfolds with greater meaning the more we engage it. The Great Code, outlined in his 1982 book, is a memory device that spells out the latent story-quest of identity, compelling us forward through the bleak ruins of lonely despair.

The McLuhan-Frye convergence forms, for all their divergences and disagreements, an ideal of restoration and the redressing of meaning. Their deepest concerns were how texts (of the world, of literary invention) make us and how we in turn make and receive more meaning.

I imagine them saying now: let there be more quests and descents into the maelstrom, more ascents up the ladder of consciousness; let there be journeys into the labyrinth; let there be a mending of our relation with the cosmos; let there be the overflow of suggestion and observation. Nietzsche said that multiple interpretations will eventually bury the original text.[31] Roberto Calasso in *K.* (2005), an indispensable study of Kafka, suggests that extended Talmudic commentary opens the mind to untold depths – an abyss for some, tormenting, petrifying because it is open-ended.[32] The openness to possibility was neither terrifying nor a terminal excess for McLuhan and Frye. They thought there was more in the texts of Nature, and in the texts of literary consciousness, than we had previously realized. In our current of artefacts and inventions that make up our environment, in the streams of seemingly disparate literary works that make up what we call tradition, we had become numb to the patterns at work. No texts, technological or literary, are shut – everything is open, waiting for us.

McLuhan and Frye were revealing secrets. In the ancient wisdom traditions, it was recognized that the world alters us, and so do our inventions. Inside the book of life we may find the grand etching of the cosmos: exodus towards identity. The point of teaching and writing is the enhancement of consciousness: revitalizations of heart, inspirations. It is vital to be iconoclastic; every age needs shamans and prophets. And so they were these, in contrasting ways: they challenged the status quo of cliché and routine.

Iconoclasm is a cleansing of vision that brings the stirrings of response. It was pivotal for them to re-creatively redeem our fall into ignorance and blind-deaf muteness.

"Mediumistically yours," McLuhan quipped when he signed a 1968 letter to the newly elected prime minister Pierre Elliott Trudeau (*Letters*, 357). The quip is packed. It plays on the reputation of his best-known aphorism, and it plays on the echoes in the word "medium": a soul who mediates, or channels, the spiritual world to the mundane plane. I find in this the merry prankster McLuhan, playing on his cult reputation. Nevertheless, he would deny he was a visionary because the word "vision" betrayed a visual bias informed by the habit of silent, solitary reading. "Visionary" was a construct that betrayed the sensory preference of the eye. He said that his work was "audile-tactile." This meant that he perceived environments in terms of the ear (listening) and of touch (pressure felt on skin): his apprehensions were therefore primarily acoustic-sensual. He acknowledged that the orality of the new electronic environments of TV, radio, telephones, computers, and satellites ("ECO-land"[33]) compose a pulsing sonic space which he explored through pun ("the medium is the massage"), performance (appearances on TV interview shows, in Woody Allen's movie *Annie Hall*), inversion of expectations (the use of cliché: "Should Old Aquinas Be Forgot?"[34]), and in deliberate agitation (what he called satire). The "Gutenberg Galaxy" of print had gone into supernova. Literature was being driven into margins. Electric flow is free-form: to catch it means taking leaps. Soon the alphabet will be backlit by emanating blue screens. Breakdown will be endemic, but so will breakthrough. What does the new look like?

Yet McLuhan's work, I have been arguing, is steeped in the ancient esoteric traditions of willed comprehension: epiphany and then commentary, initiation into the meanings behind the literal, guidance towards higher consciousness. The tradition says study all you can so that you will be lifted. The transformation of the world through technology is alchemy; the reading of the codes of that transformation is the apocalypse. His PhD dissertation, *The Classical Trivium*, underscored his subsequent work on the electronic media. Its publication in 2006 was a major discovery. It shows how McLuhan was profoundly rooted in the study of alchemy (transformation by expanded perceptual or technological means) and multilevel illuminations of the Book of Nature.

Robert Denham calls Frye's essaying "Visionary Poetics." In *Religious Visionary and Architect of the Spiritual World* (2004), Denham says, "Frye's central mission is to descend and to ascend the imaginative ladder to the ultimate level of spiritual vision."³⁵ Frye thought of titling *Anatomy of Criticism* "Structural *Poetics*" (emphasis mine). The publication of Frye's notebooks from 2000 through 2008, guided by Denham, Lee, and Michael Dolzani, revealed how Frye propelled his work with metaphysical intentions, epic-poetic analogies. The publication of his journals and notebooks were a transfiguring literary event. They spiked controversy. In what his editors have called (with some caution), *Notebooks and Lectures on the Bible and Other Religious Texts*, Frye writes, likely in 1969 or 1970, "I'm beginning to feel that I really am the man who's found the lost chord who really can, on the basis of literature, put the Tarot & alchemy & kabalism & the rest of it together into a coherent speech & language."³⁶ Frye again asserts, probably in 1976, "*I'm getting through to something, I think: the secrets of Being* ... in which the metaphorical is the literal. We can recapture this only poetically; but our poetic apprehension has to transcend everything we think of as literary into a new kind of super-'literalism'" (292, emphasis mine). Super-literalism is the achieving of visionary conditions – insight, sensory refreshment, contact with meaningfulness, heightened mental activity – through "litera," the word, or verbal construct, the focus on a book.

Frye pronounces in his *Late Notebooks, 1982–1990: Architecture of the Spiritual World* on the vocation of the prophetic teacher (i.e., himself), "I am not an historian: I'm an architect of the spiritual world."³⁷ In his most forceful declaration of his mission, he boldly affirms, "If there's no real difference between creation & criticism, *I have as much right to build palaces of criticism as Milton had to write epic poems*" (132, emphasis mine).

Cleansing the Doors of Perception, Applied Blake

Fearful Symmetry and *The Double Vision* were the Blakean visionary bookends in Frye's epic lyrical-critical quest. To enter into theoretical and theological debates through Blake is to choose a route that self-consciously challenges the canon and proposes an alternative critical focus. Blake was not central to the canon in the 1940s. He was a dissenter. The legions of the awakened walked the London streets. His Protestant London swarmed with Puritans, Levellers (or Diggers), Shakers (sometimes derisively called the Wallops), Quakers, Seekers, Ranters, Adamites, Enthusiasts, Wesleyans, Philadelphians, Anabaptists, Methodists, Moravians, Congregationalists (most of whom exiled themselves to the United States, to become the Pilgrim fathers), and the sects with the delightful Cat-in-the-Hat-like names of the Muggletonians and Grindletonians.

Nonconformists all, followers of the Inner Light, they revolted against Church and State. (Memo: the Puritans did not settle in Canada, though dissenters did enter the northern wilds through gradual immigration.)

Frye's selection of Blake – I think he would have said Blake's spirit selected him – invokes a championing of the Romantic primacy of prophetic power to resist the horror-riddled labyrinth and shackling institutions of history. The labyrinth of time can seem sealed off at both ends, a wasting nightmare with no way out. (The sealed maze metaphor serves Frye in the same way the descent into the maelstrom metaphor serves McLuhan.) Allying himself with Blake, Frye asserts the mind's capacity to forge counter-myths, and thus to reform social contracts. Liberal Romantics encourage rebellion and want concessions from the Leviathan State (and Tories fear the weaknesses that the concessions will bring).

Cromwell is said to have famously declared that the English have revolution in their bones. Blake had dissident vision encoded in the DNA of his imagination: he saw everything differently and urged his readers to do the same. Unimaginative minds descend into sour cynicism, and for them reality becomes a prison. Dissent is a way to crack the walls of the prisons of inhibition and prohibition. What looks like crankiness to the conformist is to the rebel a magical disagreement with a settled notion of reality; and to a radical dreamer like Blake, reality is mouldable; the civil war of imagination against conformity is carried on through opposition to dullness, deadness, impoverishments of spirit, dispirited and aimless wandering.

Frye learned this from Blake: every strong reading of a poem initiates radical alterations of the reader's mind. He called *Anatomy of Criticism* an encyclopedic satire in the tradition of Robert Burton's *The Anatomy of Melancholy*. Throughout his life's work we find a strain of apocalyptic satire infused with the freeing principle of Blake's *Marriage of Heaven and Hell*: the reader must awaken to the unlimited potentials of mind, the mediating energy between invisible spirit and visible matter. I find it beguiling and restorative to realize that for Blake the soul is always innocent; we can see through mundane coverings to its free spiritedness. Every new day is virginal; and if your soul prospers, the cynicism and negativity that you will inevitably encounter in the world will not poison you.

Fearful Symmetry is a manifesto of art embraced, imagination welcomed. In a 1935 letter to Helen Kemp, later his wife, Frye makes his evangelical protest clear. He defiantly (and entrancingly) states, "Now religion and art are the two most important phenomena in the world; or rather the most important phenomenon, for they are basically the same thing ... Atheism is an impossible religious position for me, just as materialism is an impossible philosophical position, and I am unable to solve the problems of religion and art by ignoring the first and distorting the second. *Read Blake or go to hell: that's my message to the modern world*"[38] (emphasis mine).

McLuhan was a devout Catholic (a convert to the Word and the ceremonies of the Church) whose dissident heresies manifested themselves in his unruly aphorisms and sly satires on power and authority. (I will be looking at this impressive contradiction in him in greater detail.) Frye was a once and future Protestant preacher, a blatant Blakean, whose catholic vision of the unity of literature manifested itself in abstract critical principles. McLuhan chose Rome and its symbolic association with the past; Frye chose the interior castle he called Jerusalem: both ended up living in Toronto, dreaming of cities of wonder. McLuhan was the specialist English literature professor who broke boundaries of study and attention; Frye – a seemingly staid theoretician whose truest motive was the cultivation of vision. These ironies and contradictions confound me at times; but they are also sources of fascination: they give me a double vision of their many sides, a vision in love with the productions of their time.

Turning to the Obscure Studies of the Two Together

Although the McLuhan-Frye convergence appears central to me, I am surprised (and perturbed) to report that there is almost nothing on the two together. Critical literature on their conjunction is sparse. There are biographical-historical references to them, passing comments in essays and chapters in books. When I began the research for this book I thought I would find volumes on their pairing. Frye muses in his notebook, possibly in 1971, on the process of alchemic combinations: "In imaginative thought there is no real knowledge of anything but similarities (ultimately of identities): knowledge of differences is merely a transition to a new knowledge of similarities."[39]

This is what I found in critical evaluations and speculations on their interweaving. The formidable theoretician of postmodernism Linda Hutcheon outlines the Frye-McLuhan association in her "Introduction: The Field Notes of a Public Critic," which prefaces the 1995 edition of Frye's seminal essay collection, *The Bush Garden: Essays on the Canadian Imagination*:

McLuhan's interest in technology and in questions of media power and control was very different from Frye's focus on the transforming and liberating power of the poetic imagination, but they have long been linked together not only as colleagues in the Department of English at the University of Toronto but as "our first genuine critics," as Louis Dudek put it in the early 1970s. However temperamentally diverse, these two thinkers were both concerned with the social role of both art and the criticism of art.[40]

Her remark about their temperamental diversity downplays the scale of their engagement with one another; the confining of their prophetic ambitions to "genuine" criticism does not absorb the influential, transformative intensities of their perceptions and essaying. Nevertheless, Hutcheon recognizes their presence and their mutuality. Her statement was a seed for my study.

The critics Ronald Bates and David Cook in their works on Frye made reference to McLuhan and a complementarity between the two.[41] There is John Fekete's antithetical deconstruction of them; I will closely read it later. However, few commentaries on McLuhan mention the presence of Frye's thought and McLuhan's responses. This is because most of the commentary on McLuhan is written by social scientists, technologists, media commentators, political theorists, postmodernist speculators, and philosophers. They are often (blithely) unaware of McLuhan's roots in the study of grammar and rhetoric.

In *McLuhan, or Modernism in Reverse* (1996), critical-theorist Glenn Willmott vividly comments on the proximity of the two apocalyptics in space and time. He calls their theorizing a profound positioning of adamant opposites: "McLuhan felt himself to be the intellectual antibook of his rival in Canadian letters, Northrop Frye, despite the fact that the latter, too, valorized the forms of art and the powers of fictive imagination towards a grasp of human reality and history."[42] Willmott provocatively reflects in his all-too-brief passages on how McLuhan was a metaphysical seer of media and Frye a "mythicist-fictionalist." By this he means that McLuhan is the observational intelligence and Frye is the poet-critic who strives to transcend reality.

Willmott revives the McLuhan charge of a dualism in the centre of Frye's thought. This is a charge I do not accept and will be exploring in my chapter on their agon. Willmott writes that Frye's dualism lies between "a sensible, aesthetic form, on the one hand, and a formless, barely representable, obscure and violent reality, on the other" (181).

He dismisses the possibility of complementarity or synergy between the visionaries, seeing them rather in terms of irreconcilable opposites: "McLuhan bears little comparison with the mythicist Frye: his media analysis from *The Gutenberg Galaxy* (1962) onward sought meaning in grounds specific to cultures and their historical systems of communication, an insistently non-literary or 'centrifugal' movement of criticism contrary to Frye's own" (ibid.). This critical judgment is common: the Frye-McLuhan debate often widely divides the advocates of one or the other; and almost no shared ground is sought.

The primary text on the McLuhan-Frye convergence remains the final chapter, "Borderlines," of Richard Cavell's *McLuhan in Space: A Cultural Geography* (2002).[43] Cavell evocatively describes and explores their agon: he makes precise reference to *The Listener* debate between McLuhan and Frye in 1970, to the arguments and innuendos we find in the back and forth of Frye's *The Modern Century* (1967) and McLuhan's *From Cliché to Archetype* (1970), to Fekete's critique, to allusions to McLuhan in essays Frye wrote after the death of his colleague – all works that my book will explore too. He also alludes to the nominal suggestions made by other critics, in particular guiding my attention to Eli Mandel's essay contribution to the anthology *Contexts of Canadian Criticism* (1971), where Mandel makes that vital link of both McLuhan and Frye with Blake. Cavell says of the two, "Each wrote a book in response to the other."[44] But his focus is on McLuhan, so the thematic concern of his title obviously indicates, and not on their conjunction or on their centrality to the founding of a prophetic seer tradition. Cavell does not read Frye's notebooks; this limits his inquiry. Frye's notebooks are peppered with sharp responses to McLuhan.

But Cavell seizes on their passion for education. Learning is a way of bringing on apocalypse. It is the dream of paradise regained. The classroom would be without walls, grace and mutuality expanding. Cavell says about the role of enlightenment, of training students to be open, "One of the major links between the work of Frye and McLuhan is the importance they granted to the educational function of their work" (219). McLuhan and Frye emerge from the humanist-scholarship traditions which emphasize analogy and correspondence (similarities in the structures of forms), and the enlightenment of students. Cavell rightly makes them central figures of the Canadian imaginative terrain (in some ways the primary figures). This was for me the most stimulating portion of his analytical enterprise. It has seeded my thoughts too.

Finally, I mention Francesco Guardiani's pioneering essay, "The Common Ground of McLuhan and Frye," published in the premiere issue of *McLuhan Studies* in 1996. It is an exploratory work that in a condensed space evokes the literary commonality – the communications' juncture – of the two. His thesis highlights their faith in learning and the capacity to revive energy and awaken sensibility; he emphasizes their awareness of the importance of the literary tradition and their hunger to encompass whole vision. He points to the focus on enriching consciousness, rising to being. This is, he says, the core of their perceptive and apprehensive cultural missions. Guardiani stresses the audacity of their Canadian perspectives. He notes the use that McLuhan and Frye made of provincial experiences, their educations in England, the marginality in Toronto from the explosions of the American literary scene, and their desire to create inspirational conditions. He makes the point that a Frye-McLuhan rivalry has been exaggerated. Similarity does not mean sameness. A mirroring or an echoing depends on two perspectives, not one. The call of questions and probes from one mind needs the response of another mind. He understands how the two offer essential analogues for one another's propositions and metamorphoses in thought.[45]

All of these critics' engagements with the McLuhan-Frye convergence, I discovered, hold this in common: one of the keys to understanding the two is the faith in the mentoring act. The training and inspiration of the deep reader of media and of literature is the elevation of the pupil (the I). Through each I comes the cosmos; each of us is a centre of perception, a channel. And so education becomes a vocation.

The McLuhan-Frye conflict and harmony provide issues that extend far beyond literary criticism into questions about perception and the nature of visionary experience. They will insist, against desolation, that vitality is everywhere, in words, in technologies. The role of education is more initiation into mysteries than it is the striving for a good grade. We are responsible for the Great Texts (technological and literary) because they embody our energy and spirit. Frye wrote of our capacity to open to light – for him the inner light of the imagination, where the soul is; McLuhan spoke of hearing and tactility (being in touch, feeling connections), our capacity to pick up traces and waves – being immersed, absorbed, inside the soul of the world.

Hearer and Seer

When reading my teachers over time I have learned how an essential element of their conflict has to do with sensibility, sensory preferences. In *The Global Village*, McLuhan makes a distinction between a hearer and a seer: "The Inuit find truth is given not by 'seeing is believing,' but through oral tradition, mysticism, intuition, all cognition – in other words, not simply by observation and measurement of physical phenomena. To them, the ocularly visible apparition is not nearly as common as the auditory one. *Hearer* would be a better title than *seer* for their holy men."[46] McLuhan listened to the throb of his age as if he were lingering on the street corner of the global theatre, receiving, sensing, breathing in, intuiting in spasms that he often spewed back in aphorisms and fragments. Frye was absorbed in his library-office and in his classrooms by books as if he were a Kabbalist scholar reading inside the labyrinths of alphabetic articulations for hidden rhymes, studying sentences for the encoded message, what waits in concealment for the converting insight of the initiate, "an inner circumference full of eyes."[47]

City streets and labyrinth paths are parallels. McLuhan and Frye were engaged in cryptic debates that penetrated to the core of what theory is and what the limits of theory must be. They questioned the circumstances and conditions of literary practice; and they made humanist inquiries into the nature and role of letters, of knowledge and wisdom in the apogees and abysses that have recomposed the Modernist and postmodernist eras.

Inspiration is uncontrollable. It creates mavericks and missionaries (sometimes martyrs). The primary aim of the seer is to see the literary object as it could be; the primary role of the hearer is to listen to and catch the overtones of the global racket and rush.

The eye has to open wide to take in the abundance of light, whether electronic or literary. Close your eyes and you risk staying in darkness. The darkness is analogous to the moment in Gethsemane when Christ experienced consuming doubt. At night, cold and shivering alone, Christ knew that the dark was enveloping him. But if you remain in the dark, eyes tightly shut, the sprawl and shout of life could become invasive, too much to bear. Then the cool darkness is a comfort. And the Garden of Gethsemane could become a home. We call this state of endless doubt alienation. Instead of being a point through which one passes,

Intentions and Overview   51

Gethsemane soon becomes a prison with no exit. So the eye must open. Then you see paths leading out. The open eye sees more light, and the soul feels more warmth. This is a visionary moment.

A seer reads a printed page and absorbs the brightness of the strongly shaped black letters on the white background. The visionary reader is born of typography and the solitary state of reading. Letters formed on a page suggest codes, latent universal structures; the white spaces between the words suggest the infinite spaces of terror and awe.

The education of the hearer means perpetual receptivity and vulnerability. The ear is the womb for seedling sound. Acoustic space is reverberant, omnidirectional. In the sensual wilderness, you feel everything. Echoes play from everywhere. Voices and vibrations pour or drum into the ear, on skin. The one sense that will not shut off in sleep is hearing. In the womb the ear is the first sensory organ to be developed. In the beginning, in conception, you hear the pulse. The world itself is bathed in sounds; it has a heartbeat in changing weather and seasons. Every place reverberates and resonates with the whisper and call of the speaking wind. To the ancients, the blind sage-poets Homer and Tiresias were moved by insight, their ear for the sea-surges of life. If hearing and touch are the primary senses (for McLuhan), then you tap ahead, feeling your way. And you breathe the atmosphere of the time to sniff out if there is something in the air.

The ear is the womb for the angel's whisper; the ear is also like a wound that lets in everything. The eye looks to horizons, seeing what is coming next; the eye is also the sensory organ that distances processes and things. The seer in extremis could be likened to an autistic person, focused on a detail to the point of hypnotized intensity; the hearer in extremis could be likened to a mad dancer whirling like a dervish, spinning in the deliria of the senses, the air alive with the thrumming of infinite vibrations.

iLiteracy

What is in the air while I write this work? It is the rumbling of digital literacies, the hypertexts of multimedia, the growth of the World Wide Web, the near universality of miniaturized electronics that compress space/time into the palm of your hand. The future of literary studies often seems in jeopardy. Most universities and colleges are moving their curricula online to accommodate students whose experiences are entirely digital. Classes grow larger, so the impersonal reigns. Publishers threaten to disappear. Bookstores in North America are folded into conglomerate warehouses that stock DVDs and candles.

McLuhan and Frye provoke questions about the role of literary study in the post-literate, or iLiterate, age. iLiteracy is a neologism.[48] Post-literacy suggested a certain place from where we came (alphabetic literacy), the implication being that the literary realm still had far-reaching influence and the printed book was the primary cultural experience. iLiteracy speaks to digital conditions beyond alphabetic literacy, referring to the ambiguities of oral-tactile communications in the electronic communion. McLuhan and Frye saw how book culture could become marginal in the mass of new information technologies. iLiteracy suggests illiteracy in the pejorative; and it suggests informational and intuitional literacy, knowledge and sensory awareness outside of the alphabetic consciousness that McLuhan called "typographic man."[49] Not all awareness comes from literary text; the day is here when orality again becomes how people receive and learn. This was a point of deep contention between them.

Still one of the reasons I go on seeking their mentoring is because they recognized a vivid, humanized, and spiritualized cosmos: a vast artefact trying to communicate through symbols and the order of words and through the media and our uses of it. They saw an intelligibility of forms beyond randomness. The tradition is not a frozen canonic order imposed on sprawling creativity. It is a commonwealth of references to the pleroma, the abundance of knowledge and beauty. An esoteric reading of McLuhan's aphorisms would raise the idea that electronica is a communion with the possibility of many worlds. An esoteric reading of Frye's essays raises the idea that literary works embody the Spirit's call to humanity. We read the books of imagination, the books of Nature and super-Nature, so that we know that we are never perceiving, or dreaming, dreadfully alone. They strove to communicate these lessons. Across breaches of miscommunication over intentions and methods they argued. In books and ideas they commune with us.

McLuhan moves us towards the light of cathode screens and electric bulbs, towards the reverberations of radios and hi-fis: the power in the hieroglyphs of electronica. He struggled to say that all artefacts are extensions of humankind, and extension means entanglement in webs of complexity. If we feel technologies have been imposed on us, then our relationship with them will be alienated. Understanding media to be extensions of us means the cosmos becomes humanized, in all the ways that this word implies. We have vast shaping power, and what we make shapes consciousness too. Perhaps electric light will one day banish darkness, awakening the transport of our souls, the passionate momentum towards serenity and wisdom.

Frye moves us towards reflections on inner light and heresies unlimited: the power we find in the private act of engaging literary works, which offer the continuous and wondrous renewal of reading for ourselves. He tried to encourage us with a hopeful teaching: when we are engulfed by darkness, then the warming of the heart must come from the imagination. If we cultivate the poetic inner eye then it may come to be that we will enter regions of awareness where, on that Blakean Glad Day, we will find that darkness and light are one.

Both Frye and McLuhan urged us to keep moving towards the quick realization that every moment can become all in all. Together they established that Canadian apocalyptic tradition which is charged, cunning, provocative, eloquent, deliberately (lyrically and playfully) off-centre from the dominant (and domineering, I regret to say) European modes of discourse of the 1970s through to the 1990s. The effect of these visionary intentions is to follow their lines of fascination so that they become ours. Spirits falter; senses can become clouded. So their re-connective efforts recast inspiration and perception into existential imperatives.

Frye discloses the urgency of the visionary path when he says close to the end of his life, in the allusive eloquence of *The Double Vision*, "One has glimpses of the immense foreshortening of time that can take place in the world of the spirit; we may speak of 'inspiration,' a word that can hardly mean anything except for the coming or breaking through of the spirit from a world beyond time ... The goal [is] enlightenment, the uniting of experience and consciousness ... the sudden critical widening of the present moment expressed by the word *kairos*."[50] The word *kairos* means "the crucial time," the opening. It is the moment when a crisis comes, a place of destiny at a crossroads where you arrive suddenly and recognize the choices appearing before you. The inspirational quality of the crossroads is essential. And the inspiration may be devastating to you. At a crossing, no matter how it appears in any time or place, a moment comes when the you must step away from your cocooned sleep and, Lazarus-like, come to the feast.

McLuhan illuminates the visionary current when he proclaims his intentions in a largely overlooked 1961 essay, "The Humanities in The Electronic Age":

> Yet today, as never before, the task of the humanities is to keep clear and lively the modes of discourse and the forms of mental life. More than ever

before humanists are called on to understand many new languages born of the new forms of knowledge ... a natural model for the humanities in the electric age ... is *the idea of the poetic of history, of a history as kind of unified language, the inner key to the creation of the spiritual energy encompassed in the ceaselessly growing life of words*. The ideal Marriage of Mercury and Philology, of spiritual values and perfected method, will be consummated, if ever, in the electronic age.[51] (emphasis mine)

Poetics are at the heart of their intellectual endeavours. Poetics: to shape, elevate into metaphor, to give liberty to associations, release verbal energies to make unexpected connections. Discursive prose and aphorisms were the techniques they developed, techniques they wore like masks. They assumed their personae (the iconoclast and the reader) with the desire and the intention of restoring a sense of beauty (symmetry) and understanding (grace). Suddenness and pattern recognition could coexist. The two launched into the frontiers of the new, making their pact with revelation.

I am aware of how their contrasting styles and sensibilities can never be wholly reconciled, nor should they be: difference is an accomplishment. But I am aware of how they marked out paths and experiences in thinking and perception in ways that can imprint their students with hope and insight. I mean by imprint something along the lines of what Jacob's wrestle with the strange angel may mean in Genesis 32. The angel's blessing, gift and wound, gives you immeasurable life but leaves you excruciatingly aware that passion and mission are parts of that life.

The track of the McLuhan-Frye convergence is not well travelled yet. My goal is to initiate a discussion of the convergence, of the conflicts, of the methods and harmonies, and of the "ideal Marriage" of communications and literature ("Mercury and Philology") which their lives and thought bravely embody. One chapter looks at their lives and controversies; the next at their agon; and the following at their harmonies; the last two speculate on an alchemy of minds and on the lessons of the elders. Initiations are always beginnings; this work before you is just that: a start down the paths where they ventured, and then on.

2
Presences and Signatures: These Figures in Their Ground

Recognitions in Toronto

See Marshall McLuhan and Northrop Frye along with me in the cruxes of their time and place. Let us look at them in the legacies of their controversies, these figures in their ground.

We begin in the present: again let us look how the memory of their presence is encoded into the landscape of Toronto and the University of Toronto. In early 2012, if you were to walk on the east side of Queen's Park Circle, then you would see the geographies of McLuhan and Frye, their eminent domains. If you walk towards Lake Ontario, still on the campus, and if you look closely, you would see how visible their names are.

Near Victoria College you will see Northrop Frye Hall. The hall is large, spacious, a building with many classrooms. It stands parallel to the Department of Music and the Edward Johnson Performance Theatre, south of the renovated Royal Ontario Museum, the cubist structures that loom over Bloor Street. The plaque announcing its name faces the music building and performance centre. Frye was an amateur pianist, an enthusiastic student of music. He played on keys, spending his life of critical study searching for the key to the imagination, to the recurrent structures and types he found in literary works. Links and associations are reverberations and rhymes; the recurrent or stubborn structures are leitmotifs. The beat through literature is the pulse of consciousness trying to know itself.

Round the circle and walk behind the medieval studies building, tucked back from Saint Michael's Library and the Catholic wing of the university, and you will find Marshall McLuhan Way. This street runs off Queen's Park Circle. It links Saint Michael's College with Bay Street and joins in narrow lanes the university grounds to the city's business section. The way is a short passage ending in intersections. McLuhan's mind was shaped by his studied retrieval of medieval scholasticism. His PhD dissertation, *The Classical Trivium*, was guided at Cambridge by the noted Shakespearean scholar Muriel C. Bradbrook, who taught him to look at the educational background of his subject, Thomas Nashe. (Bradbrook later turned her attention to T.S. Eliot.) Through his study of Thomist scholasticism, McLuhan was introduced to the Book of Nature and how we, fallen Eves and Adams, must restore original insight into its metamorphic forms or media.

One name attached to a building, the other identified with a road. I note the architectural and city-planning symbolism: a circle where people can walk and find the Frye building with its classrooms built on many levels and then find McLuhan Way, with its pathways into the campus and into economic centres. These building and street names are guideposts in the history of ideas and perceptions. Their presences continue to define our civic and national life and imaginations.

Remember how Frye spoke of "the educated imagination" in his essay of the same name, refined from CBC radio broadcasts in 1962. His stress in that phrase was obviously on the adjective "educated." He was calling our attention to the centrality and vitality of classrooms and what he called "the singing school" (the line taken from stanza two of William Butler Yeats's "Sailing to Byzantium") of instruction and illumination. Many of his books and essays were devoted to explaining how teaching could be at its most effective. One of McLuhan's last collaborative projects (with Eric McLuhan, his eldest son, and Kathryn Hutchon), was *City as Classroom: Understanding Language and Media* (1977). Students were the future, he said. Frye invoked how we must sit together (in a building) and read through the seemingly chaotic surfaces of books, guided by the learned intelligence of a Virgil-like guide, towards the awareness of the identity quest that is the prevailing literary theme. McLuhan invoked how we must each become a probe, so go out into blaring streets – the world is now a cosmopolis – and pay attention to all avant-garde configurations of media and their impact on how we think and feel, with the guidance of questions formed by another Virgilian guide or guides.

Frye Hall and McLuhan Way: each structure frames the other. Appropriately, city planners and the University of Toronto renamed structures that will always stay close to one another. Frye Hall and McLuhan Way remind us how two essential figures passed through here. They were part of the university's, and of the city's, spirit and atmosphere.

But to Frye the existential city was a noisy interruption of concentration on the poetics that matter. The true city was the utopian communitarian inner city of the imagination, the dream promise of the Jerusalem he described in *Fearful Symmetry* and *Words with Power*.[1] "Education is a matter of developing the intellect," Frye dramatically responds in the book-length *Northrop Frye in Conversation* to a question put by David Cayley, "and the imagination, which deals with reality, *and reality is always irrelevant*" (emphasis mine).[2]

To McLuhan the circuit city was our essential surround, the impressing and lulling ground of unstoppable change – a frontier for exploration, another medium. He said in *Who Was Marshall McLuhan?* (1994), "The idea is to train perception. We do not train them [students] in theories but in percepts ... *To cognize is percept. To re-cognize is concept* ... I also re-cognize, but I cognize first ... the patterns ... of everything that is happening all around us."[3]

If we go back in time we would see them passing by one another. They would have done so on the paths and in the hallways of the University of Toronto from 1946 through 1979 while Toronto sprawled round them. The city was a drab, colourless place when they first arrived, in the 1930s for Frye and in the late 1940s for McLuhan. It was an outpost – a fringe city that was low-definition, low-profile. But into the sixties and the seventies Toronto would become a babble of many languages and cultures. The city rose, not like Venice from the sea but on reclaimed land from the lake.

Offices, domes: Toronto embodied a new world mythology of banks and media centres, becoming the capital engine of the country. A joke preserves how the city changed: "How many Torontonians does it take to change a light bulb?" Answer: "Just one. But the rest of the country now goes around him."

They saw Toronto jump-start into the future. Rising over the city was the communications' needle, the CN Tower. Building began in the 1970s. They could view its injecting progress on their walks, puncturing the sky, punctuating the horizon.

The two must have had enlivening and harrowing impressions of the tower's presence. It rose like a supercharged encryption. On the literal level, it was the concrete flower of the communications' latticing, a high-voltage beacon on the hydro-grid; on the symbolic level, it was the ladder of ascent from Jacob's vision in Genesis 28, finding a weird incarnation. The tower signified a text open to sensuous receptions, one to be revised by the reading eye of imaginative power.

They would have strolled, mulling over these signs, meditating, in conversation with colleagues, around Queen's Park. They likely glanced up and gleaned the tower's heralding significance. The global theatre was ramping up; the imagination was reaching an apogee, the stories of mythic awareness transfiguring existential fact. So the global city needs images and symbols; and so life imitates art.

(I suggest that these dual impressions are representations of how the hemispheres of the brain appear to work. McLuhan referenced these neurological speculations in his late-life fascinations with the hemispheres in the "Proteus Unbound" chapter of *Laws of Media*. The tower could symbolize the right brain – the hemisphere's response to sound, pulse, wordless static, simultaneous transmissions, imagery, and signals; it was also an embodiment of the left brain's activations – a precise technological wonder, the result of logic and mathematics. The two sides of the brain engage in an intricate, infinite interplay. So the tower could represent both sides of the brain's firings.)

To seize the furore of the moment – the brash manifestations of energy – they would have to grasp the signals and signs. To follow through in their missions, they would have to be ready to interpret the hieroglyphs when they showed themselves. All of this must have seemed strange, and fortuitous, in Toronto, a marginal blip in the electric grid and imaginative terrain.

※

Still Toronto may have been far from Paris, London, Rome, Barcelona, Berlin, or (even) New York City, but inspiration can happen anywhere: you can begin your quest in any place. Some people thrive in displacement. Artists and thinkers cultivate exile. This would have been part of their educations in the great esoteric traditions: everywhere is here, if you cultivate spiritual energy. And they surely surmised: better to be living and thinking in a province than swallowed by the allure of empire. In Toronto, the arctic winds from the north periodically sweep down to cleanse your eye, refreshing your senses.

But the tower heralded: Toronto would become a hub. The city was in need of myths. What better place to be for a Mental Traveller and a student of media storms? They were citizens of the republic of ideas, so they could begin to look up, and to reflect, here in this city that was quickly transforming away from its acid nickname, Toronto the Good and Bland.

What do we mean by "here"? Where are we? The wisdom traditions (Aldous Huxley called them "The Perennial Philosophy") intimated that the identity question should be followed by that location question. ("Toto, I have a feeling we're not in Kansas anymore," Dorothy famously fretted after crash-landing in Oz. This line became one of the epigraphs to Thomas Pynchon's 1972 novel, *Gravity's Rainbow*, a novel about Second World War rocketry and occult conspiracies that fascinated both McLuhan and Frye.) Toronto was a place between, a mediation point: the United States to the south, Europe to the east, the Pacific far to the west. Therefore the city was an outsider to the imperiums (European and American), another factor in its favour.

The tower for Frye would have represented a metaphor (and archetype?) of the ascension towards higher consciousness. He would have made analogies to the upward movement of the ladder of vision, to the downward movement to "the foul rag and bone shop of the heart" that appears in the last lines of Yeats's poem "The Circus Animals' Desertion." The tower for McLuhan was a sign of how Toronto had become an echo location, volatile point of reception and transmission in borderless information networks, a centre without margins. McLuhan intuited: capitals are obsolete, museums for tourists and backdrops for movies. It was best to be a boundary-hopper and a claim-jumper.

And thus the two teachers walked around the grounds of the campus and the city. They must have crossed by one another almost daily on the university pathways. John Robert Colombo, invaluable chronicler of quotations, comments on the presence of McLuhan and Frye on the University of Toronto campus and in the city zeitgeist. These passages are apposite. They establish their bearings on one another, their signatures and evocations, the decisive influencing of the McLuhan and Frye clash and convergence; and they prepare us for explorations and exchanges to come:

> There were two enormously powerful generators of literary and cultural thought in operation on the campus of the University of Toronto in the late 1950s. Every student of the humanities knew that the currents of thought were of two kinds – DC and AC. The Direct Current emanated steadily from the office of Northrop Frye at Victoria College; the Alternating Current came in waves from the Coach House of Marshall McLuhan at St. Michael's College. If one was an undergraduate with an interest in the literary and cultural matters of the day, one could not help but be affected by one or both of these generators ... Northrop Frye was the Plato of Canada: divining

the Pure Forms, assuring us of their existence. Marshall McLuhan was the country's Aristotle, taking inventory of material causes and immaterial effects, assuring us of their interconnectedness. I attended their lectures and addresses and I read their essays in journals like the *University of Toronto Quarterly* and *Explorations*. Since then hardly a day has gone by that I have not pondered an insight or formulation, a phrase or thought, of one or the other of these two great contemporary thinkers. I selfishly believe that fate ordained it that they would have come to Toronto at the appropriate time to wield an influence over my mental development. Indeed, one of them traveled from Eastern Canada, the other from western Canada; one emerged from Protestantism, the other from Catholicism. In my mind's eye they are entwined, so entwined as to be a single, doubled-faced figure, like Janus. They function as my mental bookends. It is easy to visualize Frye and McLuhan as polar opposites, easier to see them as complementary figures, and easiest of all to benefit from their sense of what constitutes tradition and transformation.

(Colombo, quoted in McLuhan and Nevitt,
Who Was Marshall McLuhan?, 127)

I note that Colombo's observations follow the only contribution by Frye to the Barrington Nevitt and Maurice McLuhan collection of homages. In a (very) short entry Frye comments, "a reassessment of his work and its value is badly needed." In the next line Frye states, tartly and amusingly, that what he learned from McLuhan was "the role of discontinuity" (ibid., 126). I will return to his double-edged comment in my chapter on their conflicts.

I make several observations regarding Colombo's commentary. He gestures towards their impact on students and on the culture at large. He identifies their "entwined" quality. They were in their teachings themselves volatile vortices of meaning and affect. Their classrooms were experimental sites. Remember their Christian backgrounds. Frye was an ordained United Church minister. McLuhan, a fervent convert, attended noon-hour mass regularly at Saint Michael's College, often taking an interested student with him. Classrooms could be pulpits and Arcadian altars, places of congregational gatherings and of communions with the energies of their pupils.

Colombo goes on to suggest that by placing them inside one another, we would perceive "a single, doubled-faced figure, like Janus." This is an image of complementarity. He more than hints that they represent twin aspects of central questions about the application of literary studies:

to look to the texts in the tradition which expose structures and analogies; to look to the patterns of the present to be better prepared for the future. Janus was the god of gates, doors, bridges, beginnings and endings. A compound being, he was a shape-shifting divinity that yielded to new appearances according to how one looked at him. Janus had the gift of seeing the future and the past. The Janus-mask may be inspiring and intimidating: it changes, animated by enthusiasms. He was the god who oversaw the apprenticeship and education of youth, moving from one form of consciousness to another. The final note sounded on "tradition and transformation" sets the shifting text and context issue that is crucial to their undertakings. Both were figures of tradition, schooled in literary textual analysis and retention; both took that tradition and transformed it into theoretical architecture and perceptual recommendations for cognition and recognition. Their originality was embodied in their research and work and in the charisma of their classroom personae. And their presence in the Canadian environment (Colombo acknowledges) was momentous.

Frye comments on convergences of ideas and personalities, of concerns and environment, of perception and geography, of synchronous intentions and history, again in his interview with Cayley. This response helps to explain why Frye stayed in Canada. It shows that he understood how close the thinkers at the University of Toronto, by necessity, could be to one another:

> You tend to get lost in a country as big as the United States, and you have to be frantically aggressive to make much of a sense of your individuality. But in Canada there's a small enough community responding to you – I'm thinking roughly of the cultured, intellectual community – so that you do get known as a person, or any rate identified as a person ... Canadians have been obsessed with communications, which took itself out in building bridges and railways and canals in the nineteenth century and in developing very comprehensive theories of communication, like Innis's and McLuhan's in the twentieth century. I suppose I belong to some extent in that category.
>
> ... The difficulties within communication, within the very act of communicating at all, and the fact that the settlements in Canada are isolated from each other in geographical ways – these things, I think, have brought about certain affinities among people who have talked about communication in Canada.
>
> (Cayley, *Northrop Frye in Conversation*, 123–4)

McLuhan makes similar observations in *The Global Village*:

> Canada's 5000-mile borderline is unfortified and has the effect of keeping Canadians in a perpetual philosophic mood ... Canada's borderline encourages the expenditure on communication of what might otherwise be spent on armaments and fortification ... *communication rather than fortification.*
> (McLuhan and Powers, *Global Village*, 165; emphasis mine)

I restate how Frye and McLuhan direct our attention to the Canadian difference: more concerned with communication than with conquest, more concerned with revision and reforming than with overpowering or obliterating the other.

Their names have become coordinates of mythic conjecture. Colombo's evocation reminds us of their magnetic mental energies. This summons images of creative synergistic vortices from the past: the American renaissance in the transcendentalism and coinciding forces we find in the New England of Emerson, Whitman, Thoreau, Melville, Dickinson, and Beecher Stowe in the 1850s and 1860s; and in the meetings and collaborations of the Modernists Wyndham Lewis, Pound, Eliot, H.D., Virginia Woolf, and T.E. Hulme in London before the cataclysms of the First World War. There are innumerable examples of such spectacular intersections: in Paris in the 1920s and 1930s (Joyce, Stein, Proust, Picasso, Braque, Hemingway, F. Scott Fitzgerald, Henry Miller, and Anais Nin); in New York City in the 1950s and 1960s (Norman Mailer, Mary McCarthy, Dwight Macdonald, Susan Sontag); in Montreal at McGill in the 1960s and 1970s (Irving Layton, Charles Taylor, Leonard Cohen, Louis Dudek). Although these convergences of energies did not always involve academies, there were mixtures of scholarly, philosophical, imaginative, and critical intentions, interests, and obsessive pursuits. Certain places at certain times become strange centres of attraction. Why people might be drawn together at a given period, however briefly, in a city or a town should be a subject for a study of atmospheres, the impelling influence of consciousness and presence.

Inside the Classroom

Let us acknowledge how classrooms can be battlefields. I have posited that the teaching codes that McLuhan and Frye passed on were inspirational and taunting, a mix of the Romantic sublime and the satiric. But for some students, teaching can come too early, or too late. Classrooms can be politicized, soapboxes for ideologues. The classroom can be a matrix for new ideas and traditions, an unholy collision at times between revolutionary zeal and orthodoxy. No teaching experience, so McLuhan and Frye knew very well, is value-free.

Moreover, charismatic figures in classrooms invariably find rapt, and captive, audiences. We are more attuned to the power relations involved after the work of Michel Foucault. But charisma is an excess of energy, an abundance of personality and magnetic thinking. Charisma can no more be contained than inspirations can be. It is a kind of magic. McLuhan and Frye were charismatics, although their classroom styles and intentions radically differed. One jazzed leaving things loose, frequently jettisoning schedules and readings for in-the-moment improvisations and speculations; one came to each class with lecture notes prepared in advance, sometimes merely reading from those subtle notes. Further, the spiritual nature of their teaching quests – are all quests implicitly spiritual? do quests demand encounters with transcendence? – could not help but impress rooms full of youthful listeners. I knew, when I was their student, that a magnum opus was underway before my eyes; I sensed the magnitude of the occasions. I decided it was best to be quiet and receptive. (Any argument with them seemed a pointless assertion of my ego.) Some teachers supply facts. Others rewrite reality.

Pupils (think of the pun on the I in that word) open up around a charismatic teacher. They become surrogate children. A classroom can become, for a time, like a family; and like a family it can have mercurial destinies of affection and alienation. (Frye and Helen had no children; McLuhan and Corinne had six, including a set of fraternal twin daughters.) Students are changed into audiences, into avid readers of the masters' works (teaching is, after all, a way of keeping your books in the public eye). Students extend the lessons by carrying them forward. But they can distort these lessons too, and they can ferociously rebel against them.

The classroom can become a nightmare. Some students intuitively rail against the arbitrary standards of a school or a degree requirement. Facts and structures established by others could interfere with the internal story, the intuitional core, of a gifted or curious student. Your heart and soul may war against teachers and their charm.

It is well known how illustrious figures in many fields failed in the classroom. Eminence and tuition do not always harmonize. Einstein, Churchill, Thomas Mann, Kafka, Gertrude Stein, William Faulkner, Stravinsky, Gandhi, Willa Cather, Picasso, Joseph Amar, Jackson Pollock, Ellen

Glasgow, Virginia Woolf (she was schooled at home), Pearl S. Buck, John Stuart Mill, Cormac McCarthy, Christopher Dewdney: that is just a short list of the many who did not find the learning experiences of a classroom compatible with their pathways of inspiration, of stumbling and falling on their own.

I cite all this in what may appear to be a digression because I was an erratic student. "Erratic" is not an adequate word. I failed classes (mostly science and math), dropped out of high school, performed poorly at times at undergraduate school, skipped sessions with professors I found dull, avoided finishing my PhD for fifteen years. Sometimes in frank rebellion against my teachers I would desert classes and not return, or bored and uninspired I would retreat into a sullen silence at my desk, daydreaming my way out. I never liked exams, and when I became a professor of literature, I found I did not much like giving them either (though for some perverse reason I do).

Classrooms can be a blockade to learning. Nietzsche – himself an exile from the university milieu – subversively, and accusingly, claimed that no philosophy could come from any school. Success in a classroom structure is no guarantee of success in making a creative identity, in whatever circumstance. Classrooms can spawn awful rivalries and envy. The beloved charismatic teacher anoints a student to be his or her heir (and invariably it is not you).

There is evidence in the biographies of McLuhan and Frye that they were themselves students with startlingly uneven records. While they had their successes in schools – so I will show shortly – they were surely following the inward track of missionary intent: to be other.

They insistently communicated the desire to be different in the classes I attended. McLuhan preferred a small seminar's intimacy, where he could swivel in his chair and point to a student or a guest and demand a reply. (It was not unusual, however, for him to snooze during a seminar.) Frye's graduate class was larger (over thirty people attended). I saw him lecture from notes, then pause and reflect. While he was highly organized, always following the reading list set out by his course syllabus, Frye was apt to digress on recent readings. Often he said something about a poet in a way that seemed to surprise himself. He listened to intelligent questions; and sometimes he sighed and dismissed questions that were not so bright. He focused on the literary tradition, on poetics, rarely diverging from the intensity of that focus. McLuhan was sometimes insulting to his students, intolerant of shyness. He never followed the course syllabus. Tangents were epics of discovery. He was eager to hear about new technologies, new slang. ("Clint Eastwood's *A Fistful of Dollars* is called a 'spaghetti western'? Well, now, *that's* a mouthful," he said to me, after I had informed him of that description. He laughed, always welcoming an opportunity for a joke or a pun.) In private I found him nurturing and patient, though always strong-minded in his probing into my often blurry speculations. Frye in private was cordial, likely to leave you with a list of recommended readings. He had a droll wit in class, and a sly joke was apt to slide by the inattentive student.

Classrooms were seeding places for them. They were communicating the code of inspiration: to raise yourself, to make your percepts and imagination move beyond school rooms, chalk, blackboards, exams, and syllabi. It is a spiritual crime to dis-spirit others. Let a student leave a classroom demoralized and he or she is likely to nurse grievances. The two unleashed sentences to initiate openings. We were invited into the flight of words, and where we went with those words was up to us.

Origins: The Backstories

But I must ask more questions. I acknowledge the presence of McLuhan and Frye in our urban landscape and cultural history, and in the imaginations and memories of their students. Where did these two thinkers come from? How did they shape themselves? How did their charisma come to be apparent to others? How did their theoretical proposals evolve? What critical positions did they assume? What intellectual precepts and concepts did they pass on? How have their intellectual undertakings continued to hold sway? Why was each eagerly accepted and at times ruthlessly dismissed?

To Frye identity is the narrative pulse and metaphoric drive of every literary quest. "This story of the loss and regaining of identity is, I think, the framework of all literature. Inside it comes the story of the hero with a thousand faces, as one critic calls him [the critic is Joseph Campbell], whose adventures, death, disappearance, marriage or resurrection are the focal points of what later become romance and tragedy and satire and comedy" (Frye, *The Educated Imagination*, 21). McLuhan evokes the centrality of the being-becoming issue when he says in *The Global Village*, "For two centuries, at least, the frontier has taught us how to go out alone ... going out to be alone raises the ultimate question: who am I?" (McLuhan and Powers, *Global Village*, 147). McLuhan spoke of the importance of the put-on, or mask. Identity was discovered in process, constructed in medias res.

Identity was an always eloquent obsession for them. If the romance-quest is the DNA of narrative, the essential story behind the stories, the felt presence behind the material of literature, and the signatures of our environment, then let us look to the identities of McLuhan and Frye, beyond their reputations and classroom and public personae.

⁓⌘⁓

They have been called Mass Sage and Magus, the Northern Lights, "each other's Achilles' Heel" (by the late Donald Theall, another critic who studied with both McLuhan and Frye[4]), the two genii of the University of Toronto.[5] In *Northrop Frye* (1971), the critic Ronald Bates speculatively calls McLuhan "the centrifugalist" and Frye "the centripetalist" and goes on to elaborate: "the centripetalist (the priest), I would say, produces a Summa, the centrifugalist (the jester), a Geste book, with the emphasis on performance, process, gesture, and suggestion. *The one draws you in, a vortex, the other sends you out, a galaxy.* Both can be dizzying experiences" (19–20; emphasis mine).

At junctures in their careers, after the publication of *Fearful Symmetry* and *Anatomy of Criticism*, and after the publication, in quick succession, of *The Gutenberg Galaxy* and *Understanding Media*, the two men were feted and heralded. *Fearful Symmetry* was, to Edith Sitwell, "a book of great importance, and every page opens fresh doors";[6] McLuhan was called "the most important thinker since Newton, Darwin, Freud, Einstein, and Pavlov."[7] Frye was an intellectual who reached outside of the university to the common reader. Forty-one years after its first published edition, *Fearful Symmetry* is still in print (it has had ten printings); thirty-one years after its appearance, *Anatomy of Criticism* is also still in print (there have been fifteen printings). Out of Frye's writings come myth criticism and the elevation of the critic to the cult status of independent force, a strenuous seer in his or her own right. Margaret Atwood and Dennis Lee were his students. From Frye's speculations come the emphases on theoretical structure and the critical movements that have taken totalizing, predictive theory to its logical extreme. Fredric Jameson and Edward Said acknowledged their debts to Frye's "meteoric theoretical ascendancy" and established theoretical agons with him.[8]

Out of McLuhan's thought come media studies and interdisciplinary studies and the declaration that specialization is dead. Although many of his books have slipped in and out of print – and he has had to wait for posthumous confirmation of literary worth through the republication of his corpus through Gingko Press, Penguin Books, and the

University of Toronto Press – his two most influential works, *The Gutenberg Galaxy* and *Understanding Media*, have remained in the public eye. *Understanding Media* was revised by McLuhan for subsequent editions. Out of McLuhan's work come artistic responses, music by John Cage and R. Murray Schafer, the title of Haskell Wexler's film *Medium Cool* (1969), and the exegesis on the crises of classical or humanist literature in the conditions of post-literacy that we find in the writings of George Steiner, Camille Paglia, Sven Birkerts, and William Irwin Thompson.[9] In what I take to be the ultimate homage to him, the San Francisco performance group Ant Farm (founded by Chip Lord and Doug Michels) smashed a streamlined Cadillac into a burning platform of TV sets, videoing the happening in the production they (endearingly) called "Media Burn" (1975). James Cameron (of *Avatar* mega-fame, and a Canadian) once said anyone who grew up in Canada in the 1970s absorbed McLuhan's ideas through a zeitgeist osmosis. The novelists William Gibson and J.G. Ballard acknowledged their imaginative debts to McLuhan's technological vision of extended psyche and nerve ends, discarnate body, imploding senses: flesh and steel, cells and microchips now the battleground.

H. Northrop Frye

Their stories have been told separately, in various biographies. But their lives, and their fascinations, have never been set side by side, juxtaposed like tableaux. So let us look, scanning for patterns, for crossings.

Biography will help us to see. Herman Northrop Frye was born in Sherbrooke, Quebec, in 1912, the son of devout Methodists. Methodism stems from the inner light, anti-creedal side of Protestantism. His father was a hardware salesman (mostly failed); his mother, at home, was timid, prone to depressed withdrawals. He had one older sister, Vera. His only brother, Howard, was killed in the trenches of the First World War. The family transplanted to Moncton, New Brunswick, in 1919.

Frye spent his formative years in isolation, in long periods of solitary reading in the small Moncton library. (Moncton became the site of the annual International Northrop Frye Festival.) It is something of a legend that he was a successful participant in typing contests. Contrary to those legends, he did not win all of them. But something larger intervened: Frye began to experience transcendental moments.

He experienced the first of what he called his radical illuminations during his high school years. Though he was evasive about the nature of these, he cited their decisive importance. I submit they were branding conversion experiences. Their ineffability speaks to the mystical; and their transience, to the force of the epiphany and its elusiveness. Their potent effect always reminded him of states of consciousness beyond the ordinary and routine; their imprint reminded him of the emerging powers of transfiguration.

Conversions are crises. Pressures build. Then there is a spiritual detonation. A switch is thrown. This cliché contains a truth: one door closes, another opens. Frye's first illumination in Moncton (yet another nowhere) ripped away the literalist teachings of his dry, lonely Methodist upbringing. Henceforth he would say that he no longer believed the Gospels, or by inference any literary document, to be fact, conclusive historical truth. Yet he remained fascinated by the visionary, inspirations beyond the mundane plane. His transcendental experiences were his introductions to the power of understanding through metaphor.

Frye arrived in Toronto in September 1929, on the eve of the stock market crash. He entered Victoria College at the University of Toronto. The city was soon combusting with news of falling stocks, failing banks. The Depression was impending. Unemployment put desperation into the streets, hobos and beggars in vivid troubling view. In the summer at Victoria College, while working part-time at the Central Reference Library, he discovered *Blake and Modern Thought* by Denis Saurat. (Always his flight into libraries; always his need to seek books to solace his experiences.) In his second year at Victoria College he met Helen Kemp, whom he would later marry. Their early correspondence, collected in *A Glorious and Terrible Life with You* (2007), reveals a powerful immediate intimacy and avowals of literary intention.

From an early age, Frye was urged on by the hunger to know. The outwardly shy student was looking for codes to move him towards significant accomplishment. He read Oswald Spengler's two volumes of *The Decline of the West* (published together, in English, in 1932); he studied with noted scholar Pelham Edgar. His graduating degree was in both English and philosophy. In 1933 he entered Emmanuel College in Toronto, in the theology school. Those who study Frye forget that he was initially no specialist in English literature: his expertise was also in philosophy and religious studies. We should again remember that Frye was ordained in the United Church in 1935; though his experiences during a bleak summer period, when he was an itinerant minister in desolate rural Saskatchewan in 1931, had already taught him that ministering (to put it mildly) was not his vocation. Another striking epiphany – quick, clear, sharp, liberating, again transforming – in a stark motel in Edmonton told him that his vocation had to be in the study of literature. There his sense of the boundlessness of the imagination could be pivotally fulfilled. His second conversion was to literature.

In Oxford at Merton College from 1936 until 1938, Frye began his close readings of Blake. Reading was an apocalyptic process: books were openings for the epic of imaginative coherence. Frye wrote of another conversion-like illumination inspired by his experiences in Oxford, when reading Blake's prophecies. This illumination (again enigmatic; we cannot be sure if it happened in Oxford or if it happened back in Toronto, while preparing a paper on Blake's *Milton* for a class) revealed how the poet said there is a secret in literary knowledge. The key to "something bigger" could be found through poetry itself. If Hildegard von Bingen was a visionary abbess whose revelations include poetry, if Dante was a poet whose writings absorb visionary experience, then Blake was a poet for whom poetry constitutes the visionary. The secret is the unity of literature; certain forms, genres, symbols, and patterns recur so persistently that these take on the luminous power of archetypes; an intellectual energy, embodied in symbols and images, has a transcendent force that emerges from the primary texts of the literary canon. The third conversion was to Blake's poetics.

Frye never finished his PhD. (I note this: he did not endure the trials that can grind the spunk out of doctoral candidates.) He returned to Toronto to teach in contractual appointments at the University of Toronto until his first – and only – full-time appointment in 1942. Through these times of teaching, study, reflection, travelling, and illumination, he worked on the notes that he later cast into *Fearful Symmetry*.

The quiet, studious Frye was to become the militant re-imaginer of William Blake, the unclassifiable and enigmatic visionary poet and painter. *Fearful Symmetry* was written during the Second World War, in part to respond to the despair and annihilations of that period. With knowledge of razed cities, the Holocaust, the atom bomb blasts over Hiroshima and Nagasaki, and the horrors of Fascism, Frye thought his book could be indirect resistance to the demoralization of ruins. His tutor at Oxford, Edmund Blunden, had been a Fascist sympathizer. Clearly, and thankfully, none of this rubbed off on the inward-directed student, who followed his dissident inner voice (his conscience) rather than the urgings of a right-wing teacher. Frye turned to the Romantics and the liberal vision of Blake, and not then to the writings of Ezra Pound or Eliot, both of whom had alarmingly shown grim sympathy for authoritarian politics. (Pound was tried for treason at the war's end; in 1945 he was confined to the insane asylum at Saint Elizabeth's in Washington, D.C., until 1958.)

Blake upheld dissent against empire and institutional dogmatic controls of reality. He embodied in his poetry a vision of the transformation of the world, achieved through imaginative pressuring and re-visioning. "Where man is not, nature is barren," Blake memorably declares in the "Proverbs of Hell" (*Marriage of Heaven and Hell*, 152). This evokes the force of consciousness to make meaning in spite of Nature or the terrors of history. We do not find much meaning in the forms of Nature; we create our sense, and the world's, by turning within ourselves; the imagination is the conduit of the emergent divine. Blake's Los says in the prophetic poem "Jerusalem," "I must Create a System or be enslav'd by another Man's. / I will not Reason & Compare; my business is to Create" (*Complete Works of William Blake*, 629). This is a call to renegade originality. We see the visionary enterprise in these lines, the undertaking that creates mythic, metaphoric structures which absorb other structures into an explosively innovative whole. Frye's goal: to become an unprecedented critical eye. He was questing forward, in the secular-romance mirroring of the inward spiritual mission he kept (mostly) away from public attention.

At the University of Toronto Frye continued his study of archetypal forms and structures and his reflections on how the linked visionary cosmos in literature could be revealed through the activations of criticism. The dawning critical system would carry the convictions of this philosophical imperative: release the mind imprisoned in inauthentic hierarchies of thought into the realization of many dimensions of existence.

The fourth illumination struck in Seattle in 1951 while Frye was teaching a summer course at the university there. This illumination is covered in mystery. We have hints. He was confronting "anxiety, alienation, absurdity" [and anguish];[10] there are ways out of senselessness, the meaningless void. The romance-quest led from the dark forest to the sacred laughter that resists tragedy.

I have pondered what Frye saw. Was it a stage in the awareness that he was to be a prophetic figure? The first stage had been the shedding of literalism. The next two stages brought the insight that literature was his vocation and how literary content was interconnected (criticism charts boundaries, then obliterates them). The fourth stage was the flash that interconnections flow through identity. "A key to all mythologies" was the goal. This he thought he would find in "the myth of God, which is a myth of identity" (*"Third Book" Notebooks*, 69). The fourth illumination led him to the story behind all stories. But Frye was not finished with galvanizing illuminations, and the fires of illumination were not finished with him.

The Blake advocate became the champion of a new school of literary theory in *Anatomy of Criticism*. By the time of that book's publication, he had moved through various postings, becoming assistant professor in 1942 and chair of English in 1952. The publication of *Anatomy of Criticism* in 1957 brought instant recognition in literary criticism circles. Its impact was massive. Looking back at the theoretical structuralism of *Anatomy*, Murray Krieger said Frye "since the publication of his masterwork ... has had an influence – indeed an absolute hold – on a generation of developing literary critics greater and more exclusive than of any one theorist in recent critical history."[11] Harold Bloom, Angus Fletcher, and M.H. Abrams acknowledged their debt to its persuasive tonalities and overarching structural anatomies of the designs and forms at work in literature.[12] *Anatomy* boldly drew together disparate strands of criticism (historical-modal, allegoric, symbolic, archetypal) into a structuralist whole. The result of lectures given at Princeton and at the University of Toronto, the book was a polemical urging towards the recognition of the mythic, generic patterns in literary works.

Frye's subsequent lecturing and essaying took him from Toronto to Harvard and to other universities in America and Europe. But his centre remained the University of Toronto. In 1959 he became principal of Victoria College, and he remained in that position until 1967. What he said in his installation address, published in the campus magazine, *Acta Victoriana*, in December 1959, is relevant to my arguments here because it presents his prophetic mission and his call to others to rise to visionary intensity. He says, "Victoria's crest displays a sphinx, a phoenix, and an owl ... The sphinx would be a good emblem for Canada itself, put together in defiance of all natural law, yet amazingly solid and permanent ... The phoenix, the bird born of its own sacrifice, could well stand for a church made possible by the consenting of dissenters. As for the owl, proverbial both for wisdom and dullness, its kinship with academic profession has never been doubted."[13] Note Frye's compression of thought. The sphinx is the creature of riddling questions, the three-part human-beast-spirit that stands at the crossroads implicitly asking the terrible threefold: who are you, where are you going, from where have you come? (These questions come back to you, infiltrating their way into every engagement, confronting you, turning sentences sometimes into crossroads and destinations, asking you to never evade your sense of calling. They have come back to me, in my crucial readings, and in many experiences.) The phoenix is analogous to the fire of dissent and the recurrent form of the burning missionary heart. The owl is an emblem of destiny and insight.

Frye's restraint in his writings and in his scholarly career was tactical. He was (often uneasily) aware of the politics of academia and of literary reputation. He knew that to go forward, to follow his alternative path, he would have to cloak himself. He announced at this installation ceremony: "*The powers of the awakened mind are not children's toys, and the university cannot guarantee that anything it offers will be harmless ... Education can only lead to maladjustment in the ordinary world ...* it is not easy to find the tragedy of life in soap operas, if one has found it in the wrath of Achilles or the madness of King Lear" (20; emphasis mine).

Frye ends his wry oracular address by saying he hopes "for no better future for our students than a life of what William Blake calls mental fight or intellectual war" (24). I hold onto the bewitching word "maladjustment." There is no clearer statement by Frye of his faith in conflict and the necessity of readers becoming "children of light" who "go voyaging on strange seas of thought, alone."[14] I note the essential solitude of the voyage. I call this the sacred impracticality of the study of literature: it may not lead to a job, but it will lead to dreaming and thinking differently. A fighting revivalist tonality underscores Frye's civil eloquence.

We recognize Frye's influential presence on the campus and in cultural life.[15] He was named chancellor of Victoria College in 1976. In the late 1970s he toured Italian universities to great acclaim. Through this time it was known in critical circles, and to his students, that his thinking had turned to the Bible. He was about to take his work to the outer edges of theology and to present in plain sight a subversive vision of Christianity.

Through the 1960s Frye published a series of smaller books, less ambitious in their scope than *Fearful Symmetry* and *Anatomy of Criticism* but nevertheless compact and influential. His productivity was tireless. One year alone (1963) saw the publication of *The Well-Tempered Critic*, *The Educated Imagination* (now a staple on high school English department reading lists), *Fables of Identity* (absurdly, it is the only book by Frye to make it to Bloom's canonization list in *The Western Canon*, 1994), and *T.S. Eliot*. His book on Eliot annoyed Eliot and drew fire from Eliot's publisher Faber & Faber for its withering condemnation of Eliot's reactionary, anti-Semitic politics. The essay nevertheless contains some of Frye's most vivid readings of poetry through his double vision of archetypal criticism.

His fifth epiphany came in the early 1960s. It is called the Saint Clair Illumination, referring to the east-west crossroad in Toronto near where Frye lived. (Cross association: McLuhan and his family lived in this neighbourhood at that time too.) Of all his illuminations this one compels the most conjecture. No one knows what it revealed. It seems to have been a vision of the Bible's centrality to literature (though I do not think this is surprising for a United Church minister). I conjecture his illumination had more to do with seeing in literature the embodiment of the single Great Text, the spiritual magnum opus. Frye's fascination with Stéphane Mallarmé's *Le Livre, Instrument Spirituel*, and that poet's enigmatic annunciation that the world existed to be contained in a book, must have found confirmation in Frye's street epiphany: "que tout, au monde, existe pour aboutir à un livre."[16] Reading becomes augury, guiding the mind towards the secret depths of words.

I speculate that the apocalyptic moment took Frye into a Borgesian image of cosmic pages, the mysterium of leaves that he felt called upon to divine: all books becoming the book of life in the eternal library of the labyrinthine mind. Mallarmé's influence on Frye is so strong that in one notebook entry he makes the claim that "the pan-literary universe" – the idea that all books link to form one great book – is only understood by "three people ... Blake, Mallarmé, and myself. The final answer, naturally, is interpenetration."[17] The fifth conversion was to the vision of all texts forming an interpenetrating Work, the book of I, our soaring reply to the cry of the creating cosmos. From the tomb of deadened sleepwalking we resurrect to the voices that have risen too. The poets of the cosmic library are advancing through all its pages and coverings.

Was the Great Code dawning on him? Seeing the Book in all books is sensing the incarnation of the Spirit emerging in the larger body of the human imagination (Blake's Albion, Joyce's Finnegan). Seeing the unity in the world's texts in all their fluid multiplicity is perceiving the numinous mystery of the word's immediacy, in its elusive and yet felt unfolding. The reader's soul rises to see the book of identity mostly in disconnected instants; then the soul crashes, like Icarus, after his brief flight towards the sun, drawn back down to the mundane. Literary study gives wings to the reader, so that the openings of the Book can free more (and more) space and time in the soul and mind. Behind Frye's epiphany was surely Percy Bysshe Shelley's *A Defence of Poetry* (written in 1821, published posthumously in 1840) and his stirring, beautiful passage on how all poets are composing the book of being and becoming.

But Shelley was more revolutionary activist than closet mystic, and so his odd absence in Frye's pantheon of Blake, *Le Livre*, "and myself" makes some sense. (But I am haunted also by these questions: did we invent the Book, or did the Book invent us?)

In a typically perceptive passage from his *Northrop Frye: Anatomy of His Criticism*, Hamilton makes observations that suggest what was disclosed in the Saint Clair Illumination:

> Since, for Blake, "the Bible is one poem" (FS 109), Frye was led to see literature as one poem – as the same poem. Accordingly, the sense that all literary works compose one body of literature or an order of words is best described as a secular analogy to Paul's claim that all Christians become in Christ who is the word.
>
> (35)

Hamilton's description of the "one body of literature" corresponds with my proposition that Frye's intentions were prophetic – to endow his pupils with expanding eyes, expressive tongues of fire – and a reflection of a private hunger. However, I have posited that Frye's need was spiritual. The itinerant preacher became a subjective critic-lyric-seer because illuminations revealed this path.

Frye would undertake no major critical works for publication until the 1980s. There were volumes of elaborations culled from lectures: *The Stubborn Structure* (1970) and *The Secular Scripture* (1976). These well-received volumes hinted at his larger ambitions. Then at last came his essays on the Bible's impact on literature, *The Great Code*, and eight years later, *Words with Power*. In these Frye pursued the theory of the cosmological code embedded in sacred literature from the Old Testament to the Synoptic Gospels, then on to literary works like Pynchon's *Gravity's Rainbow*. Literature composed that secret spiritual opus which is our response to the universe's clouded call. In these books Frye breathed life into alternative readings of the Bible in terms of myth and metaphor, removing their story structures from historical literalism.

The theologian and critic George Grant reviewed *The Great Code* in *The Globe and Mail*. He dismissed it for trying to improve on what was for him the already "perfect Gospels."[18] Yet *The Great Code* was the fulfilment of Frye's Blakean dissidence and the culmination of his illuminations, those inspired moments that moved him towards identifying the Spirit in the letters of every verbal structure. "The prophetic vision is *fragmentary*," Frye indirectly replies in his *Late Notebooks, 1982–1990*, "and it takes busted people to expound it." "Busted" surely means you have to be cracked to let in new light. In another entry from those same days of writing, he says, sounding Mallarmé's gnomic incarnation note, "The text is the presence."[19]

In 1986 his beloved wife, Helen, died of complications that were the result of Alzheimer's disease. While he was reading into verbal structures he hoped would illumine the destiny of life – the Great Code would offer transforming energies, showing us how the cosmos vibrates with super-sensible direction – his wife was disappearing into incoherence. She had suffered from aphasia and mental confusion. Eventually she lost her memory. Frye writes of her devastation, and poignantly of his own, in his *Late Notebooks*:

> I hope to see her again; but perhaps that is a weak hope ... The one thing truly unseen, the world across death, may, according to my principle, be what enables us to see what is visible ... I begin to understand more clearly what Beatrice and Laura are all about.
>
> (137, 145)

I observe that the one book of Frye's to win the Governor General's Award for non-fiction in Canada, in 1987, was his mildly interesting essay collection, *Northrop Frye on Shakespeare*. It was not awarded to *The Great Code* or to *Words with Power*, both of which give us his epic confrontations with biblical literalism.

Frye's last years were full of academic honours. Yet in the 1970s, the 1980s, and into the 1990s his reputation began to fade. The critical revaluations had been steadily, often pointedly, dismissive, especially those by Jameson and Terry Eagleton. Although he was honoured, there was a sense that his critical theorizing was passé. In the wake of new theoretical discourses from the European titans, Jacques Derrida and Jacques Lacan, Frye's idealism, his interest in individualized dissent, in the primacy of the imagination, in the techniques of understanding through readings of archetypal patterns, in the privileging of canonic texts, in forging a Canadian prophetic stance, belonged to a Romantic tradition that was once again being demolished. Frye appeared cut off from postmodernist ironies, the concerns of race, gender, power relations, political action, psychology, and class warfare. He championed "Master Narrative" when the ideologies of master narratives, or meta-narratives, were being challenged.

Jean-Francois Lyotard's *The Post-Modernist Condition: A Report on Knowledge* (English translation: 1984) focuses on scientific and technological meta-narratives and never mentions Frye. Yet his presence obliquely pervades that essay. He is a figure who seems to lend elitist authority to themes that represent an oppressing structural imposition. It looked as though Frye had come to represent a repressive God story, turning literature into a subsection of dogmatic religion.[20] Frye had transformed from critical-theorist to a disconnected dreamer, a blithe otherworldly aesthete who, Wilde-like, preferred orderly reading to disorderly life.

Eagleton neatly summarizes these attacks (covert and overt) in this passage, which seems to endorse the polemical assaults:

> The beauty of [Frye's] approach is that it deftly combines an extreme aestheticism with an efficiently classifying "scientificity," and so maintains literature as an imaginary alternative to modern society ... It displays an iconoclastic briskness towards literary waffle, dropping each work into its appointed mythological slot with computerized efficiency, but blends this with the most Romantic of yearnings. In one sense it is scornfully "antihumanist," decentring the individual human subject and centring all on the collective literary system itself; in another sense it is the work of a committed Christian humanist (Frye is a clergyman), for whom the dynamic which drives literature and civilization – desire – will finally be fulfilled only in the kingdom of God ... *Frye offers literature as a displaced version of religion.*[21] (emphasis mine)

Frye's personal life achieved some domestic harmony, however. He married Elizabeth Brown in 1988. But a rare skin cancer began to plague him in 1990. He underwent several chemotherapy treatments. The stringency of the therapy damaged his heart, and he died of congestive heart failure in 1991. A memorial service to him was held at Convocation Hall on the university campus, eleven years after a memorial service was held at the same place for McLuhan, who had died in December 1980.

The Double Vision, his coda to his twin texts on the Bible, was published months after his passing. Outside of the notebooks and his letters, it is his most explicit declaration and exploration of spiritual meaning in the literary quest. "Man shall not live by bread alone, but by prophecies as well," Frye writes. "That is, primary concerns, for conscious human beings, must have a spiritual as well as a physical dimension. Freedom of movement is not simply the freedom to take a plane to Vancouver; it must include freedom of thought and criticism ... In the double vision of a spiritual and a physical world simultaneously present, every moment we have lived through we have also died out of into another order."[22] He proposes that the double vision is the dual lens of innocence and experience, paradise and earthly strife arranged in the harmony that permits us to see how we are each a crucial *axis mundi*, our lives an imperative metaphysical crossroads, an interpenetration of intellectual spirit and matter, soul and flesh.

The publication of his notebooks, letters, and unpublished essays was begun at the turn of the century by the University of Toronto. The notebooks alarmed critics. Bloom says in the first lines of his foreword to the fifteenth edition of *Anatomy of Criticism*, "The publication of Northrop Frye's notebooks troubled some of his old admirers, myself included. One unfortunate passage gave us Frye's affirmation that he alone, of all modern critics, possessed genius" (xii). In the notebooks the scholarly owl drops his mask. He becomes the phoenix of fiery dissent – of indelible, agonistic questioning and revelation.

The notebooks reveal Frye's often sarcastic critiques of his University of Toronto colleague McLuhan. I find Frye there at his most poetic and aphoristic, glyphic and abstruse. The notebooks present a mind like an alchemical furnace, burning with obsessive readings of texts from mysticism, Eastern religions, alternative sacred traditions, and what he dubs his "kook books." A selection of the entries was published under the surprisingly modest title *Northrop Frye Unbuttoned* in 2004, edited by the respected Frye scholar Robert D. Denham. A more accurate title would have used the words *Unbound* or *Unfettered*. In Frye's entries the outsider prophet at last stands exposed.

Frye's notebooks form a blazing, fragmentary counter-narrative to the cooled-down nuances of his published essays. We see the sparks of his soulful yearning, the complexities of his pride. His notebooks give us the discontinuities of creation to accompany the continuities of his criticism. Here is a passage from *The "Third Book" Notebooks, 1964–1972*, where Frye magnificently melds metaphor and the Gnostic coding of the day-night structure available to awakened souls: "Man is awake at night, & sees that the moon & stars are orderly as well as the sun. He also sees the sun vanish into the dark world & reappear. The Logos & Thanatos visions, then, may begin as bordering halos of one world; but each is the world, & they interpenetrate. The morning has come, and also the night" (231).

The offending passage for Bloom appears in the coda to volume 2 of *Late Notebooks, 1982–1990, Architecture of the Spiritual World*. In this statement found in *Late Notebooks, 1982–1990*, but likely composed in the 1970s, we find Frye's blunt acknowledgment of his ambition:

STATEMENT FOR THE DAY OF MY DEATH: The Twentieth Century saw an amazing development of scholarship and criticism in the humanities, carried on by people who were more intelligent, better trained, had more languages, had a better sense of proportion, and were infinitely more accurate scholars and competent professional men than I. I had genius. No one else in the field known to me had quite that.

(725)

The statement was not read aloud on the day of his death, or read in any published form that I know of until the year 2000. Frye thought genius was the higher power of Spirit that was available to anyone who tapped into it. He writes in *Notebooks and Lectures on the Bible and Other Religious Texts*, "I do feel that genius is a power of the soul and that powers of the soul can be developed by everyone ... The fact that under the stimulations of a 'great-age' or certain period of clarity in art a wider diffusion of genius becomes actual suggests to me that is always potential" (8). Genius is the following of individual mental pathways into imagination. The idea of a universal, democratic genius and a great age seems to me to be pure Whitman, but it links to Blake's voice of one crying in the wilderness, rousing humanity to throw off chains of repression.

Blake says in *The Marriage of Heaven and Hell*, "Thus men forgot that All deities reside in the human breast" (135). This aphorism is Blake's internalization of God into the imagination. God is our poetic genius, not separate from us, residing in the stories and images we ourselves create. Creation is a cognitive act. Instead of fear and trembling before an authoritarian God – Old Nobodaddy – Blake admonishes the angels and invites the prophets for dinner. This is surely what he means by having genius.

Frye understood that his theoretical architectonic was built on the Ulyssean journey of psyche and consciousness through literary works and forms. The Mental Traveller undertakes the odyssey of discovery guided by the fire of cultivated inwardness. This is Gnostic: true awareness comes from the solitary mind; it is not found in institutions or creeds. I hear an interesting echo in this of Nietzsche's declaration that theorizing is existential self-dramatizing, closet confessional. Frye's sense of being chosen haunts his boast about having genius too. I cannot sidestep what he says, and we should not; clearly, he felt himself destined. His charisma flared from his intuition that he had discovered the key to what was encased in letters.

Frye balances his boast of genius with a rueful reflection to Cayley in the posthumously published *Northrop Frye in Conversation*. He muses in 1990 on his displacement from the theoretical matrices of the 1980s and 1990s:

I am often described as somebody who is now in the past and whose reputation has collapsed. But don't I think I'm any further down skid row than the deconstructionists are.

(93)

"The Truth shall Make You Frye" ... This was on a placard I once saw hoisted during a student celebration of their teacher's presence on campus in 1980. But by the time of his passing, Frye's reputation was in eclipse. At the time that I write this, his ideas appear obscure to many, confined to an ever-diminishing coterie of readers in academia.

In an alternative channel to Frye's biographical story and historical record, we find the turbulent current called McLuhan.

H. Marshall McLuhan

Herbert Marshall McLuhan was born in Edmonton, Alberta, in 1911. Obviously we can see how McLuhan and Frye belong to the same pre–First World War generation. They were born into a world atmosphere of upheaval and revolution. McLuhan's family was Protestant, like Frye's; his father from a Baptist background, his mother a Methodist. The family moved to Winnipeg, Manitoba, in 1916. He had one brother, Maurice, who became a Protestant clergyman.

McLuhan (like Frye) never liked his early years at school. He failed Grade 6 (if such a thing is possible to do). But it soon became apparent to his teachers that this student was highly sensitive, unusually omnivorous in his readings. Biographies describe the influence of McLuhan's actress-elocutionist mother, Elsie.[23] Her impact on the sensitive boy was pronounced. She marked him with a sense of destiny.

He enrolled at the University of Manitoba. Like Frye at the University of Toronto, McLuhan majored in philosophy and English. In his journals and in his letters he reflected on how to write a great summa, a work of lasting accomplishment and effect. McLuhan's early academic career was impressively stellar. He graduated with a Gold Medal for Scholarship in 1933. In 1934 he completed his master's degree, then was accepted at Cambridge. He arrived there at Trinity Hall about to experience both intellectual revelation and religious conversion.

He quickly encountered F.R. Leavis and I.A. Richards. He heard public lectures by G.K. Chesterton, possibly ones by Ludwig Wittgenstein. It is likely that he was exposed to Wittgenstein's ideas through Leavis. Marjorie Perloff confirms in *Wittgenstein's Ladder: Poetic Language and the Strangeness of the Ordinary* (1996) that Leavis and the reclusive Wittgenstein knew each other well, often discussing literature together.[24] Leavis held Sunday afternoon teas for his students. McLuhan devotedly attended. Marchand wryly reports in his biography that McLuhan attended a lecture on campus given by Gertrude Stein: the two had an abrasive encounter after McLuhan, in a fit of youthful exuberance, heckled her (*The Medium and the Messenger*, 40).

Here is an equation of Pythagorean geometry: Frye at Oxford, McLuhan at Cambridge, each attending prestigious English universities during the Depression, when Fascism was stirring in continental Europe; each of them in England just after the intensive blasts of literary avant-garde modernism were being felt by scholars and critics inside academia. One went to the Oxford of A.J. Ayer, Blunden, and C.S. Lewis. Oxford's heritage was Royalist; the supporters of King Charles I rallied there during the English Civil War. The other went to the Cambridge of revolutionary opposition. The university sided with Cromwell and the Roundheads during the Civil War. At Cambridge the scientific-minded schools of New Criticism were forming. Leavis's study of the effect of advertising and other media in his book *Culture and Environment: The Training of Critical Awareness* (1933) stamped McLuhan's mind. Henceforth he would cast his critical eye to new textual appearances, technology's apparitions and reverberations in the world. Richards's *Practical Criticism* (1932) taught McLuhan how students read poems (they did so badly, usually in states of blank incomprehension). He was learning about contexts for reading, what surrounds the book.

McLuhan brooded on more than his intellectual life. He was experiencing a crisis of faith. Poetics were essential to him through this process of initiation into the reading of environmental frames. Poems brought the reader to cruxes, turning points of awareness; poetry was a verbal mime of the creation. Like Frye, he found apocalyptic moments in reading; like Frye, creation for McLuhan was a participatory, cognitive act.

To McLuhan the primary engagement with poetry was oral and tactile through puns and overtones, mnemonic devices and rhythmic patterning. By committing a poem to memory the reader put on or became the poem. Memorization led to performance. You carried a poem in your mind, then by this deep absorption you saw how the world changed according to the verbal, vocal, and visual tracking. By memorizing a poem you always had it close, on the tip of your tongue. Reading was a sounding out; it was depth perception, a way of tuning yourself to verbal resonances. Performances of poetry led him to reflections about what sort of soul he was to be:

> In the summer of 1932 I walked and biked through most of England carrying a copy of Palgrave's *Golden Treasury*. There had never been any doubt in my mind that art and poetry were an indictment of human insentience past and present ... In the Lake Country I reveled in Wordsworth's phrases ... Every poem ... seemed to have been written to enhance my pilgrimage ... After a conventional and devoted initiation to poetry as a romantic rebellion against mechanical industry and bureaucratic stupidity, Cambridge was a shock. Richards, Leavis, Eliot and Pound and Joyce in a few weeks opened the doors of perception on the poetic process, and its role in adjusting the reader to the contemporary world. My study of media began and remains rooted in the work of these men. Thomas Nashe was a Cambridge pet in my terms there. I did my doctoral study on him, approaching him via the process of verbal training from the Sophists through Cicero and Augustine and Dante to the Renaissance ... That art is a means of giving us new awareness through an intensification of our sensory life is obvious ... The *effects* of new media on our sensory lives are similar to the effects of new poetry. They change not our thoughts but the structure of our world.[25]

Note how for McLuhan it is a change in the structures of the world that brings about changes first in sensibility, then of mind.

The above passage, with its rare autobiographical reference, is from the foreword to *The Interior Landscape: The Literary Criticism of Marshall McLuhan, 1943–1962* (1969). It was written at the height of McLuhan-mania, when he had been transported from an academic in the world of student papers and curricula meetings into the avatar of the TV age. The passage acknowledges his debt to Cambridge. Curiously, he neglects to mention his PhD supervisor, Muriel Bradbrook. He also takes a perverse shot at the Romantic interpretation of literature as part lyric, part protest, part sublime inwardness, part imaginative expression, so represented by Blake. I believe this is an allusion to Frye's work on the Romantics. I say his comment is perverse because the anti-Romantic stance of the foreword obscures (and weirdly devalues) his scholarship on the Romantics. His references in his media books to Blake are legion; in this collection there are essays on Coleridge, Keats, Tennyson, and Poe. His comment conceals his roots in Romantic-Victorian poetry, especially in Hopkins. The sensational news of the world McLuhan found in the beauty of poetics. Moreover, he championed the idea of the Romantic outsider who must never fit into society if explorations are to stay vital. McLuhan implies that for him conversion came through recognizing the forms of existence, the *signatura rerum*, the scripture of Nature. He is setting up a division between his Cambridge initiations and training and those of the philologically rooted programs of study at Oxford.

McLuhan's experiences with the final semester exams at Cambridge were nerve-wracking – and not, in the end, accomplished. Marchand states in his biography that McLuhan's intense temperament, ever sensitive to slight and milieu, did not settle well into the examination process. McLuhan's tutor, Lionel Elvin, said this of the prospects of the mind that eventually shaped how we understand media:

> I rather pictured him then as a respected professor of English – not at Harvard or some university of that prestige, *and not somebody on the level of, say, Northrop Frye*, but quite respected and conscientious and producing two or three useful books. *Someone second rate, or rather second order.*[26] (emphasis mine)

Marchand does not date Elvin's comment in the footnotes to his biography, but it points to the abiding distrust of McLuhan's work among literary scholars. Marchand perceives in Elvin's criticism a more aggressive agon between McLuhan and Frye than I have been proposing.

McLuhan returned to North America in 1937 on the eve of war. But he did not go to the University of Toronto: he went to the University of Wisconsin, in the lowly position of teaching assistant (salary: $895 per session). There (possibly to fill his time at this out-of-the-way school) he began to observe the effects of advertising and radio on his students. In these early recognitions, McLuhan tended towards moralistic judgment (meaning he condemned the new technologies).

At this crux in the early years of his teaching, he converted to Catholicism. He later claimed that his conversion came from an epiphany, a mystical experience. He said there were signs, possibly visions. The conversion may have come in part from readings: Chesterton's books, perhaps James Joyce's work-in-progress, eventually to become *Finnegans Wake* on its publication in 1939. Catholicism brought him the intersection of the holy and the mundane in daily communions. It gave orderliness to his visions and receptivity; there is a redemption story at the heart of existential turmoil. All the universe is a language. The Bible is one expression of the Spirit. Technology would be another. Mysteries surround McLuhan's conversion. But he did say at a significant point questions end, then faith begins. You enter the church because the whole person is moved.

Janine Marchessault eloquently comments on the transforming effect of McLuhan's conversion in *Cosmic Media*: "While McLuhan's religious devotion was never part of his public persona and was never revealed in his cultural theories, it was deeply present in his thinking" (35). I admire Marchessault's study; and she has been a stalwart promoter of McLuhan's ideas in often hostile academia. But I disagree with her here. I am no longer at all sure that McLuhan hid his spiritual imperative. He mostly restricted his Catholic faith to his private life: his utterances do not depend on our sharing of his religious principles. But his apocalyptic intentions were clear: to wake us to the global theatre and the promises and perils it possesses and promotes.

Like Frye, McLuhan rarely described his life-altering experiences in confessional detail. The conversion took him from his literalist fundamentalist ground in Methodist evangelism into the symbolic and myth-based mysticism of Catholicism. Although he said that reading Chesterton's poetry, paradoxes, parables, and polemics – and specifically the essays in *Heretics* (1906) and its companion book, *Orthodoxy* (1909) – had contributed to his conversion, it appears his change of heart was rooted in direct, transcendental experience. Catholicism bound him to faith and freed him to explore. He looked back on his mystical moment and commented:

> I came in [to the Church] on my knees. That is the only way in ...
> You don't come into the Church through ideas and concepts ...
> [It gave him] complete intellectual freedom to examine any and all phenomena with the absolute assurance of their intelligibility ...
> [B]elief in God alters existence ... making it mystical and converting a leaden uninspired human into something lyrically superhuman.
> (Gordon, *Escape into Understanding*, 74–5)

Observe many of McLuhan's emphases here: on percept, on cognition, on intelligibility (all experience, all technological artefacts, can be apprehended, then provisionally described), on how our world is interpenetrated by powerful energies, and on how the user or perceiver may find inspiration and transformation through the gift of poetics, of making sense. Something is at work in the world which is greater than we are;

but this energy can be apprehended, indirectly, through "the analogical mirrors"[27] of literary study, in mechanical and electronic technologies, in the communications' media.

McLuhan's conversion did have a practical side. It opened up employment opportunities at the respected Catholic Saint Louis University. Saint Louis was also the birthplace of Eliot and William S. Burroughs, touchstone writers for McLuhan's later media studies.[28] In 1938 McLuhan met Corinne Lewis, a Texan and an actress. The letters from McLuhan to Corinne in this period are charged with affection and avowals of missionary ambitions, similar in tone and direction to Frye's letters to Helen. Marshall and Corinne were married in 1939. During the Second World War, McLuhan spent his teaching time mostly in Saint Louis, but he was still looking for more influential teaching positions elsewhere.

In 1943 he had another of the essential personal meetings that shaped his life and thought: he met Percy Wyndham Lewis, who flamboyantly called himself The Enemy. Lewis had turned his back on the European suicide – the Second World War – seeking new life in America. At the time of their meeting Lewis was lecturing at Assumption College in Windsor. This relationship is well documented in the McLuhan biographies; there is no need for me to repeat what they say so well. McLuhan would teach at the Catholic Assumption College from 1944 until 1946. But I acknowledge: McLuhan was powerfully receptive to Lewis's presence because he had engaged the polemical writings and artistic practices of the "Vortex" through Pound and Eliot while he was studying in Cambridge. He had read deeply in Joyce's work and had studied the pattern recognitions Lewis had provided in the two *Blast* editions of 1914 and 1915.[29] Through Lewis, McLuhan began to see how mass technologies were re-forging and often crushing humanity's sensibility and biology.

While his relationship with Lewis was strained – Lewis was cantankerous, notoriously edgy – the impact of his personality is impossible to underestimate. McLuhan's first mimeographed attempt at a polemical pamphlet was called *Counterblast* (1954). McLuhan appears in Lewis's novel on Toronto, *Self-Condemned* (1954), in the fictional persona of the opinionated Professor Ian McKenzie. In Lewis's exiled eye Toronto becomes Momaco (Mom & Company), a city freeze-framed in a smug provincial nothingness. A spiky pen-and-ink sketch of McLuhan exists by Lewis portraying the young scholar-critic with half his head removed. It is a half-finished image that shows McLuhan's mind vanishing into a blank space that looks suspiciously like snow (possibly a winter white out?). Lewis's portrait was prominently displayed in the entranceway to the McLuhan home at 3 Wychwood Park, until the house was sold after the death of Corinne in April 2008.

In his early meetings with Lewis, McLuhan was looking for an impressive mentoring figure to guide him and to provoke him with necessary oppositions. *Counterblast*, the title of his first foray into polemical publications, at once mimes the Lewisite techniques of blasting and blessing and provides a mild counterbalance to the severity of Lewis's Juvenalian, nihilistic eye. It is both homage and extension. This pamphlet shows McLuhan's need for another mind to measure and position himself against and to modify and transcend. McLuhan craved collaborators. His jumpy energy required frames, contexts, conversationalists, irritants, abrasive peers. Later he insisted on the methodological importance of figure/ground analogical relations in perception: apprehensions begin in awareness of an obvious figure and then follow with the exploration of subliminal (not quite visible) ground. Even in personal relations we see how he required the friction of dialogue.

Through Lewis and Pound in the 1940s and the 1950s, then through the collaborations with the founders of *Explorations*, and on to the dialogues with Frye, McLuhan was able to enlarge his thought. Isolation was starvation for him. Collaboration, like reading, was nutrition. McLuhan revised and expanded *Counterblast* in collaboration with the artist-designer Harley Parker in 1969. In the first pages McLuhan repeats the opening from his original mimeograph on the key influence of Lewis. McLuhan expands the Lewisite premises:

> In *America and Cosmic Man* Lewis saw North America as a benign rock-crusher in which all remnants of European nationalism and individualism were happily reduced to cosmic baby powder around the pendant cradle of the New Man today. The dust gets in our eyes ...
>
> The term *Counterblast* does not imply any attempt to erode or explode *Blast*. Rather it indicates the need for a counter-environment as a means of perceiving the dominant one. Today we live invested with an electric information environment that is quite as imperceptible to us as water is to fish.[30]

McLuhan and his family arrived at the University of Toronto in 1946. In the tenure track at Saint Michael's College, his field of expertise was modern poetry and criticism. And his ambitions were massive. Canada was a launching pad and an observation post. It could be the test site, point of acute friction with the rest of the world. Longing for a centre, he was hungry to shift the "Ivory Tower" to the "Control Tower" (143).

While university life could be drab and constricting, he knew its security gave him a ground for future polemical aggression. He wanted to read media texts from the Toronto nowhere. His was a singularly (and courageously) quixotic ambition. But "nowhere" contains the pun "now-here." Play with the letters in "nowhere" and we get another echo: Samuel Butler's utopian "Erewhon." Intricate webs can be spun from any text, discussion, worksite, or screen. Maelstroms erupt everywhere. McLuhan says in a letter to his mother, Elsie McLuhan,

> Occasionally I catch an oblique glimpse or illumination of Canadians, or some vivid memory is aroused and, I must confess, that at such times my heart sinks at the task awaiting the educator ... *My life in Canada will be a continual discontent.* My task as a teacher will be to shake others from their complacency – how is it possible to contemplate the products of English life (ie. Literature) without criticizing our own sterility ... *I am going to tear the hide right off Canada some day and rub salt into it.*
> (*Letters of Marshall McLuhan*, 83, 84, 86; emphases mine)

His hyperbole is evidence of his passions. McLuhan could not function without an audience.

McLuhan's move to the University of Toronto provoked controversies for years to come in the way he conducted himself with colleagues and in the way he blurted aphorisms and sent out books that were missiles designed to incite response. Sometimes, he learned, the returning response would be equally vehement.

Of his exploratory visit to the campus, McLuhan writes in a letter to Felix Giovanelli, colleague at Saint Louis,

> In Toronto I had some good visits with Frye of the dept of English ... and the rest ... They want me there. Students are of good calibre ... My plan is to start a mag. Not for Canadians by Canadians. But something serious ... One which might function well in Toronto by reason of the very hostility of the environment.
>
> (ibid.,182)

By 1947 McLuhan was fully installed as associate professor at Saint Michael's College. He reviewed *Fearful Symmetry* in the *Sewanee Review*, mingling high culture and pop culture with the insolent ease that became the trademark style and tone of his writings of the 1960s and 1970s. The review is favourable. (I examine it in detail in my next chapter.)

W. Terrence Gordon amiably says in his biography that the review demonstrates "a grandstanding ever so slightly for Frye's benefit" (*Escape into Understanding*, 141).

The next vital meeting at the university was with the political economist Harold A. Innis. McLuhan gratefully (and graciously) acknowledged the importance of this meeting directly in talks and writings by calling his work a mere footnote to the work of Innis. Innis's independent readings of communications and the media had a strong effect on Frye too.[31] I submit that McLuhan's submission to Innis is likely a corrective – the restless student of media needed yet another teacher to emulate and to radically alter. McLuhan's humble stance towards Innis, I think, is strategic. The pupil takes the teacher's promptings to even greater depths. The contrast between them is dazzlingly obvious: Innis rooted his perceptions about media in ideology and history, McLuhan rooted his in literature.

In 1951 McLuhan published his first major work, *The Mechanical Bride*. He had already said of his teaching and collaborative research aspirations, in an epigrammatic 1948 letter to Ezra Pound (at the Saint Elizabeth Asylum for the Insane): "Problem: How to achieve a milieu. How to get *10 competent people* together in one city. And keep them there to talk. To think. To write" (*Letters*, 197; emphasis mine). In another letter to Pound in 1951, he writes, "*I am an intellectual thug who has been slowly accumulating a private arsenal with every intention of using it*. In a mindless age every insight takes on the character of a lethal weapon. Every man of good will is the enemy of society ... I should prefer to de-fuse this gigantic human bomb [technological society and culture] by starting a dialogue somewhere on the side-lines to distract the trigger-men, or to needle the somnambulists" (227; emphasis mine). If his first (failed) book was not to achieve a milieu, then perhaps a magazine and public seminars would do.

From 1953 on, McLuhan's energies were directed towards the founding of *Explorations*, the seminal interdisciplinary magazine. It brought together Edmund Carpenter (from anthropology), W.T. Easterbrook (a political economist), Jacqueline Tyrwhitt (an architect and urban planner), and Carl Williams (a psychologist). The publication period, supported by corporate financing, was from 1953 to 1959. The inaugural issue published work by Robert Graves and a review by Frye of the *Oxford Dictionary of Nursery Rhymes*; in *Explorations* 4 (1955) McLuhan published Frye's essay "The Language of Poetry." There were no selections published from *Anatomy*, which Frye was writing at that time. Nevertheless,

Frye had become one of McLuhan's "ten competent people." However, I should not overestimate Frye's involvement in the *Explorations'* initiative; it was likely marginal.

The McLuhan household by the 1950s bustled with four daughters, two sons, two adults, one dog, and innumerable illustrious visitors. He must have often needed a guide to chaos. Yet he found the time to produce *The Report on the Project in Understanding New Media.* The report was rejected, its detailed and specific pedagogical recommendations ignored. From this presentation (and rejection?) came the groundwork for his explorations into the effects of movable type.

Print initiated the subliminal effects of private identity, the concerns for standardized grammar, a fixed and steady point of view. Movable type encouraged the interior space, the inwardness of the literary I. The electronic galaxy reconfigured typographic man, bringing splintering effects of turmoil and terror. The human body was being exteriorized, neural and sensory networks expanded or stretched into a glowing global network of interlacing transmissions and signals. In condensed form, these are the ideas that anticipate the quotation dynamism of *The Gutenberg Galaxy*, originally titled "The Gutenberg Era." Note the perceptual shift in the final version from the more conventional time reference ("era") to the field percepts of contemporary physics ("galaxy").

The *Galaxy* represented McLuhan's understanding of the sensory ground of radio. This is why his mosaic essaying emphasizes the schizophrenic contrast between the eye (of the solitary reader) and the ear (in the resonance of tribal drums). The text introduced the idea of the global village and the recognition of how print had been displaced from cultural, social centrality.

The Gutenberg Galaxy appeared in 1962: critical responses were strong to its originality and density. Willmott says in *McLuhan, or Modernism in Reverse*, "consider *The Gutenberg Galaxy* as a text composed entirely of ... footnotes, asserting its originality, not in idea, but in form – as a radically new kind of mapping process, an encyclopedia of references and cross-references" (115). Marchessault agrees, stressing how "*The Gutenberg Galaxy* offers Pope's Mennipean Satire, the Romantic's 'esemplastic imagination' and Joyce's stream-of-consciousness writing as means to awake from modernity and the instrumentation of all aspects of experience into a new experience" (*Cosmic Media*, 148).

Darker fields began to appear in McLuhan's mind at this time. He began to indulge his penchant for conspiracy theory, projecting his fear of isolation on others, including Frye. My agon chapter explores this. But Frye was tactfully generous in his support for his colleague. *The Gutenberg*

Galaxy was nominated for the Governor General's Award in 1962. The committee fought bitterly over its deserving stature. W. Terrence Gordon reports that McLuhan did not know – and never did know – this:

> who, as chairman of the selection committee, had locked himself up with colleagues in an Ottawa hotel room, persuading them the award should go to Canada's emerging authority on media. None other than Northrop Frye.
> (*Escape into Understanding*, 190)

McLuhan's impact was powerful enough now that he was offered the unprecedented opportunity by Claude Bissell, then president of the University of Toronto, of establishing the Centre for Culture and Technology on the campus in 1963.

The McLuhan Centre was a reinvention of Wyndham Lewis's 1914 chapter of the Rebel Art Centre in London. (I see some analogies with the Black Mountain College, founded in 1933, and in Andy Warhol's New York City studio, the legendary Factory, started up in 1962.) Lewis's idea had been to pitch a Baden-Powell-like Big Tent for artists and philosophers. The motto of the Rebel Art Centre could have been, "It's better to have everyone inside the tent working on a form of collective awareness." It was a place meant to welcome the future. But for McLuhan to breach the walls and armour-plated boxes of specialization took eerie gumption: he was already sensing how everything must cross over and meld, to make it new.

The next year, *Understanding Media* was published by the trade-book press McGraw-Hill, after much editorial haggling. The book proved to be a commercial sensation and an intellectual affront to critics, given its nonlinear mode of presentation, its tones that veered from ecstasy to alarm and from witty iconoclasm to mystical musing, its allusions to comic books and Joyce, its cavalier attitude towards scholarly precision, its mixtures of prophetic intimations and lyrical flights, and its gathering of philosophical and literary quotations and contemporary news items. *Media* represents his understanding of the sensory grounding of TV and offers a verbal mime of the effects of TV's destabilizing X-ray on the receiver. The arrays of light obsolesced privacy in an absorbing collectivity, the ionic membrane of our blue-lit viewing rooms. *Understanding Media* sold 9,000 in hardcover but the breathtaking number of over 100,000 in paperback.

Essential for our understanding of their clash, we must see now how it was at this point McLuhan took the step that troubled Frye. It was the step that excited the lasting scorn of many critics and colleagues. Two events occurred. McLuhan moved outside university circles to address popular audiences. His ideas were featured in *Vogue*, *Glamour*, *Playboy*, and *Esquire* and on TV shows. In 1965 McLuhan formed an alliance with Howard Luck Gossage and Gerald Feigen, business consultants, in Generalists Inc., to promote his ideas to corporations and politicians. Gossage and Feigen produced bumper stickers that said, "Watcha Doin Marshall McLuhan?" and "McLuhan Reads books." Tom Wolfe's myth-making profile, "What If He's Right?" appeared in *New York* magazine. To Frye, this was the beginning of McLuhan being swallowed by the media marketplace. McLuhan had begun observantly criticizing the vortices of the technological dynamo. Now he was whirled up into a cartoon figure, his ideas appearing flippant, sometimes slipshod or nitwitted. Frye commented that McLuhan did not always "agree with himself."[32] The breach came in the accusation that McLuhan had vulgarized his message into forgettable trivia. This breach between the openness of McLuhan to media and corporate affiliations and the scholarly world of literary research and annotation brought the charge that he was at best an apologist for mass manipulation, at worst a fraud.

The angry divide widens in the writings and responses between Frye and McLuhan in the late 1960s, in the 1970s, and up until McLuhan's death. The bifurcation starts with their differing interpretations of how writer-teachers (veiled prophetic-apocalyptics) should reach their audience and whether corporations and TV are unworthy objects of attention, insidiously corrosive, finally corrupting.

Frye witnessed how McLuhanism reached its exasperating publicity apogee when *The Medium is the Massage* was published in 1967. It sold a million copies worldwide. With the world renown there followed rankled controversies over the value of his work. We need only glance over the books that appeared on McLuhan – *McLuhan: Hot & Cool* and *McLuhan: Pro and Con* (the former appearing in 1967, the latter in 1968) – to see how he vexed and needled critics. A lasting perception was that he was anti-book; or that he was so confused and confounded that his work could only be a temporary, bewildering expression of pop-think; so his stardom consigned him to the ephemeral cult status of Timothy Leary and R.D. Laing. The fact that his work was taken up by artists, poets, politicians, filmmakers, and media theorists simply confirmed to many his galling scholarly unacceptability. Although he could count John Lennon, Pierre Trudeau, Frank Zappa, Norman Mailer, Woody Allen, Leslie Fiedler, and Susan Sontag as readers, this too infuriated critics into calling him a sell-out to liberal hegemony and faddishness. His contempt for academics (he called the university "a beanery," after Ezra Pound) and his *kerygma* of post-literacy appeared to announce the end of "The Book." This "once respectable literary scholar" seemed like an advocate of data darkness, whose politics and religiosity – publicly a political liberal, privately a conservative Catholic – during the 1970s appeared eccentrically disconnected from the new theoretical stirrings of deconstructionist, post-structuralist criticism. Scholars like Judith Stamps, after McLuhan's death, in a stretch of ambitious theoretical logic, attempted to place him in the contexts of the Frankfurt School or reconcile him to Marxism.[33] But it was his flustering combination of satire, mosaic presentation, suspect scholarship, his poetic flights and aphorisms, his mantic perceptions and propensity for sheer outrageousness, his witty affection for the put-on, and his willingness to admit obscure speculations that made him the fool who had shocked us into "the possibility of truth," in the words of Jonathan Miller, arguably his most peeved critic, "with a gigantic system of lies."[34] By consorting with big business people and political figures, "McLuhan" for some had come to rhyme with "Mammon."

McLuhan entered the 1970s wounded in reputation but also in mind and body. He suffered a serious of debilitating strokes; while at Fordham University in New York he experienced seizures, then an aneurism. Henceforth his ability to concentrate, and to tolerate noise and interruption, would be severely tested.

Frye was well aware of these wounds. He comments on McLuhan's struggles in the interview with Cayley, conducted during Frye's own struggle with terminal illness. It is a kindly overview of the McLuhan comet of success and the crash of his well-being:

> I thought that McLuhan was being praised to the skies for the wrong reasons and then, after the vogue passed, being ignored for the wrong reasons. I think there's a great deal of permanent value in McLuhan's insights, and I had a great sympathy for what he was trying to do. Unfortunately, he had such rotten luck with his health that he was never able really to complete what he had to say. *That's why he has come down as a kind of half-thinker who never really worked out the other part of what he was really talking about.* He talked about defense against media fallout, for example, an immensely fruitful idea ... That I would have liked to hear more about. *But, as he told me himself, he suffered such pain with the brain tumor that it just knocked him out.* Months at a time, even years at a time, he couldn't work.
> (Cayley, *Northrop Frye in Conversation*, 161–2; emphases mine)

These conversations with Cayley show Frye in an autumnal mood, summarizing and reviewing his lifelong concerns. Still the sentence about

McLuhan being a "half-thinker" triggers my reflections. It evokes fragmentation, a splintered angle, a broken trajectory of attentiveness, an unfinished career, the image of a gifted writer possessed more by vagaries and intuition than by continuity and common sense. Nevertheless, Frye evokes for us how much physical pain his colleague experienced, how desperate a time it often was for the usually vigorous McLuhan.

It is a popular perception that McLuhan's works of the 1970s signalled a "catastrophic dropping off"; so said George Steiner.[35] This was the period of his mixed-media and collaborative texts, the second version of *Counterblast*, *Culture Is Our Business* (1970), *From Cliché to Archetype* with Wilfrid Watson (husband of the novelist Sheila Watson; McLuhan had been her thesis supervisor in her work on Wyndham Lewis), *Take Today: The Executive as Dropout* (1972) with Barrington Nevitt (a major collaborator at the Centre in Toronto), and *City as Classroom* with Kathryn Hutchon and Eric McLuhan. There were plans to publish his PhD dissertation on Nashe, notes gathered for a work on media and religion.

McLuhan's driving concern in 1977 and 1978 was for the laws of media, the tetrad methodology which, he hoped, would provide its users with a technique at last for decoding, and defusing, the drowning or numbing effects of accelerating electronic currents. Many of these works contained sustained, often intensified, attacks on "Professor Frye." (Marchand says in his biography that during the 1950s and 1960s McLuhan had insisted on calling Frye "Hugo," likely a perverse misreading of Frye's first name [*The Medium and the Messenger*, 116]. There had been a set-up of a public debate at Hart House between *Explorations'* colleagues Edmund Carpenter and Frye.[36]) I once heard McLuhan dismissively call Frye's thinking "Protestant."[37]

Laws of Media was to be the apex of his discoveries. In this work he returned to the Nashe book material, culling from it the tropes of the Book of Nature and the ideal of multilevel exegesis. He would at last show how the operations of our super-Nature – the new texts – followed distinctive dynamic patterns. These were energy fields, not conceptual categories. In an anticipation of hypertext, the laws, outlined in typographic openness with statement shards and allusive aphorisms, showed structural configurations arranging themselves around crucial technologies.

Here is my take on the tetrads: each technology obeys the energy of enhancement; an artefact will expand or amplify an effect; the artefact obsolesces, or junks, another technology. Simultaneously, the new artefact recovers something ancient; in a startling twist, every technology achieves a flip point or reversal. This processing is synchronic (a chord), not diachronic (a melody). The instantaneousness is overpowering enough for us to be so blinded that the technology's effects pass unnoticed to us for years or decades. There is always jet lag in understanding media. We do not see the effects of print until radio and TV displace it: we cannot see the effects of TV until the home computer displaces it: the effects of the PC are not apparent until the iPod and cell phone displace it. The fours were to be McLuhan's mobile translating device, giving the user a key to pattern recognition.

It was the *Laws* that McLuhan worked on during the last class he gave to six students at the Centre for Culture and Technology. I was one of those six. I saw him compiling files and files of tetrads on everything from TV to semiotics. McLuhan needed his students, his son, his wife, and his associates to push perception forward.

(I was asked by Eric McLuhan at one point to glance over the files and a draft of the first chapter of *Laws of Media*, to offer my comments. My observations were perplexed, and useless.)

When Frye refers to McLuhan as a "half-thinker" who never completed his life's work, those words' ambiguity suggests an incapacity to complete a persuasively cohesive thought. He was breaking into a collectivity of ideas, moving away from private ownership, univocal authority. The new media age could not be grasped by one person or one voice. This was McLuhan's revision of Roland Barthes's "Death of the Author" into the figure of the co-creative explorer. No writer can catch the monumental shift. Words only pointed to phenomena. They neither replaced nor overcame it. The world says more than we can ever say about it.

McLuhan promoted dialogue over solitary monologue. The restrictions of scholarship were shunted aside in favour of probe and poetics. His audience was mostly outside academia. And iLiterate scanner-receivers (i.e., students) could be effectively reached only by anti-books. Moreover, his need to unseat the author's centrality showed in his insistence on oral composition. His last works were dictated: to his assistant, Margaret Stewart, and to whatever colleague he chose to work with at the time. He trusted that the voice of exploration would resound. Orality turned the making of a book into process, not a product, he said in his classroom talks. McLuhan's talk could be intuitional, automatic: the medium, himself, becoming the message. Was the stark loneliness of writing unbearable for McLuhan? Only someone who feels the acute pangs of solitude desires to communicate with an almost feverish intensity.

McLuhan liked to say he never experienced loneliness. This may be. The audience was part of a feedback he needed and the "feed-forward" that impelled him. His appearances on stage, on TV, in film, and in lecture halls could be vampy and volatile. I am tempted to argue that his claim to have never felt lonely was part of his spiritual grounding; his daily visit to communion comforted him. Still I propose that what he said is a camouflage, even an evasion: in his later years he was terribly, impatiently alone in his announcements. His books had slipped away from attention. The invitations to speak had become fewer. He had commanded multitudes, entrancing audiences, only to lose them. "The only thing harder to find than a first edition of a book by Marshall McLuhan is a second edition." This was a quip muttered (by someone unknown to me) at the Centre in 1978.

What was it like to be authentically gripped by the future? What was it like to be possessed by prophetic perceptions into the global membrane of satellite communions? To have anticipated so much? To have been at once a lightning rod and a seismograph? He said he was no soothsayer; he saw the present. I dispute his claim to have never felt loneliness because it must have been isolating in the extreme to have intuited what electronica would bring, those annunciations of the digital sublime. He was often denigrated for his perceptions (he experienced the truth of the bureaucrat's maxim: "An idea that is ten years ahead of its time is a bad idea").

And so McLuhan (understandably to me) sought occasional refuge in the cultishness that people encouraged around him at the Coach House. He talked, punned, snoozed in mid-conversation, rushed from room to room in that place, often spewing oracular statements ("In the electronic age we are living entirely by music"). But in retrospect I see how unsettling it must have been to be one of the few who saw the new coding. In his way he resembled Rimbaud and Blake, the poets he called heretics, the poets who sensed crises of spirit and perception before others knew the crises existed. The new consciousness of electronica was scratching itself into the grooves of his soul. Uncannily, his prophetic abilities addled himself, and us; and they continue to do so, into the twenty-first century that seems to have been in part sketched out by him.

(Frye was a visionary who wanted us to rise to the higher consciousness of the prophetic mind. But this assuredly is not insight into coming things. Through the sparked insights of the ignited imagination, we see with both the eye of material existence and the eye of poetry, so reality is wholly transfigured: a red rose is redder than before, the blue sky more vivid, the white smoke from a chimney like the ascension of a soul, each story we tell an allegory of love and becoming through epic and domestic wars. Frye wanted to find and free the lost code of awareness roughed in the stones of words.)

However, I believe Frye is right in part when he speaks of McLuhan's breakdowns and incompletion. McLuhan's declining health made him depend on others' help. From 1971 until his death, McLuhan experienced tiny strokes. He would have blank-outs and blackouts. He stared off in class, unblinking, suddenly dropping off into sleep. (It is possible that his small seizures were signs of epilepsy.) He lived with a constant ache in his head after the surgery for his aneurism. His sensitivity to noise was so pronounced that he flinched if someone shouted or a car backfired or music was played too loud or a movie soundtrack blared. No book, finally, could be rounded off during such experiences. His collaborators, with the exceptions of Wilfrid Watson and his son Eric, were not literary in background; so the misquotations and alterations of reference began to mount. I will reflect more at length later on what these afflictions and desperations brought to his visionary intentions. I think it is possible to read McLuhan's later works – too often dismissed by critics – in terms of obsessed urgings. His illnesses reflected his sense of emergency. His body could not keep up the pace of his clutching need to inform us of what was fuelled up, raging through the global theatre.

Aphorisms are the shorthand of the obsessed. It is the form most likely to come to the mind of one in a rush. Aphorisms can disguise stratagems of evasion. Instead of magisterial paragraphs and explanatory theses and exempla, an aphorist tries to encapsulate a summa into a line. Everything could stand or fall on the placement of a comma or a period. Extreme compression means that a word, a letter, can detonate meanings. Think of the power of the word "is." Think of how one letter can affect everything, how "message" becomes "massage" becomes "mass age" becomes "mass sage." Ratios are altered. Every figuration changes the next figure. Gaps and breaks create new alignments. You must be madly attentive. Each part of the aphorism speaks. Even the spaces between the letters have significance. If we get the sequence of play right in the letters, then the aphorist knows that his or her axiom will be remembered. It will have the feel of a fiat.

We can contrast McLuhan's mode of composition (production?) with Frye's. Frye undoubtedly shared the sense that words must have their right order in a sentence that compresses volumes. But when he came to organize his books, another energy took hold of him. He muted his force. Frye's elegant arrangements of essays, his considered lectures on the Bible, his preparation of *Creation and Recreation* and *The Great Code* at this parallel time, his steady concentrated research techniques, his constant revision of manuscripts (by hand) while he moved them towards public presentation – all show a writer revelling in his solitude. Frye reflected on the discontinuity of the aphorism technique, with his avowal of his rooting in the printed text, again in his confessional conversation with Cayley. Frye precedes his remarks with the comment that his process of thought was more like a mosaic. Then he observes,

> There is a continuity, but that's in the chronology of my writing.
> I write one book after another ... I keep notebooks in which I write very short paragraphs, and everything I write is the insertion of continuity into those aphorisms.
>
> (Cayley, *Northrop Frye in Conversation*, 146)

In September 1979 McLuhan suffered a stroke. Though he recovered enough to walk and to gesture, he was reduced in his speech to monosyllabic words. "Yes, No, Maybe, Boy oh boy" was all he could say. *Laws of Media*, and *The Global Village*, a project begun with Bruce R. Powers, were passed on to others to finish. The University of Toronto's Faculty of Arts' board elected to close the Centre, triggering a brief media controversy. On New Year's Eve 1980 McLuhan died in his sleep of another stroke. He died after celebrating mass with a visiting priest and watching a Marx Brothers' movie (*Horse Feathers*, about the anarchic hijacking of a university by the brothers) late into the night with his wife, Corinne, and his daughter, Teri.

Then began the period when McLuhan's reputation sank into a dark nadir in Canada and in America. His death was noted, but it was said that his vision of the global village belonged to the hippie 1960s, a naive, idealistic era.

In the late 1980s, the process of retrieving McLuhan began. The Oxford University Press published his *Letters* in 1987. His extensive correspondence revealed his ability to speedily improvise on his aphorisms. They recall his amusement at the world's appearances. In 1974 he says in a letter to Malcolm Muggeridge, "all of my life has been devoted to teaching and cultivating literary values. When I published *Gutenberg Galaxy* I was entirely mystified about the response which assumed it to be an attack on the printed word. I felt like a person who had turned in a fire alarm only to be branded as an arsonist" (507). However, in a 1976 letter to Sheila Watson, he speaks to the excruciating estrangements he felt at his school and in literary circles: "My own position here at the University of Toronto is no better than yours at the University of Alberta. Total isolation and futility! However, thanks to my publications, I can have serious and satisfactory relations with people off campus and abroad, leaving the local yokels to gnash their molars" (516). I wonder who the "yokels" were on campus.

Critics often scoffed at *Letters*. Michael Ignatieff reviewed the book in the *London Observer*. His review represents how certain critics (rooted in the English literary tradition of systematic argument and precise annotation) responded to McLuhan's aphorisms. Ignatieff castigates McLuhan for his writing's "pretentious claptrap ... bad habits ... crudely determinist ... substituting collage for argument ... fatal impulse towards incomprehensibility ... the shambles he left behind."[38]

Laws of Media appeared in print in 1988 after substantial alteration from the original rough-draft pages, now subtitled by Eric McLuhan *The New Science*. The other collaborative project, with Powers, *The Global Village*, appeared in 1989. Both books present outbursts against Frye that are virtually interchangeable.[39] They carry McLuhan's critique of the static "categorizing" mentality in Frye's theorizing. We find the accusation that Frye had a hidden Platonizing bias that ignores the affective ground of the alphabet, and the shift from orality to literacy, now from phonetic literacy to electronica. Frye is the only English literary critic, and the only Canadian colleague, antagonistically addressed in the two books.

Recognition came gradually. In 1993 Kevin Kelly founded *Wired* magazine and named McLuhan its patron saint. Philip Marchand's pioneering biography was published in 1989. Marshall McLuhan Catholic Secondary School opened on Avenue Road in Toronto in September 1998. The naming of Marshall McLuhan Way took place on 18 August 2004, twenty-four years after his death. (The naming of Northrop Frye Hall took place on 3 June 1983. Frye attended the ceremony and spoke at it.)

Outside English literary studies we see one of the first texts to perceive the McLuhan-Frye convergence. In 2007 the University of Toronto Press published *The Toronto School of Communication Theory: Interpretations, Extensions, Applications*, edited by Rita Watson and Menahem Blondheim, a collection of papers gathered around the proposal that there exists a school of information and communication study unique to Toronto. The papers focus on McLuhan, Frye, and Innis, weaving together patterns of cross-reference and cross-fertilization in their ideas and contact. These confirm a network of thought that is distinctly Canadian and stresses the University of Toronto's fomenting zeitgeist. The book stresses the impact of the three on political economic thinking and cultural theory. The cover shows the CN Tower in a blunt iconic skyline: the city is background, is classroom, is an entry point for evaluations and perceptions of the United States and the dawning global village, is a forum for rounding debate on images and ideas, is a theatre for the intensities of ambitious personality, is a site for a *kerygma* of original intellectual investigation. In Arthur Siegel's essay "Northrop Frye and the Toronto School of Communication Theory," we find the recognition of vital interpenetrations:

> Northrop Frye is one of the most important voices of the Toronto School of Communication Theory that had its genesis in the theories of Harold Innis and Marshall McLuhan ... [Frye's] concern with literature incorporated such concepts as identity, culture and community, which are central to communications. It was inevitable that his work would spill over into the development of communication theory ... Frye's career at the University of Toronto overlaps partly with Innis and McLuhan. They worked within a few blocks of each other, almost within shouting distance. The three renowned scholars did not interact directly [we know this in the case of McLuhan and Frye to be not so; their interaction was considerable] ... The Toronto School is not a formal institution. Rather, the name reflects the Canadian innovation in communications scholarship tied to the premise about the fundamental impact of the modes of communications on the shaping of society.[40]

Siegel, a social scientist, examines in considerable detail Frye's writings on Innis and McLuhan, referencing their disagreements but stressing their fascination for communications. The point is the recognition of intellectual affiliation, pressing convergences of thought.

The Toronto School of Communication Theory is a study of hidden networks. It is another chapter in the growing awareness of what Frye would have called the invisible singing school, the imaginative-critical space of the utopian mind that over time transforms existential situations into evolving models of aspiration through learning and illumination.

I observed how McLuhan hoped that schools in Toronto, and centres elsewhere, would open to a media *paideuma*, a radiant complex in time, into which, through which, out of which, and from which inquiries and percepts, intelligences and inspirations would flow to generations of students and electronic users. They could be snapped out of suicidal trances. This was the radical pedagogical proposal of the *Report on Project in Understanding New Media*. That immediate rejection by its intended audience – teachers – alarmed McLuhan; but the alarm inspired him to go public and to assemble and write *The Gutenberg Galaxy* and *Understanding Media*. The *Toronto School* book shows that it took decades for such potentialities of thought to find necessary reverberations, in posthumous tracings. McLuhan and Frye were feeding future energies.

In 2008, Penguin Books announced the publication of an Extraordinary Canadians series. Douglas Coupland wrote his lively biography of McLuhan. Scandalously, no book (for reasons entirely obscure to me) was written on Frye in that series.

Contra McLuhan and Frye

Let us look at a polemic discharged at the two. I want to highlight a denunciation of the McLuhan-Frye convergence. John Fekete fuses them together, their thematic association the subject of a scathing critique by this Canadian sociopolitical theorist in *The Critical Twilight: Explorations in the Ideology of Anglo-American Literary Theory from Eliot to McLuhan* (1977). The passionate polemic appeared in an international series edited by the eminent York University sociologist John O'Neill.

Certain books cry out to be reread. I first read Fekete's *Critical Twilight* decades ago. I thought that he was mistaken in his critique, but I admired his keen idealism. I returned to it for this book and still found it refreshing. He misreads them, but his deep misreading gives us a vigorous glimpse into the complementary quality of these minds.

(Appreciations of books change over time. When I was a teenager Thomas Wolfe's 1929 novel *Look Homeward, Angel* changed my life and gave me one of the first inspirations I felt to write. I have not returned to the novel in recent years. I came to the pleasures of Jorge Luis Borges later in my life. Now his essays, poems, short fictions, and reviews have become ice picks to my soul. A book can come like a nudge of concern from a friend. Some books are like compasses or watches, telling where you should turn, how much time you have before you. Fekete's book was one I set aside after my initial engaged disagreement. Picking it up again after so many years, I found it very much had kept its flash and zest. There is something to be said for his zealotry.)

Fekete acknowledges how their thinking crosses, admitting their "Janus-faced" centrality. He briskly goes on the attack. In two chapters, called respectively "Northrop Frye: The Critical Theory of Capitulation" and "Marshall McLuhan: The Critical Theory of Counterrevolution," Fekete condemns their critical methods and their evasions of political positions. He interrogates Frye first: "[His] theory, in the present analysis, embodies aesthetic capitulation to the commotive forms of domination; it proposes a view of culture structurally articulated to preclude radical historical praxis."[41] (I wish he wrote with more of an eye to the beauty of the sentence rather than with the clashing jargon of Marxism in his ear; but so be it.)

Fekete's Marxist critique develops from a school of criticism hostile to liberalism and the suspect transcendentalism of McLuhan and Frye. He sees Frye surrendering to ahistoricism. Frye's critiques become an aesthetically closed universe, a theoretical version of Wildean dandyism (a willed aesthetic solipsism). According to Fekete, Frye denies that literature has much to do with reality, thereby removing literary work from positions of opposition to specific matters of social relations. Echoing Jameson's judgments and Eagleton's complaint, Fekete calls Frye's work disengaged from any awareness of social, political, cultural, or economic imperatives: "in its analysis of the 'verbal universe,' it is arguably the first phase of that reorientation of the literary tradition that is associated with McLuhan" (108).

The Armageddon of criticism, Fekete insistently declares, comes when the Fryegian order of words links together one poem with another, and this requires systematic training through the teaching of critical structures. Henceforth in Frye's too introverted eye, criticism becomes sublime autism – ethereal, anti-historical, impractical, subjective. Romantic revolutionaries like Blake and Shelley are domesticated by Frye into idealized catalysts for quasi-mystical obsessions (purely his own). Individual consciousness matters more than collective action. Art only offers forms outside of history and geography. For Fekete, art must give us witnessing of time and space to open these to political change. Frye's emphasis on the deep course of identity in literature for Fekete becomes an egoistic obsession with Canadian identity, a kind of narcissism. Romantic dissent becomes otherworldly reverie. The result of Frye's writings – they should no longer be called "criticism" at all – is a reactionary obliviousness to "domination, exploitation, and struggle, to bureaucracy, power, hierarchy, property, the social division of labor, the political economy of the sign, surplus normatization, or revolutionary praxis, that is, to the social structures, social relations, and social collisions of real human history" (129–30).

This spirited condemnation echoes Jean-Paul Sartre's *What Is Literature?* (English translation: 1947). Literature should be witnessing, an engagement with capitalist conditions, a revolutionary transformation of false consciousness; style and form must be subordinated to the moral imperative of seeing what exploits and degrades us. Given the crucial turns of our historical period, a mandarin-like concern for "the order of words" is an abdication of social responsibility. Replace the (supposed) Blakean elaboration of a personal mythology and verbal complexities with the chronicles of suffering that we find in Dickens, Zola, Dostoevsky, Malraux, and Simone de Beauvoir.

I dispute Fekete's critique (I have said), but there is no doubt that Frye's structural poetics absorb some authors more successfully than others. His emphasis tends to be on the kind of dense metaphorical poetry that requires the decoding of a highly skilled exegete. There is little in Frye's writings on William Carlos Williams, Neruda, Henry Miller, Gorky, John Dos Passos, or John Steinbeck. Certainly, he prizes Joyce's *Finnegans Wake* over *The Grapes of Wrath*. Fekete's polemics seek to make Frye an inadvertent advocate of an ineffectual humanism. To Fekete, Frye is the desensitized cleric who sanctifies scholarship over barricade action against the degradations of capitalism.

Again, I can disagree with Fekete's confrontations but acknowledge how he identifies with oppositional gusto the weave of the McLuhan-Frye debate. In his concluding blast at Frye, he shifts to McLuhan, writing, "Frye's theoretical position capitulates to the *status quo*. McLuhan moves on from there to embrace neo-capitalist reification and to preach its dominant tendencies" (130). Fekete rightly locates McLuhan and Frye in the New Critical traditions, but he also sees their work as radical departures from that tradition, into deepening theoretical structures and patterns that reveal powerful, personal biases of imagination and perception, coupled with apocalyptic-spiritual urgency and latent metaphysical concern.

His essay on McLuhan is more denunciation than critique. McLuhan betrays criticism entirely, he says. In this, he echoes the criticism made of McLuhan from the political left. To Fekete, McLuhan is more intellectually decadent than Frye because the media guru steps away from his base in literature into corporate apologia and technological "fetishism." If Frye is a capitulator to political indifference, then McLuhan is a "counterrevolutionary" (135). A brazen determinism appears in McLuhan's theories, and so "any categories related to human self-determination – disappear without a trace."

Fekete spends the last portion of his book focused on McLuhan's strategic justifications for the new forms of electronic dominance. Fekete identifies one of the strands of interweaving thought in their work when he says, "As in Frye's structuration of the literary field, so in McLuhan's structuration of the historical field, the cultural periodization is resolved in a mythic pattern of Fall and salvation" (139). I want to explore the mythic fall-rise story that unites their thought in a later chapter. The "mythic pattern of Fall and salvation" suggests aspects of the Great Code. Fekete's equation is, I would say, more reductive than the narrative Frye decodes in the Bible. Although Fekete respects McLuhan's originality, he lambastes the technological utopianism that he identifies in *Understanding Media*. He exposes McLuhan's rejection of historical imperative and class struggle. Fekete insists that McLuhan sees the new electronic "totality" exacting "a high price: it requires 'utter human docility'" (145).

Fekete finds a terminal estrangement from the human in McLuhan's work: mind and compassion are amputated by technological extension. What is "outered" in machinery is not benign but paranoid, ruthless, coercive, and cataclysmic. McLuhan's humanism (his hopeful metaphysics) blinds him to the manipulative menace present in electronic technology. Extensions lead to nets of control. The teeming of images and sound bites is merely part of the illusory power of production. The owners of the machines reap obscene profits. Apocalypse is surely here, but it is psychotic.

Fekete ends his examination by acknowledging how important McLuhan and Frye have been to identifying context ("the medium is the message") and content ("the order of words in the imaginative expressions of literature"). His critique remains: they opened the doors of perception to new modes of theoretical discourse and then refused to step forward into critiques of domination and exploitation. Frye is the scholar par excellence who abandons citizenship; McLuhan, the critic who abandons humanity to technocratic ideology, leaving our situations vulnerable to the lies of manipulative elites. The McLuhan-Frye matrix for Fekete is an apologetic legacy for insidious tyranny. Frye's aestheticism leads to the rebuilding of the Ivory Tower. McLuhan's electronic advocacy hands the keys of the control tower over to bankers and fascistic politicians.

Fekete understands the originality of the Canadian visionaries. It is precisely their influential centrality that he wants to expose. The principal chapters of *The Critical Twilight* set up a contrary argument; without it, there can be no progression.

Interestingly, Fekete revised his opposition, staking out a new stance. He articulates this in his 1982 essay, "Massage in the Mass Age: Remembering the McLuhan Matrix."[42] In these pages he acknowledges McLuhan's radical program of enlightenment – media awareness – through interdisciplinary study. He recognizes how literary scholars avidly resisted McLuhan's nimble probes, and his strained place inside institutions. His recognition of pop cultural coding was a populist action, Fekete asserts, linking "profane culture to canonical culture" (52–3). He sees too how Frye's "formal continuity of narrative across different discourses" joins with McLuhan's approaches to environmental clusters of power. It is gratifying to see how Fekete comes to appreciate their humanism and democratic urgings. In their approaches, deep readings and the search for hidden dimensions combine. They bear the mark of a futurist visionary edge: "interpretation-communication-community" (55–6).[43]

In a letter to Donald Theall dated August 1970 that was not published in the volume of his *Letters*, McLuhan gives what I take to be a playful rebuff to Fekete's critique:

> My approach to the media is never from a point of view but is in fact a 'swarming' ... This is an exhaustible process ... It is really more fun to join the quest for discoveries than to try to classify and evaluate the processes in which I am involved ... You refer to my retaining Joyce as my major authority. Please consider that there can be no 'authority' where the game is discovery ... What I found is an enormous enjoyment and thrill in experiencing the events that are on every hand. It seems to me that this steady enjoyment of these events is a sufficient value system as it asserts the joy of mere existence. Naturally, it does not rule out the possibility of moral judgments, in particular existential situations and you know that I am not adverse to these in private.[44]

Here McLuhan expresses how joy is a form of subversion against the tyrannies of political oppression. It is through training in art that we apprehend richness and intent, precisely "the rhythmic undulations of the halos," auras of energy in everything; text is turned into "probe rather than a chart – a marriage of eye and ear."[45]

When Frye writes in the passion of his *Late Notebooks, 1982–1990*, he replies to the charge that he retreated into a scholarly cocoon:

> Marxism, Thomism, feminism, and all religions in their "fundamentalist" aspect are imperialisms. They want their power to extend throughout the whole world, and the conception of reconciliation or total agreement in propositions rationalizes some such impulse. The fallacy as always is that they use the wrong language. Culture decentralizes, and the more it does so the more readily it can communicate over vast distances of time and place and culture. Creative culture individualizes, being related to the spiritual body, where alone the world as "global village" resides. The mob-man assimilates to what's around him; the individual is equally an outgrowth of his society, but he recreates. The work of art is a symbol of that recreation, and the totality of art is the new creation.
>
> (643)

Observe two strands: Frye's slight rebuke to McLuhan in his lumping of "Thomism" (Catholic theological structures; McLuhan was an avowed Thomist) with Marxism and the absorption of McLuhan's famous phrase "global village" to refer to the utopian space of the imagination. But the final line points to a unity of thought in McLuhan and Frye: through art and imagination we turn the world towards communal artefact. Culture creates many centres. Both are positing a daring premise: politics is a subset of the imagination, another form of making meaning – poetics and consciousness first, then politics.

Summas

Let me summarize: McLuhan's major probes are encapsulated in aphorisms and discrete phrases. These are compressed bits of visionary perception, meant for unfolding by the user. "The medium is the message" illuminates the surround and its effects, how we are immersed in the speech and vibrancies of forms. Let us extend McLuhan's understanding of the energies in multiple texts: the first language is that of Nature (God's first writing); ignorance (the Fall) prevents us from reading these forms. Technological super-Nature is our second language. We see our reality largely through the rear-view mirror of nostalgia, routine, custom, and habit: thus the past becomes the frame for the present. But we have retrieved the acoustic-tactile space of tribal awareness through electronic technologies. Our present state connects us with the conditioning of electricity: speed, borderlessness, instantaneousness, simultaneity, everything everywhere at once. We are projected without bodies, minds and spirits floating and tumbling into the global ether. Electronic technology thus retrieves the ancient world of acoustic reverberation and flips it into something wholly new. Certain technologies are high definition, carrying data densities (called "hot" by McLuhan). High-definition technologies are the book and radio. Low-definition technologies convey lighter expressions of information (called "cool"). Low-definition artefacts are, or were, TV and the telephone.

Nothing is settled in swirling electrified time/space. A fixed moralizing perspective will not help us to perceive what swerves radically, at every instant. All positions are therefore provisional. Paranoia and ecstasy are twins, eternal mirrors for one another unless we shatter the mirror and examine the shards. The pun is a necessary instrument for perception because everything is happening at once. Therefore, "the medium is the message" means the forms may change all processes into mass (weight and communion: total involvement), but there is also the overtone of *mess age*, things falling apart. The later texts, from *Through the Vanishing Point* to *Laws of Media*, explore the deepening influence of electronics, how satellites and computers are wiring up shoreless, inexhaustible networks.

How should we perceive shifts in global paradigms? McLuhan's methodology relies on mosaic presentations, on readers' re-creations, on multidisciplinary references to many sources, on satiric assault on readers' expectations. Irritation and hyperbole are primary public techniques. He says in *The Book of Probes*, "For me any of the little gestures I make are all tentative probes. That's why I feel free to make sound as outrageous as possible. Until you make it extreme, probe is not very efficient" (306). McLuhan's strategy is to establish counter-environments, or counter-readings, by anecdote and flips on cliché, by lampoon, poetry, paradox, illustration, and retrieval of the ancient wisdom. The hermetic maxim "As above, so below" can be revised in light of McLuhan's suggested "As outside, so within": this elicits the premise that we live inside technologies and our technologies end up inside ourselves, processing being and becoming without our approval. "We have become like the most primitive Paleolithic man, once more global wanderers, but information gatherers rather than food gatherers. From now on the source of food, wealth and life itself will be information" (ibid., 26).

Is there determinism in his signature ideas? It appears technology predominates over the human. But technology only has the power that we grant to it. We are stamped by the cogs and webs of mechanical or electronic force. This pressing enforces unconscious behaviour. If we merge with technology without realizing we do so, our reactions will be determined. Nothing is permanently encoded. Art is the supreme instance of resistance to any sort of determinism. If we retain our power to make and to perceive, then no technology, and by inference no tyrant using that technology, can dominate us.

There is a bridge from McLuhan to Frye through their literary training. Both used verbal analogies and metaphors to comprehend concerns of consciousness and value:

> One way of stating our condition [McLuhan said in 1955] is to say that in the electronic age our entire technology has achieved the freedom and flexibility that had formerly been *available only in the verbal universe.* The metaphoric parallels and discontinuities – parataxis and syntaxis – by which mankind had first learned to structure acoustic space and create a subtle world of oral and interpersonal relations is now possible visually and spatially as well.[46] (emphasis mine)

I believe this passage illuminates McLuhan's prophetic leap: from the awareness of literary text and its properties to the awareness of electronic text and its sensible signs. Images are visible speech. What happens if the solitary reader looks up from his silent book and feels the pulse of the racing forms of electric technology?

~

Now I will summarize Frye: his essential critical movement is towards understanding the transcendental order of words in literature. In the *Late Notebooks, 1982–1990* Frye is pivotally occupied with seeking and revealing the structures of the "verbal universe." In these notebooks we find, "The only critical criterion worth a damn is the apocalyptic one" (676). Beginning in his studies of Blake and moving outwards through his theory of critical structures and genres, to his essays on education and the role of criticism in society, on to the major studies of the Bible and the last contemplation of mortality, he deepens his sense of mission. "My whole life in words: nothing is of value except finding verbal formulations that make sense ... Words are to us what water is to a fish: dwelling house of being, says Heidegger" (267). The elevating archetypes of literary texts resist the "Three A's" of anxiety, alienation, and absurdity. "What I want is an outline of the spiritual world" (272). Critical reading is an apparent withdrawal from turmoil to find the dream of arising, transfiguring sense. What does the acutely conscious critic see when he casts his eye on books? Literature offers a fable of identity against what appears to be the disorder of so-called reality. When we look into a text, we find the meaning denied to us when we are smashed up by selfishness and loneliness, violence and cruelty.

Theory for Frye is much more than scholarly categorizing. Criticism is the responsive poetic to the calling of art. We are readers lingering by the river Hebrus listening to the passing of Orpheus's head and lyre, which sings and prophesies in gnomic songs and sibylline lines while it slides by and sways, winds and waves rippling, even after the brutal dismemberment. Art and its intimate companion criticism inform a universal here that overturns what often seems to be the blank murderousness of Nature and of social disorder. Reading lifts us from raw living – the everyday may mislead us with false patterns: the deceptions of seductive propaganda – towards the revelatory. The felt presence in books is human consciousness in evolution. Through this consciousness a greater energy (the Spirit) speaks. The reader engages the persuasive dreamland of texts and is moved into communion with that which is not a social, political structure. Movements of "ecstatic metaphor" remove us from time's bondage.[47] And so ideologies give way to imaginative primacy.

Once we see the structures and genres of literature and engage their images and patterns, we move towards the visionary conditions of enthusiastic liberty: the mind expands beyond physical limitation; there is more and more to be known. This is not chaos: Frye says "a sense of articulate order comes down through the gate of horn." The liberal vision is comic, of the summer, not the winter – a hopeful transformation of consciousness that takes us into myth. We become violators of historical fact. Counter-history is mythopoetic; but if we understand myth, then we begin to see how the imagination comes alive in dream-time. "We are always in the place of beginning; there is no advance in infinity."[48]

Frye's daring proposal is that literature embodies the dream of humankind: our dream-time frames Nature *and will eventually replace it.* Frye speaks of this when he invokes his favourite Shakespearean play, *The Tempest*, and Prospero, the magus: "When Prospero's work is done, and there is nothing left to see, the vision of the brave new world becomes the world itself, and the dance of the vanishing spirits a revel that has no end."[49] The universe is broken open with the light and the reverberations of human presence. In the process we find unity with every struggling soul. The individual quest becomes every person's quest.

> To use terms which are not Milton's but express something of his attitude, the central myth of mankind is the myth of lost identity: the goal of all reason, courage and vision is the regaining of identity. The recovery of identity is not the feeling that I am myself and not another, but the realization that there is only one man, one mind, and one world, and that all walls of partition have been broken down forever.[50]

Truly Frye is an apocalyptic critic whose thinking surpasses conventional categorizations. He knew this himself: "I don't know if there really is a word for the kind of thing I am ... I am a critic who recognizes no boundaries."[51]

Frye's method is to take the traditional essay – so he informed us on that first page of *Anatomy of Criticism* – and shape his voice towards a combination of eloquent compact expressiveness and scholarly reference. His tone is often mild; his approach seemingly cautious; his exultations muted; his heresies tempered by tonal ironies; his allusive paraphrases often elliptical; his vast erudition often gnomic in its compressions; his transitions from thought to thought only seemingly supported by logic; his prose metaphors often linked to metaphors in poems and plays. Consequently, it is easy to miss his audacity. We must read him closely, in the way he compels us to read closely the patterns at work from the Bible through to *Finnegans Wake*. His verbal fecundity and his tireless book production came in part from recognizing the key to the outsider imagination in the war against repressive creedal structures, however they manifest. I have been arguing that the outsider critical imagination is a part of his Canadian vision. If all things are artifice, then the flexibility of the book-making mind is such that we must persistently create and re-create. Frye reinforces the idea of the power of poetics when he comments in "Blake's Bible," in *Myth and Metaphor* (1990), on our capacity to approach the infinite:

> We think we fall asleep at night into the illusions of dream, and wake up in our bedrooms in the morning facing reality again. But of course everything in the bedroom is a human construct, and whatever humanity has made it can remake. We gradually discover that this principle applies to everything: what is real is what we have made, and what we have not yet made: *verum factum*, as Vico says.[52]

The reader's eye peers down into the depths of a poem in a book. There the reader discovers the upward spiral voice that speaks in symbols, the essential human, trying to be heard over the scuffling noise of life's disarray. *Verum factum* roughly translates into "truth comes from what is made."

But I find nothing in Frye's work bolder than this implication: in the verbal cosmos, the sublime construct, we sense the emergent Spirit that has eternally waited for us. What is beyond the human seeks and needs the human. The Spirit is waiting for words, the evolution of consciousness through the ecstatic metaphors of our writings.

The Essential Metaphysical Drama

Their work moves far beyond the conventions of literary theory and criticism. In their writings and thoughts there is a high metaphysical drama. Many of their students (including me, when I was in my mid-twenties, at graduate school) felt and absorbed this unfolding. There was a sense of adventure in their epic quests for knowledge and perception and in their clash. We carried forward what we perceived to be the vehement quarrels of our teachers.

Teaching can be the development of antagonisms and rapports. These can linger, even fester. Sometimes the antagonisms take on a greater lustre than the rapports. The history of mentors, mahatmas, guides, shamans, visionaries, provocateurs, heretics, rebels, seers, sages, catalysts, and agents of change is always controversial. People like to take sides; when you choose one, you clarify and dignify the debate. Students can start ardent schisms, even a kind of intellectual civil war. The University of Toronto campus divided into combative camps during those days when the reputations of these elders soared.

Revealingly, W. Terrence Gordon vividly describes in *Escape into Understanding* how this drama often appeared to us:

> In my first year at Vic, I had met many students "next door" at McLuhan's home college, St. Michael's. Often they would say, "You have Northrop Frye, but *we* have Marshall McLuhan." Once I heard McLuhan speak, I thought I was beginning to understand that remark. Just beginning.
>
> (xi–xii)

I turn now to the pitch of their conflict.

3
The Critical Conflict between McLuhan and Frye

The Crux in the Crossroads

What is the crux of their conflict? To find it we must go back to their first publications and their first meetings.

McLuhan's "Inside Blake and Hollywood," his perceptive early review of Frye's *Fearful Symmetry*, appeared in the year Frye's book was published. Long out of print, it was not republished until the appearance of *Marshall McLuhan Unbound* in 2006. By 1947 McLuhan had published literary essays in the *Dalhousie Review*, *The Kenyon Review*, *The University of Toronto Quarterly*, and *The Classical Journal*. His focus had been on John Keats, Poe, Hopkins, Chesterton, and Eliot. McLuhan's literary reputation was growing. But he had not yet published a book; and he had been teaching at the University of Toronto for a short time.

His review addresses Frye's massive work in context with another work, Parker Tyler's *Magic and Myth of the Movies*. Tyler's book has dropped from sight, but Frye's study has become one of the pivotal texts of Blake studies. McLuhan recognizes Frye's accomplishment. Moreover, he perceives how Frye's voice has completely and commandingly absorbed the Blakean voice of prophecy. Frye becomes a medium for that poet's perceptions and theory of the imagination:

> *Fearful Symmetry* supplants entirely the work of Middleton Murray and Foster Damon, and of the other exegetists of Blake. For having installed himself inside Blake he does a detailed job of exploration and is able to speak of current issues as we might suppose Blake would have spoken. And, indeed, "the voice of the bard" is heard with typical emphasis on most contemporary matters, artistic and political. It is at once clear that Blake was a great

psychologist with clear insight into the mechanism of human motives and of historical periods – his own included.[1]

McLuhan launches into a critique of Blake and by inference begins to open critical fields against Frye. He sets up polarities between Blake, Joyce, and Vico, three touchstone authors for McLuhan (for Frye too, but in another context, so we shall see) in this passage:

> Unlike Vico and Joyce but like Freud, Blake mistook a psychology for metaphysics and theology. His rigorous monism had no place for "the many" save as modes of primal, divine energy. *The created world is a part of fallen godhead and is essentially evil. Existence and corruption are the same. This makes for simplicity, intensity and inclusiveness of outlook, but it may not have been of as much use to Blake the poet as he himself supposed.* (ibid., 9; emphasis mine)

In the midst of praise we can find the seed of their quarrel. McLuhan states what he sees to be Blake's, and therefore Frye's, extreme dialectical divide, a latent Manichaeism: the created world is "essentially evil," "existence and corruption are essentially the same." The phrases signal McLuhan's charge that Frye is possessed by contempt for the world. His approach to literary study is an elaborate introversion. Frye's critical theory is the embodiment of a Gnostic split between spirit and flesh (the body is hopelessly corrupt, matter a terrible trap).

To McLuhan, Blake's work represents a hermetic countering to the expressive forms of the holy cosmos. His poetry and poetics elevate personal mythmaking over the stirring abundance of existence. While this is galvanizing (it lends "simplicity" and "intensity" to the work), it is "monism" – meaning that it is reductive, categorical, arrested, confined, textual rather than contextual, and heretical. The literary monism in McLuhan's mind was solipsism: there is more to the world than anything one individual may or can say. Poetry is an analogical mirror to the complex beauty of Nature, but poetry should never be taken to be Nature herself.[2] Gazing into the mirror of art for too long can result in self-hypnosis: this mesmerism inevitably leads to intellectual narcissism.

We can sense the first stirrings of the clash. McLuhan identifies in Blake and Frye – since McLuhan supposes that Frye becomes Blake's spokesman in *Fearful Symmetry* – a dissident turning away from the world towards elaborations of his own clever devise, a sublime solipsism, a championing of aesthetic rebellion. McLuhan implies that this turn abandons the world in favour of subjective re-creation. The critic ends up alone, cultivating private responses of exquisite thinking and sensitivity. Frye was destined to be a perpetual stranger to life, burrowing himself in dusty, desolate libraries.

I understand McLuhan's veiled admonitions: Blake was (after all) a rebel who had no large reading public. At best Blake could depend on an esoteric circle of a few like-minded solitaries. The Manichaean split comes when we identify flesh and earthly life with corruption and repression. Gnosticism for the Catholic McLuhan is a synonym for the heresy of the inner light. It pits Promethean humanity against the revealed Word. If you go against orthodoxy, you go on your own. In a 1953 letter to Walter J. Ong, McLuhan writes, "H. N. Frye's *Blake* [*sic*] is best exposition of contemporary gnosticism I know" (*Letters*, 237).

All of this is expressed in McLuhan's compressed sentences. Already he is arguing by aphorism, by provocative pronouncement, by allusion, by an elliptical referencing that requires unpacking by the reader. We could understand his technique as verging on the obscure. But obscurity can be a form of engagement, a technique for probing the unknown.

While McLuhan surely praises Frye, he begins his unsettled oppositional stance in his review:

> [R]eading Professor Frye is a more satisfactory thing for most of Blake than reading Blake himself. The great poetic allegorist like Dante proceeds by simile, although the entire work is a huge metaphor. Blake proceeds by metaphor or identity of tenor and vehicle and ends up with a work which requires a key to open ... Professor Frye does not regard this as a defect since his business in his book is exegesis and not criticism.
>
> ("Inside Blake and Hollywood," 9)

By exegesis McLuhan means the fourfold technique of analogy. By criticism he means moralistic judgment. He praises Frye for avoiding didacticism. It is more useful to see, apprehend, understand, and grasp than to damn or praise without awareness. Detachment means for McLuhan (and for Frye) developing perception without allowing personal biases to block it. Opinions are the froth of the ocean, not the depths. It is this detached aspect of exegesis that often frustrated critics of both McLuhan and Frye.

At the review's end McLuhan affably mingles recommendations with thanks: "Professor Frye's inside view ... is perhaps in need of some further development from the outside ... But much gratitude is due to Professor Frye for having brought into a conclusive focus all the elements of Blake's thought and feeling" (10). There will be more of this talk by McLuhan about "inside" and "outside."

His review veers into a discussion of Hollywood images and clichés. His enthusiastic review of Tyler's book sounds a McLuhan tonality that will become part of the pulse of his writings of the 1960s and 1970s: "[Tyler] does a fine job of reading the enigmas of the fever chart from the movies but of the positive function of popular art for good or ill he says nothing" (13). Note McLuhan has swerved from Frye, Blake, theories of the imagination, and Dante to movies, pop culture, mythologies, and the effect of electric light. This would be an example of what Frye himself would later trenchantly call McLuhan's penchant for "discontinuity." That meant "the half-thinker" could not finish a thought.

Frye's response to McLuhan's review of *Fearful Symmetry* is not on record. I trust he was pleased with his new colleague at the University of Toronto.

McLuhan's Blast

Ten years later McLuhan's mild opposition erupted into fury. In 1957 Frye's *Anatomy of Criticism* was published to considerable literary critical attention and enthusiasm. His celebrity in academic circuits had begun.

McLuhan's response to *Anatomy* was more than mixed. In an unpublished essay-review called "Have with You to Madison Avenue or The Flush-Profile of Literature," McLuhan wildly veers between attack and praise. Eric McLuhan, the McLuhan archivist, was unable to tell me why the review was never published or even to where it was submitted. We should be grateful that it never appeared. It is weirdly garbled, at times unhinged by smouldering rage. McLuhan says,

> It is natural for the literary man to underestimate the relevance of Professor Frye's archetypal approach to literature. The man of letters expects the literary form to offer a good deal of private or consumer-oriented in Professor Frye's approach. The Frye approach to criticism as a science turns from the training of taste and discrimination by literary means to the collective producer-orientation of the new mass media of the electronic age. The archetypal approach is the groove of collective conformity and of group-dynamics, *which may explain why a uniquely opaque and almost unreadable book should have become a book-of-the-month choice ... In the same way, the off-Madison Avenue of the run-of-the-mill graduate student finds it quite unimportant that he does not understand Professor Frye.*[3] (emphasis mine)

The tangle of tones is hard to unbraid. He calls Frye's writing opaque and unreadable and then sarcastically claims that his fame has nothing to do with whether his readers understand him. McLuhan implies the *Anatomy* is unreadable anyway. In his agitation he begins to imply that there is a conspiratorial cult around Frye. This charge will intensify when he claims that Frye was a high-ranking member of the Masonic brotherhood.

Bewilderingly, McLuhan praises Frye for understanding "the message of the new media aright." I wonder what book McLuhan was reading. Where in the detailed examinations of genre and archetype in the *Anatomy*, and in its analyses of mythic substructures and recurrences of metaphor, does Frye mention the message of the new media? "The fixed stance of the private silent reader, identical with perspective in painting, suggested subliminally the need for an individual viewpoint in all matters." That phrase embodies a keynote McLuhan idea: the print medium created typographic man, and typographic sensibility incarnates in fixed stances and the preference for silent reading. Print elevates a selective point of view. That is projected into a position of authority. This suggestive idea is encoded elliptically in a prose that seems far away from Frye's text. The "Flush-Profile" of the title, and of several passages in the review, refers to a Madison Avenue advertising technique of pulse-taking (polling) and of flushing everything down a toilet. Is McLuhan praising Frye for understanding that literature is irrelevant to the new imagery-driven sensibilities of mass media? Or is he saying Frye has sold out to that drive by writing an "unreadable" text? His sarcasm slashes on:

> Seen from the split-level window House of Archetypes, the receding world of Western literature may look appallingly like a silent movie on a late TV show. But for those who recognize the importance of aligning all education with the dynamics of the new mass media, the deft and decent burial of literature provided by the *Anatomy of Criticism* will come as an exhilarating climax to the slower-paced preliminaries of the literary centuries.

McLuhan's implies that the *Anatomy* announces post-literacy, or iLiteracy. If this is what is left of criticism, to categorize genres and types, then the "packaging" sounds the death knell of the humanist pursuit. In private McLuhan would call Frye's text "the *autopsy* of criticism."[4] Its fame was further evidence of a necrophilia end. It is painful to note that it was McLuhan himself who would be criticized for embodying in his writings "the end of literature." No one ever said such a thing of Frye's books.

But what McLuhan is trying to express is this intuition about Frye's essays: that the more we enter the mass-media fields of attraction and repulsion, the more the guardians of book culture recede into moralistic nostalgia and rear-guard systematizing. Here is McLuhan's parting blast: "[*Anatomy of Criticism*] in turn will greatly hasten the mopping up of remnants of private awareness and expression, such as now give a confused and unsettled character to the literary and educational scene. So that what has here begun as a momentary flush-profile of literary postures will develop into a genuine chain reaction, and the remnants of a decadent form of personal reaction can be dispatched down the drain."

Marchand reports on the vehemence of McLuhan's obsession with Frye in 1957. A panel of graduate English students had been organized, Marchand describes, to discuss Frye's book. McLuhan met one of the panellists, Frederick Flahiff, and asked if he (Flahiff) would read the "Flush-Profile" essay to the gathering. In this passage Flahiff describes what happened:

> We [McLuhan and Flahiff] went out and walked around and around Queen's Park ... McLuhan was at his most obsessive. I don't mean that he was hammering away at me to do this thing, but he was obsessive about Frye and the implications of Frye's position in the same way that he had talked about black masses. It was the first time I had seen this in Marshall – or the first time I had seen it so extravagantly. As gently as possible, I indicated that I could not do this and that I was going to write my own thing ... Later, on the night of the panel, he phoned me before my appearance and asked me to read to him what I had written. I indicated that he come to the session if he wanted, and he said, "Oh, no, no."
> (Marchand, *The Medium and the Messenger*, 106)

Was this literary jealousy? Marchand thinks there was more to McLuhan's invidious response: "Frye's critical ideology also tended to make a religion of literature, a religion that McLuhan, who already had one that he considered perfectly satisfactory, heartily detested" (105).

For all McLuhan's extravagant posturing in the revealing anecdote, there is more to the conflict than academic rivalry or a Catholic's refutation of the religion of art. What Marchand misses is that with the *Anatomy* Frye had vaulted himself to the forefront of critical theory. Henceforth theory would have a powerful master narrative of encyclopedic explanation. McLuhan had developed suspicions about theory. He would damn conceptual thought itself, the meta-literary approach that he considered an imposing of structure ("light on"), and not a perception of structure, which allowed patterns to emerge and configure ("light through").[5] Frye's categorizations of literary forms in *Anatomy* pushed point of view to a massive architectonic scale. McLuhan had a master narrative – I see their agon in terms of a battle of competing myths – of orality passing into literacy and of print literacy passing into electronic iLiteracy. But he thought that what he proposed was description. What Frye proposed was explanation. This is not just jealousy. It is the revelation, McLuhan must have known, of a decisive difference of method and intent. It would take time before Frye retorted to McLuhan's campus agitations – more than ten years. But retort he would.

In Marchand's biographical detail I detect in McLuhan's voice a tone of near-desperation. The "Flush-Profile" essay contains the imperatives he expressed for the next twenty-three years. The electric world was dissolving alphabetic culture and sparking something new. Frye, his brilliant colleague, was unaccountably unaware of the incendiary streaming.

―――

Had Frye dared to make the imagination into the soul itself? Would the spiritual pilgrimage become the identity quest in literature, and in literature only? McLuhan's unease, I contend, was also over these questions. They articulated a divide for him between imagining and spiritual calling.

The great visionaries of the Catholic tradition, Hildegard von Bingen and Teresa of Avila, urged the pilgrim to beware of how the imagination could become master. They made distinctions between profound visionary experience – of the kind that leads to conversion – and acts of the creative mind. The soul is arduously finding its way through ordeals, struggling towards truth. Blissful awareness and a sense of profound harmony with the cosmos are psychic states. But the imagination has the power to turn these burning states into enchanting stories and intoxicating poetic images. Your soul invites revelations; your imagination thrives on invention. The mind can plays tricks (in short), taking images and tales to be the meaning. Ego is linked to psyche, which is linked to breath and spirit; and so ego and hubris can become almost inextinguishable when your drive towards inspired singularity leads to delusions. But the soul hungers, above all, for truth.

Frye, to McLuhan, had allied himself with Blake, a radical of the imagination. Blake turned imagination into the primary energy: this is the key to Blake's celebration of hell and Satan in the delightful inversions and ironies of *The Marriage of Heaven and Hell*. McLuhan detected this line of thought in Frye, subtly expressed in *Fearful Symmetry* and *Anatomy of Criticism*. The implications were massive. Literature, not faith, would be the site of pilgrimage. The beautiful schemata of *Anatomy* were terminal points to McLuhan because they ended practical criticism (how a poem works on us) and exalted theory (how an explanation can be greater than the poem). In theory the mind could be boundless, creating premises like a god, but ultimately becoming solitary or shadowy, the discrete intelligence easing itself with spectral pleasures. But the world, like the soul, moves ahead of our knowledge. Literature could never be a substitute for the pilgrimage towards truth for McLuhan.

Three years after this reply to Frye's book, McLuhan would write in his *Report on Project in Understanding New Media*, "What possible relevance to the student of media could a point of view be in such circumstances? He must adopt the mosaic approach. He must deal with all media at once in their daily interaction, or else pay the price of irrelevance and unreality."[6] Frye's work now appeared to McLuhan to be laboured, or worse, obsolete.

In 1959 McLuhan writes in a letter to Wilfrid Watson, "one might say that Frye's world is simply the slapping down of the poised balance on the visual side of the scale?" (*Letters*, 257). Frye's study of symbols and genres, for McLuhan, emphasizes the categorizing preferences of the visual mode. Thirty years after his first impressed reading of *Fearful Symmetry*, McLuhan writes to Cleanth Brooks of "in selecting *figures* without ground, the Norrie Frye style of classification without insight" (258).[7] Dr Robert K. Logan, noted physicist and a collaborator of McLuhan's at the Centre for Culture and Technology from 1976 through 1979, confirmed that these were McLuhan's views in an email to me on 17 September 2007:

> Marshall felt that all NF did was to do a left brain categorization of literature and a figure without ground analysis. We were in the middle of our exploration of the bicameral mind when Marshall made these remarks. Marshall criticized Frye because he operated from a point of view – a theory. As a result he was always looking for confirmation of his biases.

Here is what McLuhan is getting at: he is proposing that Frye wrote without awareness of the "massaging" of the alphabet on the sensorium. The alphabet is one of our supreme inventions, the technology that stamped and altered Western consciousness. Frye was blind, McLuhan believed, to the effects of the alphabet and also (therefore) of print technology. The book is an artefact with no absolute value. Decoding the alphabet is a product of the training of a specific cultural heritage.

Other cultures are not rooted in letters. Nor do they have the uniform elevation of the printed book to the highest value. Moreover, to elevate the book to such a degree ignores the historical context of orality, which precedes the alphabet and the Gutenberg invention of movable type by thousands of years, and the electronic retrieval of the oral-tactile condition with its fast-forward into a new tribalism of hieroglyph, what has now become a culture of motto, blurb, tweet, emoticon, GPS, and ad copy. It did not matter whether he, or Frye, liked or disliked the process: it was happening, occurring at ever faster speeds. Frye was burying his head in the sands of text. Specialization in literary studies – no matter how congenial to your sensibility – was fragmentation.

McLuhan said in a 1977 interview with Pierre Babin, "With the book, one can withdraw inward, in the egocentric and psychological sense of this term, and not, indeed, in the spiritual sense. The printed alphabet creates, in a large measure, fragmentation."[8] What McLuhan means is specialization led to a closed concern over the letter of the law, rather than the open spirit between the letters. Inwardness here means solipsism. Specialization creates schizoid conditions in which the critic concentrated his attention purely on texts. Meanwhile, the global theatre raves and blazes with the shrieks and sparks of relentless change.

Frye was taking the configurations of print to have lasting, archetypal formations. The United Church minister and fellow metaphysician was constructing counter-myths out of literary typologies, when he should have noticed that the media had become a struggle of angels and demons. In a 1969 letter to Jacques Maritain, a Catholic philosopher and critic, McLuhan outlines the demonic side of the global village: "Electric information environments being utterly ethereal fosters the illusion of the world as a spiritual substance. It is now a reasonable facsimile of the mystical body, a blatant manifestation of the anti-Christ. After all, the Prince of this World is a very great electric engineer" (*Letters*, 370). In his mercurial way, McLuhan moved to a contrasting, and even contradictory, apocalyptic perception in the *Playboy* interview of 1968. In this we find a rhapsody on media: "I expect to see the coming decades transform the planet into an art form; the new man, linked in a cosmic harmony that transcends time and space, will sensuously caress and mold and pattern every facet of the terrestrial artifact as if it were a work of art, and man himself will become an organic art form. There is a long road ahead, and the stars are only way stations, but we have begun the journey."[9] When we close the book, other doors of perception may open. If Frye went on in his deaf-blindness to the effects of media, then he would be supported by an uncritical milieu of colleagues, who also could not see beyond their fragmented specialties.

The following aphorisms I take to be McLuhan's satiric jabs from *The Book of Probes* at his "too linear" colleagues in the Department of English (i.e., Frye):

> The professional tends to classify and specialize, to accept uncritically the ground rules of the environment. The ground rules provided by the mass response of his colleagues serve as a pervasive environment of which he is contentedly unaware.
>
> (366)

> The specialist is one who never makes small mistakes while moving toward the grand fallacy.
>
> (372)

The world is the Book of Nature for McLuhan. The heavens and earth, and all things mediating between, compose the grand screen or text. This screen of texts represents the divine outline in time. It is through the appearances that we participate in the unfolding of consciousness, which is collective: what is outside reflects what is inside. The leaves of the cosmos are those mutable forms that we perceive in the natural world (a leaf of grass, a mountain, a whirlwind, a current, a rose petal, a branch, a root, a wave) and that we see are human-made or artificial (a handwritten manuscript, a statue, a bridge, a wheel, a pen, a printing press, a typewriter, a computer). Each form is a medium with a pervasively subliminal effect. We are imprinted by the world of forms and by what we make of them: more – we are pressed and influenced. All the forms, or media, are a cryptic language. The book, whether an illuminated manuscript painstakingly inscribed by a devoted monk or printed and bound by an independent-minded typesetter, is only one of the many expressions of the forms. "An insight is a contact with the life of forms," McLuhan says in *The Book of Probes* (458).

But the metaphor of the Book of Nature – so Dante would call the cosmos in *The Divine Comedy*, and Whitman called it too in his *Leaves of Grass*, his epic of subjective consciousness – has passed. It is no longer appropriate to satellite technology. The book metaphor is a vestige of the alphabetic mind. Electronica reform and deform Nature by shape-shifting it into hypertext and amphitheatre. We spin like dervishes inside the transformations of culture and society; and for many the storm uproots and devastates people, compelling them to cling to books like lifebuoys in the churning electronic sea. Insistent communications arrange and derange: "Since Sputnik and the satellites, the planet is enclosed in man-made environment that ends 'Nature' and turns the globe into a repertory theatre to be programmed ... [We live] inside a proscenium arch of satellites ... the rag-and-bone-shop of the global waste land of Shakespeare & Co."[10] This is McLuhan shifting our focus from the global village to the global theatre – and from radio and TV to satellites – in *From Cliché to Archetype*. Village becomes theatre, and then the theatre becomes the Magnetic City, where performers and couch-potato gawkers are unwitting participants in the addicted trance states of voyeurism and narcissistic self-analysis.

McLuhan's unease with Frye becomes explicit critique in *From Cliché to Archetype*. It is one of McLuhan's most subversive works. The table of contents does not appear until page 191; no introduction to the content appears until page 116 (approximately in the middle). This anti-book is structured alphabetically, beginning with a chapter called "Absurd, Theatre of the," concluding with "Theatre." Its chapter headings list "Archetype," "Consciousness," "Paradox," and "Parody." There is no index. The exempla, anecdotes, speculations, perceptions, images, symbols, leaps, breaks, and citations invoke McLuhan's now all-out war with theory. The cross-hybridization of genres and figures in his work is a latent satire on literary critical formalities. This "book" expresses breakdown.

This is where we find McLuhan's most sustained disagreement with Frye – a disagreement that takes their clash to the level of a feud. McLuhan turns polemical in the chapter "Anesthesia." In a scathing tone he calls the Frye school "*That* group of archetypalists." And he declares, "[They who] consider the linguistic form to be a recurring pattern of literary experience describe what is *antithetic* to the cliché as probe" (15; emphasis mine). McLuhan is challenging what Frye meant by archetype. For McLuhan the archetype does not have transcendental reference; there is no Platonic life of forms in another realm. The life of the forms is always here, now. We participate in their creation. What we take to be the unconscious is Nature and the media reflecting our minds back to ourselves. McLuhan did not perceive any archetypal realm beyond the relations we perpetually establish with the metamorphosing cosmos. Archetypes begin in cliché probes. These are what people use to express and interpret their experiences. If a cliché is repeated often enough it acquires status and stature in our culture and mythology. Mythology is not an eternally recurring structure, but the creation of viable interpretative stories according to a specific culture and time. Example: the attack on the World Trade Center towers on 11 September 2001 became a media myth through the replay and enhancements – the dream loop – of their images. The image of falling towers reverberates with other symbols of falling towers (in Eliot's 1922 version of *The Waste Land*), but this is because the image has recurred often enough to have achieved significance.

McLuhan denied the existence of a collective unconscious stocked with archetypal images or situations or characters or emotions. Behind his engagement there is also his profound quarrel with Freud's myths of the unconscious and Jung's fictions of the archetype.

This is the important background to his polemic against Frye. The word *polemos* (Greek) is often translated into the word "war." But I submit it can mean "contrary," in the Blakean sense of necessary opposition. McLuhan counters,

> [T]he Northrop Frye definition of archetype is: "A symbol, usually an image, which recurs often enough in literature to be recognizable as an element of one's literary experience as a whole." It doesn't matter that in the phrase "as a whole" Frye is using textbook cliché, since he is insisting that the archetypal experience is a pleasing form of somnambulism.
>
> (15)

He alludes to how Freud discovered the stages of the unconscious by using hypnosis. Hypnosis is anaesthesia for McLuhan: the deadened trance of the sleepwalker. McLuhan is suggesting that Frye prefers to be entranced by the flickering, hallucinatory dream-types on his inward eye.

In "Archetype," McLuhan cites Edmund Carpenter (one of the original collaborators on the *Explorations* project) on the classifying mind of the literary mythographer:

> like Frye, they direct their attention towards a most important problem and, like a hedgehog, build humourless, water-tight systems (and with faithful supports reading "the Book"), that instead of answering the problem or even illuminating it, block access to it.
>
> (18)

In "Centennial Metaphor," McLuhan goes on to suggest that Frye's pedagogical intentions and techniques mislead students:

> Symbolism as an art or technique meant precisely the *breaking* of connections ... The student might easily find himself in a world of chaotic conflicting suggestions as if he were to attempt to use Northrop Frye's definition of a symbol as an exploratory probe: SYMBOL: Any unit of any work of literature which can be isolated for critical attention. In general usage restricted to the smaller units, such as words, phrases, images, etc.
>
> (36)

McLuhan is enjoying himself, his iconoclastic imp surely impelling him. The joy he felt in blasting others was part of his strategy of keeping people awake. It bewildered him that others did not delight in the missiles. Further, making waves was a way of getting response. It is likely he knew no other way of confirming that someone was out there. The contrariness was light-hearted, perhaps not to be taken too seriously. We will see how Frye took the charges seriously.

Nevertheless, McLuhan becomes even more outrageous in the chapter "Genres," with its quirky subtitle, "Talent Rides Only in a Hackneyed Vehicle." He makes his most obvious counterblast against Frye in the argument that had been simmering since 1957:

> Working entirely from the medium of the printed word, Professor Frye [note how McLuhan suddenly shifts into the formal designation in this sentence] has developed a classification of literary forms that ignores not only the print process as it created a special type of writer and audience, but all other media as well.
>
> (85)

McLuhan goes on to say that Frye overlooks "the oral tradition of both preliterate and postliterate culture [and] sets up a system of classifications that apply to a recent segment of human technology and culture – a segment that is rapidly dissolving" (87). Most damning is this McLuhan declaration: pop culture, rock, jazz, song, speech, and dance set up complexities of genre that "no professor of literature can ignore."

In the "Introduction" that appears halfway through the book, Frye is challenged on the second page. This signals his importance to McLuhan. If Frye were not of eminent stature, he would not be here.

The Critical Conflict between McLuhan and Frye 123

This hyperbolic technique of attack McLuhan learned from Lewis's *Men Without Art* (1934). Lewis interrogated the novels of Hemingway and Faulkner, often condemning them, because the authors had impressive creative stature. "Never hunt anything small,"[11] McLuhan sometimes said.

In the following passages McLuhan deflates what he perceives to be Frye's dependence on the Jungian theory of archetypes. He calls Frye "the literal man," an obvious pun on "a man of letters." I believe this passage is worth quoting in full before I come to Frye's rebuttal:

> Northrop Frye [no longer called "Professor"] in *Anatomy of Criticism* defines archetype as "a symbol, usually an image, which recurs often enough in literature to be recognizable as an element of one's literary experience as a whole." Of course this particular definition is *most un-Jungian in suggesting that archetypes are human artifacts produced by much repetition – in other words, a form of cliché*. For the literary archetypalist there is always a problem of whether Oedipus Rex *or* Tom Jones *would have the same effect on an audience in the South Sea Islands as in Toronto.*
>
> (118; emphases mine)

Mischievously (and almost surrealistically) McLuhan praises Frye for sounding like McLuhan.

To McLuhan art is defined not by its content, nor by its conventions or structures (like genres), but by its effect on audiences. The frame is more interesting than the picture. The context and form of a work of art is more telling than the content of its expression. McLuhan's parting shot in the "Introduction" is to enlist W.K. Wimsatt to note that "the literary archetypalist" (Frye) has "the conventional procedure of the literary man" (128–9). McLuhan quotes Wimsatt to show how Frye's work is riddled with inevitable contradictions. McLuhan gets the publication date wrong for *Fearful Symmetry*. He says it was 1949, but it was 1947. Surely he remembered this; he had reviewed it the year it appeared. I question why he insists on showing us Wimsatt's quotation. Perhaps it is again to place Frye inside the typographic space of the scholar who cannot or will not acknowledge the ground of his own undertakings. The enclosed space makes his work "connected, continuous, homogeneous, and static." The "literal man" is a literary person snarled in letters, hypnotized by type and hence by archetypes, the theorizing which he weaves like thickening cobwebs around his sophisticated thought. Continuities exist in books.

There are mostly discontinuities in Nature. To McLuhan, Frye had fallen asleep. It was time to wake up the impassioned reader of Blake. Perhaps his probes would do this. McLuhan will never again address Frye so fully in a book.

※

There will be more: McLuhan's response to Frye in *The Listener* exchange of 1970 and the repetition of his accusations in *Laws of Media* and *The Global Village* that Frye did not understand how audiences define works of art and did not comprehend how the sensorium works. McLuhan believed the literate mind is directed by the left brain, the musical-electronic realm channelled by the right side; together they form the harmonious consort. Separated, the two hemispheres set up dichotomies that reinforce somnambulism. He returns in the accusations of *Laws of Media* and *The Global Village*, via his collaborators Eric McLuhan and Bruce Powers, to his declaration that Frye "ignored ground":

> *In the left hemisphere, however, formal cause [this is the ground,* or context, of any artefact] is translated into a kind of Platonic abstract ideal blueprint that is never perfectly realized in any given material example. Such is the understanding of Northrop Frye, one of the principal modern exponents of Platonic and Aristotelian ideas as passed through Freud and Jung. He is consistent in his left-hemisphere approach ... There is absolutely no provision [in Frye's theory] for ground of any kind: his archetype is exactly a figure minus ground (*vide* the discussion in *From Cliché to Archetype*). Otherwise it would be perfectly natural to observe, with the rhetoricians and grammarians, that the formal cause of the poem, painting, or whatever is its ground: the audience (user) and the configuration of sensibilities in the culture at the time the artifact was produced.
> (McLuhan and McLuhan, *Laws of Media*, 88–9)

Meaning for McLuhan and his collaborators is found in shifting contexts, not in what they took to be the stasis of binding text. We must stay alert to read the effects of the impressive media, in their endless distillations and conversions. Constancy comes in the faith that the Spirit of creation means well.

In a 1965 letter to Wilfrid Watson, McLuhan confesses he found Frye's work "depressing."[12] This is another note that was not included in McLuhan's *Letters*. Clearly, reading Frye had become a weight for McLuhan. This suggests a larger issue to me. McLuhan often noted the rejection of his probes by the literati and academic communities. In his letter to Watson he concludes, "Is he not the last of the visual gradient, the mirror world in which criticism itself becomes archetypal? ... His nostalgic harking back to classical decorum and medieval levels of exegesis are sufficient indicators, perhaps." McLuhan's word "depressing" has other reverberations; is there a tone of lament here? The great literary age and the refined accomplishments of print had passed. Frye is one of its last voices. McLuhan tried to reveal what was coming: the new renaissance of our super-Nature would be vitalizing, epically creative. Cinema, TV, radio, music, tribal rock and roll, performance, dance, stand-up, happenings, infotainment, texts on screens, the iconic dramas of stars and starlets, miniature communication devices, pixel images, hieroglyphs of advertising – these were the movements and moments of awakening sensibilities. But it was not likely to be a time for the production of great writers and epoch-turning books. (When *Wired* magazine adopted McLuhan as its patron saint, it was ruefully ironic; McLuhan did prefer to read books.) The "literal man" was a figure of nostalgia, likely melancholy: "The last of the visual gradient." In odd homage, McLuhan could have been saying that Frye is a visionary eye of the vanishing typographic sensibility: the I, or "aye," of solitary literary affirmation. McLuhan's aggrieved critique of Frye must have come from his insight that they were both figures that had emerged from the disappearing ground of literary training. To retrieve a quarrel between book-bound learning and orality is to resurrect the concerns of an old, nearly lost, tradition, known only to a privileged few.

McLuhan had moved a long way from his appreciation of Frye's genius in 1947.

Frye's Counterblast

Frye must have been aware of McLuhan's fulminations. How much he knew is an open question. Frye never saw the unpublished review of *Anatomy of Criticism*. Of course, McLuhan's letters were private at that time. The *Report* was unpublished. Nevertheless, in the confines of the English department and in the small world of literary exchange, the word would have been out. They continued to be diplomatic at meetings. But the current of the debate had surely been restlessly vibrant. They were renowned by the mid-1960s but travelling by then in different circles of critical discussion. McLuhan's writings of the 1970s were often responses to what he perceived to be Frye's latent antagonism. Frye's writings and private reflections did offer sharp critiques. Let us now look at what Frye was saying and thinking on his side of the agon.

Frye never mentions McLuhan in his four key works, *Fearful Symmetry*, *Anatomy of Criticism*, *The Great Code*, and *Words with Power*. To find Frye's responses, I will have to patch together passages and inferences, moving backward and forward in time. This means I will look to the shorter works, in particular to *The Modern Century* (1967), and to lines in essays. Mostly, I will be looking at certain crucial notebook entries.

Two excerpts from Frye's letters speak to what he perceived to be their collegiality and the literary roots of their educational background. Here is a droll note from Frye to Walter J. Ong in 1973: "I saw Marshall the other day at a meeting on Canadian studies, where we were discussing the question of how difficult it is for students in this bilingual country to acquire a second language when they don't possess a first one."[13] McLuhan often despaired over the state of his students' inability to function in English. Here is Frye writing in 1976 to Richard Kostelanetz: "Please don't make me an enemy of Marshall McLuhan: I am personally very fond of him, and think the campus would be a much duller place without him. I don't always agree with him, but he doesn't always agree with himself" (Frye Archives). In this I hear Frye's special tone of wry observation and affectionate humour. (His final remark is a revision of what McLuhan himself often said: "I don't always agree with myself.") Frye often shows a deflecting charm in his wit.

I observe how none of the biographers of either figure mention Frye's letters or notebooks. Two more references from his letters illuminate the crossings. This from a letter to John Garabedian in 1967: "Neither was it correct to describe me as a disciple of McLuhan, although he is a colleague and a good personal friend." From a letter to Walter Miale from 1969 – the reference is to a debate about a figure with an "anti-literary bias": "there was still the possibility that he might be, like Marshall McLuhan today, probing and prodding in directions that might turn out to be useful" (Frye Archives).

In spite of the amused tone in these letters, Frye was not always so civil when it came to McLuhan. I have been building a case for the nuanced tonalities of his prose. He frequently masks, even diverts, his strong-minded, heretical thoughts. Nowhere is this more evident than in his ambivalent pronouncements about McLuhan and in his often complicated reflections on him.

It took Frye ten years to form rejoinders after the rumour of McLuhan's disaffection with *Anatomy of Criticism* in 1957. Ayre reports in his biography on Frye's awareness of McLuhan's commotions. During an early presentation to English department colleagues of a draft called "The Function of Criticism at the Present Time," of what would become the "Polemical Introduction" to *Anatomy*, McLuhan attended and made comments. "Marshall McLuhan, rumored by one mutual friend to be out to get Frye, talked about 'essences' in a prophetically obtuse manner" (*Northrop Frye: A Biography*, 217). Ayre does not elaborate on the "rumor." And does he mean "abstruse" (gnomic, elliptical) or "obtuse" (thick, stupid) when he describes McLuhan's manner? Nevertheless, Ayre hints that Frye knew McLuhan was displeased with Frye's abstract categories. In Frye's diaries we find this subdued response to the incident:

> I got through. The attendance was mainly English ... Marshall McLuhan went after me with talk about essences & so on – Helen Garrett reported from Jack that he'd said he was out to get me. He didn't, quite, though a stranger would have been startled by his tone. Actually, I imagine he agreed with a fair amount of the paper, though he didn't say so when I went home with him.[14]

McLuhan's disagreement was deeper than Frye realized.

Still I observe how their conflict was on that day resolved in a collegial Canadian fashion. Frye describes the irony of the two journeying home together after the reading. Since neither had driver's licences, was the journey in a cab? Or did they walk? We know from Marchand's description of the "Flush-Profile" and the Flahiff incident that McLuhan's reading of *Anatomy* had riled him. These incidents are not described in Gordon's biography of McLuhan.

Frye bided his time. In *The Modern Century*, in a 1968 interview in *Le Devoir* called "L'Anti-McLuhan," in the 1970 essay debate in *The Listener*, in *The Critical Path: An Essay on the Social Context of Literary Criticism* (1971), in the notebook entries from 1967 through the early 1970s and 1980s, and in selected essays from the 1980s, we find full expression of the Frye agon with his "good personal friend."

Frye's primary charge against McLuhan is that he had become a cult figure. McLuhan had disingenuously, at best, allowed his name and ideas to be associated with business people and media celebrities, politicians and advertisers; he had sold out to the non-literate, or more precisely the anti-literary, audience. By catering to data chaos, he had betrayed his humanist roots. What is more, McLuhan had set the scene for an insidious betrayal of subjective consciousness. If we leap ahead in publication time, then we find in a 1985 essay, "The Dialectic of Belief and Vision," republished in *Myth and Metaphor*, Frye makes the point clear that he believed McLuhan had been pulverized by the media publicity machine. Further, he states what will become a consistent disagreement over the effect of the Gutenberg technology on the sensorium. The following compressed passages carry Frye's critique of the premise of *The Gutenberg Galaxy*:

> We read sequentially, moving in time from one word to the next; we understand what we have read in a simultaneous *(Gestalt)* pattern, in conceptual space as it were. For the first stage, there are conventions that what the poet is uttering is not words but music, the art that most obviously moves in time, and that the prose writer is actually speaking. For the second stage, the word *structure* has entered criticism largely because it is a metaphor drawn from the stationary or visual arts, notably criticism. Such metaphors have produced many confusions in literary theory, which I think remain confusions, even if my attempts to indicate what they are may be thought oversimplified. In Marshall McLuhan, for example, the book is equated with the linear process of reading, and the electronic media are associated with the total of simultaneous vision. This account of the matter overlooks the fact that the book has to be understood as well as read, and that it patiently waits around, repeating the same words however often it is consulted, until its readers proceed from the linear stage of attention to the next one. *The electronic media, more particularly television, greatly foreshorten the linear process, but still they require us to follow a narrative as well as make an effort of apprehension, which means in practice that many television programs make a strong immediate impression and are soon forgotten afterwards.* McLuhan came to understand this very quickly, and warns us constantly about the dangers of "media fallout," the panic caused by the sense impressions that our minds have not been adequately prepared to receive. *But in the meantime he had been ground up in a public relations blender and was unable to correct, or even modify, his absurd popular reputation as the man who said that the book was obsolete.*[15] (emphases mine)

Frye moves from medium to content in the first highlighted lines. He disagrees with the idea that "the medium is the message," disputing how the process of reading takes place. He points to what he takes to be the ephemeral nature of TV content. Content for him is still paramount over the medium. The "confusion" over this at the beginning is McLuhan's. Once McLuhan came to realize his error and the absorption of his ideas into "the public relations blender" (a double-edged image of the maelstrom), it was too late. His reputation had succumbed to "absurdity." Although Frye expresses concern for his colleague, his voicing is nuanced: between the lines I hear the implications that McLuhan was theoretically confused and that his image had been flattened into a media caricature.

Returning to the 1960s, it is in *The Modern Century* that I find Frye's disagreement at its most barbed. The essay is the only one to show Frye in a bleak sunset mood. He ruminates during Canada's centennial year on media and on the threats to Canada from the separatist cause in Quebec and from possible assimilation into American culture. *The Modern Century* was refined from a successful series of talks called the Whidden Lectures, given at McMaster University in 1967. First, let us look at the frame for what follows in a chapter ominously titled "City of the End of Things." The title is taken from Archibald Lampman's 1892 poem. Frye updates Lampman's city to modern circumstances:

> *The last stand of privacy has always been, traditionally, the inner mind.* It is quite possible however for communications media, especially the newer electronic ones, to break down the associative structures of the inner mind and replace them by the prefabricated structures of the media. A society entirely controlled by their slogans and exhortations would be introverted, because nobody would be saying anything: there would only be echo, and Echo was the mistress of Narcissus. It would also be without privacy, because it would frustrate the effort of the healthy mind to develop a view of the world which is private but not introverted, accommodating itself to opposite views.[16] (emphasis mine)

Obliquely critical this passage may appear, but it is Frye's careful prelude to his next address of McLuhan's ideas. I submit that the chapter title, "City of the End of Things" – with a William Burroughs–like evocation of urban nightmare – is a reply to the global village metaphor. Instead of the benign village, there is the terminal city. McLuhan was ambivalent about the effects of the global village atmosphere, but that is another issue at the moment. In the electronic polity privacy is eroded for Frye, individual consciousness consumed under the stamp of advertising and TV: the patterns of inner mind are damaged by this viral pressing. A grave new dystopia looms. The new contexts of media are more "con" job than utopian reconstitution or reconciliation. Essential solitude is conducted through reading books. When this singularity is displaced, what comes is the menacing Leviathan of undifferentiated mass.

I observe how Frye identifies electronic media culture with invasive noise – "slogans and exhortations" – and with narcissism ("Echo"). Narcissism is a narcotic; it tranquilizes the addicted user. McLuhan uses the metaphor of narcissism-narcosis in *Understanding Media.* Frye passes judgment here: the so-called "new" awareness from electronic media is worse than a cliché: noise batters and remoulds. The individual mind cannot maintain integrity in the jabbering upheaval. The new wiring is to junk.

Frye's next sentence triggers detonations: "The triumph of communications is the death of communications: where communication forms a total environment, there is nothing to be communicated." This sentence has been much quoted. What does it mean? It is an example of a Frye *kerygma.* Like many of his boldest declarations, it comes in the midst of a carefully arranged sequence of thoughts. The significance of this habitual rhetorical structure is that Frye guides readers rather than overtly challenges them. The effect of this style is magisterial. Frye implies that once communications media become the total field, then that field is totalitarian. Subjective consciousness, solitude, the rhythms of originality, the silence necessary for concentration, the privacy of consistent cohesive study – these are displaced. Once the world becomes a network of images and bytes where satellites transfer data and there are no borders, that is the end of communication. It spells the beginning of blur and harangue. All communication becomes miscommunication.

Frye is rarely this dire. He is, however, replying to what he perceived to be McLuhan's Aquarian conspiracy thinking: the new world of consciousness, through electronic screens, will be "nothing" more than a successful attempt at annihilating singularity, nihilism under another guise. Corporate forces impose this "nothing." These are the manipulative ways of the media, through the politicians who wish to tranquilize us with formulaic cliché, the pop cultural icons that wish to degrade us with their crudities, the images from advertising and TV which dull us with (non)consensual hallucinations, the addictions to power that come from being hooked into viral screens and networks. If the invaluable solitude of literary consciousness leaves, what slouches towards us, shadowing up to be born in the so-called renaissance of new inventions?

In Frye's following paragraph he makes this association with McLuhan at last blatant. We should not be lulled by his genteel tone and polite deference.

The role of communications media in the modern world is a subject that Professor Marshall McLuhan has made so much his own that it would be almost a discourtesy not to refer to him in a lecture which covers many of his themes. The McLuhan cult, or more accurately the McLuhan rumour, is the latest of the illusions of progress: it tells us that a number of new media are about to bring in a new form of civilization all by themselves, merely by existing. Because of this we should not, staring at a television set, wonder if we are wasting our time and develop guilt feelings accordingly: we should feel that we are evolving a new mode of apprehension. What is important about the television set is not the quality of what it exudes, which is only content, but the fact that it is there, the end of a tube with a vertical suction which "involves" the viewer. This is not all of what a serious and most original writer is trying to say, yet Professor McLuhan lends himself partly to this interpretation by throwing so many of his insights into a deterministic form. He would connect the alienation of progress with the habit of forcing a hypnotized eye to travel over thousands of miles of type, in what is so accurately called the pursuit of knowledge. But apparently he would see the Gutenberg syndrome as a cause of the alienation of progress, and not simply as one of its effects. Determinism of this kind, like the determinism which derives Confederation from the railway, is a plausible but oversimplified form of rhetoric.

(20)

There are many ideas running through this passage. Frye in his next paragraphs anatomizes the axiomatic "medium is the message" and the controversies over "hot" and "cool" media. But recognize Frye's ambivalence – his attempt to separate McLuhan himself ("serious and most original") from McLuhanism and McLuhanites – or, "McLuhanacy," so it was dubbed in the press. Obviously, "McLuhanacy" is a conflation of McLuhan's name with lunacy. The etymology of the word "lunacy," of course, links it with "Luna," the moon. I note this because the next chapter in Frye's essay is called "Clair de lune intellectuel." (I should add that Frye disagrees with George Grant's *Lament for a Nation* in these lectures; it is not just McLuhan he is addressing.)

The determinism charge against McLuhan is grave. It was, and still is, an often-levelled accusation. To Frye, McLuhan exalts technology over human consciousness and liberty. Machines prevail over identity; experience appears catapulted and shaped by energies beyond body and mind.

Even the aphorism – McLuhan's prized mode of apocalyptic communication in the global theatre – is (seemingly) determinist because it is oracular. It is an assertive pronouncement where there can be ample disagreement, but no resolution, in the way there can be, and must be, with essaying, when scholarly evidence and conclusions inform the debate. I see the "continuity" and "discontinuity" issue again looming up between them. To make things intelligible for Frye, a line of argument must establish a specific contour of theoretical presentation. The discontinuities of the aphorism turn us towards Delphic authority, hence towards theocratic authoritarianism.

This misreading of McLuhan's alleged determinism persists. I found it expressed yet again in Jonathan Hart's introduction to the 2009 reissue of *The Modern Century* in the book *City of the End of Things*. Hart is a notable Canadianist and Frye scholar (and an old colleague of mine from our student days at the University of Toronto; we had many lively conversations together). He says, "Frye contrasts his interest in the free will of the individual with Marshall McLuhan's determinism in which mass media turn out to be an illusion of progress rather than evolving mode of perception."[17] This Frye-like assertion unfortunately recycles the cliché that McLuhan believed media were greater than the human. I have been arguing that McLuhan believed media is the most human thing about us: technology is an extension of body and mind, not a form of domination. Media can be totalitarian, but human engagement and transformation are hopeful possibilities. A Catholic humanist cannot be fatalistic. There is always the story of redemption.

Arrestingly, Frye suggests that McLuhan's discontinuous mode of presentation must lead to a breakdown of subjectivity. "The deterministic form" closes argument. We do not argue with TV, only react to its oracular, imagistic intimations. Note the juncture: Frye implies that though McLuhan was a brazenly original figure, he had allowed his name to be bracketed with Media ("McLuhan Inc."). Since "the triumph of communication is the death of communication," the inference is obvious: McLuhan Inc. means the death of thought and the intellectual suicide of an important thinker.

That Frye identified McLuhan with the misguided Aquarian hopes of the 1960s is again obvious in another passage from *Myth and Metaphor*:

> [F]olksingers and rock music festivals seemed to symbolize a new conception of comradeship. It was a period of neoprimitivism, of renewed identity through ecstatic music or contemplation of a visual focus. McLuhan

suggested that the physiological impact of television and other electronic media would create a new sensibility, forming bodies of social awareness in which nations and states as we know them would wither away and be replaced by a revitalized tribal culture. In the seventies he became less sanguine about this, but something of his earlier view survives *as a vague hope that some technological gimmick will automatically take charge of the human situation.*[18] (emphasis mine)

"Vague hope" and "technological gimmick" are droll deflations. It is debatable whether McLuhan saw the new cosmos only in the raptures of rock festivals. More likely he perceived the contours of a larger structural-informational shift away from solitary literary comprehension. These processes, neither good nor bad, were the activations of our excited milieu. However, I think that Frye accurately identifies a vulnerable strain in McLuhan's thought that gives the appearance of endorsement.

Frye writes this brusque entry in his *The "Third Book" Notebooks, 1964–1972* at around the time of his composition of the Whidden Lectures: "Marshall McLuhan is a typical example [of] a reputation as great thinker based on the fact that he doesn't think at all" (146). There is this blunt remark from *Notebooks and Lectures on the Bible and Other Religious Texts*, likely from the 1960s: "Television is like a telescope, a new method of perception which tells us more, but also makes what it sees look cold, dead, and inconceivably remote" (97).

In his essay "The Quality of Life in the '70s," Frye writes of the 1960s, "It was the McLuhan age, the age of intense preoccupation with the effect of communications on society, and with the aspect of life that we call news. Many of the worst features of the late '60s, its extravagant silliness, its orgies of lying, its pointless terrorism and repression, revolved around the television set and the cult of the 'image.'"[19] Frye's rejection of TV continues in his notebooks in this editorial from the mid-1980s: "American civilization has to *de-theatricalize* itself, I think, from *the prison of television.* They can't understand themselves why they admire Reagan and would vote for him again, and yet *know* that he's a silly old man with no understanding even of his own policies. They are really in that Platonic position of staring at the shadows on the wall of the cave"[20] (emphasis mine). I find some truth in McLuhan's suggestion of a Manichaean split in Frye's thought, a division of the communications' cosmos into an "us" (the literate) versus "them" (the iLiterate) trapped in the prison of TV. Although McLuhan disliked watching much TV, he did not think it useful for intellectuals to dismiss shadows, what emanated from screens.

In their parting of the ways we see a division in the hierarchy of word over image. There is more than a hint in these passages that Frye thought the new image cults were degrading, a pulling away from the depths and layering of verbal understanding and analysis. To Frye, McLuhan had moved too much towards image, becoming an image himself, in the McLuhanesque fad. In this way, Frye allied himself with the severe critiques of media we find in George Steiner's essays gathered in *Language and Silence* (1976) and *Extraterritorial* (1976) and in Sven Birkerts's *The Gutenberg Elegies: The Fate of Reading in an Electronic Age* (1995). We see similar judgments about media in Neil Postman's *Amusing Ourselves to Death: Public Discourse in the Age of Show Business* (1985) and *Conscientious Objections* (1988). Harold Bloom, in impressively cardinal Manichaean gestures, consistently condemns Universal Television for placing image and sound, spectacle and emotion over the word. Bloom's references to the so-called irrational entertainments mark every book he has written in the decades since the publication of *The Anxiety of Influence*. But it would be doing a reductive injustice to Steiner and Postman to identify them with a polarization of word against image. While their biases favour the habit of solitude – in analytical study and literary detachment, the silence that surrounds reading, the word-by-word assembling of argument and case, words on a still white page that does not blaze with electronic light, texts that must be assembled in the intellect and not in hypertextual configurations of storage and retrieval on a vibrating cathode-ray screen, typographical space and time over digital and pixel impression – both Postman and Steiner have written admiringly of McLuhan's probes into the sensory riot of the global village.[21] Like Frye, Steiner and Postman honour McLuhan's originality. And like Frye, they lament how he was absorbed into the aerial machinery of cult and celebrity.

Is there a poignant suggestion in those writings that McLuhan was a sacrificial figure to the irradiating fields of image and icon? Through the amplification and distortion of his ideas, inevitable in the media processing of close-up and speed, we saw writ large in his volatile career the communication issues he tried to express. The solitary Frye, less comfortable with TV glare and radio replay, rarely stepped into the ferocious limelight. Perhaps he showed the greater wisdom.

Frye mourned his colleague, ironically enough, on a radio broadcast. It is in a 1981 interview for CBC Radio's *Sunday Morning*, recorded the week after McLuhan's death, that Frye expresses his awareness of the sacrificial pattern in McLuhan's boom-and-bust reputation:

He was a literary critic and that meant that he looked at the form of what was in front of him instead of at the content ... he got on the manic-depressive roller-coaster of the news media and that meant, of course, he went away to the skies like a rocket and then came down like the stick, but he himself and what he said and thought had nothing to do with that. That's what the news media do to people if you get caught in their machinery.[22]

Returning now to the later 1960s, we find Frye nevertheless expressing a crafty ambivalence about McLuhan's presence in comments he recorded for an interview in *The University of Toronto Graduate* in December 1967. He had given the Whidden Lectures at McMaster in the previous January. It is interesting to read this in light of our exploration of his less accommodating commentary in *The Modern Century*. These comments concern the role of McLuhan's Centre for Culture and Technology on the university campus. The *Graduate* was widely circulated around the university. McLuhan probably read what Frye said.

> The Centre for Culture and Technology points up another important role for this kind of academic structure. While I think it would be a good thing to have such a centre whether Marshall McLuhan were on the campus or not, his peculiar originality justifies associating a centre with him ... A scholar who is a serious and original thinker has a good deal of the charismatic leader about him. The great majority of scholars in the university are quite happy with being in one of the departments in one of the traditional disciplines, but every so often one is enough of a lone wolf for the university to want to create spaces around him ... It is particularly important for Marshall McLuhan to have this kind of space around him because he is a very enigmatic and aphoristic type of thinker, an easy person to distort and misunderstand. On the periphery, there is a large McLuhan rumour which says, "Nobody reads books anymore – Marshall McLuhan is right." This, of course, is something of an oversimplification of what a quite important thinker has to say. So I think it is important for the university to have a structure that will permit serious and dedicated people to get a bit closer to him, not only to understand him, but so they can work out their own ideas in some kind of reference to his.
>
> (12)

For all the vehemence McLuhan often showed towards Frye, the editorial shows Frye's support of the "lone wolf." The final sentence illumines the importance of McLuhan's proximity for Frye. Still I know how the prickly McLuhan would have reacted with Wilde-like speed to the qualifications of "peculiar" and "quite" placed before statements about his originality.

◦≈◦

Let us return to *The Modern Century*. Frye's preparations for his comment about the triumph of communications and the death of communications have their source in this compressed entry and exploration from *Notebooks and Lectures on the Bible and Other Religious Texts*. This is the seed from the mid-1960s:

> ... a hyper-physical world. This appears to be the world of unseen beings, angels, spirits, devils, demons, djinns, daemons, ghosts, elemental spirits, etc. It's the world of the "inspiration" of poet or prophet, of premonitions of death, telepathy, extra-sensory perception, miracle, telekinesis ... Fundamentally, it's the world of buzzing though not booming confusion that the transistor radio is a symbol of. The world of communication as total environment which inspires terror. Shakespeare's *Tempest* as heard by the imprisoned crew ... The world of drugs, multiple personality, and hallucination ... It's the polytheistic world of contending & largely unseen forces; it's the world of terror that McLuhan associates with the oral stage of culture: twitching ears, & a poor sense of direction.
>
> (90)

Frye suggests how terrifying the acoustic-tactile world of electronic mass must be for a literary "eye" person. McLuhan knew the terror well. The audile-tactile prophet is the antenna of the race. That antenna can pull in signals rife with the screeches of madness.

The litany of Frye's rejections of McLuhan's terminology continues. This is from Frye's *Late Notebooks, 1982–1990* entries in the 1980s: "I never understood why that blithering nonsense 'the medium is the message' caught on so" (234–5). Did Frye understand the meaning of the aphorism? The formidable Frye scholar Robert Denham confirmed in an interview conducted by email, "Frye had a great deal to say about McLuhan in bits and pieces over the years." Clearly, Frye struggled with the aphorism's evocation of the effect of form over content. But Denham added this dry, witty remark: "I don't know McLuhan well enough to comment." This is relevant to my book because many critics have found themselves baffled by the riddling density of McLuhan's probes.[23]

Frye writes, after consulting the I Ching in a thought experiment, "I suppose, that I was to be a 'feminine' or receptive writer ... That tiresome link with McLuhan cropped up again in the paper. McLuhan would be on the Chi'en side, I suppose: his ideas were, he said, 'probes'" (*Late Notebooks, 1982–1990*, 4). McLuhan's use of the word "probe" to describe his critical method is "a male metaphor – without social context. He supplied the context by naive determinism. Technology is alleged to create society" (ibid.). In a passage where Frye mixes metaphors with gnomic contemplation – hints and links for future essays – we find this stream of associative entries: "Information involves extricating oneself from a spider web of misinformation ... Coming to point (crazy Oedipus) where we can't afford supremacy of ideology anymore: let's have a war and smash that guy's ideology. Primary concerns must become primary ... Feeling that this is so led in sixties to revival of ecstatic metaphor: drugs, yoga, Zen, folk singers, rock music (Woodstock) would bring in a new conception of community. Revitalized tribal culture in McLuhan" (*Notebooks and Lectures on the Bible and Other Religious Texts*, 598–9). I believe there is more ambiguity than ambivalence here. It shows the twinning in the McLuhan-Frye matrix: they were more possessed by what was happening around them than they were willing to admit to one another.

When we recognize the inextricable relations between their lines of thought, we find Frye modifying his "Global village my ass" entry. In entry 115 from *Notebooks on the Bible and Other Religious Texts*, he writes a mitigating afterthought: "Every idea contains its own opposite or anti-book" (97). In this he recognizes his measuring of McLuhan. All annotations generate contraries. What comes from conflicted musings are interpretive commentary, more pages, more lectures. The more texts there are, the more textures there will be. The threads of complexity interweave.

In his notebooks Frye writes many responses to McLuhan, not all of them relevant here. Many are throwaway comments, mere marginalia. Example: he drafted in a fragment from *The "Third Book" Notebooks, 1964–1972* the "Present Idea" for a book that was to include "media & messages (McLuhan)" (20–1). This book seed was never developed.

Before I leave Frye's notebooks, let me quote him giving another quick jab: "Even if you start with a completely chaotic view of art, like McLuhan's view that art is anything that A can put over on B" (95). This is a reference to McLuhan's ad lib, often uttered in TV interviews, "Art is whatever you can get away with."[24] That is a Horatian and Quintillian notion of the practical artistic enterprise. Art is shaped by audience involvement. If people do not respond, then the artefact is not communicating, on any level.

We again encounter their oppositions. To Frye, there is the seer's stance of the Romantic sublime: a vital book overflows with intensities; the discreet reader gazes over the inspired writer's shoulder. To McLuhan, there is the hearer's sensual apprehension: text depends on response and reaction, achieving little if it passes by without immersing the user. This is (again) a division in the sensory preferences of Frye and McLuhan: the solitary and the public figures. Yet this split is by no means codified. McLuhan slips into ecstatically unique expression; Frye charges into subtle polemics. McLuhan liked to sit alone in his library at the Centre for Culture and Technology and read. Frye appeared on TV and spoke on the radio. "Ex-stasis" means eruption from the self, a transcendental notion of inspiration. *Polemos* also means strife, a perpetual striving with the other.

⁓⁓⁓

I could cite numerous passages in essays over many years where Frye wrestles with McLuhan's ideas. In several appearances his highly ambivalent (and deeply ambiguous) oppositions are pronounced. I like this one in particular: *Le Devoir*'s interview with Frye is called "L'Anti-McLuhan." The title was likely imposed without Frye's approval, a common journalistic practice. The interview appeared in 1968, coinciding with the publication of *The Modern Century* in French. That work was titled in translation *Le siecle de l'innovation* (obviously, this carries an entirely different overtone). In spite of the interview's agonistic title, Frye mentions McLuhan only once. Nor do the views he proposes sound as extreme as "L'Anti-McLuhan" portends. What concerns us is the journalist's perception that Frye was almost certainly in opposition to McLuhan. The interviewer, Naïm Kattan, asks Frye if the new orality of electronic culture announces the end of the linearity of the book and the dominance of alphabetic culture. Frye simply states that he does not agree with McLuhan on how we process print information.[25]

Nevertheless, this interview in *Le Devoir* shows how a perception prevails: Frye and McLuhan worked in contra. McLuhan saw a new culture rising; Frye resisted the apprehension. McLuhan was moving towards a description of how techno-tribal culture appears; Frye had moved into the dissidence of the literary imagination. In the blandly titled 1983 essay "The View from Here," Frye comments on the countermovements of the inspired reader. The essay is anything but bland. It is his most extreme aesthetic statement. We see Frye's Romantic resistance to fact and matter, the very constructions of reality. He exalts the imagination beyond ideologies, placing it above history and media systems:

> [M]ost of what we call "reality" is the rubbish of leftover human constructs ... Continued study of literature and the arts brings us into an entirely new world, where creation and revelation have different meanings ... It is the illusions of literature that begin to seem real, and *ordinary life, pervaded as it is with all the phony and lying myths that surround us, begins to look like the real hallucination, a parody of the genuine imaginative world.*[26] (emphasis mine)

The Offshore Debate

In July 1970 Frye wrote a powerful editorial on "Communications" for the front page of the London-based paper *The Listener*. It is his most explicit defence of print culture, his most direct confrontation with the media. His essay places McLuhan, or McLuhanism, at the heart of the debate about the values of print versus screen and radio. The editorial follows up on suggestions made in *The Modern Century* and in his notebooks. McLuhan retorted four months later. Though the debate took place offshore (I mean outside of Canada), it bluntly expresses their agon. It is possible that Frye had read *From Cliché to Archetype* by then. The tone between them was never so aggrieved. In the McLuhan circle of supporters at the Centre for Culture and Technology, the Frye editorial confirmed what they suspected was his insidious opposition to McLuhan's ideas. It affirmed that he was willing to make his antagonism public. "*The Listener* Debate" became for members of the McLuhan inner circle (primarily Carpenter and Watson) a shorthand reference to what they suspected was conspiratorial resistance to McLuhan's inquiries into how media reshapes cultural life.

Frye begins by acknowledging that he was at that time "on an advisory committee concerning Canadian radio and television ... and so I have been trying to do some reading in communication theory. I find it an exciting subject ... But I have also become aware of a more negative side to it, as to most technology. The future that is technically feasible may not be the future that society can absorb."[27] A synopsis of his case will show how he identifies mass media with a new totalitarianism, an argument similar to the one he outlines in *The Modern Century*. "My hair prickles when I hear advertisers talk of a television set simply as a means of reaching their market. It so seldom occurs to them that a television set might be their market's way of looking at them, and that the market might conceivably not like what it sees" (34). This is an image of Big Brother invading our lives. Is Frye writing an anti-capitalist polemic? He talks of outrageous acts of "counter-communication ... noisy enough to shout down that voice and spit at that image, if only for a few moments." But violence is counterproductive. Frye looks at the theory that we have returned to an "oral-tactile" culture of mantic poetry, that print represents an obsolete linear mode of thinking, and finds all this wanting.

Frye finally mentions McLuhan (column four, paragraph nine) in the by now familiar disagreement with how electronic media may be reconfiguring our sensorium into "a new 'simultaneous' or mosaic form of understanding. Contemporary unrest, in this view, is part of an attempt to adjust to a new situation and break away from the domination of print ... *I understand that for some of them the phrase 'p.o.b.,' meaning print-oriented bastard, has replaced s.o.b. as a term of abuse. It seems to me that this view is not so much wrong as perverted, the exact opposite of what is true*" (emphasis mine). The allusion to the "p.o.b." misconstrues McLuhan's shorthand reference to the "p.o.v." writer, an acronym for "point of view." It means one whose point of view becomes a prison of beliefs. Nevertheless, Frye understands this shorthand to be a flat dismissal of the values of print, rather than a satiric put-down of those who prefer the extreme stance of a hard-line position on whatever subject. Frye is identifying a strand of thought in McLuhan's followers and not, he will say, in McLuhan himself. Seldom do we see Frye so close to outrage. He matches hyperbole with hyperbole.

His current of rage is obvious (column five, paragraphs twelve to fourteen). The elements and characteristics of the oral society are compared with "the opening of *Paradise Lost* ... Satan is a rhetorician, an orator, a dictator: for use of words, everything depends on the immediate mood, where one can express agreement or disagreement only by shouting. The devils are being trained to becoming oracles, whispering or commanding voices telling man how to act and think" (35). Rhetoricians are satanic; the devils, oracular beings. Reading this, McLuhan must have taken these lines to be a personal attack: he was an expert in Elizabethan rhetoric; his aphorisms had been called an oracular form. He had been called a Delphic figure by Tom Wolfe in his famous (or infamous) profile. Frye goes on: "But there is one important difference [to the oral condition]: God is thinking of writing a book, and is outlining the plot to the angels." This would have likely struck McLuhan as a smug set-up yet again of the virtuous us (book culture) versus the demonic them (electronic culture). We grant Frye his own brand of mischief-making.

The Critical Conflict between McLuhan and Frye

Frye mentions McLuhan in the second last paragraph. Then he concludes, "Democracy and book culture are interdependent, and the rise of oral and visual media represents, not a new order to adjust to, but a subordinate order to be contained." The final sentence equates liberal democracy with the printed book, oral and visual media with technofascism. There is the fearful warning: contain what is happening before it is too late. Frye is almost never this candidly judgmental.

On October 8 McLuhan responds. He refers to Frye in the first sentence. His voice is drenched in scorn: "It is heartening to observe Northrop Frye venturing into his first steps towards understanding media."[28] McLuhan damns with faint praise: "The terrain is treacherous and beset with primitive elephant traps, as well as tiger traps. Many of these are created by those who, like Professor Frye, attempt to establish personal or private points of view about the environmental forms devised by the perennial human effort to create new service environments."

McLuhan makes only one more specific reference to Frye (column three, paragraph two). It is a corrective to Frye's learning. "In rallying to the cause of the book, Professor Frye could have found some help in *European Literature and the Latin Middle Ages* by Ernst Robert Curtius." Then in what must be by now a familiar concern for McLuhan on the clash between his percepts and Frye's concepts, we read this expansion on the Curtius reference: "The section on 'The Book as Symbol' testifies to the universality of this trope, East and West. The Book of Nature has always evoked the full energies of scientists, and was a province of ancient *grammatica*" (476). McLuhan emphasizes, "Understanding is not a point of view." An editorial is merely an expression of an angle. Just because you put yourself at the centre of everything does not mean you understand anything at all. "My personal values and attitudes, which are entirely related to the printed word, I have found it necessary to exclude from media study, so far as possible. Value judgments about the psychic and social consequences of railways and aeroplanes soon become a smog that clouds perception and judgment." Agreement should not be a factor in apprehensions. McLuhan expounds for three columns and eleven paragraphs subsequent to the responses to Frye, never mentioning him again. His strategy is to paraphrase and repeat the premises of his own books, in highly compressed form, to explore "the electric world of *audile-tactile space*, the space of encounter, confrontation, involvement and participation."

In his final paragraph he returns to his indirect admonition to Frye and quotes the terms of the 9 July editorial: "Nothing is more upsetting than such awareness to those entrenched in conventional preoccupations.

Nothing is more perverted than the party who reports that 'your house is on fire', when you are enjoying a cosy nap." The word "perverted" cries out for quotation marks. His conclusion asks the great Blake scholar to shake free from cosy cliché. Hereafter McLuhan would ominously call Frye one of his enemies.[29]

The Listener argument is the instructive debate that they should have had in person. Frye's reaction to McLuhan's retort is not on record. The two pieces have never been published side by side. I believe they should be. They are an indelible part of the Canadian visionary tradition.

Their Agon Continues

Frye persisted in his disagreements with McLuhan over how we process typographic data in *The Critical Path: An Essay on the Social Context of Literary Criticism* (1971). His essay begins with an engaging acknowledgment of how he had been lost in literary mazes, the "dark wood of Blake's prophecies," and looked "for some path that would get me out of there."[30] Nine pages on he mentions McLuhan again. The agonistic pressure is intensified in his references when he continues to suggest that McLuhan's intuitions are determinist, guided by a Thomist imperative (read: a Catholic agenda):

> More recently, Marshall McLuhan has placed a formalist theory, expressed in the phrase "the medium is the message," within the context of a neo-Marxist determinism in which communication media play the same role that instruments of production do in more orthodox Marxism. Professor McLuhan drafted his new mosaic code under a strong influence from the conservative wing of the new critical movement, and many traces of an earlier Thomist determinism can be found in *The Gutenberg Galaxy*.
>
> (21)

"The new critical movement" is an allusion to Lewis and Pound. The implied critique of "the global village" is that it is a catholic and Catholic idea: catholic, because eclectic; Catholic, because experiencing the world can become ritualized and Eucharistic. These passages show Frye was a master of the subtle counterattack.

In subsequent pages of *The Critical Path*, Frye repeats his claim that McLuhan misunderstands how the mind processes print information. He observes that McLuhan's distinction between supposed linear responses to print and the alleged "simultaneous" responses to electronic media is

The Critical Conflict between McLuhan and Frye 143

turned by him into "a portentous historical contrast" (26). The suggestion is McLuhan inflated a sensory contrast into an epic contest. Frye writes on: suppositions by McLuhan should be a prelude to criticism. The true action of the mind is when sensory bias is assimilated into theoretical protocol.

Frye points to the essential stylistic and formal difference between them. This is the outline of the "continuity" versus "discontinuity" debate which underlies their contrasting methods. He says,

> Oracular prose writers from Heraclitus to McLuhan have the sense of extra profundity that comes from leaving more time and space and less sequential connexion at the end of a sentence. The discontinuity of the Essays of Bacon, for example, where ... each sentence is really a paragraph in itself, is connected with his design "to come to men's business and bosoms," as he put it.
>
> (42)

Frye's aligning of Francis Bacon with McLuhan is highly relevant. In his PhD studies McLuhan explored Bacon's aphoristic methods. When Eric McLuhan finished *Laws of Media* for his father, he subtitled it *The New Science* to invoke Baconian techniques of engagement.

The Critical Path has passages that I find worth revisiting, but let us jump forward in time to Frye's 1994 posthumous contribution to *Who Was Marshall McLuhan?* These are the important sentences, where Frye's cagey tone disturbs what is supposed to be a eulogy. His is the briefest contribution to the book.

> Marshall was an extraordinary improviser in conversation; he could take fire instantly from a chance remark, and I have never known anyone equal to him on that score ... he was celebrated for the wrong reasons in the sixties, and then neglected for the wrong reasons later, so that *a reassessment of his work and its value is badly needed. I think what I chiefly learned from him, as an influence on me, was the role of discontinuity in communication*, which he was one of the first people to understand the significance of.
>
> (126; emphasis mine)

If we pause to consider what he says in the second paragraph, the tribute sardonically suggests again that grandiose incoherence in McLuhan's thought. Recall Frye's response to Cayley's questions that McLuhan was "a half-thinker," and we see a decisive crack in their approaches and techniques, in their ways of assembling material and of juxtaposing citation and research. The "continuity" versus "discontinuity" concern puts a strong, memorable wedge between them. Their clash becomes a conflict of style.

The Orator and the Theorist

McLuhan's aphorisms are protests against lineal thought patterns. They were a charging of the academic barricades. Aphorisms are an oral form. They depend on marriages (and sometimes abrasions) of voice and ear. Mercurial McLuhan is at his most provocative presenting complex nodes of thought in kernels. Instead of theoretical consistency and sequential discourse, he presents bursts and stabs. The term "probe," contra Frye's supposition that it was a male metaphor, came from Sputnik.

An aphorism invites dialogue. Aphorists thrive on paradoxes and contradictions. Elias Canetti once noted that all aphorists appear to have known one another, so specific is their gift for compressed thinking and echoing paraphrase. Aphorisms destabilize the reader by throwing indeterminacy in his or her path. Without a theoretical or propositional backdrop, an aphorism may appear to resist consolidation into cohesion. When adrift from a context inside a larger framework, an aphorism may seem like a smart or snide remark. The great aphorists – Nietzsche and Kierkegaard, Emerson in his essays, Wilde in his critical dialogues, Kafka in *The Blue Octavo Notebooks*, Canetti in his notebooks, Simone Weil in the notes that were gathered together and published after her death – conjure behind their abbreviated comments considerable structures of interpretation and re-creation. In an aphorism ideas become happenings.

I have said Frye had a genius for aphorism. His notebooks are packed, page after inspired page, with epigrams and apothegms. In *Northrop Frye Unbuttoned* he says, in a compressed contemplation:

> **The Aphorism.** The orator's style is continuous, but the crux is the high-style sentential, which speaks with the authority of concerned prose. An aphorism is not a cliché: it penetrates & bites. It has wit, and consequently an affinity with satire. It appeals to the instinct in us to say "I don't care if a man's right or wrong: all I care about is whether his mind is alive or dead." Naturally this will not do as a guide to thought, but it's normal & healthy as an occasional reaction. Christ speaks in aphorisms, not because they are alive, but because he is.
>
> (13)

In his *Late Notebooks, 1982–1990,* he writes, "The main difficulty in my writing ... is in translating discontinuous aphorisms into continuous argument. Continuity, in writing ... is probabilistic" (23).

When Frye's gift for the aphorism almost matches McLuhan's, I contend it is essential to address why they chose separate strategies for the public domain. The key is in what Frye says in the entry on the aphorism. The rhetorician moves in theatrical realms, wearing the mask of the playful jester. He emphasizes the impermanent tease of performance. Behind this is the performer's radical unease with publication, or with any print-based expression.

Evolutionary thought comes alive when you speak it. Poetic fact is closer to speaking than it is to verifiable arguments embodied in a text. A book can freeze the process of thought; publication interrupts the stream of words, catching breath inside the edges of letters.

McLuhan loved performing, and his aphorisms truly dance into life when they are re-enacted and debated. An aphorism cannot rest on a page. Even if a performance is not recorded, it can leave an indelible impression in its once-in-a-lifetime effect. This is how inspiration and memory mingle.

McLuhan took pleasure in switching positions quickly. This makes it almost impossible to pin him down on what his propositions represent. "I have always found questions more interesting than answers and probes more exciting than products," he writes in a 1974 letter to John Polanyi. "All of my work has been experimental in the sense of studying effects rather than causes, and perceptions rather than concepts. That this is not a normal way of proceeding in the Western world, I know only too well from the public response of distrust and disbelief concerning my motives. My motives, so far as I have been able to ascertain them, are simply an intellectual enjoyment of play and discovery" (*Letters,* 487).

When Frye describes the aphorism, he writes of the orator's style and the role of the public intellectual who strives to persuade his audience through argument. The continuities of discourse imply cohesion. Continuity in prose implies the print medium and therefore resistance to the sphere of transient speech, realm of the ear. Discontinuity implies contrarian modes of presentation and thought. "The authority of concern" persuades an audience through reasonable argument. Aphoristic wit will not do "as a guide to thought." He suggests in the final line that aphorists have an apostolic lineage (with "Christ"). Dangerously, they could have messianic tendencies. Put succinctly, discontinuous oral aphorism provokes audiences to extreme reaction.

The confused controversies that surrounded the McLuhan "rumour" showed how the aphoristic probe could be used against a brilliant improviser. McLuhan left silences around his maxims that invited more than disagreement. They invited hostility and absorption into the publicity machine. If the humanist was to engage audiences without distortion, then it was the orator's responsibility to write with care, precision, apt quotation, and cunning ambivalence. People crave continuity. The world is already broken enough. We need scrupulous guidance to artfully lead us through the dangerous apparitions of the labyrinth. The aphorist dropped and abandoned you inside a maze of thought, expecting that you would find your own exit. Frye's *Fearful Symmetry*, *Anatomy of Criticism*, *The Educated Imagination*, and *The Great Code* present a continuous surface, grounded in reference; I have described how this often camouflages his heretical nerve. Each book presents a radical resolve and revaluation: from Blake's place in the canon to the messy imprecision of the critical landscape in *Anatomy*; from the inability of school curricula to recognize the value of literature in *The Educated Imagination*, to the dogmatic literalists who pervert the coding of the Bible, a code intended to set us free. In *The "Third Book" Notebooks, 1964–1972*, we find Frye's sense of mission, nothing less than "a Divine Comedy in criticism" (127). Frye was careful to make sure that his scholarly colleagues – his readers, in part – followed his line of reasoning without being put off by the jagged enunciations of an oracular technique.

I will put McLuhan's methods succinctly: the discontinuous probe, the cut-up approach of the late texts, the tonal swerves, the stops and starts, the use of mixed modes, the use of allusion and quotation, the misquotations and errors – all are a mime of oral communication. They satirize audience expectations. He stepped forward to dislocate. Trouble, confusion, the disordering of sense, the broad gestures, and jests made engagement a drama of confounding wit.

Eric McLuhan offered an anecdotal example of what I mean: once during a Monday night seminar in 1978, McLuhan launched into an aria of improvisation on "the revolution" to those present. He remarked on how John Lennon and Yoko Ono had visited him at the Centre for Culture and Technology on 19 December 1969. They talked about the revolution. McLuhan said it was already over. Confused, Lennon asked how this could be. McLuhan said the ground of electricity transformed everything. Lennon was referring to ideological revolution, McLuhan to a revolution in sensibility. Lennon left bewildered. A student in class, on that Monday night in 1978, angrily said to McLuhan, "I don't agree with you at all." Without pausing McLuhan replied, "Well, if you don't like those ideas, I have some more. Shall we try them on?" Everyone laughed. The student's anger was defused.[31] This is an example of the orator's skill: discontinuity is epiphanic, adaptive, a reflection of electric conditions, an evocation of how metamorphic Nature evolves by leaps and twists. Waves and fields have no continuity. An atom like a spark leaps from one place to another. Theories must be provisional given our turbulent experiences. Perception is the necessity, not cautious argument.

Misquotation is also alteration. It is a way of changing the source, making it new. Misquotation is extension, again: reweaving others' texts into McLuhanesque intensities. It is an act that upsets authority. No text is sacrosanct. Every quotation could be rewired. This was part of McLuhan's exuberance, shooting his way in this direction and then that. Prophetic vision demands that we crack the boxes, transgress borders.

To McLuhan, continuity is an expression of the writer's imposition of formal consistency on thought and energy. The imposition is an expression of the conditioning of the Gutenberg technology (ABCD-mindedness). Discursive prose is only possible through the linear sequence of type. There is no scholarly verification (what McLuhan calls "matching") in orality; only repetition and improvisation, associations and echoes. The orator leaps from one intensity to another. The audience is meant to pause and ponder, to unpack utterances through discussion. Moralistic criticism is useless in volatile conditions because the right or wrong of the perception is up to the listener. A text had to become for him a discontinuous arrangement on typographic space.

His anti-books, *The Medium is the Massage* and *Take Today*, are an invitation to look beyond the letters, and beyond McLuhan himself, to the frontiers of pop culture and cyberspace. He used the print medium to tell us what plays beyond print. The McLuhan paradox is this: you have to be literary to understand what is wordless, musical, sensual, strobing, buzzing, interfusing, and iconic.

To Frye, continuity carries the ethical imperative: linked statements in time permit the reader to follow a line. Sequential paragraphs outline the critical path. The purpose of this is to establish an ethical grounding to the literary enterprise. Words have the power to enchant and harm. They must be written with care. Steady prose reflects a steady intention. Argument becomes a form of awakening to the trap of being conditioned in cliché. Understand the root and stem of the rose, and you understand the flower. The imagination, after Blake and Coleridge, is the energy that recognizes and then re-creates coherence. Since our lives are shattered we need to summon this unifying power of the mind. Critical theory, expressed in *Anatomy* and rearticulated in the compressed synopsis of *The Educated Imagination*, is the conceptual reordering of latent structures into patterns that allow the hidden to be unveiled. Metaphors spawn more metaphors.

In response to a question put by Cayley, "So metaphor is an energy that unites?" Frye says (simply), "Yes." Then he elaborates: "metaphor ... opens up a current or channel of energy between the subject and the object" (*Northrop Frye in Conversation*, 175). In other words, metaphor is the bridge over which our souls cross into new enlightened identity. Frye's most luminous books, outside of *Fearful Symmetry* and his notebooks, are often his briefest, *The Educated Imagination* and *The Double Vision*, where the quest for identity and the potential unity of the spiritual and material life are less ambiguously disclosed. Although we can find occasions in Frye's essays where he calls reality a mere construct, we must be aware of how he wrestles with ways to repair the break between alienated Nature and the humanizing imagination. In his work we see the critic-seer who strives, like an alchemical mystic, to meld the inner and outer into reconfigured light.

Two quotations from *Fearful Symmetry* support my claim. First:

> The senses are organs of the mind, therefore all knowledge comes from mental experience. Mental experience is a union of a perceiving subject and a perceived object; it is something in which the barrier "inside" and "outside" dissolves. But the power to unite comes from the subject. The work of art is the product of this creative perception, hence it is not an escape from reality but a systematic training in comprehending it.
>
> (85)

The second shows the subtle stylist Frye at his conjuring best:

> We say that the snowflake has achieved something of which we alone can see the form, and the form of snowflake is therefore a human form. It is the function of art to illuminate the human form of nature.
>
> (123)

These passages show a harmony in the McLuhan-Frye matrix; this I will demonstrate soon. They wanted to realize the cosmos in personified humanist terms, through perception of the texts that make up Nature and super-Nature, and that are both human and sacred, through the critical awareness of those books which truly reveal the quest narrative that is the Great Code of identity.

~~~

They diverge profoundly over the questions of method and theory. In the *Letters* McLuhan says, "Personally, I prefer to study the pattern minus the theory" (540). Frye presents his case for symmetries in *Anatomy*; McLuhan created teasing texts that sabotage your reading expectations. Frye wrote seemingly conventional essays that mute his growing awareness that text is not a product but "a focus of forces."[32] Another of his intellectual audacities is this: God is an energy process fulfilling its unfolding in art; we peer into the infinite through metaphors that link one association with another, and we glimpse eternity in the mythic time of many meanings, the here-now of each fully charged word and book. There is nothing outside the great text because everything we need is inside it.

We see why for Frye literary study was a calling. But bold propositions require cunning addresses. It was best to follow and unfold the threads slowly, with a cultivated persuasiveness. McLuhan had a staunch sense of both immanent and transcendental presence and intentions in Nature and super-Nature. He could not mask this in the step-by-step arguments of systematic logic. He was possessed by urgings that maddened his thinking into probes. The Magnetic City is burning up with data overload. To arrest our aroused moods, it was best to distract and disrupt audiences with witty paradoxes, outrageous misquotations.

Their strategies are still linked by humanist hope: "Only metaphorize" and "Only re-connect" could have been (and should have been?) the mottos impressed on signs placed over their doorways of their offices at, respectively, 39A Queen's Park East and Massey College.

The Practical Apocalypse Revisited

I shift now to another breach in the directions of their thought. To McLuhan, Nature and technology are shifting mirrors for one another; through art, we experience the apocalypse of this dynamism. Certain authors – Rimbaud, Hopkins, Eliot, and Joyce – effectively reveal the analogical patterning. What did McLuhan mean by the "analogical mirrors"? The mystery of life is never truly hidden. It is available to anyone "with a sacramental view."[33] The cosmos has a language which we scan for signatures, signs, forms, correspondences, grammars. In the ancient world these were called auguries. The visual languages are complemented by acoustic language. This was understood through echoes, reverberations, resonances, rhymes, rhythms. The process of pattern recognition can never be static. Like Joyce's Stephen Dedalus in the "Proteus" episode of *Ulysses*, we each have the capacity to read the signatures of things, "strandentwining cable of all flesh."[34] Electronic super-Nature amplifies protean conditions. Every day is revelatory if we live with our senses receptive. This is (once more) the "practical mysticism" that McLuhan espoused in his first published essay on Chesterton in the *Dalhousie Review* (1936). There is no estrangement from the texts of the world, whether natural or electronic, if we proceed trusting in the narrative openness and interpretative possibility manifested in them. Electronic cosmos flips into the threatening Leviathan when we recklessly absorb the razing manias of persuasion. Extension then becomes amputation.

To Frye, primary meaning, the cosmos itself, is found in the constructs of books. The metaphoric language of the world appears incoherent (and ruined) because of our slumbering state. Poetry remakes the wrecked world into the intelligible. We know Blake offered him the key: the metaphors of poetry are loaded with imaginative patterning; through our peak comprehension of this we rise from anxiety-addled moods. He also found apocalyptic content in Milton. I take Frye's critical practice to be sacramental and liberationist, the *Areopagitica* and *Paradise Regained* melded with *The Marriage of Heaven and Hell.*

Where McLuhan finds communion with the energies of the world through the multiple texts of Nature and super-Nature – prodding us towards awareness through satire and probe – Frye finds communion through cerebral contemplations of "the forces of text." In each book he worked on for publication he rarely prods, he persuades. But like Blake and Milton (and Dante and the Joyce of *Finnegans Wake*), his intentions are always defiantly prophetic. He announces,

> Language [by which Frye means literary language] is a means of intensifying consciousness, *lifting us into a new dimension of being altogether* ... There are many techniques of attaining this more highly structured awareness: there are the yogas & zazen & Sufi schools of the East, & various Western psychologies of psychosynbook, individuation, peak experiences, cosmic consciousness, & what not. I have been somewhat puzzled by the extent to which all this activity overlooks the fact that all intensified language becomes metaphorical language, & that literature is the obvious guide to

whatever passes beyond language, just as Dante's obvious guides to states of being beyond life in 13th-century Italy was Virgil.[35] (emphasis mine)

Literature is the greatest of all guides to the ineffable. And yet (ironically enough) Frye's insight was not the result of only reading Blake or Dante: it came from events, the illuminations that took place in Moncton and Edmonton. Each intuitive moment expanded spheres of comprehension (note the recurrence of the word "expand" in Frye's essays). "The main vehicle of the spirit within the soul-body is intuition: Blake's imagination is too general. It's a quality that works outside of time. I've spent nearly eighty years trying to articulate intuitions that occupied about five minutes of my entire life" (*Late Notebooks, 1982–1990*, 636). Literary texts, when properly contextualized, embody the "Epic of the Soul."[36] Some works map the structural poetics more persuasively than others: hence Frye's focus on Dante's *Divine Comedy*, Milton's *Paradise Lost* and *Paradise Regained*, Shakespeare's late plays (especially *The Tempest*), the prophetic poems of Blake, Emily Dickinson's lyrics, Eliot's *Waste Land* and *Four Quartets*, Joyce's *Ulysses* and *Finnegans Wake*, and the oeuvre of Wallace Stevens. From literature Frye receives the enlarging epiphany: we live inside artificial structures which articulate, and sometimes contain, Nature. Nature can only be fervently redeemed by our constructs. The interweaving Book is our visionary pursuit – "a metaphorical unity of different things"[37] – and our remaking is the world beginning again, in the way our dreams (and too often our nightmares) wish it to be. "I've thought all my life," he writes in his *Late Notebooks*, "of a metaphorical universal map" (146).

The essential frame for Frye's later critical studies is, of course, the Bible: "a work of literature plus."[38] "God," Frye says in his interview with Cayley in *Northrop Frye in Conversation*, "is a linguistic event" (189). What is the "linguistic event" trying teach those who study literature with apocalyptic vigilance? "God wants liberty for man" (98). In the silent study of the literary critic, alone contemplating his books, the radiance comes. In that private place each may find the integrity of sole consciousness. Reading becomes both fusion and rapture: the reader on the critical path transports himself through pages. The path helps to release the associations in symbols. Once he or she is illuminated, the solitary scholar enters the classroom to direct the circumspective eye, the inward gaze of students moved towards a similar brightening enthusiasm.

Thus Frye moves into a poetic signature all his own: the stirring style of the scholar turned diviner. If the movement of the mind must be towards comprehending the texts and subtexts of verbal constructs, then gradually we become conscious that there is a rhythm in the centre of what seems like a sealed labyrinth, where snares appear in forbidding apparitions. The language of the Word, incarnated in metaphors and myths, is the language of the renewed heart.

Words with Power is a work of revival and reverie. In this writing that came late in his life we find these discharges of beauty and exuberance:

> "More is the cry of a mistaken soul," said Blake: "less than all cannot satisfy man." Here the difference between "all" and "all things" is very clear. The world of all things, as know it now, is the material world, and matter is energy congealed to the point at which we can live with it. In the spiritual vision we recover the sense of energy to the extent that we identify with the creating power, and have come from Yeats's polluted heart where all ladders are planted to the place where all ladders end. But where the ladder of progressive steps ends the dance of liberated movement begins.
>
> (176)

Note the number of times in *Words with Power* that Frye speaks of moving "beyond." In the following passage he revises a notebook entry quoted earlier, adding another spirited dimension to drive his words towards the "metaliterature" that he desired for his last willed testament:

> [L]iterature is not only the obvious but the inescapable guide to higher journeys of consciousness ... Virgil represents literature in its Arnoldian function as a "criticism of life," the vision of existence, detached but not withdrawn from it, that is at its most inclusive in the imaginative mode. *Beyond Virgil there is Beatrice, who represents among other things a criticism or higher awareness of the limits of the Virgilian vision ... what looks like a limit from a distance often turns out to be an open gate to something else when we reach it.*
>
> (39; emphasis mine)

Indirectly in his prose poetry, he is allowing for the first time the female muse figure, Beatrice, to enter. We are a long way from an early Frye notebook entry where he gruffly (and annoyingly) says, "I wish Beatrice didn't blither so: she's the most tedious & driveling spinster in literature."[39]

Here are crucial points in their paths. McLuhan turned in his perceptions towards multiple texts, and towards consciousness becoming the mediating energy between them. The cosmos of media perpetually speaks. Frye turned in his conceptualizing mind towards books and the heightening of consciousness that comes from the devotional study of enduring literary forms. The order of words on the page perpetually speaks. We train ourselves to read the lines and between the lines to stitch metaphors together. They may have turned in different directions, but they still shared this humane recognition: everything is within our grasp.

The Dark Frame of Paranoia

I come now to the question of conspiracy. McLuhan had an abiding obsession to know, Who rules? What are the energies at work in institutions that could reroute and even block new thought? Heightened perceptive states can flip easily into paranoia. It is another opportunity (after all) to make, or receive, meanings. The darker framing of paranoia is another way of making processes and encounters intelligible. Paranoia is vitalist: to the paranoid, the world always pulsates with intentions (usually not your own).

From the midpoint of the 1970s on, when his reputation began to go into eclipse, his penchant for paranoid conspiracy theories grew. His penchant did not just grow. It stewed and boiled over.

McLuhan detected conspiracies in what he thought were covens in the university and in the art scene. He often divided the world into his own Manichaean extremes of enemies and supporters. In his 1953 letter to Walter Ong, McLuhan darkly broods,

> For the past year I've been exploring the relations between the Secret Societies and the arts. A grisly business. I don't know what you know, but I know there isn't a living artist or critic of *repute* who isn't playing their game. I mean their rituals and doctrines as basis of artistic organization ... Eric Voegelein's recent *The New Science of Politics* ... is a denunciation of the Gnostic sects from Joachim of Flora ... to Marx. Sees "Reformation" as re-emergence of these sects into the open ... H.N. Frye's *Blake* [sic] is best exposition of contemporary gnosticism I know.
>
> (*Letters*, 237–8)

I think it is important to decode that last line on Frye's Gnosticism. To McLuhan Gnosticism was a treacherous tradition that threatened the stability of the catholic world (small "c" catholic; this refers to the idea of a visible, viable community of struggling souls). Blake did in part represent the cult of art for McLuhan. This cult was hubristic and demonic if it set up an alternative cosmos to the one prescribed by scripture. Where McLuhan goes farther is in the imputing of a Gnostic presence in the entire art world: success, failure, recognition, fame, even money came from membership in elite crowds or in-clubs. Some of this anxiety on McLuhan's part came from being part of what he called the minority culture of Catholicism in Canada (it is in fact not a minority culture at all: more than thirty-five percent of the population professes the Catholic faith; it is – and was – the largest of the Chrstian communities in the country; moreover, many prime ministers, Sir Wilfrid Laurier, Louis St Laurent, Pierre Elliott Trudeau, and Joe Clark, among others, were Catholics). But McLuhan relished his outsider status, using it to strategic effect. We have noted his contact with Lewis and the title of McLuhan's "Counterblast" pamphlet. In *Through the Vanishing Point*, he exalts the role of the artist-sleuth: "the artist has in many circles in the past century been called the enemy, the criminal ... the detective since Poe's Dupuin has tended to be a probe, an artist of the big town, an artist-enemy ... society is always one phase back" (246). This passage comes after a quotation from a biography of Picasso, where the great cubist celebrates "the antisocial being" that terrifies the status quo. McLuhan cites this with gleeful approval.

Nevertheless, McLuhan's sense of being an outsider meant being at times distanced from powerful inner circles. It meant acute awareness of how those circles were informed by people (he thought) he knew. In another letter to Ong in 1954, he goes into detail about conspiratorial cliques:

> I don't see how it is possible to teach English literature, or any literature, or any European lit. without full knowledge of the "secret doctrine" for which arts are the sole means of grace. I realize now that my own rejection of philosophy as a study in my pre-Catholic days was owing to the sense that it was a meaningless truncation. Not that my present interest is due to any conviction of truth in the secret doctrine. Quite the contrary. It is rather to a sense of it as the fecund source of lies and misconceptions. e.g. Puritan Inner Light ... Can you think of any reason why Catholic students of philosophy and lit. today should not be given the facts about these "secrets?" I can find nobody here who can or will discuss the question.[40]

"Puritan Inner Light" refers to the Protestant inner fire tradition of inward knowledge and wisdom. I believe the reference is to Frye.

According to McLuhan's wild insinuation, Frye was part of a Masonic cult at the University of Toronto. Frye's success – extraordinary and inexplicable to McLuhan, since Blake's prophetic poems were obscure and *Anatomy* was "opaque and unreadable" – had to be due to inside connections. The Catholic part of the university (Saint Michael's) was to McLuhan like an island inside the decidedly Protestant campus. The edgy tone in his conspiracy theorizing echoes Pound's crackpot obsession with banking cabals and trilateral commissions. In a 1951 letter to Pound – incarcerated for treason in Saint Elizabeth's Hospital – McLuhan mimics the poet's often crazed cadences: "I agree with your analysis of Foundation administrators and the beaneries ... The beaneries are on their knees to these gents. They regard them as Santa Claus. They will do 'research' on anything that Santa Claus approves ... To get published they must be dull, and stupid, and harmless" (*Letters*, 226).

The unacknowledged power struggle to the Catholic McLuhan was between forces of inner light, heresy, and those of revealed light, orthodoxy. The 1917 Papal Code of Canon Law unambiguously stated that being a Freemason would bring on excommunication. To this day Holy Communion is denied to anyone suspected of joining Freemasonry. Irreconcilable with the doctrine of the Church, Freemasonry appeared to champion occult practices (white magic, séances, channelling, astrological charting, automatic writing, the study of auras, consulting the Tarot). Post–Vatican II revisions have muted these edicts but not eliminated them. The devout McLuhan was conscious of the doctrine of the Church to which he had converted.

There is theatricality in any cultivation of a conspiracy theory. It lends glamour to seething invisible energies that appear to guide events. Membership in covert societies spelled for McLuhan the possibility of alternative narratives to official ones. Someone out there is in charge of things. Illuminati scatter clues. Governments are run by family dynasties, backroom compacts, sects, brotherhoods, cabals. Something happens beyond the normal channels of perception. Ciphers are active everywhere. You succeed in life by making connections. Money suddenly, inexplicably, keeps flowing for select people from sources behind the scenes.

The turning point of perceiving the mutuality of all energies, technological, natural, spiritual, and personal, is conspiracy theory. Data pressure has to be controlled by an invisible will; to a mind well versed in the reading vectors of force, a conspiracy is a gorgeously seductive line of explanation. Paranoia, Thomas Pynchon and Don DeLillo have shown us in the taut narratives of *The Crying of Lot 49* (1965) and *Libra* (1988), is extreme sensitivity to the convergence of hidden organizations, pitiless powers shaping life without our consent. If all images link together, if one symbol leads to another, then the dark mirroring of this is the paranoid's paradigm. Instead of enlightened patterns of association, we find sinister agendas of control.

In his biography of McLuhan, Marchand reflects on McLuhan's belief that Frye was working not only against him, but in league with a larger, supposedly satanic force. It appears that the usually dependable and sensible Marchand is in some sympathy with McLuhan in these "discoveries."

> One vital discovery he thought he had made [in 1951] was the influence of secret societies, particularly the vast and occult powers of the Masonic order ... McLuhan made the leap from noting that such lore persisted from the Renaissance to the twentieth century to positing that actual elite secret societies promoted it in every area of contemporary life ... Even opposition to him from the colleagues at the University of Toronto could be explained as centered in a secret society or two flourishing in other colleges ... They posed a deadly threat to the Catholic Church, which, along with Aristotle, insisted that the senses did not deceive the mind and that the material world was dependably real ... The foremost of the secret societies, in McLuhan's view, was the Masonic order ... McLuhan began to see the history of the West as having been shaped in unknown ways by the works of the Masons ... He certainly never abandoned his belief that his great rival in the English department of the University of Toronto, Northrop Frye, was a Mason at heart, if not in fact ... Frye's school of literary criticism, aside from its tendency to put literature into a series of intellectual straitjackets, is closely linked to the timeless, unearthly visions of gnosticism and Neo-Platonism that McLuhan detected in the secret societies.
>
> (*The Medium and the Messenger*, 102, 105)

Does Marchand understand Gnosticism? There is no cross-referencing in his biography or in his notes to any of the essential texts; there is no reflective consideration of the subject; no Basilides or Valentinus, no Gospel According to Thomas; no readings of Gershom Scholem, Moshe Idel, Hans Jonas, or Bentley Layton. Donald Theall, in the interviews I conducted with him in December 2007 (five months before his death), spoke of his collaborative studies with McLuhan in the 1950s: McLuhan, Theall said, was aware of the then recent discoveries in Gnostic texts and was fascinated by their unorthodox descriptions of Christian theological origins. I find a definitive Gnostic strain in McLuhan's iconoclasm, if we understand the Gnostic urge to be anti-dogmatic, counter-institutional, metaphor-based, searching, and immanent (the things of this world burn with the fires of meaning). Bloom examines the impact of Gnosticism on writers in *Genius: A Mosaic of One Hundred Exemplary Creative Minds* (2002), where he exalts the agons of genius: ardent, often idiosyncratic drives to forge master narratives and counter-myths. These are traits we can easily discern in McLuhan's work. McLuhan may have collaborated with many other critics and artists, but the result in every book and in every pronouncement is audaciously, and unmistakably, him: H.M.M. (the initials of McLuhan's full name), an Adam in the ferocity and frolic of the second creation – the new detonation – called electronica.

Gordon's biography of McLuhan, with official sanction from Corinne McLuhan, does not mention conspiracies. Nor does Ayre's book mention a Masonic connection. In my nine years of readings and research into Frye's work I have yet to find anything that would give credence to McLuhan's suspicion. Still McLuhan's pre–Vatican II Catholicism would have put him at odds with Frye's United Church Inner Light liberalism. Although McLuhan became a political liberal – a supporter of Pierre Elliott Trudeau and of Jimmy Carter – his religious views were orthodox. I have already traced Frye's thought through the dissenting heritage of the Muggletonian Blake and the Puritan republican Milton. While Frye's personal life was mostly uneventful – he was no supporter of the hippie protest movements of the 1960s – his writings do embody Romantic contrariness: the poet is a blasphemous creator-God in whom personal revelations flare; the reader becomes critic and thus co-creator when he allows the epiphanies of poetry to burn in his mind too. But to McLuhan, poetry and art return us to cognitive wholeness: the gestalt of perception guides us to the re-cognition that ordinary life is miraculous.

Some McLuhan followers have pushed anti-Fryeism to extremes. They turn a theatrical agon into a war for the soul. Frank Zingrone's *The Media Symplex: At the Edge of Meaning in the Age of Chaos* (2001) is a formidable work of conjunctive thinking. However, Zingrone suddenly shifts from his perceptive premise, that media can reduce meaning to inhibiting "symplexes" rather than diversifying complexes, to an editorial about an anti-McLuhan Masonic conspiracy clique at the University of Toronto. Zingrone accurately identifies the Gnostic iconoclasm in McLuhan's thinking and confirms that McLuhan's doctoral work was in part on the alchemical-Hermetist Albertus Magnus. Zingrone then echoes McLuhan's accusation:

> He was certain that the highest senior officials and colleagues at the University of Toronto were top-ranking Masons conspiring to hold power secretly.

The arch-exponent of this condition was Northrop Frye, whom McLuhan believed to be a thirty-third degree Mason. Why did he concern himself with these things?[41]

Zingrone argues that McLuhan's paranoia represents the flip side of his investigation into invisible influences. I agree. Electricity is known by its effects; we are unconscious users of energies. Sensitivity to hidden influences has a paranormal flavour: there seem to be forces, spirits, dominions, demons, codes, and agencies at play. Recall the ambiguities of the word "medium" in McLuhan's "the medium is the message." It evokes the possibilities of séance, mediations between realms visible and invisible, esoteric gnosis, a Yeatsian communion with supernatural beings, open channels between Spirit and matter. Electric process places us back inside the mysterious mutuality of the *participation mystique* (the mystical unity between persons and processes). Media effects are not only physical, they are psychic. All energetic forces and processes are wholly ambiguous, sometimes mere traces that quickly fade or transform into something unexpected.

I described earlier how the quicksilver McLuhan liked to switch back and forth between recognizing the occult powers of media in terms of a demonic and angelic scrap. A metaphysical interest is a concern for energies outside and beside and beyond and below the body. How did Frye fit in? By allying himself with the Masons, McLuhan's reasoning goes, Frye turned his work towards the championing of human protest without creedal sanction. Frye became department chair, then principal of Victoria College. His career was a model of academic acclaim. Meanwhile (Zingrone reminds us), McLuhan's ideas continued to be rudely dismissed by literary scholars.

This is why McLuhan's attitude towards Frye turns vehement in the unpublished "Flush-Profile" essay, in *From Cliché to Archetype* and the *Listener* rejoinder, in the repeated passages in *Laws of Media* and *The Global Village*. If we pursue Zingrone's explorations of hidden grounds in *The Media Symplex*, then this vehemence was part of McLuhan's acute receptivity to networks. The benign Frye must have been shocked by the extremes of the charges that came from the Coach House. On the other hand, so I have been charting through the documentation of Frye's responses to McLuhan, we can sense a subtle judgmental tone in his writings. Frye identified McLuhanism with Thomism and with totalitarian tendencies in the media. He railed in his notebooks against Vatican edicts. Although that was fair game in the matrix and agon of homage and dissent that they shared over the years, there is no doubt McLuhan would have said this was evidence that his perceptions and his religious faith were being denigrated. He never tired of saying that he did not like the globalization of electronic media, but preference was not the point: we must perceive without judgment. McLuhan's increasing sense of isolation in the 1970s amplified his feeling of alienation from colleagues and from the kind of literary reputation that Frye enjoyed.

The irony is McLuhan's thinking approaches heresy by Catholic standards. The impact of Pierre Teilhard de Chardin's works on McLuhan is well known. In my next chapter I will look at McLuhan's homage to Teilhard in the "Spoken Word" section of *Understanding Media*. The global village is an adaptation of Teilhard's idea of the noosphere: human consciousness evolving into an orbiting planetary mind, the earth rising towards a pulse of emotion and thought. Electronic technology represents the significant convergence of mind and matter, spirit and force. The convergence has enlightening effects: people throughout the world appear to be experiencing the *om* (unity) of longing and desire, the omega of destiny (the apogee point) in the communion of common hopes, and the closeness of all hearts and minds in the collective recognition of individual value which we see in the decisive championing of human rights; and it has terrifying, darkening effects – the abyss of suffering and injustice, the overheating of rage, greater opportunities of totalitarian politics, a mass suicidal impulse in the development of the atom bomb and other appalling weapons. But apogees and abysses are irrevocably upon us. We are living through a build-up of our own spiritual-emotional force, positive-negative. This is why our world is subject to collective nervous breakdown (witness reactions to tragic news reports) and to sympathetic juncture (the outpouring of help for the victims of catastrophe).

Teilhard was silenced by the Church in the 1940s and 1950s for his speculations on cosmic destiny, the *opus humanum*. During the latter part of his life Teilhard was exiled to remote archaeological digs in Asia by his Vatican superiors. His books did not receive wide circulation until the 1960s and 1970s, well after his death in 1955. Nevertheless, his provocative mystical ideas found their way into Catholic intellectual circles. He made his evolutionary claims in books that conceived of the noosphere, the thinking pulse that is the new world of telecommunications, before the effects of radio, television, telephones, and computers were obvious.[42] McLuhan knew Teilhard's prophetic insights and absorbed them. He projected heretical intentions on Frye but often obscured his own dissident pathways of thought.

Robert Denham has a pointed comment to make on the Masonic conspiracy theory. In a 2008 email to me, he describes a personal encounter with McLuhan's close associates and their abiding suspicions:

> Many years ago a friend of mine at York, Bob Cluett, took me to a Party at Frank Zingrone's home. Eric McLuhan was in attendance. They told me that it was common knowledge that Frye was a Mason. When I asked how they knew that, they remained tongue-tied. Frye certainly read some things about Freemasonry, which would have been another of the many imaginative constructs that he found in esoterica ... I've read almost everything that Frye wrote ... and I've never run across even a hint (in his notebooks and diaries and correspondence and other private papers) that he was a Mason. One wouldn't, I hope, let stand in the essay of a first-year student the kind of argument that Zingrone and Eric McLuhan offer.

The silence and the lack of evidence are a signal to students of conspiracy that their hunches are true. But the Freemasonry charge against Frye had much to do with orthodoxy versus heresy, doctrine versus individual speculation and dissident strangeness.

Was the suspicion part of McLuhan's desire to adhere to Catholic dogma no matter what? Freemasonry is identified with non-creedal gatherings of Protestant reformers, anti-monarchists, intellectuals, cosmopolitans, free thinkers, and revolutionary democrats. I cringe thinking of the morally upright, congenial McLuhan dropping down into an abyss of fear and accusation. But he was a complicated man, harnessed to his passions; eccentricity runs rampant through his wisdom. The strain of his intensity on his health was clear to anyone who knew him. Catholic ceremony inspired and rooted him. Faith gave him patience and trust in his explorations. Forgiveness freed his soul, giving him the liberty to probe. Dogma was, I would argue, his protection against the chaos brought on by his sensations and imagination.

Freemasonry has such an elusive history that I suppose it could be construed to be conspiratorial. Yet even if there was direct evidence of Frye's initiation into Freemasonry, this would have pointed to a shared mysticism, their divine discontent. McLuhan and Frye were attempting to read the meaning of the hieroglyphs written on our lives both by ourselves and by the source. Freemasonry was (is) indeed concerned with the architecture of the Spirit: the processes of Nature are not random. Numbers, proportions, ratios, letters, measures, time: each is a factor in the construction of the world. Through exacting study of the imprints and patterns, the effects and signs, we can discern the story of human destiny. God had placed in Nature and in books – and for McLuhan, in super-Nature – all we needed to know about making things endure, the geometries of the soul in its profound interaction with the Spirit's design. Art comes in our work, the free building of our ground, our daily contemplations and communions.

Frye's reputation faded in the decades after McLuhan's death. If he was being supported by a behind-the-scenes network of influential people, they clearly flagged in their activities. The 100th anniversary of McLuhan's birth in 2011 was marked throughout Canada, the United States, and continental Europe with celebrations at universities and theatres. Toronto newspapers recognized McLuhan's prophetic genius. Frye's centenary in 2012 was, in contrast, honoured by university events, but the celebrations were muted, isolated into smaller gatherings. Toronto newspapers had trouble paraphrasing his theories, relegating that duty to breezy columnists. However, in October 2012, Darren Byers and Fred Harrison presented on the Victoria College grounds their memorial-like statue of Frye, seated (serene, legs crossed), surrounded by seven books. It shows him, quizzical and contemplative, gazing upwards. The book on his lap is open.

The Ancient Quarrel between Orators and Writers

What is the point of their intellectual duelling? Why should we comprehend the quarrels of the two in a Canadian visionary-prophetic lineage? It is time to move towards a larger articulation of what their feuding forms. By doing so, we restore them to our attentive speculations in a web of call and response.

My proposal is this: the McLuhan-Frye clash was a battle of the books. It was a revival of the ancient contest between the grammarians (orators) and the dialecticians (writers). This was the subject of McLuhan's dissertation, ostensibly on Thomas Nashe, in which he spends most of its pages explicating the background debate between "the ancients and the moderns." Orators were debaters. Truth came in communal arrangements, round tables. Orality depended on presence and encounter. Dialecticians were devoted to assembling persuasive argument in texts; writing depended on a concentration on letters, inscriptions on paper. Both were devoted to disclosure. Their methods for achieving revelation radically differed.

We can now see McLuhan and Frye in this age-old context. They were sparring over a larger intellectual issue located in the difference between the orator who prizes the ambiguities of performance and the radical contingencies of truth and the prose writer who prizes orderly classification and the truth of the words set out in exact and exacting sentences in a text. It is the difference between performance (acting) and book-bound persuasions. In McLuhan's terms, the orator is the pre-Socratic ancient; the prose writer is the Platonic modern. Although this simplifies the complexities of their thoughts, it helps us to focus how McLuhan defined the clash and how Frye defined it in his responses. Frye was right when he saw in McLuhan's bickering pronouncements a hyperbolic expansion of ideas into an epic conflict. They were putting on a show. But the show had importance. It was far from entertainment or a mere pleasurable pastime on a sometimes sleepy university campus in a city that often seemed like a provincial outpost in an overlooked colony. McLuhan triggered the agon with his first essay salvos in 1957 (though they were unpublished) and his assertions thereafter around the university campus. But Frye came to see how important their wrangle truly was to the Toronto School of Communication Theory. In the end, there was no one else at the University of Toronto, or in the country, who possessed a similar yearning or range.

What is the ancient quarrel? In McLuhan's 1946 essay, "An Ancient Quarrel in Modern America (Sophists vs. Grammarians)," he outlines the structure of the contest. While the article looks at a debate on the future of education in the United States during the post-war period, McLuhan draws analogies to the debate between the encyclopedic virtuosi of the oral comprehensivists (aphorists and satirists) and the specialists of the new written texts (philosophers and legalists). He says, "My explanation of the modern quarrel is in terms of the old quarrel between the grammarians and rhetoricians on one hand and the dialecticians on the other hand ... Patristic humanism subordinated dialectics to grammar and rhetoric until this same quarrel broke out afresh in the twelfth century when Peter Abelard set up dialectics as the supreme method in theological discussion."[43] This may seem arcane. But it illuminates the debate McLuhan believed was the ground to the figure of contemporary controversies over the direction for education. By grammar, he means the four simultaneous levels of exegesis. By oratory, he means the techniques of persuasion a public speaker uses to engage an audience, to elicit response.

This is what the orator does: truths are discovered in mutual exploration, never pontificated. They are homiletic and learned through experience and parables, ironies, paradoxes, aphorisms, and illustrations, not by command. The orator taunts audiences into being; an eloquent speaker can be sabotaging and arch. Oration is different from dictation. The orator's emphasis is on reverberations, punning, elaboration, verbal skill, allusion. We come to know truths by comparing lies. The wonder of words will lift us; and words should dazzle us. We must take home the memorable remarks and meditate on them, unfolding their dimensions. Eloquent wisdom is an open hand, not a closed fist.

The orator is a citizen of the cosmopolis, constantly tweaking the perceptions of audiences. When McLuhan says that in the twelfth century dialectics is set "as the supreme method," he means in his definition that classification, sequence, conceptual thinking, system, abstraction, verifiable scholarship, and argument came to trump "Patristic humanism." This is, McLuhan suggests, a conflict between the sounds of orality and the silence of literacy, between the public speaker and "the man of letters." However, the conflict is only apparent: literary text is informed by voice, the oral inspires the order of words on the page. In McLuhan's scheme, orators subordinated the ideal to action, but writers subordinated action to the ideal. The ancients invited us into dialogue so that we can be kindled into wisdom. The moderns gave us books through which we can be led to the truth through explanation. Once one knew the truth, all premises fell into place; the theoretical architecture follows this logic.

Let me clarify the polarity. The ancients emphasized the play of ideas, preferring probing aphorisms and recitals of verse and quotations. The brevity of an aphorism hints at common knowledge; it is as if we, the receivers, are in on it. The aphorism includes our paraphrases and explications, even if the aphorism itself remains mystifyingly irreducible. Memorization is essential to an orator: knowing poems or stories by heart is greater than consulting a text. The moderns emphasized the structure of truth, preferring knowledge and system, the sequence of an argument, the logical arrangement of sentences. What you say must match the data; the research should support the conclusions. By leading the reader from point to point, the author establishes authority. The steadiness of a voice, of a point of view, evokes the steady ethical perspective. Being persuasive means supplying the necessary references and research. A book has rare power when it encodes a point of view. It is obvious from this dichotomy that McLuhan thought the history of ideas and interpretation could be neatly divided between the ancient pre-Socratics (the humanists) and the modern Platonists and Aristotelians (the moralists). If we push forward in time and exaggerate the contours of McLuhan's argument, then his proposition exemplifies the difference between Oscar Wilde and Matthew Arnold: the former delivers ideas through paradoxes, fables, quips, aphorisms, and dialogues; the latter offers the sombre, consistent analyses of *Culture and Anarchy.*

How does the McLuhan-Frye contest represent a rebirth of the battle of the books? It comes in the new ground of iLiteracy. In a succinct explanation in *The Electronic Word: Democracy, Technology, and the Arts* (1995), Richard A. Lanham astutely summarizes what I mean:

> The main intellectual debate of our time ... is best understood as a resurrection of the ancient quarrel between the philosophers and the rhetoricians ... Print ... is philosophic medium, the electronic screen a deeply "rhetorical" one.[44]

He goes on to say,

> In the archetypal quarrel between the philosophers and the rhetoricians to which I have so often returned, the rhetoricians took human society as it was, messy with conflicting interests and attention-structures, and tried through the stylized techniques of two-sided arguments to bring some order – always temporary and shifting – to the human barnyard ... Plato taught the philosophers to take the opposite approach, to despise the messy human reality and imagine a much tidier one.
>
> (248)

Lanham often cites McLuhan through his essays and identifies the hostility towards his probes in this context of a conflict between "messy" rhetoric and "tidy" dialectics. "[T]he whole Aristotelian basis of literary criticism is undermined by electronic expression" (xi). He extends the McLuhanesque idea that readers of the printed word court mesmerism by looking at, rather than through, "fixed black-and-white surface of verbal symbols to the conceptual world beyond ... the printed prose style [is] an aesthetic of controlled self-denial and suppressed visual and auditory suggestibility" (26, 73–4).

Lanham clarifies the argument I have been building about the McLuhan-Frye agon. He overdramatizes the case, but exaggeration is what orators do:

> "McLuhanesque" became and has remained a standard dyslogic epithet that critics used to disparage any discussion of electronic media ... *electronic technology meant the end of literacy and the return of orality. Since literacy, for most*

people, is *Western culture, electronic technology immediately generates* formidable opposition ...
   The oral/literate distinction takes us to the heart of McLuhan's arguments ...
   If, however, you read McLuhan from a philosophical *point of view, he is not didactic but "outrageous."*
                              (201, 202, 203; emphases mine)

We recognize the formidable opposition that McLuhan's ideas met and how "McLuhanesque" became a term of abuse by some critics. Frye often sought to distinguish McLuhan the thinker from his followers and the "outrageous" effects of his propositions. Lanham suggests that the context of the battle of the books was rarely given an opportunity to be exposed. And so the battle's premises were vividly disclosed in the critiques discharged at McLuhan.
   Lanham argues that neither the orator nor the scribe should be viewed in isolation. Neither has privileged access to truth. The ancient and the modern are dependent on each other. The oracular and the prosaic must exist side by side. Dynamic thinking requires oscillations between the two positions. The ancient and modern debate composes the yin and yang of critical discourse. Lanham seeds the argument that I will be making in subsequent chapters about the necessity of embracing the McLuhan-Frye matrix and agon:

We want both Rousseau and Quintilian, the Romantic central self with its unique originality and the role playing rhetorical self that makes society possible.
                              (146)

I believe it is likely a simplification to polarize McLuhan and Frye's thought in this way. But the simplifying spotlights the intensity of their debate. The polarity of the ancient and the modern infused McLuhan's mind. We can hear in Frye's quarrel with McLuhan his unease with the "jazzing," the apparent flouting of fixed coordinates, the easing into the world of publicity and celebrity, the apparent desertion of book culture, the seeming preference for the new tribalism, the comfort with images over verbal formulation, the probing of the experience beyond words. Did Frye think, Where are the values here? How could McLuhan tolerate noise? Why did he lend his considerable critical intelligence to the understanding of TV, surely a lesser medium? Why did McLuhan proceed by leaps and gaps, when our cracked lives need bridges? Why did he addle and aggrieve people to the point where they would reject him entirely? Why be interested in pop culture when canonic literature brings to the mind the intensities of the awareness that we need?

We see how for Frye the courtier in the court of media betrayed the truth. Step into the jaws of the media Leviathan and you will be swallowed. If there is no inward self and no eternal archetypes, no unconscious stocked with a structure of symbols, no stable textual structure in which the order of words can be discerned, then there is likely nothing. Universal TV is pullulating data. Computer culture, with its hypertext and imagistic screens, is merely a distraction, even a degradation of culture. Once out in full naked view, ideas can lose their integrity, even their mystery, hence their power to lead and heal. Intellectual reputations can become matters of gossip and appearance, how you sound on the radio, how you dress on TV. Books provide the indispensable rhythm of the inwardness that spells out the refined patterns of the Spirit. Alphabetic literacy is the basis of a civilization that cherishes singular awareness. Through the swarming by electronic media, "the literal man" becomes a light in a dark woods, journeying in solitude away from the chatter and jitter of data overload. All gradual exposures of thought will be untimely then. The power of an intellectual flame demands privacy and silence, time and concentration. A book is truly one person speaking to one person.

Bloom eulogizes Frye in his 2000 foreword to *Anatomy* and in autumnal tones summarizes the polarized position:

> If *Anatomy of Criticism* begins to seem a period piece, so does *The Sacred Wood* of T.S. Eliot. Literary criticism, to survive, must abandon the universities, where "cultural criticism" is a triumphant beast not to be expelled ... Critical reading, the discipline of how to read and why, will survive in those solitary scholars, out in society, whose single candles Emerson prophesied and Wallace Stevens celebrated. Such scholars, turning Frye's pages, will find copious precepts and examples to help sustain them in their solitude.
>
> (xi)

McLuhan's quarrel with Frye is over the rigidity of a point of view. This narrows reality into a steeled perspective. McLuhan likely saw Frye withdrawing into a book-lined den where the only light that burns is that of the self-directed ego: the self becoming God, engaging in readings that concern almost no one. Truth is contextual (he never said there is no truth). The single candle will be blown out by the torrential blasts of change. Perhaps McLuhan would explain: the wise fool jazzes because cosmic forms are a vast improvisation; seeds fall on fallow or barren ground; what rises up never resembles what came before. Electric technology is here, and if Nature invites participation and super-Nature is an extension of our nervous systems and thoughts, then all processes can be comprehended.

McLuhan said of his preference for books, "As a Professor of Literature, I am entirely on the side of print."[45] But he knew one person's opinion hardly matters in the wake of enormous transformations. If the cosmos is unfolding as it should, why not chronicle the cyclone and see if it can be transfigured into a radiant vortex? Why presume that literature embodies the single candle? Why not appreciate an array of collective lightings? Why be a gloom-pourer? Is it our destiny to be at play in the fields of the Lord? Is the war between screen and printed text a false polarization? What is beyond words, in the spaces beyond rows of type, in the images and sounds that are part of our metamorphic cosmos? Why highlight books over painting, or music, or numbers, sculpture or dance? Images and music are signatures. Do we have a duty to understand our culture and offer comprehending ways? It is possible that the new world of communications is a reverberation of the cosmic communion, the elements and the Spirit speaking and resounding with greater force than ever before. What you take to be noise may be the music of the spheres to another. The ability to assemble a scholarly, fully annotated argument is not necessarily a sign of enlightenment. A culture can have a sensory bias that is invisible to its citizens: propaganda prevails when we take our surround for granted.

Agons can be woundingly divisive. The originality of the McLuhan-Frye clash directs us elsewhere. My premise is their contest suggests a debate between orality and literacy, between the public comet and the single candle. They would have preferred it – in their indelible devotion to educating consciousness – if we focused our attention on the dynamism. Contraries, Blake tirelessly tried to show, are only divisively annihilating to those whose minds and spirits dwell in darkness. McLuhan and Frye needed to vivify and sustain their minds; through their debate they measured the other's spirit and so found the intellectual necessity to enlarge their range of percepts and concepts. They knowingly cultivated the clash of the orator and the writer into an epic rivalry. It was an aesthetic adventuring, too, and an intrepid act of imagination.

They were Canadian contraries. And their joint effort in originating a visionary tradition appears in these ways: they were audacious and evasive, subtle and explicit, at once ancient and modern, equally engaged in a movement towards pleroma. This tradition presents a radical envisioning available at every moment: probing, poetic, pedagogical, and prophetic. In McLuhan's first published essay of any significance, "G.K. Chesterton: A Practical Mystic" (he would have been a mere twenty-five at the time of the publication), he says with crusading clarity, "The mysteries revealed by Mr. Chesterton are the daily miracles of sense and consciousness. His ecstasy and gratitude are for what has been given to all men ... Mr. Chesterton has stepped beyond the frontiers of poetry, to what M. Maritain in speaking of Rimbaud calls 'The Eucharistic passion which he finds in the heart of life.'"[46] I juxtapose McLuhan's statement with an observation by Frye from the "General Note: Blake's Mysticism," the coda of *Fearful Symmetry*. Frye was thirty-six at the time of the book's publication. "If mysticism means primarily a contemplative quietism, mysticism is something abhorrent to Blake ... if it means primarily a spiritual illumination expressing itself in ... unspeculative piety ... the word still does not fit him. But if mysticism means primarily the vision of the prodigious and unthinkable metamorphosis of the human mind ... then Blake is one of the mystics" (345). Although McLuhan and Frye differed in methods and terminology, in the focus of their energies (one turns to observational communality; one turns to theoretic and imaginative reconstruction), they did not differ in their sense of vocation, the intellectual furnace of their mindful directions. Nor did they differ in their desire to leave significant imprints, the need to change their readers and their time.

They knew there is the writing on the wall and the writing in the soul. The patterns of discord and concord can (and they thought should) yield to forms of hopeful apocalypse. Their quarrel gives off more light than heat. And it is now into their harmonies, and towards their synergy, that I go.

4
The Harmonies in Two Seers: Orchestrations and Complementarities

McLuhan-Frye Dynamics

Contraria sunt complementa: "opposites are complementary." Hidden harmonies are often greater than obvious conflicts. I know it will not do to reduce the formidable intellects and personalities of Marshall McLuhan and Northrop Frye to a soup of sameness; something of them must remain forever contrary. Blake passionately asserted, in various fiery expressions, how "Opposition is true Friendship." But something of the two speaks to patterns that cross, overlap, briefly break, then combine again in coinciding lines of energy.

The word "complementarity" comes from physics and refers to the paradoxical phenomenon that light can be both wave and particle. A wave is an undulating structure; a particle, a cluster of compressed force. Louis de Broglie and Erwin Schrödinger pioneered this understanding of light. The alternating patterns depend on how we look at them. Light will sometimes look like a particle, sometimes a wave. The duality is only apparent, however. Niels Bohr called these profound contingencies complementarity: an electron behaving in two ways at once. The contradictory formations should be perceived simultaneously, which is impossible for our eyes to see and difficult for us to imagine, yet the phenomenon exists in Nature. Light is a particle field, a rise and a fall. A paradox is a double vision. Paradoxes are an example of figure/ground tensions in interplay. The perception of this condition leads to a dynamism that is the end of any static pattern.

Fritjof Capra explains complementarity:

> Niels Bohr ... considered the particle picture and the wave picture as two complementary descriptions of the same reality, each of them being only

partly correct ... Each picture is needed to give a full description of the atomic reality ... The Chinese sages represented this complementarity of opposites by the archetypal poles *yin* and *yang* and saw their dynamic interplay as the essence of all natural phenomena and all human situations.

Capra says that "physicists prefer to speak about interactions, rather than about forces."[1] Oddly, the normally quick-eyed Frye called Capra's *Tao* one of the "nut books." In his *Late Notebooks, 1982–1990* he confesses to getting "nothing out" of it. He snorts, "Commonplace mind." But he goes on to admit that David Bohm's writings – his works are indebted to Capra's – were useful. His entry, incidentally, begins with another quirky amendment of McLuhan's thought: "[His] point is that multiple models are the great 20th c. discovery ... I'd say it was the rediscovery of the variation form" (713).

This is a centre in my argument: we should see the McLuhan-Frye matrix in terms of "dynamic interplay." I have been charting their crossings. It is difficult to divide them from their ground of teaching in the English department at the University of Toronto or from their shared background of literary and religious studies. Nor can we sever them from their Canadian context, from their Romanticism and Modernism, from their long, sometimes visible, often oblique, conversation and quarrel. When we talk of the two, we move back and forth, travelling in oscillations between their waves and fields.

So I move from agon to gnosis, from oppositions and contests to perceptive knowledge and unities. They pursued poetics: the tongues in TV, the spiritual signature in the book of life; and in their passion for apocalypse, their revelation of the universal forms in electronic media and literary texts, in their comprehensive visions, their humanist concern for sharing learning (let us call this the process of heroic education), in their mutual metaphysical concern that once we are awakened we will find all shall be well ("What will be will be well – for what is is well," Whitman rhapsodizes in *Leaves of Grass*), we will know their cogent complementarities. I have said they needed one another for sparring and spurring. In their quixotic crossings, McLuhan gives us contemporary contexts for reading (the media), and Frye gives us the story – the quest – through the blaze of iLiteracy. We need them for our definitions.

Of fields and waves, McLuhan says in his first major statement, *The Mechanical Bride*, "There is no logical connection between Bergson and

Proust. But they certainly belong in the same world. Put side by side, they throw a good deal of light on each other" (50). In an earlier passage from the same book he writes about "orchestrating human arts, interests, and pursuits rather than fusing them ... Orchestration permits discontinuity and endless variety without universal imposition ... it can entertain a harmony that is not unilateral, monistic, or tyrannical ... while welcoming the new in a simultaneous present" (34).

In 1981, after McLuhan's death, Frye lectured at the American Academy of Arts and Sciences in Boston, where he eloquently spoke of "The Double Mirror." This is the idea, elaborated in *The Double Vision*, that there is a coinciding of two metaphors, or essential fictions, in art, in the Bible: one of matter, the other of Spirit. The proper job of the critic is co-creation, to alchemically weld the latent coinciding energies. Then Frye writes this stirring moment in the last paragraph of his address: "The rhetoric of proclamation is a welcoming and approaching rhetoric, in contrast to rhetoric where the aim is victory in argument or drawing an audience together into a more exclusive unit. It speaks, according to Paul, the language of love, which he says is likely to last longer than most forms of communication." Frye shape-shifts from critic to preacher, moving from identifying themes and ideas to imagining unities, emphasizing how harmonies ("welcoming and approaching") are possibly more lasting than excluding conclusions ("victory in argument"). In his finale he emphasizes how metaphor is "made for man and not man for metaphor" (metaphors are always links, bridges), then ends with this sweeping reference: "as my late friend and much beloved colleague, Marshall McLuhan used to say, man's reach should exceed his grasp, or what's a metaphor?"[2] His implication: conjunction over specialization, vision and revision over fragmentation. Frye concludes with a question, and a question always initiates and guides the quest. It is significant that Frye concludes with a punning statement from McLuhan to invoke the values they shared.

McLuhan, ever the ironist, describes a meeting between himself and Frye at the University of Toronto, in this 1973 letter to former student Hugh Kenner:

> [William] Wimsatt was here recently to give a lecture and a seminar, and I was present when he dined with William Empson and Norrie Frye, *making a very strange gestalt indeed!* Empson has been up at York since October, totally ignored by the University of Toronto until I brought him down for dinner.
>
> (464; emphasis mine)

"Making a very strange gestalt indeed." Apocalyptic orchestration suggests a consort of energies for the purpose of perception. The relationships are not logical but analogical: the juxtaposition of patterns and pattern makers, each of whom were voyaging towards the new. What is the "strange" gestalt? We find it in their devotion to being part of the marginality of the Canadian experience; I find it in their desire to pursue inspirations, to turn scholarship towards meaningful reconstructions, to the implications in their thought of spiritual hope, in their cosmopolitan readings of pivotal literary works; and I find it in their refusal to have followers (though we, their students, were cut and cast by their ideas and styles) and in their belief in the transcendent power of the mind even to overcome death.

They came to crossroads where they saw rising forces where the ancient and the modern coincided: the CN Tower represented both a spiritual ache and a hypodermic syringe; nowhere and the noosphere had somehow come together in Toronto. Their moment in history was charged with apogees of accomplishment, abysses of suffering. McLuhan and Frye were disturbed by madness and mazes, portals of discovery opening, the paranoid sense that something was closing in: thrown-ness and terror, activating principles in their minds. I noted Frye's hope that the three A's – of anxiety, alienation, absurdity – (and the fourth he rarely mentioned: anguish) could be overturned, transfigured by the educated imagination. To McLuhan we pad ourselves inside our inventions, mindlessly lurching from one oblivious act to another, unconscious of the torrential, toppling effects of the new artefacts we extend from ourselves. In the University of Being and Becoming, they strove to kindle users and readers.

The obvious expression of their complementarity is their commitment to the humanities in Canada. But their country remained a point of ambivalent awareness for them. Frye said, or is reputed to have said, "Americans like to make money; Canadians like to audit it"; McLuhan, equally acerbic about his home and native land, was often heard to mutter that his country was "deliberately dull" (emphasis on the adverb "deliberately"): this gave Canadians the peculiar advantage of being provincial, guileless, uncultivated, and bland, therefore capable of quiet fearlessness, resourcefulness, observation, immersion, and surprise. McLuhan speaks for both when he says in a 1971 letter to the University of Toronto president Claude Bissell,

My motive in returning to Canada [after Fordham] was then, as now, my fear of acceptance. I knew there was no danger of this in Canada. It is very salutary to have a daily charade of human malice and stupidity mingled with warmth and insight. In the U.S., surrounded with an atmosphere of success and acceptance, I could have lost my bearings very quickly.

(*Letters*, 430)

Ayre's biography of Frye and the biographies of McLuhan show how Bissell ensured that the two stayed at the University of Toronto. He provided them with support staff and office spaces and stayed out of their way. The wise Bissell observed the injunction that a university bureaucrat should be seen and not heard. Bissell (wily university president from 1958 until 1971) was well aware of the importance of the Frye-McLuhan matrix for idealistic educational purposes and research imperatives, ambitious cultural influence, and an embryonic intellectual and critical tradition. He knew their lightning-rod conductivities had consequences for what we are and could become.

Their advocates and apostles, like Bissell, have their histories too. There should be more studies, profiles in depth; the networks of support and influence should be traced and illuminated. It is beyond the scope of my work to do this. But there were pathways set out by Derrick de Kerckhove, Eric McLuhan, Elena Lamberti, T.C. McLuhan, Liss Jeffrey, Arthur and MariLouise Kroker, Robert K. Logan, Robert Denham, Ian Balfour, and Margaret Atwood that are part of the McLuhan-Frye legacies. The two left unfinished ideas and implications for others to develop. Their enterprises were invitations to grow our souls and minds. I call this the invisible school. Its unseen roots go down to the source of their ideas; the school without borders rises upward in our imaginations and spirits. The networks of connections are waiting for our recognitions.

A Luminous Canadian Communiqué

What kept them in Toronto? What rooted them in an edge culture, a place on the margins? They had tenure at a major university; they had eager students and support for their activities by the administration. But their decision to stay, I believe, was more philosophical than practical.

Frye speaks of a Canadian's ambiguous position in the world in his conclusion to *The Modern Century*. He sets us inside our paradoxes, revelling in the contradictions of spirit (imagination) and matter (geography and the body):

> I should like to suggest that our identity, like the real identity of all nations, is the one we have failed to achieve. It is expressed in our culture, but not attained in our life, just as Blake's new Jerusalem to be built in England's green and pleasant land is no less a genuine ideal for not having been built there. What there is left of the Canadian nation may well be destroyed by the kind of sectarian bickering which is so much more interesting to many people than genuine human life. But, as we enter a second century contemplating a world where power and success express themselves so much in stentorian lying, hypnotized leadership, and panic-stricken suppression of freedom and criticism, *the uncreated identity of Canada* may be after all not so bad heritage to take with us.
>
> (69–70; emphasis mine)

The uncreated identity ... Frye's gentle assertion echoes many of McLuhan's probes that Canadians have no identity. This is our idiosyncratic, chameleon power. It gives a cultural flexibility in the new transnationalism of communications. The global theatre makes us capable of assuming many selves. Social networking is the self unleashed into the daily and nightly sluice of reinventions.

Frye's essays in *The Bush Garden* and *Divisions on a Ground: Essays on Canadian Culture* (1982) outline a view of Canada with a "garrison mentality," his famous formulation that Canadians inform their sensibilities and consciousness with a protective shield of words and ideas. The "garrison" is an image of insulation, of a fireproofing, as it were, against Nature, but also against aggressive political-social voices and views, through the cultivation of the inward space of mythic time. While the metaphor seems exclusionary, Frye's "garrison mentality" shares with McLuhan this: the Canadian experience is a primary imaginative and observational construct, a civil and quirky quarantine that cushions and inculcates.

Frye was engaged with Canadian literature from the start of his literary vocation. He was aware that it was essential to cultivate voices and to praise the traces of distinctive vision. I believe he (sensibly) wanted to create a vital culture to encourage voices so that his own work could be received and could evolve. Intensive communications through reviewing and editing make a solitary mind less riddled by the duality of reverie and isolation. Linda Hutcheon expressively comments on the complex relationship that Frye had with the fledging literary community in her "Introduction: The Field Notes of a Public Critic." She notes how Frye's engagements initiated necessary controversies:

> Over time, some commentators have come to feel that its [Frye's *The Bush Garden*] influence on Canadian literature and criticism has been pervasive but destructive; others have felt it to be minor and overestimated. But when *The Bush Garden* appeared in 1971, the reviews were pretty well unanimous in hailing it as a landmark text. This is not to say that there were not the usual accusations that Frye had fathered a brood of myth-obsessed poets, whose erudite and academic work he paternally protected in his reviews ... Yet, in one reviewer's terms, the "witty malice" of Frye's detractors had to contend with the "noisy reverence" of his fans ... The specific reasons for controversy are inevitably going to be different today, but Frye's provocative visions of the Canadian imagination – mentally garrisoned against a terrifying nature, frostbitten by a colonial history – is a vision that still has the power to provoke.
>
> (vii–ix)

McLuhan never wrote or planned to write a book that would organize his essays and aphorisms on being Canadian. Yet his books, especially *Counterblast* and *The Global Village*, allude to his awareness of the paradoxes of the Canadian proposal, the place where the identity quest becomes elusive and amorphous, open and hybrid, in the model of a counter-nation.

Though I admire Hutcheon's lucidity and eloquence, I disagree with her definition of the "garrison mentality." She opts for a history-based critical reading of the phrase: Frye's proposition evokes protective insularity against the northern ferocities of isolation and climate. His phrase does this on a literal level. But it is a metaphor, and therefore open to understanding on the anagogic level. The garrison may be analogous with the DEW-line (Distant Early Warning line), a receiving and transmitting point, open in the centre. Garrison walls intensify the focus of the mind's eye. Think of the garrison in terms of a place where light could be like a sudden shaft beaming upwards (and downwards). The garrison then reverses from fortress into outpost, a place staked on frontiers of the Spirit. The garrison is a unifying point where many others of differing backgrounds can gather to trace the shimmer of the lightened focus. It becomes a summoning centre that protects creation and poetics.

(And we should recall how for Frye, Orphic poetics and the principles in fables, the truths in the imagination, prevail over ideology and history.)

The Frye garrison, the McLuhan DEW-line: in spite of what seems like bellicose images of defence while under attack, these are metaphors of wise receptivity; they encourage reflection. They are part of their perception of the Canadian difference. Frye clarifies the expanding and harmonizing dimensions of the garrison metaphor when he says in "Conclusion to a *Literary History of Canada*," one of the signal essays of *The Bush Garden*, "Separatism, whether English or French, is culturally the most sterile of all creeds. But at present I am concerned rather with a more creative side of the garrison mentality, one that has had positive effects on our intellectual life" (228).

From inside the garrison we can chronicle and channel the hurtling news of the world. Again, Frye's concept of the garrison mentality parallels the DEW-line metaphor that McLuhan evolved to articulate marginality. Being on a margin is simultaneously wounding and strengthening. DEW-line and garrison become points of meditation, of reception and transmission. A garrison may have walls, but like an agora, or like a gash, it is receptive (open) in the centre to what showers down from above. A DEW-line is a warning system that, like flesh, absorbs, filters, translates, and then communicates the information surround. The DEW-line and the garrison mentality offer twin images of Ariel-Canada and Caliban-Canada: the possibility of lightness and liberty, and the reversal into monstrous survivalist self-absorption. Ariel-Canada alludes to the lightness of identity – many people residing in varied cultural backgrounds, speaking different languages; Caliban-Canada alludes to the fracturing that seems an inescapable part of our internal dialogues about linguistic separation and alienated regions.[3]

In *McLuhan, or Modernism in Reverse*, Willmott comments on "Canada's different and post-colonial cultural history" (201) and justly observes, "[T]he intersection of multiple empires and languages [is] a unique version of the dialogic form of collective consciousness." Perhaps unconsciously (he resists a bracketing of the two thinkers), he goes on to sound the McLuhan-Frye note about the subtle Canadian imaginative space/time, the bearable lightness of being and becoming:

> The Canadian utopia is not a withdrawal from history-making in the return to some pastoral nature, but an "eternal frontier" or limit, proper to the modern world above all, at which the natural and the historical – or the ontological and the technological – must somehow be recognized together.
> (203)

The Harmonies in Two Seers

In a 1968 letter to the newly elected prime minister, Pierre Trudeau, McLuhan amusingly says, "Canada is the only country in the world that has never had a national identity. In an age when all homogenous nations are losing their identity images through rapid technological change, Canada alone can 'keep its cool'" (*Letters*, 359). Frye says suggestively, and perhaps more anxiously, in this musing in *Notebooks and Lectures on the Bible and Other Religious Texts* from the late 1960s, "Canada is a symbol of the new world that floats in space & has no centre the world of cars & motels & shopping centres, & high-rise apartments that's replacing the sense of a fixed centre" (70). Being backwards allows you to peacefully observe spectacle, anything revving in fast-forward.

They stayed in Toronto, in their English department at their university – itself garrison and DEW-line, ivory tower and control tower – to perpetuate humanizing concerns. Technology, for McLuhan, is not divorced from us, though its effects can be alienating, fragmenting. The broad incoherence of literary works could be reviewed for Frye and transformed into an embracing metaphysical formation, away from the alienation that deflects us into plagued, voiceless despair.

When I piece together McLuhan's and Frye's writings about Canada, I see the pattern of what becomes their luminous communiqué. They were producing a joint message about Canada's marginality that glimmers – and reverberates – with us still. Theirs is a critical, visionary tradition akin to the transcendentalist poetic and philosophical configurations of Emerson and Whitman. Though their communiqué shares elements with our American counterparts – we settled a new land; we consider newness an opportunity to find expressions unprecedented by European standards – the decisive difference comes in our desire to always live on borderlines. Canada will never be an empire. Frye would have understood from Blake how empires tragically become bloated tyrannies. McLuhan spoke of the importance of flourishing centres and of intervals (breaks, lines, gaps, fissures between forces, the surprising zigzagging of atoms). Canadian cosmopolitanism would surely prosper by translating Euro-American styles and forms into unique expressions but could advance into something else again.

The following passage highlights McLuhan's version of the communiqué:

> Borderlines as such are a form of political "ecumenism," the meeting place of diverse worlds and conditions. One of the most important manifestations

of Canadian ecumenism on the Canadian borderline is the interface between the common law tradition (oral) and the American Roman law (written) ... Borderlines maintain an attitude of alertness and mutual study which gives a cosmopolitan character to Canada ... The borderlines is an area of spiraling repetition and replay, both inputs and feedback, both of interlace and interface, an area of "double ends joined," of rebirth and metamorphosis.[4]

I note how in these lines from *The Global Village* McLuhan says nothing of political revolution. Notice too how he makes allusion to Joyce's *Finnegans Wake.* Canada is the polyphonic realm of "Doublends Jined"; many meanings coincide. (I will soon show how *Finnegans Wake* fascinated McLuhan and Frye.)

In the next passage from the notebooks I find Frye's version of the communiqué:

I have a limited faith in historical process myself: I cannot believe that the Canadian nation will blunder and bungle its way out of history into oblivion, raising with its name only ridicule or at best a sympathetic smile from the rest of the free world. I do not remember any other time in history when a nation disintegrated merely through a lack of will to survive, nor do I think ours will.[5]

His remark at the end of *The Modern Century* that Canadians have "an uncreated identity" is surely an echo, not only of McLuhan's concern but of Stephen Dedalus's at the end of *A Portrait of the Artist as a Young Man.* Joyce, through Stephen's diary entry, invokes the epic identity quest of going on to forge "the uncreated conscience of my race."[6] The two deeply felt a connection to Joyce: they too were thinkers from a marginal country, aspirants to the moulding of encyclopedic works, discoverers of identity through the process of heroic quests, romancers of the punning depths of language. Forgery is fabrication: the *verum factum* principle. You become what you make. We study them to know a reinvention of Canadian letters, how they shaped criticism and media studies into enterprises of perception and synopsis and shaped theoretical protocols into literature. I also read them and reread them for their energetic and ingenious styles.

I find arresting contradictions in their communiqué. Frye – resister to constructs of fact, advocate of mythic counter-historical structures – wrote essay after essay in the 1950s and 1960s about Canadian writers and their struggle for original voices and presences. He squabbled with Irving Layton; celebrated E.J. Pratt and Margaret Atwood; editorialized for *Canadian Forum*; sat on CRTC boards; reviewed new books of poems; and cobbled together articles on the garrison mentality for a book, at the bequest of the admirable poet Dennis Lee. The edition of *Northrop Frye's On Canada* (2003), edited by Jean O'Grady and David Staines, in the *Collected Works* series, runs to a mammoth and impressive 741 pages.

McLuhan was equally committed to the Canadian geography of perception and imagination. But he rarely wrote anything about individual Canadian writers – with the notable exception of Lewis. (Lewis is a forerunner of the hyphenated Canadian citizen: born on a yacht on stormy waters in the harbour at Amherst, Nova Scotia, to an American mother and a British father, an uprooted cosmopolitan, a restless pilgrim spirit who wrote about advertising and pop culture but preferred European high culture, he nevertheless carried a Canadian passport all his life.) McLuhan constantly blessed and blasted Canadian shape-shifting, our useful cultural anonymity, though he almost never commented on specific movements or notable writers, or, for that matter, on recently published novels and poems. McLuhan's occasional note to a local author in his *Letters* – for example, to Margaret Atwood on 22 November 1972 – usually becomes a platform for an abrupt explanation of his probes into psyche and borderlines. His correspondence with Trudeau, however, is of supreme cultural importance. These letters were opportunities from 1968 until 1979 for McLuhan to offer agile insights into the paradoxes and camouflages of the Canadian persona. His letters to Trudeau tried to gently nudge the prime minister towards a greater enlightenment.

Just before McLuhan's death, Frye wrote an important reflection in his essay "Across the River and out of the Trees" on the Canadian communications' thematic essence. Written for the *University of Toronto Quarterly*, this musing is worthy of our attention for a quartet of reasons: first, it was written when McLuhan's reputation was at its nadir and he was ill with aphasia; second, it speaks in a more conciliatory tone about McLuhan than Frye tended to do in the 1960s; third, it is a recognition by Frye of the communications' network of insight and foresight represented by McLuhan, Innis, and himself; fourth, it calls to readers who might one day engage the Canadian promise of a vivid democracy without lasting borders erected between cultures and languages. Frye's title is a (somewhat) witty revision of the Confederate general Stonewall Jackson's statement on his deathbed, uttered after an accidental ambush by his own troops: "Let us cross the river, and rest under the shade of the trees." But Frye sheers away from the bloody conflict of the American Civil War to the distinguishing originality of the Canadian civil discourse and poetics. (Another cross-reference: his title obliquely alludes to Ernest Hemingway's novel *Across the River and Into the Trees*.) I am happy to report that there are no predictable references here to snow or the bush:

> Marshall McLuhan, a literary critic interested originally in Elizabethan rhetoric and its expression in both oral and written forms, followed up other issues connected with the technology of communication, some of them leads from Innis. His relation to the public was the opposite of Innis's: he was caught up in the manic-depressive roller-coaster of the news media, so that he was hysterically celebrated in the 1960s and unreasonably neglected thereafter. *It is likely that the theory of communications will be the aspect of the great critical pot-pourri of our time which will particularly interest Canadians, and to which they will make their most distinctive contribution.* So it is perhaps *time for a sympathetic rereading of* The Gutenberg Galaxy *and* Understanding Media *and a re-absorption of McLuhan's influence*, though no adequate treatment of this topic can be attempted here.[7] (emphases mine)

Frye recognizes how it is communications that could become for Canadians "their most distinctive contribution." This signals a harmony of minds about their unusual locale, a place with the candour of fantastic voices – felt speech, where understandings and misunderstandings could prosper, this fringe whose permanent destination is the future.

Charismatic Personae

They were charismatics with influential personalities. Charismatic personalities carry the blessing, the sense of being chosen to live life with strange and lucky energy. A charismatic personality is seldom containable by conventions. Charisma appears in people with an abundance of enthusiasm (they seem to glow with life). Enthusiasm is linked to inspiration; charisma, too. To be inspired means to be carried by the wind of God (or the gods), to be singled out. Yes, McLuhan was dramatic in his flair and verbal flourishes; Frye seemed passively genteel in comparison. But Frye could quietly and steadily compel the attention of hundreds in a lecture hall. Their personalities were defining forces in their cultural stature.

Both were men of considerable spiritual pride. McLuhan and Frye believed, with Blake and Milton, that the prophet-scholar-writer-teacher must engage their pupils and their age, their readers and critics, and raise them to new levels of perceptive, critical awareness. I have been arguing through this book that their intentions were apocalyptic. Any figures who take on such grand ambitions must have been following restless egoistic drives in their personalities. It is manifested in their awareness of destiny, which their letters and notes certainly show, and in their frequent admission of how they carried the mark of provocative genius. There is ample (and necessary) pride in their "stubborn structures" and "laws."

They shared the pride of vocation and felt called upon to cause disturbances. When Frye was attending Oxford, he discovered Denis Saurat's *Blake and Modern Thought* (1929) and, more important to my book, *Blake and Milton* (1922). Ayre contends that it was Saurat's work which initiated Frye into the complexities of the call, the eloquent openness to original mythmaking and metaphoric necessity of Blake's prophetic poetry. Saurat's monograph on Blake and Milton interprets the dynamism of those he took to be the two primary English epic poets (he omits Spenser and Wordsworth, for some reason). My argument uses Saurat's model for understanding the sense of vocation that steered McLuhan and Frye onward. Saurat writes of how Blake "in the midst of his gigantic and terrifying chaos of angry phantoms ... remains calm and master of himself. Such intense and appalling visions as his should probably have ended in veritable madness ... Milton also had his strength in himself ... Both in Milton and Blake then there is the same high-spirited attitude in their exploration of the unknown world."[8] While Blake and Milton emerged from the Puritan dissenting sects of the inner light, Saurat's observations nevertheless help to reveal the reinvention we find in the Frye and McLuhan prophetic engagement with their time and place. Prophecy for them primarily meant perceiving patterns now invisible to most. We should not underestimate how powerful their sense of calling could be: enthusiasms prompted them. Anyone who encountered them, singly or together (which I did when I attended their seminars and lectures), felt their charismatic shepherding. This came in their gifts for crystallizing metaphors and myths and in the considerable presence of mind they showed when they spoke to you individually.

Frye says of the prophetic empowering of his criticism, "Something must arise from contemplating the infinite variety of literature, of the sort indicated in the epilogue to *The Tempest*. Of course *this makes the literary critic a prophet, or at least gives him a prophetic function, but I can't help that. Hear the voice of the bard* ... Criticism is the primary act of human awareness: it expresses detachment without separation ... *Then imagination moves from actualities to possibilities, involving primary concern, and the criticism of that leads to spiritual vision*"[9] (emphases mine). The Puritan scholar had consecrated himself to the literary quest: he would stake his personal convictions in his work instead of in institutional authority. The seer in Frye kept cracking other systems of thought to let in searching light.

In a 1948 letter to Dorothy Shakespear Pound, McLuhan proudly expounds on his ability to annoy people. He exhorts the urgency of perception training: "*The appeal must be to the young*. But the young have been robbed of their energies by association with ... mental sad-sacks. Worse, they have been systematically deprived of all the linguistic tools by which they could nourish their own perceptions at first hand at the usual traditional sources. In the name of the sacred and unimpeded unfolding of their little egos the old have withheld all linguistic training from the young ... They are easily discouraged when they see what ground they have to make up ... Personally I'm not tired or discouraged. *So I am a cause of much annoyance and discomfort wherever I happen to be*"[10] (emphases mine).

I sometimes had the impression that they thought the future of literary studies, of criticism, of media awareness, of sensory life, depended on their activities. Their pride was practical and generous, however. They loved teaching others and passing on their readings and discoveries. Frye's pride was ruled over by his exacting scholarship and pedagogical precision in the classroom. McLuhan's pride was much more untrammelled. His dissident disposition led to endless upsets with perceived adversaries. However, Eric McLuhan offers anecdotal evidence of the generosity of the two in their teaching. He reports how both made themselves available to the often wayward questioning of their students in office hour conversations and after lectures.[11] To mould minds is the activist aspect of the prophetic imagination. To irritate people into perception is one of the goals of the orator.

They nurtured their minds on Dante, Shakespeare, Milton, Tennyson, Rimbaud, Baudelaire, Poe, Joyce, Eliot, and Stevens. While it is obvious that Frye did so, it continues to astound critics that this was also true for McLuhan. I have no doubt that an artistic and spiritual pride – towards envisioning wholes, empowering readers, encouraging theoretical extension and making essential verbal distinctions, rebalancing ratios of perception – animated prodigious encounters with the most difficult books of the literary canon, their study of complex cultural cycles, their intellectual endeavours, the restless addressing of artefacts. One aspect of their complementarity, for example, must be their mutual obsession with Joyce's enigmatic ouroboros, *Finnegans Wake*. And the complex ambitions of personality spurred them towards the composition, or the last urgent assembling, of compendia: Frye's meditations on the Bible, McLuhan's in the end fragmentary outlining of the laws of media.

The following passages from *The Educated Imagination* and *Through the Vanishing Point* speak to their ambitions. These passages are phrased in the detached tones Frye and McLuhan sometimes prized and strategically posed. Still they reveal their prompting intelligences commanding our attention, seeking the encompassing vision to be found either in theory or oracular pronouncements. Their texts were meant to be living organisms that arrange and focus, investigate and prod. Frye says in *The Educated Imagination*, "Our impressions of human life are picked up one by one, and remain for most of us loose and disorganized. But we constantly find things in literature that suddenly co-ordinate and bring into focus a great many such impressions, and this is part of what Aristotle means by the typical or universal human event" (25). My paraphrase: life, like literary experience, is ruptured, inchoate, until a critic or philosopher helps us to discern structural and thematic consistencies. Thus impressions are focused, thereby transmuted into universalities. McLuhan says in *Through the Vanishing Point*, again self-consciously igniting controversy, "This may, indeed, be a primary function of art: to make tangible and to subject to scrutiny the nameless psychic dimensions of new experience ... In a pre-literate society art serves as a means of merging the individual and the environment, not as a means of training perception of the environment ... Thus to put the artifacts from such a culture into a museum or anti-environment is an act of nullification rather than revelation" (28, 243). My paraphrase: life can be wrenching and pleasurable but seemingly incommunicable; we do not see the forms without the help of the artist-hearer. We cannot understand the effects of the forms in the waxworks of an exhibit. Institutionalized thought inhibits perception. We strive to apprehend artefacts in the experience of thriving grounds.

The McLuhan catalyst roves in society, assertively alerting people to forms and inventions. The critic is *a man of action*, evocator and messenger, incarnate psychic probe. The Magnetic City – the cosmopolis forum – draws the media-diviner deeper into the maelstroms and arte-*facts* of postmodern situations. Fire-cracking controversy is a sign of success.

Frye's furore resides in the energy of criticism to re-envision the forms of the imagination. Blake taught him these are more real than the facts of the world. Through our intentional linking of texts together we seek the order of words that possesses talismanic presence. The critic becomes *a powerful revisionary; the critic-reader is a transformer.* When we dwell in the mental Jerusalem, we gain the hope that over time we will transfigure our existential city into the utopian conjecture: "I give you the end of a golden string, / Only wind it into a ball, / It will lead you in at Heaven's gate / Built in Jerusalem's wall."[12] There is no death in the literary cosmos. The inner fire reconfigures matter through energy and will.

Two minds like great wheels of fire: without their frictional egos, there would have been no progression.

The Call to Restore Wonder

I return to prophecy and disclosure, those keywords for understanding McLuhan and Frye. If the feel of the spiritual call was deep in them, I want to ask how that call appeared in their work. If McLuhan and Frye initiated an apocalyptic tradition in Canada, then what is it they apprehended?

I have posited how one is a seer and one a hearer, so we need to grasp what they were seeing and receiving. McLuhan said, "Breakdown is breakthrough."[13] Breakdown is a forceful, sometimes barbaric, cracking of old structures. McLuhan keenly said, "You can't read the writing on the wall until your face is up against it."[14] Frye adapted the term *kerygma* to identify what he meant by the announcement of heightened being: "Kerygma is *spiritual* rhetoric ... It's the actualized form of the 'myth to live by,' assuming that the real life is a spiritual one, delivered once for all from all ideologies or rationalizations of power." Spiritual rhetoric is inherently revelatory: "a world where God speaks. That's where the kerygmatic voice comes from: a hell of a good universe next door. Or sometimes, just hell."[15]

McLuhan's method of breakdown-breakthrough is epitomized in the way we must decode his aphorisms. They give insight into the play of the forms. The hypnotizing figure breaks (this is iconoclasm); the ground is revealed (epiphany). The world is composed of interpenetrating natural and artificial texts, Nature and the media. These we must learn how to comprehend on multiple levels. His pivotal aphorism, "the medium is the message," leads to meditation. By such deft attentiveness we learn how to focus our attention in the midst of chaos. Aphorisms are a portable wisdom which we can use to reflect on what rockets around us.

Frye's grail was the identity code, the double helix of literature. "All attempts to find out what that point is are religious quests" (*Frye Unbuttoned*, 233). The Great Code came in meditations on those central books and poems that led to illumination. Deep study is epiphanic, a way of learning how to say "thus: I am"; it was Frye's intellectual yoga, a way of intensifying the inward or expanding eye. He says in *Notebooks and Lectures on the Bible and Other Religious Texts*, "Revelation is not visualized, but it is a 'seeing' ... From there it passes into the reader and becomes the participating apocalypse, which is also a new type of creation" (364). He cites the yogic importance of reading when he says in *The "Third Book" Notebooks, 1964–1972*: "When the mind takes over from the body it holds the body quiet, in study or concentration. Sense perception is directed & controlled. Some programmes of experience, such as yoga, assume a spirit-mind relationship parallel to the mind-body one. They say that the spirit is the real self, but can't emerge until the mind is kept quiet" (40).

The identity code for Frye is most fully revealed in the dynamic content of the essential medium of the printed word. (I emphasize the noun "content" here.) It is "one of the most efficient technological instruments ever devised."[16] The book is efficient because it is the portable verbal incarnation, the movable feast, the symbol of continuity, the perpetual orgy of knowledge, the artefact of the continuous dream, itself a vehicle of transport, a site for sequential contemplations. The printed word paradoxically becomes the still point in the turning world, the typographic crossroads of mind and Spirit, where the interpenetrations of realms take place. In those moments when we quiet our scattered minds in the practice of reading, then Ulysses and Penelope, Jesus and Mary, Lear and Cordelia, Heathcliff and Catherine, the quester-knight and the hyacinth girl, Poldy and Molly – and all the types they represent – come calling, always.

A life without imagination means an existence in which Achilles, Helen, Priam, Beatrice, Romeo and Juliet, Lear, Jane Eyre, Rochester,

Natasha and Pierre, blind Tiresias, Blanche and Stanley, Vladimir and Estragon, the judge and the kid have no presence. It would be a banquet without God, gods, goddesses, sprites, imps, angels, devils, heroes, and anti-heroes. Life might be easier, less dramatic, without them, but the epochal story of the quest for the soul would likely vanish. Without these characters and their part in the central story of identity, we would be overcome by grinding desperation and aimless ennui. We need the imagination to spark ourselves back to dreamland, where adventure beckons and the capacity to create seems eternal. Wandering thus returns to pilgrimage.

The prophetic focus in McLuhan's work, however, took him from page to screen, from black-and-white typographical space to vibrating electronic surfaces. When it was first published, *Understanding Media* was condemned for its style and diction. The book was called repetitive and contradictory. Yet it was his attempt to evoke the flux of electric processes, in a fluid paradigm for the Magnetic City that required a fresh vocabulary and metaphors. It was possible that the new panoramas could not be reached, or even comprehended, by conventional literary phrasings, even by verbal means. We are transforming beyond the leaves of books. If this is so, then it is a moot point how any book could express what is not containable. The printed word was already doomed, he thought, to become the entitled concern of an insular coterie.

Two passages point to this paradoxical condition of employing the printed word to look through the black marks and white spacing of its row-by-row typographic design. The first from an earlier work has euphoric beauty, an enigmatic diction that makes its authorial stance almost impossible to evaluate:

> At electric speeds the hieroglyphs of the page of Nature become readily intelligible and the Book in the World becomes a kind of Orphic hymn of revelation.[17]

The next is possibly the most passionately debated of all the passages in McLuhan's work. It is this articulation from "The Spoken Word: Flower of Evil," a chapter in the first edition of *Understanding Media*:

> Today computers hold out the promise of a means of instant translation of any code or language into any other code or language. The computer, in short, promises by technology a Pentecostal condition of universal understanding and unity. The next logical step would seem to be, not to translate,

but to bypass languages in favour of a general cosmic consciousness which might be very like the collective unconscious dreamt of by Bergson. The condition of "weightlessness," that biologists say promises a physical immortality, may be paralleled by the condition of speechlessness that could confer a perpetuity of collective harmony and peace.[18]

Dennis Duffy sees in this passage the "mystical overtones of McLuhan's vision of the new world coming to be through electronics" in his study *Marshall McLuhan* (1969).[19] In *McLuhan, or Modernism in Reverse*, the critical-theorist Willmott isolates this startling evocation of the galvanized Pentecost and cosmic consciousness, but calls it a biting example of McLuhan's wit, a bitter crystallization of satiric hyperbole (64). There is an echo of Jean Baudrillard in Willmott's sense of the terror implied in a mythopoetic speculation that is at once reverie and caveat. Marchand says in his biography that it is difficult to decipher McLuhan's tone (*The Medium and the Messenger*, 169–70). Is it ironic? ... elated? ... mocking? ... admiring? ... prophetic grandstanding? Erik Davis says, in his book *Techgnosis: Myth, Magic and Mysticism in the Age of Information*, the McLuhan style is an arrangement of "patented rhetorical shocks."[20] George Steiner notably calls the paragraph a moment of pure Blakean mythmaking.[21] In this passage observer melds with the poet in a cognitive rapture; but recall how for McLuhan the poet has the nearly sacred position of being at once the enemy of society – the outsider perceiver – and the maker of meaning (an unacknowledged legislator).

Davis's critique of this passage in *Techgnosis* suggests that McLuhan was aware of "symbolic technology ... magical images that tap the hidden currents of the cosmos" (21–2). A line of words arranged in the right abracadabra order will open volume after volume. I believe this passage pays homage to Teilhard's formulations of the noosphere, the mysterious powers of electronic telepathy flowing through the etherized signals of TV, radio, computers, and telephones. McLuhan compacts and conflates allusions: Teilhard's vision of a universal consciousness is associated with Richard Maurice Bucke's *Cosmic Consciousness* (1901), with Bergsonian flux, and with the Pentecost (on the anagogic plane, the instant when we become mediums for spiritual messages) and the promise of a worldwide apocalypse of perception and the peace which passes understanding in the Amen and the *om shanti shanti shanti* of prayer and mantra. Then there is McLuhan's vague reference to "biologists" (who are they?). Meaning for McLuhan is multileveled, therefore contingent. Revelatory responses must be elusive. Meaning resides in many visible places, elsewhere, in the user, and simultaneously in the invisible eternity. Every reading and misreading, even if absurd, become a possibility.

This well-known passage occurs precisely one quarter of the way into *Understanding Media*. (The active verb of the title evokes immersion; it is not the product of a mind that has packaged perceptions into prescriptive analyses.) With its grand tone, its embrace of the multiple forms of consciousness and technology, the paragraph could have been the concluding one for the book, a Teilhard-like Omega point. It is not; it appears at a point where the book ripples outwards in many directions. This is a McLuhan trigger passage: an oral detonation. It is a node (radiant or otherwise) meant to provide a context for commentary and re-creation. We are on the frontier where words are not enough. McLuhan says in *The Book of Probes*, "Men on frontiers, whether of time or space, abandon their previous identities. Neighbourhoods give identity. Frontiers snatch it away" (493). It follows that in the electronic interface where the screen absorbs the printed word, the frontier may only be described through magic invocation and allusion, the dance of jests and gestures. Out in the wilderness, the immovable type of the "literal man" will not last.

In an important passage from *Cosmic Media* that could be a gloss on McLuhan's Pentecostal vision, Marchessault says,

> The electric galaxy is a metaphor for a new consciousness and expressive culture that is organic, simultaneous, pattern-and-process oriented, driven by the interval, acoustic and tactile, defined by the breaking down of boundaries and categories of a previous era of impersonal assembly line linearity. Electrical media create new forms of interdependence, interpenetration, interdisciplinarity and interactivity.
>
> (150)

And she perceptively adds, in reference to his latent spirituality, "There is a mystical aspect to McLuhan's choice of light, which underlies his utopian view of the electric galaxy as a return to orality and a mystical unity" (174). I believe Marchessault and her colleague Elena Lamberti in *Marshall McLuhans Mosaic: Probing the Literary Origins of Media Studies* (2012), a seminal study of the humanist literary roots in media ecology, are advancing the vision that McLuhan was showering facts with volatile light: the possibility of enlightenment.

To McLuhan the cosmos is a reverberating orchestra of forms, each interacting, interfusing. No one form has primacy, except in terms of individual bias. "Art is an expression of an enormous preference," he said, quoting Lewis. We were in an era – depicted and eerily evoked in the alternating tones of rhapsody and dismay (concord and discord) that distinguish *Understanding Media* and his mixed-media anti-books, *The Medium is the Massage* and its follow-up, *War and Peace in the Global Village* (1968) – of an extension of nerves and senses through communications' technologies. The epigraph to that latter book is, "Globes make my head spin. By the time I locate the place, they've changed the boundaries."[22] Prophecy can drive us out of our minds. So McLuhan says in *The Book of Probes*, "By electricity we have not been driven out of our senses so much as our senses have been driven out of us. Today man's nerves surround us – they have gone outside as electrical environment" (375). Identity is radically quicksilver: in electronic space/time we quickly flip masks and moods, and our thoughts are exteriorized; being diffused and defused, we slip into discarnate states, searing selves through the worldwide communications' seal, individual minds transferring and vaulting upwards into the collective hive-mind. Ironically, it is amusing to see how McLuhan's provocative point about the limitations of the printed word never stopped him from producing books, papers, essays, pamphlets, or letters.

To Frye the printed book counters existential decay: "One of the things relevant to the intensifying of consciousness, the growth from seeing into vision, is beauty."[23] Criticism is a transcendental act. In the singular poetic book *Le Livre, Instrument Spirituel* – metamorphosing from Homer's epics, Ovid's lyrics, Virgil's epics and lyrics, from the Bible, through Shakespeare, Milton, Blake, and Shelley, Dickinson and Browning, and on to Joyce, Eliot, and certain exemplary contemporaries (Pynchon and Toni Morrison) – we discover the evolving universal human form, through all variations of tongues and styles, "maternity and paternity" (Whitman said, describing the library of liberty in his preface to his 1855 *Leaves of Grass*) in supple, rich experience. In the magnum opus we each compose, the poets show and the critic reveals: everything joins with everything else.

Frye's defining statement appears in *Northrop Frye Unbuttoned*, under the title "What Poets Say." This passage places his thinking in counterpoint to McLuhan's recognition of the electric super-Nature of the post-print world.

They say that everything is everywhere at once.
They say that all nature is alive.
They say that creation is dialectic, separating heaven & hell.

They say that the material world neither is nor isn't, but disappears.
They say that the created world neither is nor isn't, but appears.
They say that the containing form of real experience is myth.
They say that time & space are disappearing categories.
They say that men are Man, as gods are God.

(308)

This lyrical passage announces what poetry – the cultivated poetics of the inspired furore – makes available to any reader.

The above passage pivotally shows the critic becoming a seer. A work of criticism could be cryptic, energetically enigmatic – an eminent, if subtly hushed, prose poem, compelling commentary. When literary works become one conspicuous text, centuries mean little; lives come and go, empires conquer and collapse, but the great work composed of calls and responses unfolds.

Ayre reports in his biography (on the back jacket) that McLuhan once observed, "Norrie is not struggling for his place in the sun. He is the sun" (*Northrop Frye: A Biography*). Ayre seems inexplicably unaware of McLuhan's playful (sarcastic?) tone here. McLuhan is suggesting that Frye's ambitions verge on hubris. Nevertheless, I believe McLuhan's comment blends awe and critique: he is surely saying Frye's prodigious undertaking replaces all texts with his own categorizations and revisions; but his sublime conceit (surely) gives off new light.

Their harmony appears again in Frye's "What Poets Say." Frye's *kerygma* reveals the latent structure of literature. The same passage could be adapted to McLuhan's kinetic media perceptions: to reveal what is available to the users of electronic instruments. Every person in the global theatre has at their touch the poetic power that Frye describes. We become poets and potentially demonic addicts of power, in the intricate (over)heated wirings of digital information networks. McLuhan's aphorism, "User is content," simultaneously invokes the enlightened musical glass-bead game Hermann Hesse describes in *Magister Ludi* (English translation: 1969) and the calamitous drugged-out realm of William Burroughs's *Naked Lunch* (1959). "User" is slang for a pimp and a drug fiend. It is also shorthand for a participant. "Content" carries overtones of subject matter and contentment (delight and serenity). "User is content" evokes Ariel and Caliban on the isle of artefacts, in the global theatre: the high-flying sprite, the slouching beast; you can be an ecstatic player of keys and a monstrous user of machines. Behind Frye's "What Poets

Say," I hear this allusion to A.N. Whitehead's observation in *Science and the Modern World* (1925):

> In a certain sense everything is everywhere at all times. For every location involves an aspect of itself in every other location. Thus every spatio-temporal standpoint mirrors the world.[24]

It should be no surprise by now to know that McLuhan was influenced by Whitehead's passage. Whitehead is quoted in *The Gutenberg Galaxy* and *Understanding Media.*

McLuhan and Frye were concerned with multidimensional levels of awareness – apprehending through, but beyond, the literal. Recall that Frye said in his notebooks that the metaphorical emerges in the literal; recall how McLuhan said that it is through the literal that metaphors, symbols, allegorical patterns, subtexts, and contexts weave and reweave. "The medium is the message" and "user is content" evoke figure/ground interplays of sense and sensibility. This is another articulation of what Frye calls the double vision, after Blake: it is the ability, whetted by literary study and theoretical challenge and concentration, to see how reality is multifaceted, so that your organizing, poetic consciousness learns to see presences and experiences in terms of making and remaking. The imagination *is* consciousness. Or we could say, the imagination is the highest expression of consciousness. The urge for us to see life in vital interactions of Spirit and matter, of content and context, Frye presented in the essay he prepared for publication just before his passing, *The Double Vision*. This is his epigraph from Blake's letter to Thomas Butts:

> For double the vision my eyes do see,
> And a double vision is always with me:
> With my inward Eye 'tis an old Man grey;
> With my outward, a Thistle, across my way.[25]

In the following mosaic of aphorisms from McLuhan's *Culture Is Our Business* (1970), the Blakean note is clear. They apply the double vision to show how meaning surges in what may seem trivial. These aphorisms mime the graffiti and slogans, blurbs and bytes of pop culture, our new Rosetta stone, and show "a literal man" looking through the blips and spaces of post-Gutenberg texts. The pop world not only speaks, it pounds and flashes. The way to respond to unstable time is through parody, plagiaristic revision, samplings, unexpected lyrical flights:

> Poetry is the means of opening the doors of perception on areas of experience otherwise inaccessible ... *The new electric environment is a collective poem* ... In the electric age the connection in narrative and art is omitted, as in the telegraph press. There is no story line in modern art or news, just a date line. There is no past or future, just an inclusive present. In an all-at-once world of jets and circuits, the open road has become the inner trip ... All experience is a metamorphosing of reality.
>
> (270, 112, 132; emphasis mine)

I have made many remarks on their fascination with Blake. Here are two more passages by them that show this. These passages amplify the recognition that imaginative, sensual life depends on the ability to see spiritual and material energies operating all at once. The phrase "all at once," of course, suggests simultaneity and urgency. Frye says in *Fearful Symmetry*,

> It is, then, through art that we understand why perception is superior to abstraction, why perception is meaningless without an imaginative ordering of it, why the validity of such ordering depends on the normality of the perceiving mind, why that normality must be associated with genius rather than mediocrity, and why genius must be associated with the creative power of the artist. This last, which is what Blake means by "vision," is the goal of all freedom, energy and wisdom.
>
> (25)

This, written twenty-one years after Frye's statement, comes from McLuhan's 1968 text, *Through the Vanishing Point*:

> [T]he kind of "single vision" that William Blake later deprecated as "single vision and Newton's sleep" ... consists basically in a process of matching outer and inner representation. That which was faithfully represented or repeated has ever since been held to be the very criterion of rationality and reality. When there is a failure of such correspondence, a person is thought to be either hallucinating or living in a world of self-deception ... The *sensus communis* as the interplay of all the senses creates an involvement that unifies the imaginative life in the way sought by William Blake.
>
> (16)

Is McLuhan referencing Frye? They surely shared visions: the world and the texts are communing. Blake was alive in their minds; and through the phenomena of the electrified world and the printed book, McLuhan and Frye directly and indirectly spoke to one another and to us.

Admittedly, I can see how these passages appear to place genius and the artist in a hierarchy of superior, refined being. John Fekete, among others, levelled the charge that they were idealists, transcendentalist Romantics, closet religionists, and ersatz priests. Is this true? They were privileged people; I do not dispute this. They lived in the rarefied atmosphere of tenure and academic debate. Neither of them had much formative experience outside schools – or outside North America and England. (And neither fought in the Second World War.)

Still Frye thought "the powers of genius" are available to everyone. And McLuhan thought we gain the capacity to be hearers and seers through the clairaudient, clairvoyant enhancements of art. Electronic communications form the text that could extend humanity into a communion that is elevating and troubling. The classroom for Frye became a congregational place where each student could, with mentoring and contact with texts that carried the essential verbal energies, raise himself or herself to the level of prophetic insight. From the classroom the student could move on to the weaving together of the threads each literary work embodies. Education must go beyond libraries and schools and the TV or PC room. The learning experience is culture-bearing, a pitch to society. There is ethical purpose to teaching and probing. Focus leads to questioning. Questions will lead to the divine discontent. But the Blakean references in their work clearly show how they swerved away from ideological constructs towards the claims and demands of revelation and poetics. The getting of wisdom is strenuous – a contest in itself – and perpetual.

How closely were they reading one another? It is hard to be categorical about this. Still the more I place passages from their works side by side, the more parallels – harmonies – I begin to see.

In the late 1960s and early 1970s Frye and McLuhan wrote passages in their texts that sound remarkably similar in their acknowledgments of the call to knowledge, the code of awareness. Frye proclaims in *Divisions on a Ground*, "We enter into a body of thought and try to add to it ... Wisdom consists in the possession, by the community as a whole, of the essential axioms for sanity and survival. By ignoring or undervaluing this common wisdom in favour of expertise, education becomes a pernicious form of mass hypnosis."²⁶ McLuhan announces in *The Medium is the Massage*, "The method of our time is to use not a single but multiple models for exploration ... Education must shift from instruction, from imposing of stencils, to discovery – to probing and exploration of language forms" (69, 100).

❦

But I do not doubt that what they meant in part by the call of awareness was the imprint of faith. They experienced conversions, I have noted – Frye, to the United Church ministry (and away from it); McLuhan, from Protestantism to Catholicism (and later an unapologetic pre–Vatican II version of it). To postmodern ideologues for whom spirituality is just another construct or fiction, inexplicable in a contemporary sensibility, this harmony must remain baffling, even off-putting. Spirituality in universities is the new perversity. Certainly, critics have suggested that any true religion we will find in their writings will be in their theoretical architectures, the master narratives (the holy lies, in Nietzsche's phrase) that they wove out of their inventive independent energies. However, the two were not evangelical; I never saw either of them try to encourage conversion. That McLuhan escaped to the sanctuary of communion every day at noon at Saint Michael's was well known to me. It was not unusual for priests and nuns to be present in conversation at the Centre for Culture and Technology. Most students knew that Frye was an ordained United Church minister with an itinerant preacher past. "My Christian position," Frye muses in his *Late Notebooks, 1982–1990,* "is that of Blake reinforced by Emily Dickinson" (714). This statement melds the haunted voice of one crying in the wilderness with the deliberately introverted, isolate voice that declares, "The Soul selects its own Society – Then – shuts the Door – ."

Faith, trust, inspiration, idealism – these values and imperatives profoundly differentiate them from deconstructionist trends. Frye comments on McLuhan's and his own religious rooting in a telling passage from his "Conclusion to the Second Edition of *Literary History of Canada*" (1976). Reflecting on those contributors to the *History* who remark on the underpinnings of spirituality and faith in certain Canadian figures, Frye says, "[W]hat Canadian philosophy does have is a strong emphasis on religion, so remarkable as to be worth pausing on for a moment ... much is said in this book and elsewhere about the religious drive in George Grant, in McLuhan, in myself. In [Donald] Creighton the drive may not be technically religious, but it is certainly prophetic ... *I had long realized that the religious context of so many Canadian intellectuals had something to do with the peripheral situation of Canada*" (460–1; emphasis mine). Revealingly, Frye continues in the essay to align his spiritual centering and McLuhan's – by inference their marginal dissidence against the nihilistic, power-mad aspects of modernity – with the eccentric Canadian sublime: "Canada has been steadily building up something like a North American counter-culture against the United States which is now big and complex enough to be examined on its own terms. *Once more, 'against' simply means differentiation*"[27] (emphasis mine).

My book is permeated with paraphrases from Frye's notebooks to spell out how his literary endeavour was underscored by a spiritual quest. His life was impelled by momentary transcendental shocks. Denham's *Religious Visionary and Architect of the Spiritual World* is dedicated to the proposition that "the central feature of the superstructure Frye built is its religious base" (ix). This is what Frye said in the *Late Notebooks, 1982–1990*, about how the vocations of lecturer, missionary, critic, writer, teacher, and prophetic visionary could cohere in a person's life:

> Any biography, including Ayre's, would say that I dropped preaching for academic life: that's the opposite of what my spiritual autobiography would say, that I fled into academia for refuge and have since tried to peek out into the congregation and make a preacher of myself.
>
> (621)

McLuhan's Catholicism so steadily informs his thinking that I propose it should form a separate study. He wrangled with religious questions from an early age. His letters attest to his spiritual affirmations. Of his privacy on these issues, McLuhan said in a 1969 letter to Edward Hall,

> I deliberately keep Christianity out of all these discussions lest perception be diverted from structural processes by doctrinal sectarian passions. My own attitude to Christianity is, itself, awareness of process.
>
> (*Letters*, 384)

I do not believe that this is entirely so: a mystical Christian presence is evident in his work. I see it confirmed even in the passage above, where he emphasizes "awareness of process." It is this awareness – often on the brink of words, always at the edge of an aphorism, often in the play of humour, always in a gesture or an image – that he sought to encourage in "users." Further, his thinking is rooted in the Catholic symbolism of liturgy and communion. In a 1970 interview with Hubert Hoskins, published in *The Listener*, in the same year that the Frye-McLuhan exchange took place in those pages, McLuhan makes exoteric what he usually kept esoteric. Note the context of his response. His typically ambivalent musings follow Hoskins's reading of that notoriously allusive, elusive passage on the Pentecostal conditions of mass communication in *Understanding Media*. They are an annotation to the 1964 text. In this probe he makes the sensational claim that media can transcend our physicality:

> *[W]e are post-history and timeless.* Instant awareness of all the varieties of human expression reconstitutes the mythic type of consciousness, of *once-upon-a-time*-ness, which means all-time, out of time ... the *surround* of information that we now experience electrically is an extension of consciousness itself ... Many people simply resort instantly to the occult, to ESP, and every form of hidden awareness in response to this new surround of electric information. *And so we live, in the vulgar sense, in an extremely religious age. I think that the age we are moving into will probably seem the most religious ever. We are already there.*
> (88; emphasis mine)

Frye's work has explicit theological repercussions. His premises in *The Great Code* and *Words with Power* helped to inspire and formulate the ideas put forward by the theologian Tom Harpur in his polemical meditation, *The Pagan Christ: Recovering the Lost Light* (2004). Harpur's book begins with a description of the effect of Frye's understanding of the metaphoric dimension of the Bible. He cites how Frye's undergraduate lectures on the Bible – likely the twenty-four lectures Frye gave in his course the Mythological Framework of Western Culture, at Victoria College in 1981 and 1982 (and gathered in the last sections of the 2003 edition of *Northrop Frye's Notebooks and Lectures on the Bible and Other Religious Texts*) – profoundly addled a student (himself). Harpur was permanently unsettled by Frye's proclamation that the Bible was a collection of myths. Frye's thought incited Harpur's challenge to those who insist on historical readings of the origins of Christianity and to their literalist articulations of the synoptic Gospels.[28]

A good Blakean Protestant, Frye seems at times to dissent against the idea of the Church (Catholic, Anglican), or of any church whatsoever. This dissent made him sceptical about the premises of Protestantism and its evangelical roots in factual readings of the Bible. His essays and notebooks on religion do show that he thought well of most spiritual practices, except when he felt he had to comment on the Vatican; then Frye becomes resolutely Protestant.

McLuhan's observation that Frye opposed papism – the framework of the Church – was sound: Frye relished subtle heresies. I say "subtle" because of the subdued tonalities he invariably uses in his essays. He championed Blake's firebrand poetics, but he himself did not often sound much like a marooned prophet denouncing the boredom and restrictions of his age (the notebooks are frequently the exception to this). He was perhaps too much the Canadian academic, and English department servant, to authentically preach thunder from the desert or tower (unless you wish to call a committee gathering a desert or a classroom space a tower). Frye's essays do not carry anything of the revolutionary zeal of an Old Testament prophet. Nevertheless, there is a nudging in his shy proclamations – an addling, a destabilizing, an undercurrent of muted gospel militancy, a nuanced moving of the reader and the pupil towards a turning point, the "change of heart" of the Gospel of Matthew's admonition in 18:3.

Any reflection that I could present on Frye's challenge to fundamentalist, history-based religion risks reductionism. Nevertheless, I think it is important to review it because his challenge speaks to the paradoxes of his life: he was a minister and an iconoclast, a literary specialist and a visionary. My review should show how spiritual convictions goaded him into territories that promise to be unsettling. His arguments are embodied in the three books that form his last critical testaments, the third being *The Double Vision*. The trilogy becomes a tetralogy when we add the lectures that were published more than a decade after his death in *Notebooks and Lectures on the Bible*.

If all language-based texts from the Bible to Blake to *Gravity's Rainbow* exist in a continuum, in which every metaphoric statement exists now, then these constructs form a counter-history. The Bible offers myth – a heightened form of fiction – not fact, empirical descriptions with a verifiable chronology. Prophetic poetics may refer to events – absorbing them, incorporating actual people – but myths are not finally dependent on history or biography. There is no factual life in the imagination. Religion (in short) is myth misunderstood; and religion is (in fact) properly the dream-like poetics of the people: it is the way we enter into the vast essential misreading that reveals our capacity to make and remake meanings. This is a wild, beguiling heresy. In his quiet way Frye was sweeping away everything ever written on the historical basis of the Bible.

What is the metaphoric basis of the Bible? Metaphors, Frye says, "are verbal energy-currents carrying out the first act of consciousness, trying to overcome the gap between subject and object. Creation wasn't necessarily made for the sake of human consciousness, but consciousness is the human response to creation."[29] Verbal energy-currents sometimes refer to dates in time, but the spirit of imagination is directed elsewhere: towards myth. Pivotal for Frye is how myth differs "from the pseudo-historical fantasies that make up so much of Biblical scholarship. The mythical 'this happened/couldn't have happened' presentation is a parable: here's the story; what do you make of it? You ask, but how much of it is true? The answer is, all of it and none of it: it's the only story you're going to get: what do you make of it? *Verum factum*. My question is: what do the poets make of it?" (28). (He echoes here McLuhan's proposition that true operations of mind, perception, imagination and apprehension are "making, not matching.") An enigmatic preacher and wise-man named Yeshua (Aramaic), Iesous (Greek), Iesus (Latin), Joshua (his Hebrew name), or Jesus (his seventeenth-century English name) began a brief passionate mission in Palestine during the turn of the first millennium, teaching and performing acts of healing magic. But our concern through the written documents – which do not seem to verify the existence of a real person – must be with the mythic dimension of the figure: the Christos. We engage a fictive presence journeying, struggling. But this mythic-allegoric form, once understood, transforms our sense of history. It is then we wake from history's claustrophobic nightmare into the vision of hope and compassion. Through the continuum of metaphor, the Spirit tries to seep through and reach us, inspiring us to speech and action.

Eternity wants to enter into the productions of time, I believe Frye would have said. Reading is (potentially) a radical transference of spiritual energy to the reader, who becomes a primary critic, in Frye's conception of revisionary awareness. This reinterpretation of the myths and metaphors of the Bible would pose a threat to the literalists of Protestant evangelism, who sometimes crudely and violently insist on a historical Jesus.

Frye is refreshingly blunt in his notebooks. In *Words with Power*, where the torrential eloquence of the journals does make its way into a public essay, Frye still subdues his claims. His experiences in Protestant churches must have told him how dangerous a metaphoric reading of the Bible is. Given that right-wing politicians in the United States and in Canada have curried support from evangelical conservative extremists, I see his point. Tom Harpur received death threats from his charitable Christian brethren. The Anglican minister had to move to northern Ontario, to an undisclosed address, to protect himself and his family.[30] Frye acknowledges the dangers of literalism in his notebooks: "I find the Gospels most unpleasant reading for the most part ... The Christian Church with all its manias had started to form when the Gospels were written, & one can see it at work smoothing things away & making it possible for Christianity to be kidnapped by a deformed & neurotic society."[31]

But it is impossible to read through Frye's later books and notebooks without recognizing how he was moved by the deepest impulses of spirituality. His humanism is infused with the energies of giving, of compassion, of learning what our destinies may hold, of searching in the letters for the key that will unlock the Spirit's hidden codes. He scoured through books looking for the signs and symbols where humanity might be found after finding ourselves crashing down and marooned. Frye's sermons are collected in *Reading the World: Selected Writings, 1935–1976* (1990). In this passage he gives a moving and near-mystical interpretation of the medium and the message in terms that suggest Pentecostal possession:

> T.S. Eliot compares the poet's mind to a catalyst that is present at, without taking part in, a chemical reaction. We can call this the unconscious or inspiration or whatever vague abstraction we choose, but *whatever we call it, it seems to be a sense of being a medium or transmitter of poetry rather than a possessor of it* ... *The point is not that "I think;" the point is rather that somebody or something is thinking with me* ... the moment when "I know" goes into reverse and becomes something more like *"I am known."*[32] (emphases mine)

McLuhan died before the publication of Frye's theological works. The Catholic McLuhan would have balked at Frye's inner light readings. I imagine, had McLuhan lived long enough to read them, he might have found his reply in Chesterton's *Heretics*: "Like his master Pater and all the aesthetes," Chesterton writes of George Moore, "his real quarrel is with life that is not a dream that can be molded by the dreamer. It is not the dogma of the reality of the other world that troubles him, but the dogma of the reality of this world."[33] From *Orthodoxy* McLuhan might have selected this: "That Jones shall worship the god within him turns out ultimately to mean that Jones shall worship Jones ... Christianity came into the world firstly in order to assert with violence that a man had not only to look inwards, but to look outwards..."[34]

Have we returned to their clash? No, my argument directs us to the deepest aspect of their harmony: their faith. Many of the McLuhan-Frye dialogues and disagreements can be framed in a spiritual and religious discussion. Everything happening in this life for them carried transcendental and immanent importance. Moreover, both were sufficiently open-minded – "Old men should be explorers," T.S. Eliot said in the "East Coker" poems in *Four Quartets* (1944)[35] – to admit the possibility that "something" (a recurrent Frye word) beyond spoke through them and in what they comprehended. Remember McLuhan's jocular sign-off in his letter to Pierre Trudeau: "Mediumistically Yours." They used the words soul and spirit without quotation marks. Writing and teaching were invitations to voyages: producing perception and new conception meant enhancements of possibility. The sheer prodigality of their work suggests a war against dejection. Faith drove their dissidence. "I am a metaphysician," McLuhan wrote in a 1970 letter to another collaborator, J.G. Keogh, "interested in the life of the forms and their surprising modalities. That is why I have no interest at all in the academic world and its attempt at tidying up experience" (*Letters*, 413). Their religious backgrounds taught them the power of rallying unity (and gave them confidence). Everything is one thing, and we participate in its extensions and its deepening.

McLuhan's *The Medium and the Light: Reflections on Religion* (1999) is an indispensable posthumous work. In it we see his Catholic humanism anchoring his insights. The editors assembled essays, interviews, letters, reviews, and aphorisms that show how his sensory apprehensions were infused by an apologia of hope. Nothing in or of the world was finally divided from our manifold senses. His paranoia about Masonic conspiracies at the University of Toronto or his outbursts of cynicism about politics and business – "Stupidity is a normal human condition," he often said[36] – should not obscure his dedication to perceiving the paradoxes of truth. The fragments and the ruins in life, the dissociation of sensibility, could be brought back into consort, the spell of being liberated from the cage of insensitivity.

The following passages from *The Medium and the Light* summarize the essence of the McLuhan–Frye harmony. Their metaphors of investigation through X-rays or expanding eyes offer a pattern of alternating currents. The passages become more relevant when we understand them through my seer-hearer analogy. They show the difference between sensibilities that preferred the sensory-psychic bias of the eye or of the acoustic-tactile. But remember that McLuhan was, like Frye, a "literal man," his sensibility imprinted by book culture:

For Western man, literate man ... time is continuous and homogeneous, and space is likewise ... for the auditory man, no two times, no two spaces could be alike ... Everything has its own structure ... In terms of eye and ear, both are completely right, but when one begins making value judgments about the other ... the trouble begins ... With the book, one can withdraw inward ... The printed alphabet creates, in large measure, fragmentation ... But now an electric world is unfolding, acoustic in nature because it is instantaneous and simultaneous. It is formed as a vast global resonant unity ... *the solution lies in the complementary nature of the two cerebral hemispheres ... These two hemispheres are complementary, and not exclusive. Neither mode is more important except in transitional forms of awareness. It is a culture that makes one or the other dominant and exclusive. A culture builds itself on a preference for one or the other hemisphere instead of basing itself on both.*
(44, 47, 49–50, 53; emphasis mine)

I began this book by claiming that McLuhan and Frye wait ahead of us at a crossroads. This juncture must be clearer now. At the crucial turning point, the transition from book culture (domain of the literate I; the room with a view) to electric culture (the sphere of the audile-tactile; theatre with the jitters of sensation) was embodied in their dialogues. Their debate personalized profound structural shifts. They gazed into the whirlwind of the present, into the maze of texts; and they read these in terms that grew from a need to find "fearful symmetries." Frye took literary text to be a counter-sphere to a craven, disabling world; McLuhan took the maddened, flamboyant world to be his text. There is the Spirit in words, literary works offering the sublime aesthetic rebellion of inspiration; there is the Spirit charging through the global forum, all things animated.

We arc moving closer to the essence of their crossing; and a crossroads is an image of complementarity, the cruxes where energies meet, when a wandering becomes a wondering.

The Book of Doublends Jined (Finn, Again!)

One of these cruxes is Joyce's *Finnegans Wake*. Who reads the *Wake?* Few do, or can. Who has a key to it? These two read it, deeply. Both claimed to have a key to it and to draw out from its new web of words a key to present fears and conditions. I have read the *Wake* off and on over many years. Sometimes I read it out loud to myself; I believe Joyce wanted us to hear it more than he wanted us to silently peruse it. It is meant for performance, comic skits – "roar-atorios" riffing on a word or two. My readings have moved in alternating currents of bafflement and pleasure, insight and confusion. It is one of the supreme gnomic books of our literature – arguably, the most demanding of all the deliberately difficult works of modernism. Virginia Woolf's *The Waves*, Pound's *Cantos*, Fernando Pessoa's *The Book of Disquiet*, Robert Musil's *The Man Without Qualities*, Paul Celan's post-Holocaust poems – all present magnificent challenges for reading, all are elusive in highly individualized ways. But the *Wake* takes us into the language of dreams, puns unlimited. What to make of it?

McLuhan and Frye were always seeking keys, codes, laws, signals: how to enter into dynamic processes – of the imagination and of technological effect – and to evoke and describe them. So when we arrive at Joyce's last work, we find what was for them a canonic text. They were gripped by the intertextual complexity of Joyce's book because it offered the kind of rewarding difficulty they deemed indispensable. The prodigality of its verbal ingenuity lured them. *Finnegans Wake* is tightly organized around Giambattista Vico's cyclic patterns. Mythopoetic, it is an amusing book of "outer nocense,"[37] a slipping off into dreams after the drowsy words of Molly's soliloquy at the end of *Ulysses*; and a polyglot punning "mamafesta" (104), the first work of modernism to represent the effects of theatre, radio, TV, and cinema.

Frye and McLuhan focused with precision and passion on the first page and on the last page of "the book of Doublends Jined" (20). Following their lead, I will reflect on these virtuoso passages, to the best of my limited ability when it comes to the *Wake*. (I confess, though, that its enigmatic power always attracts me. The *Wake* rises, and then even this often groggy reader will not sleep.)

McLuhan's references to *Finnegans Wake* are myriad. They begin in *The Gutenberg Galaxy* and continue to the posthumous collaborations. Every McLuhan text after 1962 mentions Joyce and his writings. There is a well-known and entrancing story that tells of McLuhan being asked by a journalist what books he would take with him to a desert island. "All of them by James Joyce," he quipped. *War and Peace in the Global Village* is set in a stylistic *essai concrete*, its marginalia made of quotations from the *Wake*. Three pages of *War and Peace* (46–8) are a recitation of the ten thunders that appear throughout Joyce's book. The *Wake* becomes for

McLuhan a set of verbal clues, and cues, for decoding and comprehending the global theatre.

Frye's references to *Finnegans Wake* are legion too. In *Northrop Frye Unbuttoned*, he writes, "[It] is a kind of hypnagogic structure, words reverberating on themselves without pointing to objects ... This may be the hallucinatory verbal world within which God speaks" (95). Hypnagogic works make reverie books. These mesmerize the reader into receptive states. Joyce's novel (if we can call his genre-melding a novel) is for Frye the most refined expression of the pure verbal cosmos in which the outside world is condensed into dream pages. Frye reworks and extends the passage from his notebook – he often did this – in a published statement, this time in *Words with Power*. Frye mixes the allegorical deep structure of the quest-romance, the journey towards identity, with Joyce's verbal oneiromancy. It is Frye's explicit pronouncement of a book becoming a convergence point (crucible) for invisible Spirit (or imagination) and visible matter (words).

> The motto of Delphi was "Know thyself," which suggests that the self intended was a conscience far below the ego with the anxieties of self-interest, far below all social and cultural conditioning, in short the spiritual self. For that self to "know itself" would constitute the unity of Word and Spirit in which all consciousness begins and ends. Such a spirit could produce its own oracles, and they would be not only genuinely prophetic but genuinely witty. *Finnegans Wake* is the only book I know which is devoted entirely *to this hidden intercommunion of Word and Spirit*, with no emergence into the outside world at any point, but of course the creative energy involved has produced all literature.
>
> (232; emphasis mine)

Frye's phrase "hidden intercommunion" is a parallel to my notions here of harmony and complementarity.

Finnegans Wake was for McLuhan and Frye a step beyond literature, a movement into exuberant meta-expression. Its appeal powerfully magical, this book joins insight into modern city life with laughter, textual innovation with mythic allusion, cyclical patterns of exile with return, precise wordplay with the widest (wildest) possible allusiveness. One voice in the *Wake* speaks of the grand intention: "to tear a round and tease their partners lovesoftfun at Finnegan's Wake" (607). Joyce's gamble at creating unlimited form and expression dramatically, comically, reconfirmed for McLuhan and Frye the necessity of reversing the effects of our fallen state – Tim Finnegan the everyman crashes drunk down from scaffolding, like Humpty Dumpty (an analogue), and must rise, or wake, over and over ("Finn, again!") – into the new teeming. A wake is a whiskey-soaked occasion ("whiskey" is the "wise key"). The *Wake*, to McLuhan, "is not the world of Adam and Eve, but one in which there is a priority of Eve over Adam."[38] Making has the priority over matching, creation and re-creation over the closure of a terminal point.

All crossings are beginnings. By our utterances we give birth to ourselves. In an essay aptly called "Cycle and Apocalypse in *Finnegans Wake*" in his 1990 collection, *Myth and Metaphor*, Frye concludes with a meditation on one Joycean phrase, the evocative hybrid "tillthousendsthee." Frye reflects on how this mystical phrase lifts into view "the imagery of the cycle" and expresses "whatever is beyond the cycle."[39] I will come back to what they both might have meant by "beyond."

How are "Teems of times and happy returns" articulated in the *Wake* (215)? In my close study of its last words I will show how Joyce evokes the Adamic fall, then tries to reverse it, and what it is that McLuhan and Frye saw in this re-cycling back to Eve. The book (or Book) ends with the monologue by Anna Livia Plurabelle (ALP). Justly called one of Joyce's most beautiful writings, it is a lingering meditation on death and resurrection. (The *Wake* was published on the eve of the Second World War, and two years before Joyce's death.) In ALP's reverie she murmurs and mothers, remembers and ponders, envisions and listens, dreams and sees, identifies and invokes, meanders and moans; turning and returning, she melds night and morning, water and wind, into words and sounds. These pages reveal neologism and onomatopoeia at an apogee. The puns become oracular entry points. It is the only time in literature when a sigh and a breath become eloquent. This is from the 1992 edition: "So soft this morning ours. Yes. Carry me along, taddy, like you done through the toy fair ... I sink I'd die down over his feet, humbly dumbly, only to washup. Yes, tid. There's where. First. We pass through grass behush the bush to. Whish! A gull. Gulls. Far calls. Coming, far! End here. Us then. Finn, again! Take. Bussoftlhee, mememormee! Till thousendsthee. Lps. The keys to. Given! A way a lone a last a loved a long the" (628).

A wake is a watch, an observance. The word has Teutonic roots in *WAK*, which means "to be brisk" and "to be vigorous." In an Irish wake there is a calling after the dead. The corpse is raised up from its coffin to join in the festivities. A wake is a rejoicing. A wake is also the track of a ship. Wakes are often called "the ship's way." A wake can be wet track through ice and through a row of high damp grass. The verb "waken" carries the overtone of watchfulness. Who first watched us? The stars, the sun, the moon, and the planets looked down. What are the wakes of the ship of life? They are breath and water.

ALP calls to the night sky, her father, and to her husband, Humphrey Chimpden Earwicker (HCE: Haveth Childers Everywhere and Here Comes Everybody), herself becoming air, morphing into waves. Like Orpheus's head but metamorphosed into a female head, ALP floats down the Liffey in Dublin – hear the overtones of leaf, levy, leafy, lift, if, live, and Livia in the river's name – softly poeticizing and prophesying. In Joyce's profound mythic imagination the Ovidian transformation has been reinvented, becoming comic, not tragic. ALP is Isis, an Irish washerwoman, a flower, and the current of life. A redemptive Eve and a redeemed Ophelia, ALP sings to a sleeping mankind, her beloved, her wandering Adam: "Finn, again! ... The keys to. Given!"

Joyce ends the *Wake* with a lyrical line, a sentence forged into a new hybrid formation of gaps: "A way a lone a last a loved a long the" There is no full stop; a pregnant pause, perhaps. (Once drawn into the *Wake*, I start punning along with Joyce.) It is a miracle of a monologue (witty and elegiac at once), and it is a surrendering to death. So mesmerizing is the sensual stream of its maternal murmur that the reader is apt to miss this plaintive fact. ALP floats away drifting into ... rapture, perhaps rupture: the white light of the blank page, where you and I are asked to begin again, to reread, doubling and joining the "etyms" and ends.

We flow into silence. To McLuhan, the lack of a period would have indicated discontinuity: a break, a gap, an interval, a space between. The action is in the white space. The reader must interpret, revising and weaving threads of meaning. Gaps leave an open place for each of us to step through. The user is thus the content. The blank after "the" (a definite preposition, not an indefinite one like the five articles, "a," that precede it) gestures towards what is outside the page. Mysteriously, it beckons into the unutterable in any and all human terms, perhaps a question of faith. The silence is charged with the inexpressible and the ineffable

But outside the blank there are other ways of communicating, many spheres of human expression. Music, silence, dance, gesture, numbers, symbols, signs, hieroglyphics, and images: these are "History as her is harped" (486). The white space at the end of the book for McLuhan did not spell "closing time" but opening time: the gesture towards screens and the soft white noise of phones and lights. In *Finnegans Wake* Joyce speaks of the effects of the "verbivocovisual presentment" (341) and "the faroscope of television, (this nightlife instrument ...)" (150). Joyce described "telephony" and the "teleframe," "the charge of a light barricade" (349) in the 1930s, decades before the universality of TV, PCs, or cell phones, the portable sites where channels flow and merge. The white space after "the" sluices towards what comes after, invoking how the books of Nature and super-Nature are still to be written and still write us.

After "the," we can go back to the book's beginning ("... again!"). We re-cycle to the *once upon a time* that starts each story, "riverrun, past Eve and Adams, from swerve of shore to bend of bay, brings us by a commodius vicus of recirculation back to Howth Castle and Environs" (3). (*A Portrait of the Artist as a Young Man* begins, "Once upon a time, and a very good time it was ...") With no capitalization on "riverrun," ALP flows joyfully back to HCE ("Howth Castle and Environs"). The river runs through everything, returning us to the source and the eternal story ("Eve and Adams"), now in a city that is every city (Howth Castle in Dublin looks out over the River Liffey).

The *ricorso* could suggest a closed cyclical inevitability, but when we circle back to beginnings, we return possessing new information and lessons. The sphere of knowledge is widened, consciousness expanded. Flow is the not-so-secret process; though no river, Heraclitus said, can ever offer the same experience twice. Water, like Tim Finnegan's whisky, is the reviving elixir.

Gilles Deleuze and Félix Guattari identify the key role of the flux-flow for McLuhan's iconoclasm in their *Anti-Oedipus* (English translation: 1983). Stream of consciousness becomes the overflowing stream of the post-Gutenberg current:

> [W]hat exactly is meant when someone announces the collapse of the "Gutenberg galaxy"? ... This seems to us to be the *significance of McLuhan's analyses: to have shown what a language of decoded flows is,* as opposed to a signifier that strangles and overcodes the flows. In the first place, for nonsignifying language anything will do: whether it be phonic, graphic, gestural, etc., no flow is privileged in this language, which remains indifferent to its substance or its support, inasmuch as the latter is an amorphous continuum. *The electric flow can be considered as the realization of such a flow that is indeterminate as such.* But a substance is said to be formed when a flow enters into a relationship with another flow, such that the first defines a content and the second, an expression. The deterritorialized flows of content and expression are in a state of conjunction or reciprocal precondition that constitutes

figures as the ultimate units of both content and expression. ... Hence the figures, that is, the schizzes or break-flows are in no way "figurative"; they become figurative only in a particular constellation that dissolves in order to be replaced by another one.[40] (emphases mine)

The *Wake* for McLuhan incarnates "the language of decoded flows" by pouring out linguistic associations into its readers. We are meant to become drunk with its word libations, its liberating spirit(s).

The *Wake* represents a crisis in consciousness, so McLuhan recognized. It embodies a joyful wisdom, however. Language can do this; it can break boundaries, flood borders. The comic dance of the *Wake* appealed to his faith in the *commedia* of life, of all our inventions. All is flowing, all shall be well.

Where else does the white space at the end of the *Wake* go? Emily Dickinson and Paul Celan are masters of the dash and of white space, the typographic void. The blank at the end of their lines breaks with coherence: emptiness shatters the sense of sentences. Blank space implies a slant towards the irreducible or towards catastrophe. Perhaps there is a grasping after the mystical; perhaps not: the silence is unstable, often dark. Dickinson questions all premises in her poetry; Celan's poetry registers the shattering of his sensibility through his horrifying experiences of the Holocaust. The eerie blanks in their poetry may be meant to maintain the surround of an incommunicable, even bewildering, nothing. Or it is the place of Mystery, or devastation and Mystery, both. The blanks may speak; then again words may not be enough.

Joyce's blank space rolls us into the open. The empty place is not terrifying – it is a canvas waiting to be filled. The voracious, inventive Joyce, hungry for new words, was avid for anything that made us (or just himself) laugh. The passing into death and blankness never ends, truly; we keep coming back to the "riverrun" of bewitching renewal.

The *Wake* inspires other associations for Frye. The *ricorso* invokes the primal story, the poetry before the poems: "the map of the souls' groupography rose in relief" (476). Soon after circling back to the source, Joyce writes in part 1, "There extand by now one thousand and one stories, all told, of the same" (5). His book is a mapping on synchronic levels of the rapturous story falling and rising through, and invigorating, Western literature. Yet the fall-rise story cannot be told or received in the same way: it is always being reinvented. To awake from "the nightmare of history" – the phrase uttered by Stephen Dedalus in *Ulysses* (28) – the critic-seer traces the current, diving deeper into verbal depths. The return is to reinterpretation, moulding the text in new contexts. With each *ricorso*, the cosmos of the Book sounds more reverberations, forges more links.

Joyce's structuring of the *Wake* confirmed for Frye the everlasting wave-form of revision. Each pun is a world. The *Wake* represents the "pan-literary" dream: a hypnagogic structure, into which readers may fall and then rise to identification of latent patterns: "And as I was jogging along in a dream as dozing I was dawdling, arrah, methought broadtone was heard and the creepers and the gliders and flivvers of the earth breath and the dancetongues of the woodfires and the hummers in their ground all vociferated echoating" (404). In Joyce's dream-time we awaken to the powers of myth and metaphor. Outside the book's pages reality sleeps.

The *Wake* reinforced the insight Frye had into *The Tempest*: the isle of art is a utopian ("Phoenix Park") theatre where the cell of dream-life eventually, ideally, overcomes a reality all too often estranged from our higher selves. The night of the *Wake* is no darkness. It is the space-time of the imagination, Spirit and Word in "intercommunion." The *Wake* is end-negating: "fin negans," in this the French word for "end" and a pun on negation. In its sibylline whispers are intimations of imaginative restoration, its prose poetry seeping through frontiers of discrete identity and saturating us with a greater humanity, all voices speaking, including the re-creative reader's.

There is more to the *Wake* than this. In ALP's last aria she sings of "the keys." The musical analogy is obvious. But the keys are given ... to what? I think it is to opening the doors of perception and of conception; imaginative life unbound. Frye's *Anatomy of Criticism* clarifies:

> If I have read the last chapter of *Finnegans Wake* correctly, what happens there is that the dreamer, after spending the night in communion with a vast body of metaphorical identifications, wakens and goes about his business forgetting his dream, like Nebuchadnezzar, failing to use, or even to realize that he can use, the "keys to dreamland." What he fails to do, the "ideal reader suffering from an ideal insomnia," as Joyce calls him, in other words the critic. Some such activity as this of reforging the broken links between creation and knowledge, art and science, myth and concept, is what I envisage for criticism.
>
> (354)

Frye announces his supreme project: a synthesis-book that through criticism achieves the Renaissance ideal of art and science together. Joyce does not use the phrase "keys to dreamland" in the *Wake*. It is a Frye portmanteau line. Still the dreamland he envisions is where there is an embrace of the investigative techniques found in philosophy, poetry, art, politics, and science in a resonant whole. Frye's view of science is not post-Cartesian naturalism, specialized and fragmentary: it is comprehensive. He says in his notebooks, "To unite the dream world with the waking world is to create."[41] His reference to the *Wake* on the last page of the *Anatomy* is to the making of new consciousness. The term "critic" for Frye (we have seen) is wide-ranging: it turns the common reader into the uncommon artist of seemingly disparate literary strands.

McLuhan understood science in the same comprehensive way. The allusion to the Renaissance view of science and knowledge, art and myth, in a harmony of exploratory understanding is evoked in the Baconian and Viconian subtitle to *Laws of Media: The New Science*. The subtitle is meant to synchronize with McLuhan's PhD dissertation on Nashe and the essential emphasis he put on seeing art and science, grammar and rhetoric in a cluster of interacting disciplines. In *Laws of Media*, McLuhan describes the codes at work in media processes and offers a key through the tetrads, to filtering and transfiguring the flooding effects of the media-sea.

He condemned Frye for a classifying mania in *Anatomy*. Yet they shared similar aspirations: to unite fields of inquiry, to find keys and laws (in sacred geometrical patterns), to overcome alienation, to offer sage axioms. *Finnegans Wake* provided a key to the recharging forces of the cosmopolis and a key to the imaginative power that melds spirit and word. *Verum factum*: what is true is what is made. They read through the *Wake* towards revisions of Vico's axiom: we are our inventions, and the truth is in our inventions.

Vico's phrase from *De Antiquissima Italorum Sapientia* is often quoted in its abbreviated form. The axiom reads when I restore it, *verum esse ipsum factum*. "Truth is in itself a construction." I have found innumerable translations of it. One lively version that I very much like runs like this: "We only know what we ourselves have made." But this translation likely urges the quote towards solipsism, albeit a sublime one, like an exalted imaginative swaddling. It implies "self-begetting." This would be in keeping with Frye's Blakean-Miltonic prophetic-lyrical-critical ambitions. McLuhan's take on the Viconian maxim would urge us into extension beyond the Romantic Self. Technology (what we have made) becomes us, extends us, remoulding and shaping. The axiom may mean our inventions are a foundation for truth. But truth, we glean from McLuhan and Frye, is found in process and discovery: it is lived, never a static position.

In the last passage from *Anatomy* Frye points to Joyce's incomplete last sentence. The Book of Being and Becoming is not finished. One book opens to another. The silence at the end of the *Wake* is not a signal of desperation. The visionary reader must insert him or herself. *Verum factum* is therefore the poetic principle, the root of creation. In his declaration about "reforging the broken links" at the end of his opus, Frye says this principle continues. This is the great yes said to the human opus.

The white space at the end of the *Wake* is a place where echoes begin. It is where we pick up the keys, which are clues too. Of course, McLuhan and Frye read the same book with differing interpretations of its alchemical dream. But by adding their rereadings and their imaginative extensions they confirmed its importance to modernity and to their quests.

In a 1977 letter to Walter J. Ong (written just before Christmas), Frye speaks of a recommendation made by a student:

> [O]ne of his proposals was that he and Marshall [McLuhan] and I should form a seminar to discuss *Finnegans Wake*, which hardly fitted my working schedule, or I should imagine, Marshall's.[42]

It does not surprise me to hear it was once suggested at the Department of English that the two conduct a joint seminar on the *Wake*. Their love for it was obvious to every student. Their classroom methods would never have meshed, however; I know this from my experiences in their seminars. McLuhan conducted his graduate seminars in conditions of quick improvisation; Frye read from lecture notes and sketched out diagrams on blackboards. He says in the letter that he did not have the time to prepare for such an event. Perhaps he could not imagine sharing a classroom with the "jazzing" McLuhan either. There is no mention of the proposal in McLuhan's letters. Yet for all their differences, and their contrasting styles when dealing with students, it is one of the missed opportunities of literature that a seminar conducted by the two on the *Wake* never took place.

⚜

McLuhan said in *The Medium and the Light* that complementarity must be understood in terms of doubling – shifting and multiplying figures and grounds. Joyce says early in the *Wake*, "So This Is Dyoublong? ... Hush! Caution! Echoland!" (13). McLuhan and Frye read the *Wake* and carried its echoes into their fascinations. The metalanguage of the *Wake* propelled them into the opening time (of pages and screens), where relationships of unique intensity could exist. "If there is a future in every past that is present," Joyce writes towards the end of part 3 of *Wake*, "Stump! His producers are they not his consumers? Your exagmination round his factification for incamination of a warping process" (496, 497).

The Designs of Light, Revisionaries of Style

I have said that this study of my teachers is more appreciation – and extension – then it is an expression of my confrontation or squabbles with them. One of my lines of appreciation is for their style, McLuhan's genius for aphorism and quip, Frye's genius for prose-lyric essaying. Each cultivated a public style, in their writings and pronouncements; each has a hermetic complexity concealed inside his most well-known thoughts. I want to look at Frye's cultivation of a muted manner, the spreading calm in the deliberately restrained rhetoric of his prose, and to engage McLuhan's lines of audacity in his aphorisms. McLuhan's books were sometimes called unreadable, which usually meant they violated the logical sequence of a traditional scholarly work. But if I am right that we should be understanding their missions to be both poetic and apocalyptic, then the gaze they turned on their subjects had to burn: McLuhan's sensibility burned through the data he gathered and arranged, Frye's burned into the notable unified Book he perceived.

I explored their battle of the books, the dispute between the orator and the author. Frye welcomed the essay tradition, working comfortably in it when he prepared texts for scholars and students. Some of his most arresting, synthetic work is found in books where he becomes the public intellectual, *The Educated Imagination* and *The Double Vision*. These remain in print. Surprisingly, Penguin Books published the difficult, uncommercial books *The Great Code* and *Words with Power* in companion paperback editions. They engage the Bible in those rich terms of mythic and metaphoric elaboration. They are religious, but not in any creedal way. The twin texts carry powerful subtexts of looking through the Bible towards the latent mythic story, the code of rise-fall, creation, exile, exodus and mission, and apocalypse. (I will read Frye's master narrative in my next chapter, in a bracketing with McLuhan's explorations in media ecology.) But I repeat, these books are not meant for browsing.

The editors at the Gingko Press in California bravely undertook the process of republishing major McLuhan texts that had slipped out of print. The most significant of these is, I contend, *The Book of Probes*, which presents his aphorisms against a crafty, imagistic backdrop of designs and photographs. McLuhan's texts after 1967 moved towards multimedia presentation, mixed modes. The riddling trickster needed co-authors to help sort out the twists of his quicksilver sensibility. His later texts are often called inaccessible and incoherent. I disagree. They show him delighting in spasm and vital appropriation. His was rapidly becoming a "found" philosophy of graffiti and imitative ad copy, showing a brazen cultural kleptomania, his mind borrowing and paraphrasing innumerable sources.

On the surface their styles seem inimical: Frye, the well-tempered scholar of literary theory; McLuhan, the mass sage sampling quotations from every conceivable site. Frye prized sequential theoretical prose, promoting long periodic paragraphs; McLuhan over time denied he had a theory and promoted an aesthetic of suddenness. Frye refined his essays into models of stabilizing wisdom; McLuhan relished disruption. McLuhan's bold declarations mask the ambiguity and ambivalences of what he felt and thought; Frye's nuanced ambivalences mask his audacious undertaking. I have often had the impression when engaging their tireless productivity that they hardly ever slept.

But writer-intellectuals who strive for awakenings in others must be constantly tuning and retuning their manner and methods. Imagination is the inner star, for Frye: the ideal reader is a solar figure, heating up and illuminating patterns and structures to achieve the higher world of premonition and prophecy. It is that higher world that is paradise, the realm we (or most people) want to find again. The electronic whorl is both light and mass, perspectives are always being reconfigured, for McLuhan: the cosmopolitan citizen experiences every time at once, and there is no absolute viewing point anywhere. Perspective is a shifting kaleidoscope.

I submit the two shared a passion for presentation and effect, for high verbal engagement, "the vocation of eloquence." They reflected deeply on how to take readers into spirited feuding and then back into contemplative, re-creative stillness, in the currency conditions of noise, of confusion, of distraction, of fragmented concentration and soft addictions to the inner trips of movies and TV, of infiltrating informational networks.

We have observed the oppositions and replies to one another in their writings and declarations. Frye said, likely in 1967, in *The "Third Book" Notebooks, 1964–1972*, "McLuhan has enormously expanded my book about the return of irony to myth" (145). Frye said in 1970, "The more I think about McLuhan's *obiter dicta*, the more the exact opposite of what he says seems to be true" (237). In his late collaborations, *Laws of Media* and *The Global Village*, McLuhan took to that scolding of his colleague over his blindness to an audience's role in shaping form and content. Nevertheless, Eric McLuhan and Frank Zingrone, in their preface to *Essential McLuhan* (1995), acknowledge Frye's presence: he was "the other pole in the intellectual field that configured world attention about Toronto during the last 40 years."[43] McLuhan and Frye may have been opposing magnetic poles in their thoughts and compositional techniques, but in their call and response, we find the shared passion for shapely, memorable articulations.

McLuhan anticipates hypertext in his verbal burlesques and encyclopedic references. A revaluation of the anti-books of the late 1960s and the 1970s – *Through the Vanishing Point, From Cliché to Archetype, Culture Is Our Business*, and *Take Today: The Executive as Dropout* – will reveal McLuhan at his most undaunted, in a hungry channeling, pushing his collaborators towards L=A=N=G=U=A=G=E-like interplays of image and quotation and marginalia and observation. In these works McLuhan becomes part parodist, part poet, part joyful plagiarist, part Orphic scientist exploring data, edging up to the cusp of a new kind of critical-mythic-ecological premise.

How do you reveal what is so new that it is likely wordless? His style was by then wholly guided by the immediacy, the mediumistic mesmerism, of dictation. (He showered ideas and aphorisms on visitors to the Coach House, who were often reduced to stammering replies.) The result was an evocation of, and a pronounced creative receptivity to, the "media echology," so he called it. The audile-tactile surround demanded an accelerated, compressed style and flexible forms. This processing required trust on the part of the catalyst. Nowhere else do we find McLuhan stuttering more adamantly towards the inexpressible than we do in the risky final pages of *Take Today*.

Let us look first at the punning title. It invokes possession (being taken), a film or TV clip (called a take), urgency (seize the moment), cliché ("Hey, like, see this"), a bruising fight (take that, today), memorable exempla (here are takes on the present), storming the barricades (take back the moment before it is too late), exhorted command (take hold of this book now), endurance (putting up with fear), theft (steal the moment), and transport (carry the moment away). I found twenty more different meanings for "take" in the *Oxford Synonym Finder.*

> **DO-IT-YOURSELF FATE**
> *Everyman as Finn Awake ...*
> ... There are managers galore for the global theater ...
> New treasures for all ...
> "To borrow,
> To burrow,
> To barrow."
> H.C.E.
> with
> KEYS
> TO
> GIVEN (295)

Amusement and invention mingle here. Obscure allusion and subversion cross over in teasing, jagged forays into the white noise of typographic space. He absorbs neologisms from the *Wake.* It is McLuhan's later texts, like this one, that have had the greatest influence on the mixed modes and exploratory performance essays of Jean Baudrillard, John Cage, Camille Paglia, and Arthur and MariLouise Kroker and on the installation art of Jenny Holzer.

Truly one of the most arresting enterprises we could undertake in reading McLuhan is to read his books backwards: then we could travel from the blanks and concerns for ESP and the global soul and the sampling and puns, back to his first published essay on Chesterton, "Practical Mystic." If we shift in our readings from *The Book of Probes* to his PhD thesis, then the trajectory would be hauntingly clear: he emerged from his literary base, and in rapid time, overrun by urgency, and by the governing insight that the printed word was about to become obsolete in the collectivities of information discharge, he imploded into white noise. His faith grounded him, but his quickened insights accelerated his vision into the hypertexts of his last years. I submit that McLuhan's sensitivities were so acute that he could actually sense the fears and ecstasies, something in electricity that was strangely perceptive, or carrying a kind of embryonic consciousness, the mind extending into the new technologies, sometimes becoming auto-destructive, like a machine with its ignition button stuck in On or *om.*

In the "Spirit and Symbol" chapter of *Words with Power* Frye goes to the outer edge of essaying, to what I call oracular criticism. He had, in earlier pages of his summa, said that the Bible is "a work of literature plus" (6). He looked for ways to reach his readers, a breaking free from theoretical structuring into direct communiqué, the furore of ecstatic words. His notebooks shatter genres. But he did not guide the notations into publication. They should be reviewed in terms of editorial interventions, and therefore in a ghostly, posthumous collaboration with intrepid scholars.

Frye wrote *Words with Power* knowing that death was close. In the "Spirit and Symbol" pages of the book he approaches "the mysterious borderlands between the poetic and the kerygmatic" (111). We find Frye reflecting on how some maddened writers move from description and commentary to oracular utterance, the passion that penetrates defences, creating intimate channels of response. Ironically, he had expressed reservations about the oracular mode in *The Modern Century*. Yet he had long battled with divergent energies: his genius for aphorism in his notebooks, and what could be the non-verbal (expression beyond text). In a fashion we are by now familiar with in Frye's writings, he places his germane revisionary reflection in the middle of the chapter. "According to Vico, communication from an unknown world began with a thunderclap ... This symbol is incorporated into Joyce's *Finnegans Wake*" (112). The apocalyptic is compounded with the critical: "Eliot later spoke of wanting to go beyond poetry in the *Quartets*, and Pound expanded – exploded would perhaps be a better word – into even broader dimensions" (115). There are moments where Frye pushes towards turning essaying into a vehicle for the meta-literary. His fuses reference, allusion, paraphrase, commentary, metaphor, compressed imagery, and analogy until they reach an alchemical heat in another chapter, "First Variation: The Mountain." In the following Frye speaks of tower analogues – his lifelong obsession with the rise-fall coding in literature and, by extension, in our imaginative lives. Associations fire quickly. His analogical furore seems to burn up his technical ability, leaving him uncharacteristically close to being speechless:

> The rising tower, then, soon turns into the falling tower, with its attendant confusion of tongues, hence Babel is really a cyclical symbol, an example of the rising and falling of great kingdoms that forms a kind of counterpoint to Biblical history ... In *Finnegans Wake*, after Finnegan has fallen off his

ladder, he falls into the sleep of history, which moves in the cyclical rotation indicated by one of Joyce's chief mentors, Vico. This turning cycle, which includes awakening and rebirth but never a climb up the original ladder again, is a kind of parody which encircles the whole book, as the sentence left unfinished on the last page is continued on the first. In Yeats too there is a cyclical movement in history, a sequence of alternating "primary" and "antithetical" periods, one democratic and the other heroic in tendency. In the Tarot pack of cards ... the wheel of fortune and the falling towers are featured, and both are referred to in *The Waste Land* ... The closed cycle, the Tower of Babel built and abandoned innumerable times, is traditionally symbolized by the *ouroboros*, the serpent with its tail in its mouth. The *ouroboros* – and closed circles generally – is sometimes said to be an emblem of eternity ... if the *ouroboros* is actually feeding on itself, it is presumably a spiral narrowing into nothingness. I am aware that ... the circular structure of the benzene molecule was inspired by a dream of the *ouroboros*, just as I am aware that the DNA molecule has affinities with a double spiral. But I am not sure just what to do with these analogies.

(156–7)

Frye goes on to feed his imaginative flame with Jacob's ladder, angels, Dylan Thomas, prophetic parables from the New Testament, the Incarnation, reaching upwards towards "Ladders, temples, mountains, world-trees ... now all images of a verbal revolution." Images begin to break free from argument. His rage for a mystic order takes place in a mere two pages.

The crescendo of images shows Frye's mind on the brink of the unlimited. It shows a mind dizzied by the vertigo of infinite association. McLuhan's break-up of sentences into spasms is comparable to Frye's new mode of marking on the page, "a structural model of intensified consciousness" (165). These pages express analogy plus. Like McLuhan (struggling with illnesses at the time of his last dictations), Frye's late-life urgencies possessed his style: the images found scattered in the world have melded with the symbols rooted in our imagination. Frye's gloss on this interpenetration comes in a notebook entry written during the composition of *Words with Power*: "Nothing is discovered out there that isn't in some sense already here."[44] Note in Frye's pages the allusions to the symbolic patterns of the *Wake*.

When discussing *The Critical Path*, the always helpful A.C. Hamilton remarks on Frye's use of the demotic (conversational style highlighted by verbal elaboration and layering) and the hieratic (or oracular).

Hamilton's insights are apposite because they elucidate the moments in *Words with Power* when Frye's prose chafes against the limitations of diction and syntax, burning in an upward flame towards the lyrical and the inexpressible, the place outside the black marks and white spaces of print. Hamilton could be speaking of McLuhan when he says,

> The high demotic style brings "a recognition of something like verbal truth," because it places the literary work within literature as a whole; the high hieratic style brings "a recognition of something like verbal beauty" … because it places the reader at the centre of the verbal universe. Hence Frye claims that the high demotic style "travels outward from the imaginative into the 'real' world," while in the high hieratic style "what we read suddenly becomes a focus of our whole literary experience and imaginative life."
>
> (*Northrop Frye: Anatomy of His Criticism*, 170)

Their awakenings to what is beyond text must stir awakenings in us. These examples from their late works reveal an extreme intellectual and sensory pressure applied on words and sentences, on fragments and intimations, on lines of analogy and argument, on shifts in voice. It is as if the printed page cannot bear what they want to impress on it. The two were firing themselves up towards more than words can say. These passages disclose deep stylistic and formal aspirations: they wanted to break directly into catching the traces of apocalypse, with the (paradoxical) freedom to still reflect on this transcendence through words.

The *Wake* was one of the essential works that provided them with myths by which they could speak and teach. The metaphors are of waking (surfing on tidal waves of change) and awakening (to the transcendent, radiant dreamland incarnated in literature). They were offering something greater than metaphor: they were mustering minds, towards the dream that could re-create the world, to the world's rapidly altering state. It is taking time to realize the power in their late writings and assertions. We are slowly waking up to their poetics and style, the range of two literary critics who aspired to the prophetic.[45]

Now Do Without Us

They claimed that there should be no followers. And for all their need to establish vortices of thought at the University of Toronto and promote the Toronto School of Communication Theory (an invisible school of the mind, a centre without walls), they resisted being blatantly apostolic. Charismatic people are prone to cult followings; but they tried to put these off.

McLuhan said, in an interview published in *McLuhan: Hot & Cool* (1967),

> You can be quite sure that if there are going to be McLuhanites, I am not going to be one of them. I know that anyone who learns anything will learn it slightly askew. I can imagine that having disciples would become a very great bother.[46]

At times it seems McLuhan sets out to willfully evade the reader. His divergences from "sense," his obscurities, his mosaics of citations, his ellipses, and his denial of theoretical consistency are a strategy to accomplish what he describes in the comment above. His cavalier attitude towards fact-checking could be attributed to a strategic denial of disciples. I noted earlier how his texts are laced with misquotations. Some of his fiercest critics spend chapters simply listing these.[47] Texts that are not authoritative cannot be used for dogma or codification. Allusions can set up a realm of echoes; but no one can hold on to an echo. (And it is hard to be a follower of someone who is moving very fast.)

Aphorisms resist tidy theorizing. McLuhan's revisions of others' quotations must throw the finality of any statement into doubt. They represent intellectual knowledge in terms of re-creative poetics, where error has a place. This also raises the point I have been making that McLuhan's aphorisms are artefacts in themselves. We can luxuriate in their expressive ingenuity.

His insistence that his work was "satirical" points to deliberate toying with audience reaction. All is put-on and play in the global theatre. Talking nonsense has a ritual role. "I satirize at all times," he said in a chastening 1971 letter to William Kuhns, "and my hyperboles are as nothing compared to the events to which they refer." In the same letter to Kuhns he testily explains his use of error: "I would be grateful to you if could give me any examples where I have *mis-stated* any fact whatever. My canvasses are surrealist, and to call them 'theories' is to miss my satirical intent altogether. As you will find in my literary essays, I can write the ordinary kind of rationalistic prose any time I choose to do so. You are in great need of some intense training in perception in the arts" (*Letters*, 448). More than an admirer of McLuhan's work, Kuhns was an enthusiast. McLuhan's reply was intended to ward him off.

I established how McLuhan needed collaborators. But this can be understood too in terms of a resistance to founding a cult philosophy to which he alone held the key. Quixotically, McLuhan's style is utterly personal. His aphorisms are so original that they earned him a designation in the French dictionary: *McLuhanisme*. His seeming disappearance behind the impersonality of the aphorism – he hardly ever uses an "I" in them – became emblematic. McLuhan claimed that he preferred conversation and collaboration (and clowning and controversy), and yet he wrote and spoke with a rare trust and presence that gave him the aura of a spiritual authority.

Still no self-avowed satirist or shape-shifting fool can afford to have uncritical disciples. Moreover, inspired states and deranged episodes may mirror one another. One way or another, if the shape-shifter pursues new perception, it may sometimes appear that he or she is out of his or her mind. Borderlines collapse or vanish. Even your body might feel permeable. Offense and outrage follow. Altered states of consciousness, McLuhan intuited, come about with the use of new technologies, and especially with the electronica that are extensions of our own power, our brainwaves radically changing in the swelter of the interactions.

Satire demands that audiences shape-shift too. The members of the audience, McLuhan's ground, must think and feel for themselves: provocation implies that we must rise to voice and then finally transcend the initial provocation (the First Nations people magically call this a rising to "sacred idiocy"). "User is content" is (again) the attendant aphorism to "the medium is the message." It directs us towards understanding how the forms of Nature and technology find meaning through the mental exercise of the user. McLuhan's aphorisms are prods. But he knew that his strategies did not always break through to recognition and re-creation. His producers sometimes became mere consumers. In one of his sharpest attacks on why there should be no McLuhanites (or McLuhanatics), he says in a 1974 letter to Marshall Fishwick,

> One major misunderstanding concerns my "style" which happens to be a very *good* style for getting attention. As for *understanding*, that depends entirely upon the reader. The user is always the content, and the user is often very evasive, or very stupid.
>
> (*Letters*, 505)

He was revising Zarathustra's injunction, "Now do without me," into his own cautionary injunction, "The user will always do without me."

Nevertheless, I noted before how in later years at the Centre for Culture and Technology, McLuhan did encourage some cultishness. That increasing isolation he experienced, with his books out of print and the celebrity spotlight far less intense, led him to need a supportive circle of followers. The gregarious McLuhan needed companionship. But this amazing detail has struck me over the years since I was in that last class of six students: I never saw McLuhan write anything. He talked; others noted down what he said. Paper accumulated on his desks; file folders began to bulge. He was constantly expounding aphorisms, spinning witty remarks, and I wrote them down too. But I never saw him with a pen in hand.

Frye also tried to resist the ardour of his followers. In spite of a lifetime devoted to developing pedagogical techniques, to honing curricula, he was careful about letting his readers and students find their own pathways through the labyrinth. He sometimes expressed a sense that his work was satiric – though I take his meaning to be very different from what McLuhan intended. In the fourth essay of the *Anatomy*, "Theory of Genres," Frye writes of the conceptual difficulty in identifying what certain literary works may be. He recommends "Mennipean satire" for "fictions" by "Petronius, Apuleuis, Rabelais, Swift, and Voltaire." We may include those unclassifiable fictions by Joyce and Aldous Huxley *(Brave New World)*. The important point is Frye's identification of satire with anatomy. In an understated, indirectly revealing passage, Frye refers to Burton's *The Anatomy of Melancholy*:

> Here human society is studied in terms of the intellectual pattern provided by the conception of melancholy, a symposium of books replaces dialogue ... The word "anatomy" in Burton's title means a dissection or analysis, and expresses very accurately the intellectualized approach of his form. We may as well adopt it as a convenient name to replace the cumbersome and in modern times rather misleading "Mennipean satire."
>
> (308, 312)

In the Renaissance understanding of the word, "melancholy" suggests late-night readings in silence. It invokes sublime aloneness: the inwardness of contemplation, the sanctity of the singular mind. Melancholy (not a synonym for bipolar depression) connotes the saturnalian mood. The inward temper is developed in the schooling of surrounding darkness and flickering light. Solitary time is when devoted students proclaim silence, study, leisure, and ease and direct their minds to meditations on words and images, preparing their receptivity for a flow of intuitions. Inspiration comes when the senses are stirred into wakefulness; technique is the courting and honing of skill.

The *Penseroso* mood evokes a temper (or humour) that combines the wilderness voice of Blake with the introversion of Emily Dickinson. Frye's evocation of melancholy is partly an apologia for his shyness in crowds and the powerful aspirations of his work. He implies that his work is meant to be an exhaustive and exhausting synoptic enterprise, assembling and detailing intellectual structures in literary criticism and then doing so in a symposium of books (that "*replaces dialogue*"; emphasis mine), which we see in the encyclopedic range of the *Anatomy*.[48]

Anatomy is another word, in Frye's cloaked lexicon, for summa, the most unclassifiable and arcane of genres. A summa may clear the view of criticism for others. But it remains highly speculative, and therefore singular. Frye's theorizing is so allusively far-reaching that it appears to take him to the rim of theory, towards its limitations. The urge to totalize must reverse into the awareness that while theory lends intensity to the expanding eye, it can never take in everything. Essaying is provisional. Frye acknowledges this by calling the closing chapters of his *Anatomy* "tentative."

And yet a summa is implicitly autobiographical. It must be, because the author is arranging his subjects according to the passions of his eye. But in the *Anatomy*, the seer-critic is giving voice to what is other: this is Frye's rebirth in the guise of the literary magus, welding together seemingly unrelated works through the magic of his perceptions. The goal is utopian: cultural awareness and salvation through books. Hence the pattern of fours in his compendium. Literature is made out of earlier literature; all books develop into one master narrative, which is the apocalypse of a cosmic human consciousness; people cannot live nakedly in Nature but in and through the dream structures of the imagining: in the imagination there are types and images, emblazoned with transcendent force.

Although Frye's impact on literary studies of the 1950s and 1960s was enormous, his diminished influence was, I believe, inevitable. His imprint on theory marks him as an original, but it is as if we find ourselves at times quietly looking over his shoulder at how he is organizing his readings. (He seldom reads a poem with any line-by-line closeness; he is much more interested in mythopoetic patterns.) *Verum factum*: Frye was creating his foundations for viewing the poetic principle, truths in process. Such an illuminating originality generates agreement and opposition in equal measure.

The melancholic temperament selects its own society. Here is an association: Giorgio de Chirico's 1919 painting "Hermetic Melancholy" mysteriously depicts a philosopher's face gazing down darkly, sorrowfully, through a window into a shadowed room. In the room there is an open box (a coffin? a symbol of resurrection?) and a blue rod (a divining staff?). This haunting painting leaves impressions of secretive concerns; it is an alchemist's space encoded with exquisite enigmas. Night has come. But the night holds no terrors. It is welcomed, because it speaks of the solitude that is necessary for the pursuit of the arcane arts. The painting recalls for me Frye's pensive temper and love of mystery. In "Expanding Eyes," in *Spiritus Mundi: Essays on Literature, Myth, and Society* (1976), Frye tactfully explains why there should be and can be no disciples:

> The sense of being something of a loner has always been in any case rather exceptionally true of me, with my introverted temperament, indolent habits and Canadian nationality ... I have had some influence, I know, but I neither want nor trust disciples, at least as that term is generally understood. I should be horrified to hear of anyone proposing to make his own work revolve around mine, unless I were sure that he meant a genuine freedom for him. And if I have no disciples I have no school. I think I have found a trail, and all I can do is to keep sniffing along it until either scent or nose fails me.[49]

He was revising Zarathustra's injunction to say, "I follow my own path. Watch along if you wish."

But in the composition of a summa there are strange contradictory urges. A summa ends an epoch: it reviews and summarizes, but it also ushers in new thought. It carries the imperative of the inspired solitary who wants to overcome categorization, and yet its author cultivates categories and lists. A summa emerges from a private reading of a vast number of books, and it is a proclamation to a public: it is part of the democratic *paideuma*, the desire to enlighten through education. In a summa a writer seeds his or her personal destiny; but the seer steps forward to map for others the shape of the identity quest.

Clearly, Frye and McLuhan disagreed on the definition of satire. To McLuhan, satire was directed at audience awareness; it was a prod, a jabbing outwards. To Frye, satire is that unclassifiable hybrid of various sources, themes, structures, and symbols: the open genre that excludes nothing. Yet in spite of their disagreement on the definitions, the complementarity of the McLuhan-Frye matrix holds: they each used satire, but through a mirroring comprehension of what the word can mean.

They claimed scrupulousness in eluding cultishness. Nevertheless, the four biographies confirm how devotees lined up. Pride has no end. McLuhan and Frye were ambitious enough to have that fierce pride of spiritual and intellectual destiny, tracing pathways they knew were unique to their sensibilities. Yet the hearer and the seer had to know that what they made was incomplete. All literary structures and visions are finally fragmentary. In ecstatic moments they may have thought that they had found the keys and the laws, but in humble moments they must have realized that there is meaning beyond everyone's sentences, always ahead of articulation. If they were elusive, then so is what they pursued.

When I was their student, Eliot's *Four Quartets* was the one literary work that appeared on both of their lists in those graduate seminars of the late 1970s. In these elegies Eliot reminds us how experiences may deceive and delude us, how words can elude us. Eliot writes in "East Coker,"

> ... and every attempt
> Is a wholly new start, and a different kind of failure
> Because one has only learnt to get the better of words
> For the thing one no longer has to say.
> (21-2)

If there is no end to ambitious pride, and to the complexities of consciousness and personality, then there can be (or should be?) no end to humility. This is not the humility of demurring modesty, a Uriah Heep–like obsequiousness. It is the sense that you are always at the beginning. All learning is provisional. We remember how McLuhan and Frye remained devout all their lives, no matter how they may have masked that faith. So they tempered apocalyptic ambitions by their trust in their respective Catholic and Protestant devotions. Literature was after all only one part of their activities: McLuhan had his large family, Frye his love for Helen; each attended prayer times at chapels. I cite all this to remind myself how humility came to them through an acknowledgment of spiritual ground and domesticity: they were not entirely unhinged in their lives by their lofty conceptual thoughts or wildfire perceptions.

Let us meditate on the single candle of solitary intelligence that Bloom eloquently describes in his foreword to *Anatomy of Criticism*. The single candle image likely retrieves 2 Esdras 14:25 from the Apocrypha, when God speaks to Ezra to "come hither" so that He may "light a candle of understanding in thine heart." Proverbs 9:10 exalts understanding, one of the motifs of wisdom. A candle is an image of singularity, its flicker emblematic of receptivity and vulnerability. Transitory light speaks to aspiration – and to the awakening of sensuality. "To burn with a gemlike flame": Walter Pater's imperative became a motto for modernism. But this image of pure inspiration and aesthetic splendor must be tempered by the wisdom of knowing that in the flicker comes sorrow: the slants of isolation and transience. A darkness sometimes seems to be waiting for the moment when it can engulf and snuff out a flame.

Surely the perception of implacable darkness – of ignorance, limitation, exclusion, blankness, brutality, and injustice, of loneliness and incapacity – is meant to preserve humility too. These remind you of boundaries and of the unknown: they speak to the fragility of each flame. No flame is like another; and no flame lasts, we know. In Buddhist thought, the flame of a candle is a metaphor for the proof of the successive transformations of the soul. The base is our roots in the earth, the wick is our spirit, the flame is consciousness, the smoke the soul teeming into the invisible.

A flame continues to burn, offering warmth in legacies when we revisit our mentors and what we have learned from them and loved in them. I can attest to their affability and to their receptivity (most of the time) to questions. And to their moments of humility: they would on occasions acknowledge how they lacked wisdom on some subjects. I am now convinced this is why McLuhan had collaborators, why Frye invited students to speak to him after class.

They were learning from us.

The Enigma of Numbers

I offer here a last reflection on their harmonies. I do so by returning to the role of fours in their thought and work. Their radical declarations came in the quartet of opening, disclosure, inspiration, and direction. They dealt in fours to form them into ecstatic and meditative quadrants. Both followed Blake's constant turning to the fourfold. But the fourfolding was not merely poetic gloss, a concentrating of numeric force. The pattern of fours is what mystics call the ratios of sacred learning: the silence of reflection, the action of writing and speaking, the observation of changing details, and the quest for grace (another word for understanding). It is all this that must be passed on, through the elder to the student.

The essence of literature for Frye is found in the romance-quest and in its variations of "know thy self." To McLuhan all things in Nature and super-Nature interpenetrate and interact. To both, the literary cosmos and the media work in fields of complementarity. This is not alienation – estranged force: it is the reconstitution of wholeness, processes in yin-yang patterns; breakdown and breakthrough are simultaneous. And to both, the instrument of mind is alchemical because what we process and experience is moved by our longing to communicate: we need the call-and-response antiphony to prosper.

McLuhan and Frye shared the awareness they found in their studies: this was the hermetic message, what must be revealed from the stone of our materials. All levels of knowledge and experience can be perceived to be operating harmoniously. To know this grants us some spiritual freedom: we turn into a thought, and a thought moves into atmospheres, into lives, like the Spirit. There is the diachronic, lineal pattern of existential engagement (history, fact); and there is the synchronic simultaneous pattern of imagination (intuition, poetry). In the Torah, knowledge of the levels is called *Pardes* – roughly, "paradise." In Christian theology – Catholic and Protestant – this awareness is called "The Way." In the Christian mythology that deeply informed their minds the moment when knowledge and experience intersect is represented by the cruciform.

Frye visualizes the cruciform, with "some 'audio-visual aids,'" in a passage from *T.S. Eliot: An Introduction*. This passage shows his first use of the diachronic-synchronic metaphor (the vertical-horizontal pattern), which he will call the *axis mundi*, after Yeats. He outlines the form that will express the visionary structure of *Four Quartets*. Towards the end, note how Frye manages – in a considerable leap, itself an act of imagination – to unite the conservative Eliot with the radical Blake:

> Draw a horizontal line on a page, then a vertical line of the same length cutting it in two and forming a cross, then a circle of which these lines are diameters, then a smaller circle inside the same centre. The horizontal line is clock time, the Heraclitean flux, the river into which no one steps twice. The vertical line is the presence of God descending into time, and crossing it at the Incarnation, forming the "still point of the turning world." The top and the bottom of the vertical line represent the goals of the way up and

the way down, though we cannot show that they are the same point in two dimensions. The top and bottom halves of the larger circle are the visions of plentitude and of vacancy respectively; the top and bottom halves of the smaller circle are the world of the rose-garden and ... the subway, innocence and experience.[50]

In *The Book of Probes* McLuhan adapts the lineal-simultaneous pattern to refer to how he became aware of the effects of electricity on society and culture:

My method is vertical rather than horizontal also the scenery does not change but the texture does.

(327)

In his gnomic way, he invokes the presence of the cruciform in his methods and apprehensions too. McLuhan and Frye acknowledged that the more we read into a word, the more we increase the potencies of the word. We extend text (and the Text) by adding textures. They shared the understanding that mysteries hide in plain sight.

The patterning of fours rooted them, the number like a numinous encryption: four essays in *Anatomy*; fourfold chaptering in *Words with Power*; the tetrads in McLuhan's *Laws of Media*, *The Global Village*, and *The Book of Probes*. While McLuhan used the five-part order of rhetoric in some essays to lend cohesive power to his pronouncements (A.E.I.O.U.: the five letters correspond with a sequence of address to the reader: "Art Education I Owe You"; also, all Shakespearean plays have five-part structures), this should not deflect us from recognizing the centrality of fours to him.

In *Cosmic Media*, Marchessault affirms the contemplative magic of the fours in McLuhan's "long line of creative intellectual probes." It begins in his work on the medieval trivium and quadrivium curricula in his PhD dissertation and culminates in *Laws of Media*. I find her argument strikingly convincing. She proposes that McLuhan's motive was to counter the restrictive model of the triad; hence in his mind "the book-anti-book-synbook structure of the Hegelian and Marxist dialectic" (223–4). To McLuhan a three-part system leads to paralyzing stasis. A tripartite structure of departure, initiation, and return leads to recurrence, not to revelation and therefore to the possibility of more openings. Fourfold motion ensures dynamic process, eternal translations into multidimensional thought. There is no ending in the tetrad. Each part unfolds into another. The compassing of the fours leads to hermeneutics, therefore reviving the four levels of simultaneous readings and re-creation. Arguably, the tetrads are a multidimensional amplification of analogical thinking, which is the key to divining, the practice of conceiving poetically, in infinite associations. The openness is the democratic apocalypse: we may each learn how to accomplish it. The connections Marchessault makes with Vico's cyclical vision of history – and with crises of understanding, the powers of perception, and especially with teaching – are especially pertinent; her connections link with this book.

In *Anatomy of His Criticism*, Hamilton illustrates the power of the organizational focus (the intensity) that comes from tetradic principles. In a mimetic homage, he shapes his argument around the compass of fours. He absorbs numerology because through the just placement of numbers there will be reverberations, chords. Hamilton outlines Frye's critical tenets, and by inference, his sense of cosmic meaningfulness, by presenting his own keynote paraphrases (192–4). First, Hamilton proposes the power of romance to shape literature into the secular scripture. (He overlooks how Frye's intentions are heretical: myth and metaphors organize religious language; therefore religion for him is misinterpreted poetry.) Second, reading a literary work is a co-creative act. (I have proposed that Frye's notion of reading is revisionary and thus it carries a vocational imperative.) Third, all verbal discourses combine to inform the mythological universe. (This is Frye's assuming of Mallarmé's pan-literary cosmos: every book becoming one, which we enlarge through composition and commentary.) Fourth, literature lightens us, nudging us towards a keen citizenship, because we could now be emboldened by vision. (Frye's Pentecostal intent is to turn us into realizing visionaries, spiritual realists, practical dreamers, insightful pupils of the Spirit.)

Consciousness rises and falls: these are the changeling phases of our experiences. Education, deep reading, are ways of comprehending the elevating patterns. Fourfolding is cubist: embracing complexity, many sides at once. The truest revolution comes in revelation, when we abandon encrusted thoughts and cross through dead structures, into the air that inspirits us, becoming liquid fire, in the empyrean of cognition and tuition. Thus we leave the literalist horrors of fundamentalism far, far behind. Enlightenment then means living in the joy of being and even non-being. Consciousness is the capacity to make connections: and though illumination is not always peaceful, study and reflection may bring the visible fragments of the Spirit into incarnations of welcome and serenity.

They knew modernity confronts us with crises. The origin of the word "crisis" links, again, with coming to a crossroads. But when we break through to prophetic understanding, then we enter the vibrant here. This is likely why McLuhan's essential aphorisms are cast in the present tense. They are structured with ambiguous nouns linked by the perpetual now of "is." The "is" becomes both linking verb and proclamation. Frye uses the "is" construction in his *kerygma* pronouncements. In McLuhan's perception of the simultaneity and instantaneousness of the global theatre, there is a sharing of minds and sensibilities in persistent epiphanies. In Frye's idea of the critic-seer, and in his propositions about the educated imagination, there is the possibility that book and reader, spirit and word, can rise together and converge in the mythic present. The last sentences of Frye's *The Double Vision* approach this: "There is nothing so unique about death as such, where we may be too distracted by illness or sunk in senility to have much identity at all. In the double vision of a spiritual and a physical world simultaneously present, every moment we have lived through, we have also died out of into another order. Our life in the resurrection is already here, and waiting to be recognized" (85). In *Take Today* McLuhan exuberantly expresses a similar perception: "Tomorrow is our permanent address" (224).

I conclude with two illuminating incidents: one comes from the Frye archives, the other from interviews with Corinne McLuhan. The first is from a 2001 recollection by the noted scholar David Staines. I disagree with the passage where Staines claims that Frye became less religious in later years. The publication of what I call Frye's spiritual tetralogy – *The Great Code*, *Words with Power*, *The Double Vision*, and the notebook volume *Architecture of the Spiritual World* – spells out a thematic spiritual quest contrary to what Staines asserts. But we should again make the distinction between orthodoxy and private spirituality, Catholic and dissenter. Still here is Staines's vivid and sympathetic recollection, relayed through Dan Schick's recording:

> Staines ... reflected on the Canadian literary critic Northrop Frye, who had a complex professional relationship with McLuhan. While they personally shared many beliefs and values, career success did not always come at the same time. Frye's success was celebrated in the 1970s while McLuhan's work was becoming undervalued. Frye, who was a United Church minister, also became less religious over the years, creating another source of tension.

Staines remembered walking through the University of Toronto campus with McLuhan from the Catholic St. Michael's College past Frye's Victoria College where he would joke "the truth shall make you Frye." But there was deep respect between the two men and Frye, especially early in his career, looked to McLuhan for inspiration. After McLuhan died, Frye said to Corinne McLuhan, "I always wanted to be closer to Marshall than I was."

(quoted in Frye Archives, 32)

In 2005, I asked Corinne McLuhan about the legendary friction between Frye and her husband. Our conversation took place in the quiet dining room at the McLuhan home in Wychwood Park. The frail Corinne, then in her nineties, was still capable of sharp response. She waved her hand airily, as if dismissing the rumours. She said, in the clear tone of her Texan drawl, "Norrie was always very kind to me. And to *Marshall*." Then she became thoughtful, her look a little perplexed. "But you know," she sighed, "how *Marshall* could be, sometimes."[51]

Let us see now what happens when we meld McLuhan's percepts with Frye's concepts. Can there be an alchemy between the hearer and the seer? Imagine what configurations may come in a synergy of media ecology – the surround is the message – and the Great Code story of creation, fall, exodus, and apocalypse.

We have become students of their inspirations. Let us adapt them for the purpose of fusion. They were crisis thinkers: and it sometimes seems like we are hazing out sunlight and replacing it with a global city-night where we have trouble seeing the stars, and because we are still in the midst of oppressions and depressions, often falling upwards and downwards with no apparent horizon and no bottom, we should move quickly along in their wake, their voices and presences marking a way ahead.

5
Alchemy: Synergy in the Thinking of McLuhan and Frye

Radical Propositions

What happens if we combine "the medium is the message" with the Great Code? I want to propose a new synergic premise for the visionary-seer tradition. Our technologized milieu is alive, massaging us into new, unfamiliar shapes. The media surround often seems more chaos than cosmos. But a fool does not see the same PC that a wise soul may see. Media dynamism needs a story. The Great Code, in Frye's conception, is the story we are telling in infinite variations. It is the tale of how we came to be lost and of how we may come to be found again. I propose this synergy, where we are aware of our media environment and come to recognize the personal myth we each must tell during our quest for value and meaning.

Communication becoming communion: this is the bridge between McLuhan and Frye. Their sense of necessity was not only intellectual; it was a powerful longing. They were moved by maelstroms and mazes, by the desire to ascend and sometimes to descend the ladders of perception. Heightened consciousness, expanding eyes: they take us to revelatory cusps where we are asked to look up, look down, listen deeply, touch the pulse in the flow of our time. The utopian premise in their work emerges in their desire to restore radical innocence to perception and to readings (comprehending anew), and to bring a laughter that is from delight and not from cruelty or condescension. The spiritual Jerusalem breaks through into life when we recharge our spirits, and the tinges of paradise seep through our words. Paradise is where exuberance is always beautiful.

Intercommunion is a key to McLuhan and Frye. One of McLuhan's most intriguing legacies is his apprehension that we each possess a natural clairvoyance through electronic extension and convergence. Telepathic awareness develops when the media confers searing instantaneous changes in perception and consciousness. You switch on your PC and click to the world news: instantly you are sent to the Middle East or to Washington: you see faces of politicians and celebrities that are now so familiar they are inescapable to you. You blog opinions, you scan the words and emoticons of people you will likely never meet. In *The Book of Probes* McLuhan says, "Today man has no physical body. He is translated into information, or an image ... There are no connections in resonant space. There are only interfaces and metamorphoses" (92, 74). What once seemed occult and esoteric, remote from everyday life, is now a part of our technological make-up, our wiring into the electronic forms. Poetics has become our essential practice in the worldwide poem (the web) we are making.

Frye's finest realization is his identification of the perpetual allegory at the heart of literature. He recognizes that the imagination is made of symbols and profound structures. The principle of identity is the Great Code, the story of human struggle and apocalypse. There are inklings of the narrative structure in *Fearful Symmetry*, but Frye makes them manifest, strangely enough, in the almost-forgotten *T.S. Eliot*, one of his least successful works, critically or commercially. (It has been long out of print.) There we find his original evocation of the romance-quest cycle that will define his writings to come. His voicing of the code is one of his contributions to understanding the evolutionary edges of darkness and light. He says,

> The archetype of this cycle is the Bible, which begins with the story of man in a garden. Man then falls into a wilderness or waste land, and into a still deeper chaos symbolized by a flood. At the end of time he is restored to his garden, and to the tree and water of life that he lost with it. But by that time the garden has become a city as well, a fiery city glowing with gold and precious stones, so that the tree of life (symbolized in Dante by a rose) is a tree in which "the fire and the rose are one."
>
> (79)

Communication is the struggle for comprehension, miscommunication another breakdown that could (possibly) be a breakthrough. McLuhan insisted that communication was not mere transmission, agency from one point to another. It is participation and feedback, echoing and reverberation. It is feed-forward: probe and propulsion into response and revision, into remaking and extension. Frye taught that communication is contact with ideas and symbols, all the literary typologies, and with the past in those books where the dead come alive again, their voices tongued with inspirational fire.

We have looked at how McLuhan became a galvanizing and polarizing symbol in the media celebrity circles he courted. He carried within himself the disruptive energies of the 1960s and 1970s; he was bound to the gnawing spirit of the times. His stenographic style is symptomatic of his prophetic stance: everything must be said immediately. Frye evaded that sort of sacrificial fame. But there was in his writings a message to fellow readers, a signal call. In book after book and in his compressed notebook writings, he wrote out of intimations that it was time to forge the divine comedy of criticism. This was not mere egoistic pride (though it was that too): it came from his knowledge that a summa was essential. A summing up, or anatomy, is a vast gathering, an imperative recalling. Something was in danger of slipping away.

I posit that both men intuited the dawning iLiteracy. McLuhan called Frye "the literal man" in *From Cliché to Archetype* in scornful bewilderment: how could illustrious Frye miss the shifting ground of his culture? He did not miss it. His essays compose a corpus of resistance against the waves of forgetting and ignorance that often disturb iLiteracy. In the combination of shyness and gall that typify his writing, his rhetoric was, and is, an indirect counterpoint, even a counter-charge, to the diminishing importance of literary communications in the global theatre.

~~~

If we accept the premise that McLuhan and Frye put communication and communion at the heart of their enterprise, then we must look at how miscommunication looms. Mass communications can mean intercommunion, but it can mean weight and pressure – excess and saturation. Breakthrough can become another pretext for breakdown. Patterns may shatter into fragments. And fragmentation, like specialization, is the beginning of isolation.

"These fragments I have shored against my ruins," Eliot's quester-knight muses on the dry shore of the arid plains in the last stanza of the 1922 version of "What the Thunder Said." The lyric fascinated Frye. He mused on it in his classroom discussions. McLuhan uttered it obsessively.[1] It must have spoken to his urgencies, his spasmodic sense of isolation. The Magnetic City could become a frantic, violent storm centre. In Frye's later years the self-defined solitary reader said to Cayley that he belonged with McLuhan and Innis in the Toronto School of Communication Theory. This insight was a question of redefinition and pattern recognition. Utopia can reverse, in the secular mirror, into inferno. The

Alchemy: Synergy in the Thinking of McLuhan and Frye

McLuhan-Frye matrix of conflict and harmony was a necessary way of shoring themselves up against ruins of thrown-ness and upheaval, against infernos and cyclones. They were each other's guides, at times. Agitation is still companionship, of a kind.

~~~

Alchemy and synergy: to comprehend the shape of the McLuhan-Frye recombination, we should turn from their errant communications to communion, a compounding – and transubstantiation – of intellectual spirits. What comes in a synergy and alchemy of the two? Complementarities mean both/and, not either/or. In my examination of the McLuhan-Frye premises there is obvious evidence of their exploratory and experimental spirits. Let us see what happens in the proposal of alchemy when we mix the two together.

To McLuhan conditions of mixing inform the electric ground of the global Magnetic City. In *Take Today* McLuhan says we live in "the processes of ECO-land, all gaps become prime sources of discovery ... Nothing has its meaning alone ... A note alone is not music ... The 'meaning of meaning' is relationship. When young activists harp on 'relevance,' they are asking for interface or the abrasion of dialogue; they are Eco-sounding to discover where *it's at* ... Truth is not matching. It is neither label nor a 'mental reflection.' It is something we make it the encounter with a world that is making us" (3).

In electric fields no juncture is permanent. *Verum factum* exists in our day-to-day reality through the power of digital technology to place us everywhere at once. We can recast our identities at high speeds, in every angelic and demonic instant, and we sit entranced before pixel screens, suddenly transported into euphoric and depressive responses. News of the world-soul is unavoidable. Satellites crisscross the global surface, shooting signals back and forth in an unstoppable array, no psychic barriers blocking the global present. Thus the electronic media field becomes the entire message.

In its ideal state the electric condition is one where hybrids and interfaces occur in swift epiphanies. McLuhan says in *The Book of Probes*, "Interface refers to the interaction of substances in a kind of mutual irritation. In art and poetry this is precisely the technique of symbolism" (482). These processes converge on everyone, he says in these aphorisms:

> In television, images are projected at you. You are the screen. The images wrap around you. You are the vanishing point.
> (195)

An interface is the moment when two seemingly disparate strands interweave, providing enough friction to create the new. In alchemy the chemical stirring of contrary energies was intended to yield up another compound entirely. Alchemy is a metaphor for the metamorphosis of being through the combining of apparently unmixable opposites. Synchronicity suggests seeing what happens when two energies meet, suddenly becoming a field for one another. It is the moment when works or stories do more than meet: they operate in coinciding pattern – reflecting and refracting one another, playing in concord before splitting off again into discrete forms. Differences can never be completely transcended on this plane. Synergies do not synthesize patterns into stasis. But alchemy and synergy may offer a vista before morphing into something else.

McLuhan gives us media ecology – "EVERY-WHERE IS NOW HERE IN ECO-LAND" (297), he says in *Take Today* – essential metaphors for understanding our electronic surround. The source-energy never freezes. But Nature has been made obsolete by technology, and we live in an artificial communications envelope. Its influence is subliminal but pervasive. Inside our trembling neon-lit envelope we carom like astonished tribal members obeying the omens and biddings, without knowing that an automatic auguring is underway.

In three aphorisms McLuhan illuminates, and exaggerates, the environmental stunning and processing. I am taking these from *The Book of Probes*, in which McLuhan's rhetoric moves into spheres of deliberate disturbance: "We are as numb in our electric world as the native involved in our literate and mechanical culture ... The age of writing has passed. We must invent a new metaphor, restructure our thoughts and feelings ... Societies have always been shaped more by the nature of the media by which humans communicate than by the content of the communication" (8–9, 22–23, 17). These aphorisms appear at the beginning of *The Book of Probes*, pages before the author's name, the title page, the publishing information, and the table of contents. The book was edited and arranged by David Carson with help from Eric McLuhan, William Kuhns, and Terrence Gordon. So important are these probes that the editors chose to place them before the author and book information. The aphorisms accentuate McLuhan's concern for our numbing down in the wake of change and his perception of how the avatars of book culture prefer to judge rather than probe: the forms of media, of super-Nature, are more influential than any content could ever be.

McLuhan is engaged in observing the milieu; Frye gives us its story. He replies to McLuhan's probes with his *kerygma* and allegorical narrative. Frye is "user as content," seeking the message in the medium. Frye answers his own question posed in *The Educated Imagination*: "What good is the study of literature?" (1). His writings represent the poetics of *verum factum* shifted away from mass media, back to singular consciousness. His is the reading eye sifting through verbal data for the latent romance-quest at the heart of what appears yahoo destructive, psychotically incomprehensible. Where do we find primary expression of the message? In the binding of literature, the configurations of the printed word.

Frye sometimes expresses doubt about conciliatory compounds. Can we harmonize contrary modes of thought? And should we do so? This is from a 1968 entry to *The "Third Book" Notebooks, 1964–1972*:

> I have always distrusted what I call Reuben the Reconciler in thought: the syncretism that "reconciles" Plato & Aristotle or St. Thomas & Marx. I think every great structure of thought or imagination is a universe in itself identical with & interpenetrating every other, but not similar or harmonizable with any other. Syncretism is Coleridge's fancy playing with fixities & definities, and it leads to the net of relations, not to the archetypal universal unique ... *What I now want to do is pick epiphanies out of them for my own purposes.*
>
> (39; emphasis mine)

With typical intellectual honesty, he reverses himself into another kind of recognition. This is an entry from the same notebook, probably written in the same year:

> I seize on every resemblance there is, invent a great many there aren't, and disregard all differences, determined to find an analogy in the teeth of the facts – *not that there are any facts, of course* ... Right now, Poe's *Eureka* is turning up on my agenda again.
>
> (211, 212; emphasis mine)

Frye, like McLuhan, was inspired by the prospects of discovery. In spite of Frye's accusation that McLuhan was freeze-framed into a media cliché, and McLuhan's accusation that Frye was assigning static patterns in "depressing" formulae, they were equally motivated by the energy to seek and find. But in the quotation above Frye swerves away from pronouncements about the end of Typographic Man, away from McLuhan's assertion of the primacy of communicating forms over the force of the individual mind. In this notebook entry Frye revels in a powerful Romantic dissident solitude: "*not that there are any facts.*" There is more to what he is saying, so we shall see.

Alchemy and synergy: they are hybrid formations. In *Understanding Media*, McLuhan declares in the chapter "Hybrid Energy,"

> *The crossings or hybridizations of the media release great new force and energy as by fission or fusion.* There need be no blindness in these matters once we have been notified that there is anything to observe ... the parallel between two media holds us on the frontiers between forms that snap us out of the Narcissus-narcosis.
>
> (48, 55; emphasis mine)

Hybridization is an analogue for recombination (and conversion).

Frye refers to mysterious, furious energies of alchemy in the aptly named "Fourth Variation: The Furnace," the last chapter of *Words with Power*. In two passages, he offers literary figures for the metaphor of hybridization and then crystallizes my point here:

> The release of titanic powers in man through invention is feared and dreaded at every stage in history, partly because of the intertwining of the titanic and the demonic, and partly because technology, having no will of its own, is readily projected as a mysterious, external and sinister force ... Yeats's "Byzantium" also describes a mysterious technological-purgatorial-alchemical world in which "blood-begotten-spirits" cross water at their death to be processed in "smithies," and go through a purgatorial oblivion which involves dance, fire and transformation into "glory of changeless metal." ... *this is one of those either-or questions that have to be turned into both-and answers before it makes sense.*
>
> (270, 276; emphasis mine)

Hybrid structures are symbols of purgation and participation. "Mythical thinking," Frye writes in the *"Third Book" Notebooks, 1964–1972*, "is what it is now fashionable to call both-and thinking" (82). In the *Late*

Alchemy: Synergy in the Thinking of McLuhan and Frye 237

Notebooks, 1982–1990, he says cryptically, "The simultaneous yes-and-no statements of myth and metaphor" (537). To look at McLuhan and Frye "all-at-once" in the pattern that emerges when we do so confirms their seeding of a visionary-prophetic tradition. So we begin to evolve beyond the theories and myths they premised, to another shaping.

I propose that we will find a clear expression of their visionary-prophetic tradition in the joining of "the medium is the message" with the Great Code story. The communicating forms that McLuhan identifies need our re-creations of content. This content could be the code that Frye strove to express in the decades after *Fearful Symmetry* and *Anatomy of Criticism.* "The medium is the message" alludes to the impact of changing surrounds on our sensibilities, subliminal shifts that occur too rapidly for our senses to keep pace with them. I have established how for McLuhan the forms of Nature – the electronic machines, the Eco-land, the Magnetic City, the satellite-scanned global theatre – can have an ascendant impact. Humanity sleeps through transformations; but when we are awakened we are aroused to the trauma and euphoria of our condition. Then the machines stop being a disservice and become potentially a service.

McLuhan's transformation from literary scholar to media ecologist was fraught with the dangers of misunderstanding. Relentlessly, in an astonishingly short period from 1951 until 1979, from *Explorations* on to his last scramble to assemble manuscripts with collaborators (who were often much less astute about what he perceived), he spoke, wrote, taught, and taunted to snap the trances of conditioning. That he was one of the first to do so speaks to the obliviousness he dashed to expose.

Nevertheless, McLuhan's perception-quest was left in probing pieces. His resistance to the label "theorist" was partially comic, partially a refusal to classify his thoughts. He was volubly alive in his shape-shifting, always seeking the new. This had to mean he would leave those great gaps in his thinking. They are intervals in which we may enter with our psychic, intellectual, theoretical, and poetic reconstructions. (This also means some of his ideas should be discarded if they do not serve the purpose of inciting discussion.) His pioneering means frontiers are still open. The open territory is the question of identity. "And who are you?" This is the second-to-last line of *The Medium is the Massage.* It is scrawled across a page showing an image from *Alice in Wonderland.* Tucked in the lower left-hand corner of the back page, we find an A.N. Whitehead quotation, "It is the business of the future to be dangerous" (153, 160).

"Who are you?" The Who song says (this chorus line became the herald of the *CSI: Crime Scene Investigation* TV series). McLuhan elaborates on the identity issue in *From Cliché to Archetype*:

> In *War and Peace in the Global Village* the principal theme is the quest for identity through violence in a world of rapidly shifting technologies. A sudden change of environment through major technological innovations blurs the identity image of generations old and new. They then begin a tragic *agon* of redefinition of their image of identity.
>
> (114)

The overwhelming question put to the quester at the Chapel Perilous in the wasteland is, in all probability, "Who are you?" Culture and society for McLuhan sometimes seemed a junk pile of old ideas and identities, like an information wasteland. The quotations and probes should show how McLuhan knew that the identity question would drive the new century; it is the apocalypse of the post-book phase. The Magnetic City surveyed from outer space is an array of blazing electric light, an "Interzone" where individual lights often seem extinguished. Terror comes when everything drops from under us. "Our ground," McLuhan says in *Take Today*, "is literally in the sky" (294).

Place the narrative code, the soul of the story, inside the jangling forms of electronic information, and we will see the synergy of McLuhan and Frye. The question of "who are you?" inspired Frye, from *The Educated Imagination* to *The Double Vision*, to find a key, or *the* key. But like McLuhan, Frye hesitated to give definitive answers; they place restrictions on thought. Instead of platitudes he offers the story code that he discerns in the Bible. His riddling obsession from his early studies of Blake, the Great Code becomes the artful concern of most of his later essaying. The code is the tale that tells the story of individual apocalypse; it is the path encrypted in the imagination that could offer a way out of the darkening maze of history: and the imagination has been with us from the beginning of time.

In Frye's *Notebooks and Lectures on the Bible and Other Religious Texts*, the prophetic pressure on words becomes paramount. In his "wild pitch," written possibly in the 1940s (dating is often difficult with the entries), he speculates that the nineteenth century belonged to Kant's thinking. This was the critical approach to speculative reasoning. The twentieth century belonged to Hegel's dialectic and its epochal inversion by Marx and Engels into the revolutionary, materialist version of the spiritual cycle of exile and liberation. The twenty-first century would be the time when "myth and revelation could possibly come through" (623). The wild pitch is Frye's Romantic-Modernist vision, the recognition of a narrative heart inside the crises we endure. The twenty-first century would drive people towards the discovery of the inward agency that connects them to the living realm of symbolic narrative.

The Aerial Roots of the Eternal Story

What is the Great Code? There are double strands of meaning. The book's subtitle seems a modest deflection from the grandness of the main theme: *The Bible and Literature*, not, I note, the Bible in literature. *The Great Code* confirms that without the study of biblical themes and typologies, literature from Dante to Milton to Blake, from Hopkins and Dickinson to D.H. Lawrence and Eliot, is not intelligible. However, Frye admits that his essay cannot be categorized: "just as the 'scholarly/ unscholarly' antibook had somehow to be got over, whether evaded or transcended, so the 'personal/impersonal' antibook had to be got over too ... One emerges on the other side of this realizing once again that *all knowledge is personal knowledge*, but with some hope that the person may have been, to whatever degree, transformed in the meantime"[2] (emphasis mine). Eight pages later he identifies where he found his title: from Blake, of course, "The Old and New Testaments are the Great Code of Art." One strand of Frye's line of attention is to chart how the typologies of the Bible – the book which "evades all literary criteria" – may nevertheless be understood in their effect on the shapes we find in the literary imagination.

The subtextual code, the arcane strand, begins in the introduction. It appears (spoken almost in a murmur) in two places. First:

> Those who do succeed in reading the Bible from beginning to end will discover that at least it has a beginning and an end, and some traces of a total structure. It begins where time begins, with the creation of the world; it ends where time ends, with the Apocalypse, and it surveys human history in between, or the aspects of literature it is interested in, under the symbolic names of Adam and Israel. There is also a body of concrete images: city, mountain, river, garden, tree, oil, fountain, bread, wine, bride, sheep, and many others, which recur so often that they clearly indicate some kind of

unifying principle. That unifying principle, for a critic, would have to be one of shape rather than meaning; or, more accurately, no book can have a coherent meaning unless there is some coherence in its shape.

(xiii)

The unifying principle is the poetic principle. The shape of meaning is the perpetual allegory. However, Frye does not expose the nuanced detail of the narrative structure until later:

> [W]hat I isolate as seven phases of what is traditionally called revelation: creation, exodus, law, wisdom, prophecy, gospel, and apocalypse. Two forms of apocalyptic vision are postulated, making eight in all, the eighth bringing us back to ... the role of the reader.
>
> (xxii)

The phases of revelation compose the story code of thrown-ness, exile, wandering, and revelation. Although this narrative is attributed to the overall unifying structure of the Bible, it is Frye's key cryptogram. It is the central story pattern of the Western literary imagination for Frye: "Creation, exodus, law, wisdom, prophecy, gospel, and apocalypse." This principle appears transfigured, in many guises and permutations.

How can we read the code? Frye's understated sentences suggest this: the underlying story, from creation to apocalypse, is the quest. It is the irreducible communion of spiritual crisis and pining, in our long struggle towards love and plenitude; and it is what makes us human and joins each individual to the greater community of lonely searching souls. The code shapes the necessary fiction that offers a metaphor for our hunger for beauty, the bearing which could overcome the depleting ravages of time.

The Great Code is the identity quest that Frye had illuminated at the centre of literature in *The Educated Imagination*. Here is the structure of this epic of growing consciousness: creation, fall, wandering, struggle, the call back to wisdom, redemption, the coming of clarity (gospel), and then the sudden recognition of the pattern at work, which is the apocalypse. The quest story is the archetypal narrative in all prophecies, poetry, fiction, and art. It is revealed in glimpses, through overtones, between the lines, in recurring images and symbols.

What Frye heretically suggests is this: *the core of reality is imaginary* (at least in part). Facts are one side of life; the deep side of life takes place in the allegoric narrative that gives shape to what often seems baffling. Through symbols and recurrent types, the universal language of the imagination, the story code becomes Rimbaud's longed-for alphabet of the soul.

―――

The code is the story we tell ourselves. It is the tale of how we fell. It begins in creation: when we open our eyes, *fiat lux*. This is the beginning, *once upon a time, ab ovo*. So the story always begins, in the opening of our mind and of our senses. But once we rise from darkness into light we almost immediately find ourselves alienated. Somehow we have become exiled from light and enlightenment. We have fallen. This condition of exile has many names. But the breakage feels very real. We were elsewhere, and now our lives seem desperate, disillusioned, disjointed, strained, and botched. "As I said (but didn't say in GC [*The Great Code*]) everybody has a lost soul, and should make sure that it gets good and lost. But the lost soul is perhaps the only one we have."[3] The feeling of being lost is the appeal of stories charged with characters on the verge of cracking, from Achilles's wrath to Hamlet's so-called madness, from Milton's rebel angels to Vaughan and James's obsessive fascination for the twisted metal of ruined cars in J.G. Ballard's *Crash* (1973). Storylines abound with images of descent into storms, into volcanoes, into darkness, into pits of suffering. We identify with them because we are caught falling too. And how long have we been falling? Has the fall always been this painful and raw? Are we falling even faster in the long haul down without any bearings whatsoever? Will we fall forever? And is our fall so steep and fast that all we feel is irresistible descent into deeper chasms? Have we fallen in love with our descent, preferring it to ascent?

Yet the story carries redemptive hope. This comes in the exodus myth. Souls throw off their chains, surge free, and wander into the wilderness, away from tyranny. We are falling, but we yearn to get back to love, plenty, peace, welcome, home. The wandering *towards* will take generations. So in the wilderness we experience hallucinations and see apparitions; but we will also receive prophecies and wisdom. Proverbs and psalms will be told or sung. These carry the inklings of supra-consciousness, epiphany awareness, that there is more to the wandering than we often see: there is purpose. We may recall the purpose, or through prophecy be recalled to it. Once awakened, we may come to knowledge of gospel or the mission. Call this knowledge of the quest. The quester is a pilgrim – heroic, or otherwise – voyaging to the home he or she has lost.

The story has a hook, however. It is crucifixion, the time of piercing pain. In any mission there must come appalling doubt. We are seized by the trial – Kafka's parable of inexplicable arrest and punishment is exemplary here – symbolically represented by the agony on Golgotha. But Calvary is more than the experience of suffering. It is the fall again, this time more excruciatingly felt because it is done with knowledge of the exodus, of the wandering, the law, the wisdom, the promise of prophecy. The story says that in the test time there will be the uncovering: we die to rise now. Once resurrected in our hearts and minds, we gaze back over the story, recognizing the glaze of pattern. This is why there is always the double apocalypse: an ending, a beginning. "[C]reation is the revelation of the cosmos to human consciousness," Frye writes in his *Late Notebooks, 1982–1990* (723).

In every literary work, in all works of art, the story falls through time. The allegoric principle intimates a rise follows the fall. This is our solace. The rising is the imperative of the imagination: to understand the cycles of the tale and how each re-cycling will be different. We see why the *Wake* had impressive symbolic importance for Frye. The story code takes place between morning and night: every day it plays out; but without certain illuminating texts (the Bible, *Ulysses*), we may not sense its presence.

Let us stand back and review the fall-rise imprint: there is the story we are told, and there is the story we discover for ourselves. There is the story code we take from others; and there is the story we tell from our own perspective. The story tells us to find the place where the Spirit or the wind moves us. This can occur anywhere. One version of the code could inspire you to go out adventuring, like Ulysses; another version could find you staying at home, like Penelope. The Spirit, like the wind, goes where it wants.

The storyteller, or the singer, will die. But the story code, like our dreams, can never completely decay. Trust the tale, then, not the teller (all narrators are unreliable, to some extent). The storytellers are reinventing the code, sometimes injecting massive doses of irony or telling tales of epic misconstruing. You can trust the tale; it flows on, even if those who tell it misunderstand it or evade it.

Is the Great Code a variant of the personal legend? I think it is: the story that we should tell of our lives and show to the cosmos (whoever may be watching and listening). Each person must live the code in his or her auspicious way. All that is required is some measure of novelty, of value, of valour, of passion, of love. Presumably, the Spirit will guide us towards living a story that elevates us to a higher consciousness, and not toward utter viciousness. Nevertheless, what is needed is self-mythologizing. You become a character in your own mythmaking, no matter how confused or chaotic your quest may appear to you (and to others). It could be that the legend will appear when you are organizing a local theatre piece, rearranging your home, becoming a politician or a lawyer, being with your children, listening to the wind, playing a musical instrument, going on a trip to a new city or country; it appears when you raise what you do to a height of intensity. (Be sweet and wild, and the gods, or the Spirit, will attend and take note.) Each of us therefore carries the seed of the code in the form of our personal myth. Our obsession with recording ourselves, with documenting our experiences, flowers from this seed.

The Great Code says: perceive and live deeply. This is why we need the great works, the books that vividly depict the fall and rise. They articulate, and mirror, our hunger to find life and to tell the story of our pursuit of it. The critic becomes a knowledgeable seer the more he or she can show us the code's workings.

A realist would reply, this is pure anthropomorphism, a blind solipsistic humanism that projects on the terrible blank screen of the churning universe. The code is no more than an aesthetic invention, the realist would say: an enticing proposition. The show we make is a spectacle full of the sound and the fury, signifying nothing. At a point a pilgrimage will likely become mere tourism. And at some point the soul's story could turn into a horrifying joke or a subversive lie told with inexplicable malice (the quester then becoming more like Iago than Don Quixote).

Nevertheless, I believe there is a hint in Frye's conjecture that the code, like the alchemical magnum opus, is played out for the benefit of larger forces, the Spirit. Hence the intensity of the drama, its comic and tragic features. Milton's heaven and hell are both observation posts for the angels and devils of *Paradise Lost.* Like the invasive divinities of Homer's epics, the angels and demons command people to choose and live once we step outside the protective pastoral of Eden: we must journey and find the crossroads. I wonder if Frye supposed, Gnostic-like, that the code was implanted in our souls, etched into our hearts, so that we must discover it or wither into dust. It must be bravely disinterred from matter (the pages and words of books are like stones).

The presence of the code in both psyche and book may account for our irresistible gravitations towards the lives of impressive figures, politicians and celebrities, sports heroes and artists, who live with special fire. They carry the code to an extreme for us, their audience. And they reveal it vividly, avidly, for our contemplations and critiques. A wasted life is therefore a wasted story. But are there wasted stories, truly? If the code reveals that we must live and voyage at a pitch of intent, then every person, every family, will have a myth to tell others, in whatever form. Consider the stories we tell of the dead at funerals, the stories we tell of lovers and marriages, the stories we spiel about colleagues at roasts; witness our relish over gossip and innuendos at workplaces. On the Web we find a crazed sprawl of conspiracy theories and extravagant tales about motives and events. I imagine McLuhan saying to Frye, this is evidence of the Great Code (the allegoric principle) operating at hyper-speed. In other words, whether implanted or re-created, whether encased in the matter of texts or documented on disc for our families, the code persists.

But the allegoric story does not depend on historical record. The fable of identity is an imaginative reference to the potential of the independent mind. Sometimes the personal legend will come in criticism, in philosophy, in scientific theorem, in a teaching. "Life," Frye writes in *T.S. Eliot*, "is a parabola" (75). The word "parabola" echoes in the word "parable." The parable, or fable, is a form of narrative that resembles the aphorism because of its brevity. Its compression leads to an infinite number of readings, all the possibilities that the mind can bring to bear.

All the work Frye did to identify conventions, typologies, images, genres, and ethical dimensions revolves around his searing vision of the fall-rise story. Yes, the Great Code is a master narrative but one that does not stall us in authoritarian stasis. On the contrary, the code is meant to liberate; no one tells it in the same way. It provides "a condition of complete simplicity/(Costing not less than everything)."[4] There is not necessarily a religious implication to the allegoric principle. It can be "the secular scripture."

The code is transgressive. It violates the repressive orders of Nobodaddies: the tyrannies arresting us in single vision, in dark-satanic wheels, the flat-line experience of exploitation and cynicism, the temporary manipulations of monomaniacal political or ad campaigns. The code insists on a transcendental super-story that revolts against bondage. Nothing is irreversible about our fallen state. Moreover, the code unites the individual with humanity because the story recurs in every culture, in all times.

Alchemy: Synergy in the Thinking of McLuhan and Frye   245

The synchrony is clear: inside the electronic vortices, the great tale of "who are you?" endures. Poe's "A Descent into the Maelstrom" – essential to McLuhan (and to Frye, Poe was "The Greatest Literary Genius after Blake"[5]) – serves to recall: McLuhan seized the whirlwind and took field notes; Frye envisioned the whirlwind and saw the story varied but recurrent.

Frye makes the critic-seer the ultimate reader suffering from the ultimate insomnia. This promotes the crucial inwardness for the process of interpretation. It is through the power of text, in the aesthetic arrangements of its disciplined dreaming, and in the metaphors and symbols of that dream-time we call literature that we find the code of the counter-quest. Why is it a counter-movement? Once more, it is imaginative resistance to worldly experience which often seems devoid of meaning. I rephrase (and recast, in my way) the movements in the story: journey, challenge, withdrawal, epiphany, higher vision, dark night, and brightening. The prophetic epiphany comes in the moment when this structure is fully revealed and the darkness and the light become part of the whole. With the narrative principle come the images and the archetypes of wilderness and wasteland, of mountains and valleys (aspiration and anxiety), of towers and ladders (intersections), of furnaces (the fires of creation), of the restoration of the garden which can blossom into a redeemed lotus city. Meditative inwardness through reading is not, finally, solipsism, a retreat from the world: it is the encouraging re-creation of the allegoric principle according to each person's solitude. This is why Frye in *The Great Code* emphasizes "the role of the reader." All readers have the liberty to open pages and the freedom to open themselves and participate in the story if they choose to exercise re-creative energies. Each reading is potentially a turning point; the profound intersection of book with history is apocalypse. Frye quotes the Zen philosopher D.T. Suzuki to represent his definitive view of apocalypse: it is "an infinite mutual fusion or penetration of all things, each with its individuality yet with something universal in it" (168). In the mutuality of the microcosm-macrocosm we can each hold infinity in the palm of our hand, eternity in an hour.

Frye elucidates the mystical implications of the code (his "old fetish") in this notebook entry, from the time when he was writing *Words with Power*:

> I think of my eight phrases of revelation as a progressive dialogue of Word and Spirit. Creation is the first epiphany ... the presentation of a world with

things in it to consciousness ... Exodus is the first response of the Spirit, in the form of the nation of Israel. Law is then the second epiphany of the Word, where the seven days become the Sabbath observance ... Wisdom, the individualizing of the law, is the second response of the Spirit to this, and is symbolized by Solomon ... Prophecy is the third epiphany of the Word, born mostly out of defeat and humiliation ... Gospel is the third response of the Spirit ... The panoramic apocalypse is the final epiphany of the Word, obviously, and the participating one the final response of the Spirit.[6]

The code can span an individual's lifetime. It may spell out the parabolic challenge of the twenty-four-hour cycle too. The day world provides us with the realism of heroic and absurd history – tragic and foolish events, often ruinous passions; the night world is erotic reverie, the womb-time of myth and newness. *Ulysses* and the *Wake* form one version of the metaphoric whole – a day's odyssey, a night's dream – of the quest-parable through the modern maze. Where does Joyce locate his complementary evocations of how the code plays through every day and night? In his city, Dublin; Frye had learned the journey begins wherever you happen to find yourself. "The goal of the quest," he says in his *"Third Book" Notebooks* (likely in 1969), "is to integrate what we're getting with what we've got, and the only way to reach the goal is to wake up & find ourselves in the same place" (243).

Versions of the Mystery

Again, is the Great Code nothing more than a fine fiction, a persuasive story forged out of our desperate need? Is it Nietzsche's holy lie, reimagined? Is it just the sometimes virtuosic story we have to tell to comfort ourselves against darkness? Is it a way to deflect anxiety? Is it just another way to subdue facts, the agitations and absurdities of reality? Is it insulation against the shock of death? Is it a triumph of aesthetic clarity when life is always muddled? It could be all these; the code dignifies the observer: stunning random data now has a profound unfolding. Step outside the book, blink in daylight on a grubby street, and ask, Does the fiction still make sense? The story may be what we must (preposterously) tell ourselves to stave off what seems the inevitability of mental decline, among other terrors. The symmetries of fiction may be just that – a sentimental application of hope against overwhelming evidence to the contrary (reality makes no sense whatsoever).

Alchemy: Synergy in the Thinking of McLuhan and Frye 247

But the code was surely not all that for Frye (nor is it so for me). It is what inspires the emerging inner I. Further, the code is a myth which overflows from our reconstructions into reality and then seeks to transfigure it, when the cracked world and Prospero's brave new world unite. Frye's proposal becomes essential, I submit, when we find ourselves in the Magnetic City being shell-shocked or shellacked by the deluge of raw images and the glosses of text messaging.

"In the electric age we wear all mankind as our skin."[7] This McLuhan aphorism opens at once towards a harmony of blissful absorption into utopian unity and towards the acute paranoia about what presses and depresses us. If sunlight burns and spiritual light wounds – so we learn from Jacob's wrestling with the strange angel in Genesis 32 – then what can electric light do? "The electric light is pure information. It is a medium without a message" (*The Book of Probes*, 391). The forms always speak, always imprint or scar. They may not have a message, but they are living representations.

Environments are actions for McLuhan, and the forms are agencies. Even without obvious content there is vibration, impact, prickling, dynamism. The electric cosmos itself is a kind of influential supra-consciousness. We are therefore continually trying to hear "What the Thunder Said." *War and Peace in the Global Village* takes the ten Joycean thunders from the *Wake* and tries to decode each of their verbal-vocal vortices.[8] Eric McLuhan valuably continued his father's study of Joyce's text in his own exegetical work *The Role of Thunder in Finnegans Wake* (1997).[9] Understanding makes us, like Jacob, wrestling participants in the phenomena. This is for McLuhan the reversal of the fall, which is for him the descent into unconscious destructiveness. The user is empowered to become creative: a significant producer, not a consumer.

Laws of Media concludes with the merging voices of the collaborators. The merging is so complete it is difficult to know who is speaking, McLuhan Sr. or McLuhan Jr.

> The goal of science and of art and of education for the next generation must be to decipher *not the genetic but the perceptual code*. In a global information environment, the old pattern of education in answer-finding is of no avail: one is surrounded by answers, millions of them, moving and mutating at electric speed. Survival and control will depend on the ability to probe and to question in the proper way and place. As the information that constitutes

the environment is perpetually in flux, so the need is not for fixed concepts but rather for ancient skill of reading that book, for navigating through an ever uncharted milieu. Else we will have no more control of this technology and environment than we have of the wind and the tides.

(239; emphasis mine)

The Great Code and "the perceptual code" are not identical. But in any intersection where McLuhan and Frye speak through their ideas, across the breaches of their miscommunications, the "pure information" of electricity (the energy that impels) summons our need for the unfolding story of inward agency. The dynamism of our environments calls out for the imagination's response. Orpheus's head tears down the electric current, singing, prophesying, babbling, muttering, and telling the tale while we eternal critics on the shorelines pick up the traces, decoding and retelling. Through literary works from Homer to Ovid, from the Bible to Dante, from Shakespeare to Milton, from Blake to Dickinson, from Joyce to Atwood – even if these books are now deciphered in the margins of the electrified globe – the code gradually becomes clearer and greater.

In the flux of information, the disarrays of our century's turnings, we are each in search of codes – anything that will help. Electronic modernity shows us how every person is a centre in the Magnetic City. Through certain disciplines (study, poetry, art, faith, education, ritual, yoga) we may achieve intellectual focus and meditative concentration. In our experiences of media and of books, there are the signatures of the source and the presence of the tale, the mystery of being and becoming in all its exciting expressions.

We need McLuhan and Frye both, and the recombination of "the medium is the message" with the Great Code makes them new. The new comes in the vibrant shifts between the cultivation of mental travelling and the recognitions of electronic phenomena. We may perceive the surround through a discontinuous aphorism, which gives us a compass; and we may follow the storyline of the quest-code, which gives us the transports of the essential tale. Pattern recognition and narrative comprehension could then exist side by side in synchrony. Discontinuity and continuity interfuse in a paradox. By allowing them to move together in this arrangement, we may find a way to resist single vision. McLuhan's experimentalism and Frye's essaying scholarship need not be exclusive from one another.

They preferred to understand their work in comic terms: the comedy of the media, the divine comedy of criticism. Comedy is conciliatory, resistant to tragic anxiety, "the very pet purpose of subsequent recombination," so Joyce says in the *Wake*; or, rather, so McLuhan claims that Joyce says in that book.[10]

In 1947, fresh from completing *Fearful Symmetry*, Frye was impassioned by the prospects of the fresh start found when you recognize the infinite in the imagination. In an entry from *Notebooks and Lectures on the Bible and Other Religious Texts* Frye shatters his subdued phrasing, the product of layering revision. His rhetoric retrieves poetic power, sometimes bluntness. It is hell-fired writing:

> Nevertheless it isn't new knowledge but a new power of knowledge, a new courage to know, that's important ... We must cling to a God who approves of blasphemy because he hates Jehovah & Nobodaddy & Zeus & Isvara & all the other kings of terrors & tyrants of the soul. To a God who appreciates obscenity because he looks not into the secrets of our hearts but into the hearts of our secrets, & knows that our bloodfilled genitals & cocking guts are the real battlefields.
>
> (256)

It takes blasphemy to illuminate orthodoxy, and the orthodox may contain heresies. One drives the other; when they collide, crises occur.

McLuhan sometimes oscillated between criticism and delirium, becoming a medium (the midway point, the possessed), feeling, responding, thinking, and speaking so quickly that his aphorisms seemed to surprise him. To allow intuitional flow, the user must be willing to be used. If an aphorism is meant to be an aggressive friction for the receiver, then what becomes of the aphorist himself? Aphorisms can amuse and stun. They may do more than direct attention: they could outline a pathway of being. He says in one of the interviews reprinted in *The Medium and the Light* with Pierre Babin,

> MCLUHAN: The electric world, which is acoustic, intuitive, holistic, that is global and total ... it invites them [us?] into total immersion, and it doesn't lead towards goals or objectives but focuses only on a certain quality of life.
>
> BABIN: Could we call this a return to mysticism?

MCLUHAN: I think so. Gutenberg emphasized the process of outering and Marconi marked the start of its ebb. At the speed of light, the inner trip is all that's left ... *To become a knight errant or nomad is easy today thanks to the telephone, the car, and the jet.*

(97; emphasis mine)

When I go all the way back from this interview with Babin to McLuhan's first published essay on Chesterton, then I find his acknowledgment of the presence of the code, what he calls the allegoric principle. This is the evolutionary principle of emerging consciousness. He approves of Chesterton's assertion:

Mr. Chesterton regards the soul of a story as "the ordeal of a free man," "... There is no such thing as a Hegelian story, or a monist story, or a determinist story ... *Every short story does truly begin with the creation and end with the last judgment.*"[11] (emphasis mine)

McLuhan's and Frye's shared metaphysical concerns led them to see an allegoric subtext to the fall-rise (or rise-fall) in every life, in the everyday.

Frye expresses his recognition of the presence of the transforming code in an entry likely written in 1948 in *Notebooks and Lectures on the Bible and Other Religious Texts*. We find him, in the naked way of his journaling, identifying the story at the heart of our dilemmas. It is a rare moment when Frye becomes more Henry Miller than a commentator on Milton:

[T]he soul is an immaculate virgin, ready for the divine child. Then it goes out and gets fucked by the world all day long, & staggers back a baggy-eyed old whore, still hoping after sleep the Moment of purification will come again.

(27)

At this point I want to speculate more about the McLuhan-Frye synchronicity. I think it is important to reflect again on why these two powerful iconic intellects happened to appear at the same time, in the same place, in a city that was truly off-centre from the volatile, hungry empire to the south.

It is strange, and deeply absorbing to me, to consider this. They were writing and teaching for decades mere footsteps away from one another.

Alchemy: Synergy in the Thinking of McLuhan and Frye 251

They centred their work in revisions of esoteric questions from the wisdom traditions. Can we take their books and see beyond the words towards knowledge of something known, something apprehended? Can we see in their theoretical undertakings recognition of the source of life? Can we find the cyclical pattern, awakening then falling asleep then awakening again? Can we find in their work how we, their students, could become perpetual pupils of darkness and light?

I have no answers for these enigmas. But the two arrived at a country's centre to become the centre of a visionary legacy. The mystery of their coinciding energy should impel others.

Recombinations, Oppositions

Alchemy is based – according to the legends of its practice – on the conjunctions of opposites. I have been proposing that contraries bring about new arrangements. Hybrid energies are like conversion experiences: you shift from one state into another. And hybrid energy is one of the key teachings of the esoteric traditions in the ancient wisdom: "Make it New" (Ezra Pound's and H.D.'s exhortation) is the urging to seize what you find and combine it with marvellous, surprising ideas or dreams or reconfigurations or objects. They can be translations, samplings: Picasso's African masks, Jackson Pollock's drip paintings that transformed the space of the canvas; George Gershwin's quotations from jazz and classical masters; Allen Ginsberg's risqué sexuality set beside incantations of spells and allusions to Blake and Mohammed in *Howl* (1956); the Beatles using the background noise of the streets in recordings; Francis Ford Coppola's collages of images in the opening of his film *Apocalypse Now* (1979) and his resetting of Joseph Conrad's *Heart of Darkness* (1899) in the Vietnam war; Stan Lee's comic-book visualizations of strange beings who are half human, half insect or part human and part unearthly god: all these demonstrate the collisions and mergers of old and new. Strong premises invite the new through debate and disagreement. McLuhan and Frye, in the considerable power of their writings and statements, seemed to demand opposition, insisting on contrary positions which reforge other essays and books, the spilling over into bursts and vistas.

Thoughts are actions that can bring reactions. Given their latent comprehensions of the divine comedy unfolding in electronic space/time and in the literary imagination, we can see why they drew critical fire. Not every critic or philosopher shared their sense of intercommunion; truly, not many shared it at all. Opposition broke out quickly and forcefully. Their ideas stirred others into alchemical recombinations of thought and avid resistances.

I will take Fredric Jameson, Umberto Eco, and Jean Baudrillard to be representative critics. They are major critical-theorists who countered the Janus-faced philosophers of the Toronto School of Communication Theory. These critics understood the not-so-concealed spiritual imperatives and grand story of the McLuhan-Frye matrix and recognized how the two were Romantic-Modernists addressing contemporary conditions. Critics who put ideology (primarily Marxist) above perception or aesthetics found plenty to loathe in McLuhan's jazzing and Frye's not-so-in-the-closet Christian mysticism. It has often appeared to critics and sceptics alike that McLuhan and Frye were both conducting classes in a Toronto mystery school of ethereal initiation.

I begin with this contrary voice, one of the sharpest. In Jameson's influential book *The Political Unconscious: Narrative as a Socially Symbolic Act* (1981), he at once admires Frye and lambastes him. Jameson has vast ambitions to be an influential, thought-setting critic too; he wants to overcome Frye and Freud. In order for Jameson to do so, he honours them (a respectful way to start); then he replaces psychology and literary criticism with Marxist cultural theory. I find it interesting that he takes over many of Frye's structural patterns from *Anatomy* – the four levels of exegesis – and applies them to political structures (30, 31). The primary allegory for Jameson, however, is not the identity quest. To him the deep story of history is that of social-political alienation, exploitation, and inequity. Identity concerns are a kind of narcissism for Jameson; while we concern ourselves with ourselves, the powers that be continue to abuse us, turning us into slaves.

Like John Fekete, the Marxist Jameson resists Frye's spiritual intentions. Unlike Fekete, Jameson does so by juxtaposing Frye's achievement in interpretative theory with a critique of that accomplishment. In the following passage Jameson places Freud and Frye on a historical plane of dialectical polarity. Jameson challenges the question of theoretical narratives:

> [T]he trajectory of our discussion, from Freud to Northrop Frye, is an emblematic one: for any contemporary reevaluation of the problem of interpretation, the most vital exchange of energies inevitably takes place between the two poles of the psychoanalytic and the theological ...

between ... the diagnostic genius of Freud himself ... and ... the problems and dynamics of interpretation, commentary, allegory and multiple meanings ... primarily organized around the central text of the Bible ... preserved in the religious tradition.

(69)

Although Jameson acknowledges "the greatness of Frye," he attacks Frye's fostering of the illusions of religion.

Jameson's primarily charges Frye with (allegedly) turning his attention away from community to the individual. To Jameson, Frye revels in solitude and mythmaking, the essentials of inwardness, a sublimely deliberate solipsism. While Jameson approves of Frye's Blakean notion of each of us participating in a larger sleeping human body, he remains uneasy with the obscurities of Frye's undertaking. Jameson identifies Frye's vision of the stirring Blakean Albion (communal heart and mind) with Joyce's HCE, both landscape (Howth Castle and Environs) and humanity (Here Comes Everybody; though Jameson misses the merriment in Joyce: HCE is also "Hocus Crocus, Esquilocus"). But Frye's limits his "greatness" by diminishing the importance of the political-historical dimension in the allegoric principle.[12] Before Frye wrote of myth as counter-history (perhaps his reply to *The Political Unconscious?*), Jameson criticizes Frye's celebrations of imaginative timelessness, where suffering is transfigured by the panorama of poetics. Multinational capitalism is a ruthless corporate body that consumes us; it does not turn us towards poems and visions of community.

Jameson's well-known first line of his book is "Always historicize" (9). Translation: seize the political moment. I can imagine Frye's rebuttal to him being, "Always metaphorize." Translation: seize the essential in the Great Code.

Jameson puts history above myth: "History is what hurts" (102). The political narrative of the fall of mankind into capital and of the redemption through revolution trumps the individual quest with its roots in theology. Whatever you may think of Jameson's critique, you can agree with his insight into the direction of Frye's mythic speculations: towards the intersections of Spirit and matter that are represented for Frye in the canonic literary works that demand maximum critical focus. Frye's dissenting spirit (his visionary discipleship) is not enough for Jameson. It must be attached to the revolutionary agenda; no one person overcomes history. Jameson accurately sees how for Frye individual imaginative transformation precedes economic change. The outer world is dissolved into figurative energies, image and symbol. These in turn become the *ricorso* to edenic consciousness. Read Blake, Frye said: we will be exalted in our awareness; then comes social reform. Poetry is the first conversion.

Jameson calls Frye's vision of the romance-quest a "Magical Narrative" (103, 110, 112). I believe this is an accurate rephrasing of the allegoric principle. The romance-quest narrative is "a process of *transforming* ordinary reality" and containing it (110). All the puns in the word "contain" – to hold, to possess, to mitigate, to enwomb – are not lost on Jameson. He leaves Frye to move on to read other texts. But Jameson is crucial at this juncture because he perceives the apocalyptic-prophetic implications of the quest. It addresses, with a shamanistic summoning, the soul's rising; for Jameson, this is a mere wish-fulfilment fantasy. Revolutionary change is postponed in favour of private revelations, which are difficult to express, if not, Frye saw in *Words with Power*, ecstatically beyond words.

Jameson sees how the romance-quest absorbed Frye's thought. He identifies the shadow of Frye's (insular?) concept of the spiritual storyline. Jameson insists that Frye's disregard of the imperative of institutional-political change cut him off from the concerns of class war, of race and gender, of economic disparity, of the voiceless and the oppressed.

In parting, it is interesting to see how Jameson mentions McLuhan briefly in *The Political Unconscious*. "[T]hat technological determinism of which MacLuhanism [*sic*] remains the most interesting contemporary expression" (25; emphasis mine). The misspelling of McLuhan's full name is repeated in the index (303). It appears that Marxist critics have trouble proofreading too.

※

Umberto Eco's lacerating critique of McLuhan appears in his essay "Towards a Semiological Guerrilla Warfare," in the chapter of his *Travels in Hyperreality* (1986) called "Reports from the Global Village." Like Jameson on Frye, Eco zeroes in on the prophetic McLuhan. Eco's trenchant scepticism is directed towards McLuhan's "utopian" scan of the global village. He perceives McLuhan's implicit metaphysical concern. He calls McLuhan one of the "apocalyptics." Eco is not in any way praising him for his originality. Scornfully, he writes,

> McLuhan ... concludes that, when the mass media triumph, the Gutenbergian human being dies, and a new man is born, accustomed to perceive the world in another way ... Where the apocalyptics saw the end of the world, McLuhan sees the beginning of a new phase of history. This is exactly what

Alchemy: Synergy in the Thinking of McLuhan and Frye 255

happens when a prim vegetarian argues with a user of LSD: The former sees the drug as the end of reason, the latter as the beginning of a new sensitivity ... But the communications scholar must ask himself this question: Is the chemical composition of every communicative act the same? ... [T]o those who believe that "the medium is the message," I would like to recall an image ... of the cannibal chief who is wearing an alarm clock as a necklace ... The world of communications ... is full of cannibals who transform an instrument for measuring time into an "op" jewel ... [I]t is not true that the medium is the message ... The move from the Gutenberg Galaxy to the new Village of Total Communication will not prevent the eternal drama of infidelity and jealousy from exploding for me, my girlfriend, and her husband.[13]

Eco concludes his biting critique by discussing the differences between Signal, Message, empty form, Addressee, and Code (136, 139). His use of the word "code" differs from how Frye means it. A code for Eco is something to be broken. It is a brand, a purchasing entry point like a credit card, a slogan, a corporate maxim, a tabloid logo, a splashy TV headline, a jargon shared only by corporatists and political elites.

Eco proposes guerrilla warfare to disrupt media massiveness. He sees its weight in terms of tyranny: media is the new monster, Leviathan reborn. Philosophical differences are fair game; and Eco is setting up an agon of differentiation with McLuhan. Eco dehumanizes information media: it is now titanic, depersonalized, crass, gross, and grotesque. McLuhan's "medium is the message" is reduced in Eco's formulation to an equation of forms without effect: it is a formula for how people vulgarize communications. This leaves media masters free to impose their often sinister (or sleazy) agendas. Eco's interpretation aside, what he accurately directs us to is the environmental apocalypse that McLuhan caught in his famous aphorism. Mass communications have changed our relations in ways that we could never have foreseen and should not, in Eco's combative terms, surrender to or absorb. Eco dismisses what McLuhan appears to mean. But he agrees that the milieu has altered. Mass media becomes the oppression of the totalitarian signal to Eco. By ignoring the political dimensions of the media, McLuhan confined his thought to questions of technique. It was inevitable that McLuhan would be blind to questions of class warfare.

Eco surely illuminates the epochal shift; but the media surround (for him) is an intolerable swell of corporate messaging. He suggests this has not changed the secular story of human struggle. At the heart of the New

Village of Total Communication is the vision of what we do to find ourselves and one another. The tragedy of control is destabilized by guerrilla interventions. The mass media seem truly new, but inside their processes we find the age-old tale of the return of Moloch, the false god devouring his own children.

I believe Eco thinks that media users should become Wiki-leakers, practitioners of pastiche, gawkers and cyber-bandits, part of the Anonymous movement that outs videos and images, hacking Pentagon files and rants by celebrity Scientologists. We should be whistle-blowing, compromising government sites, learning how to sabotage the global system that supports the beast of control in the Electronic Disturbance Theatre (EDT) of Hacktivism. Cultural jamming is available on the Internet; and tactics of street disruptions can be taken to the Web. Weirdness is still free, which we see on the shock sites ("Operation Payback") that ridicule political and commercial slogans.

Eco cannot shake off the McLuhan and Frye synergy, though: the domineering machine that is the global theatre reverberates with the human quest; it needs the rebellions of our prankish trolling. We have to push back at big media. It has become excessive, replacing our struggle for justice with BS. Eco stakes out his contrary position by making his context and content an existential construct, without reference to the transcendent and immanent. In his eyes, there is only heroic resistance to the predatory mass-media-Moloch. The savvy use of Web sites by the Occupy Wall Street movement in 2011, where protestors kept ahead of police by text messaging, would confirm Eco's faith in cyber-banditry. (Hacktivist sites and flash protests are to the twenty-first-century virtual community what pamphlets and newspaper editorials were to eighteenth-century revolutionaries.)

⁂

Baudrillard goes beyond Eco in his critique of McLuhan. But Baudrillard's critique is an extension of McLuhan's thought; it is difficult to read him without seeing how influenced by McLuhan he is. Baudrillard recognized in his essay *Simulations* (1983) how far McLuhan had gone in his perceptions of mass media.

In *Paroxysm* (1998), Phillippe Petit interviews Baudrillard and summarizes his positions in a succinct style. The interviews imply what happens when a thinker takes McLuhan's probes to an igniting flip point. Remove humanism, the valuing of each soul, the primacy of education, the faith in cosmic intelligibility, the metaphysical concern, the rooting in literary tradition, and what do we have? Take away the yearning of the identity quest from the human romance, erase it from the consciousness of literary and media users, and what would the world resemble? Obliterate the transcendental hope of the McLuhan-Frye matrix and what is left? Take out the premise that communication is possible between the world forms and people's senses, between text and readers, between individuals of contrary modes of perception and thought, between waking mind and dream-time, and what appears? Extinguish the esoteric subtext of the McLuhan-Frye alchemy, the proposition that all that falls must rise, and what hurtles towards us?

Baudrillard is the truest successor to McLuhan, but only if we take the global theatre to be an excremental heap. All media ecstasies for Baudrillard are intoxicating addictions. The pleroma of the sacred has been stripped away in his uneasy vision by the overstimulations of mass media.

A paroxysm is a spasm before a violent Armageddon. Media "culture" is coming to that end, for Baudrillard. "We dreamt of a transgressive, excessive mutation of values. What is coming about is a regressive, recessive, involutive mutation ... The true cancels itself in the truer-than-true, the too-true-to-be-true, the reign of simulation."[14] He refutes Jameson and Eco; no political action is effective against media engulfment. "I set out from the idea that we shall not get back to history as it was before information and the media, that the excess of history or the excess of eventfulness cancelled out the very possibility of historical action" (7).

To Baudrillard, and like Eco, the media is our world: there is no escaping its total permeation into our psyches. Unlike Eco, he believes that we cannot intervene, even through Anonymous prank sites. There is no authentic communication and no miscommunication. Instead of pleroma there is glut. Media simulacra have become "a spectral, virtual universe, a devitalized, lobotomized form ... My object might rather be said to be a society losing its transcendence, from which the social, the very idea of the social has withdrawn. Hence the concept of mass, of silent majority. The masses ... are a kind of amorphous agency, a sort of silent prophecy or anti-potency, an indefinable antimatter of the social" (39–40).

By pushing McLuhan's idea to extremes, Baudrillard posits a place beyond the texts of humanist literacy. He gives precise evocations of the nihilistic aspects of iLiteracy: "Mirror-stage has given way to the video-stage. Nothing escapes this kind of image-recording, sound-recording, this immediate, simultaneous consciousness-recording, any more. Nothing takes place now without a screen." The Great Code no longer riddles through the labyrinths of time. "Identity is a dream pathetic in its absurdity ... Living identity, the identity of the subject, implied the mirror, the element of reflection. Even in the shattered mirror of alienation, the Student of Prague [an oblique reference to Kafka?] rediscovered his image on the verge of death. We no longer have such good fortune" (50). Murderous gangs re-emerge at the same time orbital technology and global commerce annihilate borders. We are so hyper-stimulated that our normal condition is now stupor, or the addled pursuit of unsatisfying pleasures. Mass pop culture overturns Nature so that young people reference icons and machines, never trees or seas. God, metaphysics, morality, revolution – these are all meaningless tropes, sentimental attachments. The capital of the world is Times Square in New York City, because there all is burning electric light and pixel-signal, a new entity that dwarfs and parodies humanity. We swarm around screens in ant-like obedience. Politics has become a simulation of a theme park (already in itself a simulation). We are reborn in test-tube electronica, growing up to become Bozos the clones.

This is Baudrillard's highly original insight: if there is no God, no Nietzsche, no Marx, no Freud – no higher being, no possibility of the Overman, no feasible political revolution, no interior realm to be readdressed – then there is nothing left but media images. Simulation, stimulation: in the arena of images, there is no ground, no bottom, no frame of reference, no metaphysics; the loop of images is everything. Like McLuhan, he sees media as the supreme new embrace, the simulacra. Unlike McLuhan, Baudrillard sees no perceptual process that transforms and reintegrates electronica; the media are not a representation of cosmic energies, nor an activation of the impression by forms and their re-creation. We will find no allegoric narrative set inside books because literature (every aspect of alphabetic culture) has been absorbed into the digital delirium, the pixel-clustering of image and text. Even libraries are obsolete when access is available to any PC user.

In the conditions of media allatonceness, the simulacrum refers to itself. Machine speaks to machine in telebanking networks. TV culture becomes ravening: "Reality TV" is a home invasion, dissolving boundaries between the real and fiction. It is always shock and awe in the media reel. Instead of the tyrannies of maniac leaders, we have the insidious tyranny of financial computer codes. McLuhan's "the medium is the message" is scorched into "the virtual is the message."

Baudrillard implies that the humane and devout McLuhan, a reader of poetry, a lover of truth, fell short in his visionary awareness. Electronic machines turn us into extensions of them. (McLuhan once quipped that the egg hatched the idea of the chicken in order to get more eggs. Now electronica encourages the proliferation of TVs and PCs to get more screens.) Media becomes a unified field of meaninglessness. We rattle around in claustrophobic cells, becoming voyeurs and exhibitionists inside the circuitries of the closed cosmos.

What if Baudrillard is right? I hope not. But he powerfully catches the paranoid side of electronica with an eloquence that McLuhan never achieved. The difference between them remains this: technology is unnatural to Baudrillard. All technology extends is itself. The virtual state is a global entity, without soul, merely feeding on data and morphing. There is no alienation because there is no way out. Even nihilism is absorbed into our daily dose of information.

It is as if McLuhan's aphorisms had waited for Baudrillard's dark variations. The global village becomes a synonym for the catastrophe of globalization. This is electronic media raging in extremis. "Information exhausts itself within itself, and absorbs its own ends. Television says nothing but: I'm information, everything's information ... Globalization is built on the basis of the supremacy of the medium and then neutralization of the message ... Global integration is achieved on the basis of nullity" (72). The sometimes dire prophetic sides of McLuhan and Frye find fulfilment in Baudrillard's cataclysmic but eerily entertaining toxic-city.

There is some irony in Baudrillard's essaying. "It is no longer the human which thinks the world. Today, it is the inhuman which thinks us" (115). The end of the end is the conclusion of humanism; the new consumption resists the legacies of the past. Our freaky science-fiction condition – where we screen images and are screened simultaneously – requires an unachieved (and likely unachievable) heroism.

Baudrillard talks of "renunciation": no more totalizing ideas or humanist agendas, no spiritual imperatives, no more transcendence, and no solitude. It will not do to see romance-quests or media communions or stories of awakened consciousness or finely woven nets of literary analogy. Yet does critique flicker in the margins? "A thinking that is no stranger to imposture" (116). The world cannot bear whole schemes. Theories will be swallowed by the machines, sent back to us in ephemeral pictures, mesmerizing raptures. We have to devise ways to flee, becoming emigrants of the media alpha and omega. The alphabetic code is not enough to map where the mind must go. Communications come in samplings, which we recycle in sound and picture bytes. The things that do not kill us will make us stranger.

Baudrillard's thought is the terminal destination of McLuhanism. His philosophy reaches the phase where the apocalyptic-prophetic is another dangerous seduction. Apocalypse becomes a cliché in the way that "revolution" is used in ad copy for spring fashions. McLuhan became a figure of quaint moral concern for Baudrillard; he was a thinker shaped by the alphabetic culture he seemingly critiqued, defined by an (embarrassing) hope, rooted in an irrational, sacrificial faith.

While I obviously sympathize with the missionary intentions of McLuhan and Frye, I find something weirdly compelling about Baudrillard's intensity. I have moments of doubt when I think his vision is more than a premise: it is documentary.

He is saying there is nothing beyond the global theatre. McLuhan implied this was so too. But his humanism, and his faith, forbade any final condemnation of it. No story had closure. Every image, every tale, every epiphany, every sign opens to another. It would be arrogance to presume we can know how we are meant to evolve; all we require is trust, inspiration, stamina, patience, wisdom, courage, insight.

Jameson, Eco, and Baudrillard offer postmodernist contrasts to the visionary humanism that McLuhan and Frye represent. Indebted to the two in one way or another, the triad of philosopher-critics are nevertheless more familiar voices of late twentieth-century critical thought and theoretical proposition. If you take their voices together, they often sound like a chorus of negation. The Canadian theorists Arthur and MariLouise Kroker often daringly extend Baudrillard in their collaborative writings.[15] But the Krokers ground their work powerfully in the intellectual theoretical line of McLuhan, Innis, and Grant and so remain connected to their humanism and to the alternative time/space that all three thinkers thought Canada provided.

I know there are great differences between these critical-theorists. Jameson's examinations of postmodernity are conducted under the aegis of Marxist humanism, a revolutionary address to the problem of alienation. Eco's semiotic theories are often swallowed by the inventiveness of his novels. Baudrillard's ideas become dazzling play: to name is to impishly deflect. Calling image culture a new holy order is a deliberate derangement of the senses. Nevertheless, Baudrillard stops me cold with his implicit question: Did the apocalyptic intentions of McLuhan and Frye falter? Did they idealize criticism and writers, the electronic media and its players? What if we opened the doors of perception and found ourselves swamped by garbage? What if we opened what we thought were the gates of paradise and found Kafka's ghost instead?

These critics put the quotation marks of sceptical, even cynical, distance around the McLuhan-Frye School of Communication Theory. McLuhan and Frye seem part of a nostalgic liberal bequest that presupposes the existence of soul and truth. Illumination and enlightenment, the passions of the human journey and expanded eyes – these can seem like corny concerns to those who have experienced the feverish appeal of media loops. McLuhan and Frye presume the existence of a core self, "the citadel of individual consciousness,"[16] indelible under surface spectacle, transcending cocaine-fuelled partying and special effects. They conducted a struggle of reading and misreading, but this may now be of interest only to tenured scholars and bookish introverts. In the blink of a postmodernist retrospective, how strange it must seem to see how for McLuhan Nature and super-Nature impress us through their forms; how we are capable of turning the cosmos into art; and how for Frye the spiritual energy in one book links to another, and we seek finer articulation through re-creation, while in our readings we become "numinous presences ourselves."[17] They tried to write paradise, when it is easy to stay in purgatory and in hell – and easier yet to write nothing at all.

The University of Being and Becoming

It is with great relief that I return to the McLuhan-Frye synergy. Their conjunction appears again in McLuhan's recognitions of the media surround and in Frye's necessary cultivation of the Mental Traveller. McLuhan acknowledges alchemical recombinations in a 1960 letter to Bernard Muller-Thym. His statement is a rare admission, written before he was engulfed by the shimmer of transitory media celebrity. He states how the complementary patterns of the external and the internal could inform both individual creative energy and the communal formation of ideas. Alienation is a given, but never inevitable. Institutions could be reformed by new ideas. He says,

> I see no reason to neglect the notion that with each of our senses becoming externalized electronically, we encounter the sensus communis in a collective form for the first time, and can and need to know very much more about the operations of the private sensus communis ... Renshaw urged

me to contact Bell Telephone Labs where he said I would find teams of researchers happy to tackle my hypotheses ... *And so by a commodious vicus of recirculation ... we come back to Bernard, Eckhart, and the University of Being.*
(Letters, 271, 272; emphasis mine)

The passage is an echo chamber: Joyce's *Wake* reverberates with Saint Bernard of Clairvaux – mentor for Hildegard von Bingen – and Meister Eckhart's mysticism. It was Eckhart who wrote of the University of Being. McLuhan is musing aloud about the humanist goal: to remake our minds and the world into a luminous unity. In a synoptic phase he evokes a living tradition of reconstituted learning, incorporating literature, business, spirituality, media. His tone is delighted. It is obvious that the alchemy is meant to meld disparate energies, in communiqués that speak harmonies, not poisoned polarities. There is good will – perhaps a cultivated Blakean innocence and experience together – in his letter.

Frye writes on the alchemy of education in "Expanding Eyes." He reflects on how learning must move from reverie and study to contact with others. This is a refutation of the Jameson challenge that Frye's premises herald an obscurantist withdrawal. His meditation focuses with good will at the implications of teaching beyond grade requirements and skills building. In alchemy Frye finds a metaphor for his activities in mixing the minds of readers and students with literary art: the inference is that chemical bonding makes a new person. He expresses his hope for a University of Being too:

> [Jung] ... treats the "great work" of the alchemists as an allegory of self-transformation ... Such a work of transformation is the work specifically of saints, mystics and yogis. However the alchemists managed, it seems to require teachers, oral instruction, and joining a school, and it is so unimaginably difficult that very few get far along the way, though they undoubtedly make a difference to the world when they do ...
>
> Gurdjieff ... distinguishes two elements in man: the essence and the persona, what a man really is and what he has taken on through his social relationships. Gurdjieff clearly thought of the kind of training that he could give us essentially a developing and educating of the essence. Perhaps there is also a way to development through the persona, through transforming oneself into a focus of a community. *This includes all the activity that we ordinarily call creative, and is shown at its clearest in the production of the arts. What is particularly interesting about alchemy is the way in which it uses the same kind of symbolism that we find in literature to describe the "great work" of the mystic. If*

spiritual seeker and poet share a common language, perhaps we cannot fully understand either without some reference to the other.
(*Spiritus Mundi*, 119, 120; emphasis mine)

In this there is Frye's abiding fascination with the "great work," the alchemical opus of the self. Every transformation requires an agent of change.

Can we put their hope for a University of Being and Becoming into succinct phrases? Education transforms culture and society into environments of learning, for McLuhan: this is where the ladders start. We are asleep in dreamland and must learn to dream awake. To Frye, education trains us to become critics. While this seems like the sort of specialization that McLuhan decried, Frye develops a method that helps us to find a prophetic key in literature – to open the patterns of recurrent symbols and seize the Great Code. Literature is the dreamland that asks us to awaken into greater imaginative life. Critics after Frye had to engage his suppositions before they could move on. And for all McLuhan's hope that his work would be taken for science, empirically based and therefore verifiable, his accomplishments are idiosyncratically inventive. He made media studies out of his study of literature.

Let me extend the vision of the University of Being and Becoming. In the mythology of syncretism, where all forms and expressions of knowledge can combine, there is what is called the *museion* (in Greek). One translation is *musaeum*. In Alexandria, the ancient library stood magnificently at the centre of education: one of the wonders of the world, it was called the *museion*, established to welcome the muses. The word "muse" is the origin of the words "museum" and "music"; it has echoes in musing and amused. The Alexandrian School was the site where intellectual and spiritual energies were conserved and potentialities converged. People of different faiths met and mingled. Eastern mystic traditions merged with Western philosophies. According to legend, the library was burned down by Julius Caesar's conquering legions; most of the codices were devoured by flames. (Also according to legend, the library rose again and then was torched another three times.) So the library is perhaps more myth than history; but we have learned from Frye how myth rises like the proverbial phoenix from fact into another influential form. That form is the romance-quest for knowledge: know yourself. The syncretic *museion* would have found affinities with the interdisciplinary education program that McLuhan proposed in his 1960 *Report on Project in Understanding New Media*, an idealized project: idyllic, utopian.

Why has the myth of the Alexandrian *museion* persisted down through the ages? I propose it is because of the story of conservation: the *museion* embodies the imperatives – to restore and to perpetuate. It is the transcendental kingdom of knowledge, the community of souls joined in learning. Macaria, the New Atlantis, the New Jerusalem, the academies of the Florentine Renaissance, Castalia; the *museion* has appeared in many places and stories and has had many names. It was an isle of art that granted peace to its guides and students. This was not a peace that brought financial security or social usefulness. It was the peace of contemplation where finer qualities of soul and mind prevailed. The library was the heart of the myth of cosmopolis, where the citizens of cultures not only peacefully coexisted but learned from one another.

In the syncretic vision the cosmos is alive, and we are the children of its light. See the world alive, and we will flourish; see it in darkness, and we deaden ourselves. The Alexandrian *museion* was metaphorically a mixing bowl of elements. It was multilingual, multiethnic. Out of narrowness and ignorance, out of pessimism and despair, out of fatigue and fear, out of slavery and oppression, out of religious difference and conflicts, people found peace in learning, in recognitions of the harmonies between ideas. In the *museion* pagans, Jews, and Christians (and later, Muslims) met with Buddhists and Hindus from India. They shared symbols and lessons. We can take from this the importance of breaking down walls. Education is part of the warming of the soul. The study of many texts – however they may appear – will teach us affinities. Alexandria finds an analogue in Yeats's golden city of Byzantium and in Frye's singing school of the Spirit. I suggest that syncretism is the (possibly) utopian model for planetary culture and world citizenship, the global consciousness that Teilhard de Chardin called the noosphere.

Did McLuhan and Frye idealize the possibilities of a *museion* in their city and their time? I submit that the Alexandrian dream haunted them. I have said that they should be seen together in perennial conflict and complementarity, in their seemingly marginal Canadian *museion*. But every place is both centre and margin in the global theatre. In Toronto there could be a marriage of philology and Mercury. Thus their oppositions are not ultimately divisive. Sympathy connects; antipathy drives the abysses between people. We have seen how their charismatic personalities and intentions did not (and could not) always harmonize, but their desire to make ideas and probes central to understanding is harmonious.

McLuhan and Frye knew that their nearness to one another was essential for the compounding of contraries.

The alchemists' goal was the refining of lead into gold. The heaviness and thickness of one metal becomes the lightness and reflective power of another.

The symbols of this mixing are the volcanic crater and the bowl, metaphors for mental processing. In the ashes of the fire bowl a rose like a phoenix rises. According to Frances Yates in *The Art of Memory*, the domed cranium structure of the head represented the theatre of the mind to the Renaissance Hermetists. A theatre can be like a bowl. We talk of theatre "in the round." Shakespeare's theatres were round; one called, significantly enough, the Rose, the other (of course) the Globe.[18]

The alchemical mixing bowl is an analogue for reception and welcome. It is a symbol of openness. In the liturgy of communion one forms one's hands into a bowl to receive bread, the manna, which on the symbolic plane is spiritual food: wisdom. The pursuit of gold is a metaphor for enlightenment, radiant consciousness, the wisdom of the knowledgeable and perceptive self. Gold is the colour of the sun, of light.

The McLuhan-Frye initiations into "echoland," into critical arrangements of generic and thematic concerns, are attempts to bring to light currents and structures of sensational effect and thought. Apocalypse is not catastrophic; remembering is not nostalgia. *Kerygma* recharges the spiritual battery. Paranoia may travel at the speed of light, but so can wisdom. Against evangelical sermons or theories of imminent dread, there is the romance-quest of identity, which never ends, and our participation in cosmic phenomena, which may never end. When imagination dissents and perceptions bloom, the toxic-city is for a time reversed into the syncretistic city. It only takes one or two voices to say so.

The Toronto School of Communication Theory was a moment when syncretism rose and found a place again. Something stirred; an opening came. There was an awakening in the circles, paths, buildings, and classrooms. Two teachers crossed each other's paths and made pathways over abysses, through labyrinths. For a time they proposed an ideal of deeper communication. They gave us the double vision: one saw the new reality we share, one intuited and comprehended other dimensions. Contrary souls met and recognized one another, sometimes distorted one another, sometimes goaded and inspired and blamed and praised the other, then inevitably passed by and on.

Return to the university grounds, and walk northward and then east, around the circle at Queen's Park, back to Frye Hall and McLuhan Way. Their names and the places are memory theatres or memory systems. Naming is a compass, not just a way of honouring.

Coincidentia oppositorum: this means the coinciding of opposites. In alchemy, the Latin phrase refers to conjunction, the goal of the fires of love and wisdom. The phrase also reveals that those things you thought were divided in fact share more in common than you realized. McLuhan and Frye were tireless in their spinning of ideas and of texts. That energy itself is warming. And when such thoughts come into a time and place, the vast negation, the long fall, that often grips the world is briefly suspended. Seeing the world in the Blakean and Joycean terms of an enlarged human body involving all is not an image of globalization. Perhaps one day the lions of instruction may seem wiser than the tigers of postmodernist wrath.

Restoring Humanism

I turn to one more convergence in my explorations. It is another expression of hidden harmonies. The roots of wisdom are in the air, so the current of ideas may appear in many manifestations.

Sometimes you find echoes of the McLuhan-Frye synergy in surprising places. I found sympathetic vibrations in Gayatri Chakravorty Spivak's *Death of a Discipline* (2003). I suppose the only reason that her postcolonial polemic surprised me is because many theoreticians of deconstruction have been hostile to the apocalyptic-seers of the University of Toronto. But Spivak talks in her essay of crossing borders and of comparative literary studies, a necessary interdisciplinarity. Boldly, she turns from "hostility, fear, and half solutions" towards "a politics of friendship to come."[19] And she, I think nobly, invokes the ideal of "planetarity" to replace the concept of globalization. That word is tainted by rampaging capitalism, the rule of economies by unelected corporations. The global theatre is an image of the noosphere, not of a branding by big business. "Today it is planetarity that we are called to imagine" (81).

Spivak does not mention Frye or McLuhan until late in her essay, but she makes the case for a synergy of the ideas they conveyed. Identity and the media-scape require new articulations. "[I]f as teachers of literature we teach reading, literature can be our teacher as well as our object of investigations" (23). Literature may be marginalized, certainly not the central means of communiqué in the corporatist milieu, but it has purpose. What is that purpose? "The question *'who we are'* is part of the pedagogic exercise" (26; emphasis mine). Imagination is "the calling forth" of the spirit to address the world and to remake it. Truth is unverifiable, but there is reference beyond the text. That reference is to otherness, "alterity," the infinity of meanings in people and phenomena. Otherness or strangeness, the mystery in everyone (and in everything), is irreducible. Her significant secular revision of the romance-quest is to substitute "we" for "I." I mean by this that she recognizes how communications' technologies collectivize before they individualize. I blinked when I read her prophetic words. Her essay was published years before Tumblr, YouTube, Kindle, Facebook, Twitter, and other social networks enlisted user-populations the size of nations.

When she describes the crossing of borders, we can see an analogy to "breakdown leads to breakthrough." When we recognize "planetarity," we should take this to mean the Magnetic City is a reality, not just a slogan. The noosphere is not a theoretical, ideological construct: it is what the world has become, and we must use richly poetic language (influenced by Teilhard de Chardin) to trace and track it. Machines may commune with other machines, but your heart still seeds and needs other hearts.

Spivak's subtle reading of Virginia Woolf's *A Room of One's Own* (1929) leads her to recognize how inwardness (solitude) could meet with community. The individual angle can be isolating, but it can rise in responding to other inquiring and suffering spirits.

> [T]he mysterious imaginative undertaking of Woolf's book can still kick in; 1928 is somewhere between Shelley and the Internet.
>
> (50)

Reading, education, the question of identity (of multiple selves), the issue of what it means to be literate — these carry imperatives in planetarity. Spivak sees that the thematic core of literature and the study of many texts generate resistance to the homogenizing force of financial globalization, "the imposition of the same system of exchange everywhere" (72). Literature escapes that system by offering visionary alternatives, refreshing our engagement with difference. Yet we cannot escape the impact of the media surround:

> In the Tumblr gridwork of electronic capital, we achieve that abstract ball covered in latitudes and longitudes, cut by virtual lines, once the equator and the

tropics and so on, now drawn by the requirements of Geographical Information Systems.

(72)

Again sounding the global village note, she writes, "[T]he Earth is a bigger concept-metaphor than bounded nations, located cities" (93). Towards the end of her essay Spivak invokes Frye. Although she chastises him for trying to make criticism into a science in the *Anatomy* – she takes Frye to mean hard science (a debatable interpretation of what he meant) – she sees that he grants what she calls "the incommunicable experience in the center of criticism" (101). What Spivak means by the "incommunicable experience" is fourfold imagination: arguably, she is pointing to the myriad meanings of the romance-quest; then she may also be referring to how the ineffable – the inspiring source – can be expressed indirectly through metaphor only. In cryptic terms she may allude to how meanings are contingent on the reader's background and ways of understanding ("user is content"). Then she may be suggesting how the infinite mystery at the heart of literature resists final voicing; this is the mental travelling that ventures forward in perpetual voyaging.

Spivak theorizes that imagination, when represented in literature, embraces the unlimited. Something surges through books that unites us in shared humanity. The quest to know who we are, however, should be read in the global technological context. "I know the cartographic markers of the TV in the arm of my [airplane] seat. Planetarity cannot deny globalization" (93). Now our imaginations, she implies, must break free from categories. Literary text has to meet technology's context. When we imagine what the planet is becoming, we grasp the moment in all its manifestations. If literacy is one of the keys, then what door of perception will it unlock? We open it to the vista of the ideal city that transcends particularities.

A (possible) paraphrase: we multiply machines, becoming more ingenious with our instruments, creating simulations of the source, the natural energy fields of electricity. Our contact with one another now needs open-heartedness, so that we may realize good will and harmonies of intention. We are going ahead into the glow-mind (the light off of screens, from all wired cities) that seems to want to reduce the night, if not to wholly subdue it. Through circuitry – the emergent planetary consciousness – we recognize the true tale of the hunger for exodus (liberation).

The current of electricity is the flush of Nature and super-Nature, made up of individual currents (ourselves), melding into the Magnetic City. There are no nations, only infinite worlds (possibilities) in us. Each station, and site, is an entry point, an orb or "urb," mothered by energy.

McLuhan and Frye asked their time to overcome alienating impoverishments. The call for interdisciplinarity and for a community of souls is an echo of their probes and quests. "There are no passengers on Spaceship Earth. We are all crew," McLuhan said.[20] (He absorbed this precept from Buckminster Fuller.) "Electricity ... creates musical politics," McLuhan says in *Counterblast* (113). The aphorism can mean now is the time in the global village when ideology and orthodoxies give way to harmonies. Synergy is a chord played for an instant before other melodies and chords come. This is "The Phoenix Pattern: End as Beginning."[21] These are aphorisms that Spivak and Frye, for all their differences of reference and style and their differences of political conviction and theological urgency, would surely have endorsed.

We are back to apocalypse. At the start of my book I argued that McLuhan and Frye are the originators of a prophetic-visionary tradition in Canada. Yet the effect of their visions and apprehensions transcends provincial borders. This is in keeping with McLuhan's idea of the borderless global theatre and with Frye's belief that the primary power of the imagination is to interpenetrate realities. In McLuhan's poetic aphorisms there is criticism; in Frye's criticism there is poetry. In their aspirations there is the willed creation of intensities. These are found in Frye's coherent patterns of thought and in his implied discontinuities, the leaps he makes in linking metaphors. McLuhan's intensity is embodied in aphorisms that shift from satire to rhapsody. Pride is an inward flame: Frye burned his flame towards the pages of Blake and Milton, Shakespeare and Joyce; McLuhan turned the burn of his intelligence towards electricity, the element of fire. The visionary-prophetic starts not when the material world ends but in the moment when insight begins.

The apocalyptic mode creates instabilities, however. In the McLuhan-Frye matrix their provocations and pronouncements are instabilities that I believe are meant to be inspirational. In the Book that literature composes and we compose through our rereadings, singular inwardness emerges, for Frye; with that rising, there is a convergence of images and symbols that could overcome anxiety. To McLuhan, the recognitions of media power are meant to tell us how we share in the phenomena. We proceed and ascend from visible to invisible energies: the physical plane (text) rises to the spiritual plane (or imaginative); we go from the medium (artefact) to the message (the effect of the forms).

Apocalypse comes when we know that these cruxes take place every day and night. The Great Code is dormant in our sleeping consciousness until critical voices wake us. The electronic cosmos turns this literary metaphor into the potential practice of every person who picks up a cellular and switches on a screen. Computer storage promises that there will be no disappearance, no limits to knowledge. Access to electricity means we are open to the soft sell of instant massaging and the battery cell of life. In the electronic polity there is a constant coming together, an availability that too easily becomes vulnerability. The arc of the romance-quest always exists in multiple genres and texts, alphabetic and digital. The revelatory mode can feel dislocating, omnidirectional. This is why McLuhan and Frye assumed the roles of the guiding seers, investigators of the spirit (human or otherwise). We need a path through the phenomena; and we need visionary company.

One definition of prophecy means foretelling the future. It is misleading to always think that prophetic figures are crystal-gazers, hectoring Cassandras. But the prophetic tradition says now is the doorway through which all time and space pass. Prophecy is faith in the future; by possessing the present, you might realize tomorrow by allowing it to be. Divination means moving deeply into what is before you. The present, when you read a book and when you scan a screen and hear the global beat, pours over us; we are transported into the unifying moment that speaks to what comes. The moment is neither hallucinatory nor nostalgic. Again, in Frye's understanding of genius, our higher selves emerge when we engage the order of words. The immediacy may be exultant or disturbing. It reveals that we are connected.

I will set out two sets of passages that disclose how Frye and McLuhan understood their place in the prophetic tradition. The first is from *Notebooks on the Bible and Other Religious Texts*. It appears in a place where Frye meditates on the meaning of intensified reading. This passage implies how for Frye concentration can become like a taking leave of the senses, as it were, to soar intellectually. A private meditation on the mandala pattern of a literary form is more than an organizational tool. Solitary readings of literature are paradoxically Pentecostal, the dawning of communal meaning. The privacy of the school of night is a womb. Melancholy becomes exalted introversion, a prelude to inspiration and to the reverie or prophetic state:

> Every once in a while in studying symbolism I feel a surge forward as though my unconscious has handed me another cabbalistic symbol from a kind of universal Tarot. Freemasonry I understand systematizes this into a technique. I think a similar process is the central part of the New Testament conception of the gift of tongues: whether actual languages in the literal

sense were produced by collective excitement I don't know: doubtless it's possible, but would it be anything more spiritually valuable than a curiosity if it did happen? *Surely the feeling of a pattern of a universal meaning coming clear piece by piece, so that those who understand it could talk to each other in shorthand, would be predominant, & would be part of the so-called gift of prophesying.*

(38; emphasis mine)

Prophecy becomes the ability to read the characters, even if they only appear in fragments. We learn to commune with each other in shorthand, through mutual understanding of the signs.

The second set of passages, from *The Global Village*, shows McLuhan improvising, yoking contrary images. The condensed speech suggests quick oral dictation. I find it impossible to know for certain where Powers begins taking down the discharge and where McLuhan stops (if he does). Pentecostal communication becomes the streaming of two voices. The sermonizing could be McLuhan's, a critical outburst before the devastation of his paralytic near-silence; it could be Powers's. Whoever is speaking, the words rush and leap. Prophetic speech is discontinuous. These are lines I have selected from five pages of the text:

> All media are a reconstruction, a model of some biologic capacity speeded up beyond the human ability to perform: the wheel is an extension of the foot, the book is an extension of the eye, clothing an extension of the skin, and electronic circuitry is an extension of the central nervous system. Each medium is brought to the pinnacle of vertical strength, with the power to mesmerize us. *When media act together they can so change our consciousness as to create whole new universes of psychic meaning ... All individuals, their desires and satisfactions, are co-present in the age of communication.* But computer banks dissolve the human image ... Electronic man wears his brain outside his skull and his nervous system on top of his skin ... He is like an exposed spider squatting in a thrumming web.

The passages then segue without connection into this aria:

> Earth in the next century will have its collective consciousness lifted off the planet's surface into a dense electronic symphony where all nations – if they still exist as separate entities – may live in a clutch of spontaneous synesthesia, painfully aware of the triumphs and wounds of one another. *"After such knowledge, what forgiveness."*

(87, 94–5; emphases mine)

The extreme compression in these selections is telegraphic. The allusions are to Genesis 32, but now the struggle with the angel becomes a symphonic sounding, with the blessing and the wounding occurring between communal bodies, between nations. The uncredited quotation is from Eliot's "Gerontion." The prophetic intention is clear: all this is present.

The prophetic stream led McLuhan and Frye into a sublime aesthetics. The revelations of the patterns in literature, and of the global theatre's phenomena, are matched by the depths and ironies of their expressiveness. Metaphoric elaboration and tonal shifts distinguish the Puritan-dissenter scholasticism of Frye's writings. The discontinuous breaks of aphorism, the tonal shifts between celebration and condemnation (often in one controversial sentence) mark McLuhan's pronouncements. Few Canadian writers are so quotable; few provide such allusive densities.

Still those who pursue originality will never entirely fit in anywhere. McLuhan and Frye idealized prophetic outsiders: Milton, Blake, Joyce, and Picasso. The two may have had hermetic reasons for doing so: in their content each called for the universal and the communal, but in their styles each remains distinct. Both spoke of Canadian identity in terms of the unmade, the yet to be. It is a cultural mythology that does not fit, does not settle.

(Reverberations: being original makes both men dangerously similar and similarly dangerous. By dangerous I mean that the vigorous scope of their visionary undertakings implies that anyone who engages them risks absorption. You could disappear into their voices. Their originality poses a special risk to Canadian readers. Canada is a country, an anti-nation truly, whose culture has often sidestepped the implications of rambunctious greatness, the terror and delight of the sublime. We will let our brawling American neighbours fight the big battles of the abyss; let them contend with power and fate. We will leave to European intellectuals the task of exploding what came before, in the intricate demolitions of inherited constructs. Let us exist on the margins of epics, eternal Starbucks to the deliria of Ahabs. But on the razor's edge of the margins, alarm and awe will surely seep, even surge. The Canadian lightness of being is bearable because we have willed it to be so. This lightness often means evading anything wildly unsettling to the peace and order we take to be our fate – or destiny. But between the lines of Frye's prose, in the gaps around McLuhan's aphorisms, there are magnitudes, implications great enough to be possessing and tacitly impelling.)

Did they speak in the nuanced rhythms of veiled autobiography? Their essays, lectures, aphorisms, and interviews conjure the Canadian

Alchemy: Synergy in the Thinking of McLuhan and Frye

obsession with the unfinished identity quest. I surmise they were referring to themselves and to their undertakings. Their books and lectures, letters and notes signal an incompletion that invites us to inject ourselves. Apocalypse means beginning again, not an Armageddon closing. The Canadian imaginative space and time is lighter than our American counterpart. But in the spaces of the McLuhan-Frye matrix, in their labyrinths and breaks, we will go on finding the perceptions and conceptions of their works; these must lead to incessant revision. If we are unfinished beings in the activating state called the Magnetic City, then these collaborators in the *Explorations* project become essential recorders of ecstatic metaphor and the powers of super-Nature. When all books form one Book, then mine is part of theirs too.

I read them to find them in the white space after an aphorism, in the silence that surrounds aching questions. "What speaks to us across death? ... What speaks to us across our own death?" Frye writes in the final pages of *The Great Code* (230). "The power to read the language of environments was the province of the seer ... the secrets he discovered were great breakthroughs ... [a] showing forth of the divine through environmental veils"; thus spoke McLuhan in *The Medium is the Massage* (59). When I read the signatures of McLuhan and Frye, I am moved into paradoxes, the ambiguities of Spirit and matter. Jacob Boehme, mystic philosopher, articulates the attempted readings of Spirit and identity, essaying into the transient intersections of word and being:

> If I read myself, I read God's book, and you my brothers are the alphabet which I read in myself, for my mind will find you within me. I wish from my heart you would also find me.[22]

The McLuhan-Frye matrix often looks like a reconfiguration of Romanticism-Modernism; but their explorations breach the future through the visionary strain. We are not finished with them, and they are not finished with us.

What follows the McLuhan-Frye visionary-apocalyptic? The intricate memory banks of cyberspace reinvent inspirational codes, perhaps even reinventing the muses themselves. The average student is likely to be more computer literate – becoming a Web adept or a Facebook familiar – than informed by alphabetic figures of speech. Reading on a screen is not a strain for some eyes. (I admit that it is so for me; I cannot proofread on a screen at all.) YouTube turns its users into performers and voyeurs; cell phones are event recorders; instead of holding a single candle or a match on ritual occasions, people hold up cells (the shorthand name reveals a molecular connection; not only nerve ends are extended but so are body cells). Text messaging is a necessity for "tweeps" and "screenagers," mouse potatoes and cyberslackers who bridge silences in communications with captions, abbreviations, dashes, geotagging, and the smiling or sad faces of expressive punctuation.

Ruefully, I observe the fascinating para-literary terminologies that have evolved in cyberspace: selfie, dataveillance, surfing, chat room, search engine, cursor, aggro, boregasm, showbooking, upness, flame war, yolo. New words are clearly signs of vitality. Already the Oxford English Dictionary has added PC terms, sometimes defining them with Joycean élan (circa the *Wake*): see especially the entries on photobombing and LARPing (live action role-playing online). Computer competence is a condition for advancement in most careers. Kindle 2, Amazon.com's electronic reader, pencil thin, holds upwards of 1,500 books. All literary works will soon be available for downloading on iPhones. "Our vision," Amazon CEO Jeff Bezos said, "is every book ever printed, in any language, all available in less than 60 seconds." No password protection is secure enough in this data flow.

Every month the innovations rush: flexible paper displays, where image and text and graphics and colour combine, appear with the tag "e-paper." In the terminology of virtuality, note the names: Kindle and Twitter, with their eerie reverberations of burning and birdcall, sparks and snickering. Google carries overtones of agog, ogling, goo, and giggle. Devoted use of that search engine is called Goog-apocalypse. Mobile texting creates cybervilles where personal libraries are composed of movies and blurbs, songs and photographs. On Twitter, where ideas and moods can be posted at regular intervals any time, readers are called "followers"; a million followers access the thoughts of one person through a process called "breaking." I received a forwarded email about online identities from a student in Europe who said, "Furthermore, I share with you a tool I have created with Draceina Pinion (avatar name). Is Brainflowing and is designed for doing brainstorm in Second Life and transfer the contents generated to rea[l] life. I guess you will like it." I am still trying to decode this message.[23]

I found an Internet cliché that runs, "On and on it goes and where it stops only Marshall McLuhan knows." It is difficult to imagine, in the electronica of Direct2Drive and iTunes, meta-verses and 3D environments, how the subtleties of Frye's books, with their inference of wide reading in canonic literary works, would find a common readership that can absorb anything more than a few discrete lines. Is it breakthrough leading to breakdown? It is likely not an either/or proposition. Literacy has become so elastic a term that it encompasses mathematics, physics, TV, music, painting, sculpture, architecture, and biogenetics. The word "literacy" is appropriately deployed now in the plural neologism, "literacies," to indicate an ambitious, perhaps improbable, comprehensiveness.

We scan signs, the omens of earth, sky, towers, stars, and endless wires. Sometimes we make out their sense; sometimes the signs do not cohere. The mythic gnosis says, for the romance-quest to begin again, a Penelope and Ulysses must be reawakened in us. Abysses are openings. Is the silence at the page's edge a sign of irreparable breakage and something more? Do waves (in all forms) carry memories of their transformations while we beat on, hearts and minds evolving inside the current?

In a passage from his inquiry *The Passion of the Western Mind* (1991), Richard Tarnas beautifully blends Blake's visionary intensity with environmental consciousness. In this I find an expansion of the McLuhan-Frye urgencies, in what I take to be a meeting of "the medium is the message" and the Great Code:

> The twentieth century's massive and radical breakdown of so many structures – cultural, philosophical, scientific, religious, moral, artistic, social, economic, political, atomic, ecological – all this suggests the necessary deconstruction prior to a new birth. And why is there evident now such a widespread and constantly growing collective impetus in the western mind to articulate a holistic and participatory world view, visible in virtually every field? The collective psyche seems to be in the grip of a powerfully archetypal dynamic in which the long-alienated modern mind is breaking through, out of the contractions of its birth process, out of what Blake called its "mind-forg'd manacles," to rediscover its intimate relationship with nature and the larger cosmos ... we can recognize ... one long meta-trajectory, beginning with the primordial *participation mystique* and, in a sense, culminating before our eyes.[24]

6
The Lessons of Two Teachers: Guidance and Signs

Can inspiration be taught? Can an apocalypse of understanding come through teaching and the readings of books for a class? Enlightenment implies the lessons of a steady practice; apocalypse suggests conversion, the radical turn. The old word "afflatus" translates into the modern word "inspiration"; but the original carries the meaning of wind, of breath, of energies moving, of lifting your spirits. It preserves the sense of being astonished or overwhelmed; the muses, the Spirit itself, have come calling; you receive. Something outside of yourself rouses your senses. The ancient word "afflatus" preserves the strange, sacred turmoil of the moment. You are changed and charged. Inspiration means to be influenced, streaming in the flux, breathing deeply. To be charged means to be called upon, to be assigned a mission, to be accused, to be attacked, to be possessed, to be electrified, to be asked to pay a price.

Can you bring on the prophetic mindset? Can the practices and methods of these teachers will apocalypse and bestow the gift of understanding? In my appreciation of my elders I have come to many conclusions. This stands out: their primary gift was their attempt to provide ways to let us soar. McLuhan and Frye proposed through their writing and teaching, public lecturing and controversies that if you reform education and attentiveness, you inspire society. How is reform accomplished? It is done through poetics and art, sensory cognition and provocative knowledge, whether in classrooms, on the printed page, through screens, in symposia, in private conversations, in seemingly throwaway suggestions. McLuhan says in *The Book of Probes*, "The art of remaking the world eternally new is achieved by careful and delicate dislocation of ordinary perceptions" (510). He says on the same page of that work, "The artist has merely to reveal, not to forge, the signatures of existence. But he can only put these in order by discovering the orchestral analogies in things themselves." Frye sounds the defining note of his imperative when he says in *The Double Vision*, "In proportion as spiritual perception begins to enter the scene, we are released from the bondage of being 'subjected' to a looming and threatening objective world, whether natural or social. In the spiritual world everywhere is here, and both a centre and a circumference" (40). The arts of perception and inspiration can change a reader into a seer: each deep reading of the cosmos means rebirth must be perpetual. The fall-rise story comes to us every day.

I have questioned whether inspiration means assuming my mentors' shadows. Their mentoring has certainly entered my imagination. Through imagining them I have come to know them best. I have often found that they are most useful to me when they are not easy to understand. I prefer the gnomic McLuhan, Frye when he is most heretical. Then I start to delve and delve, and I find no end to the reflections. McLuhan's magpie insights stay with me; so does Frye's envisioning of all literature becoming one Book. The histrionic McLuhan contrasts sharply with the pious Frye, it seems; but these are masks: McLuhan was a pious Catholic who attended mass every day; Frye was a Gnostic heretic dreaming his alternative readings of the Bible in the lonely room of his library at Massey College. If I continue to wrestle with them, then this is because I have been impressed by their presence, inflamed by their inspirational fire, even branded by it. "Perceptions are not facts, they are processes," McLuhan liked to remind us. And Frye said, at his most attractively iconoclastic, "not that there are any facts anyway." We counter history to find eternity; and we create the anti-environments of art to penetrate the screens of existence.

McLuhan was uncanny in his insights into the future of communications technologies. Few in his time saw the wit in his maxims; he was ambivalent to the point of ambiguity. Some critics take Frye to be some reincarnated form of Christian moralists like C.S. Lewis, when his truest antecedents are Blake and Milton. Readers do not always recognize Frye's and McLuhan's visionary centrality to the Canadian literary tradition because neither were novelists nor poets. They did not give birth to any personae other than themselves (which was a formidable birthing). But they saw more and dreamed with more power than almost any we have yet produced. What also remains with me is the scale of their endeavours, their "wild pitch." When I need to draw inspiration from them, I contemplate their demands on us, and their spirits re-enter my room.

Confession: I am faced with the limitations in my understanding of the prophetic when I absorb their lessons. I could stand in the sphere of the new in the way McLuhan urged and see only crowded streets. The cell phone may buzz and my PC may require an upgrade, but in these I do not see the outlines of the future. (Any time I offer prognoses, they are invariably wrong.) Somehow McLuhan intuited the shape of things to come. Frye wanted us to rise to the sublime; and I have studied his writings and taught his books to receptive students. But neither the prophetic eye nor the premonitory ear have become my day-to-day. I romanticize the one great Book and see its strands in all that I read; but I still stub my foot on the step leading into my home.

Another confession: at times I react in frustration over whether you can find their dark depths. I am not sure whether it is, finally, necessary to do so, but it seems to me that I should ask, where are their zones of darkness? I wonder if they did descend – crash – into desperate places. But in my readings, all my studies of them I have yet to find what William James called "the dust-and-ashes state of mind." Romanticism and Modernism are littered with the wreckage of reckless souls. And there are moments of sad fatigue in McLuhan and Frye. McLuhan expresses in his letters the frustration he felt in trying to light the fire of perception in his circle. His aphasia brought pained silence, gaps in speech. He must have had the weary realization that any recovery of his health was unlikely. Frye hints at sorrow and depletion in his notebooks; Helen's passing into dementia brought deep mourning for the loss of his beloved wife. Both were concerned that their messages were not getting through to readers; but that is the anxiety of every creator.

I search in vain through their words for signs of despair, moments of lost faith, "the valley of ashes," "the dry bones." They do not seem to be there. Seemingly inspired every day, they filled the air and pages with thought and surmises and quotations and puns and aphorisms. I have asked myself, do I want to find darkness in them so that they seem less towering? They would not appear so formidable, perhaps, if they had moments when they faltered. Readers have overlooked their ironies: McLuhan disliked much of what he envisioned in emergent media; Frye's high ambition to burn from critic into a Blakean-Miltonic holder of the key to dreamland seems to have eluded most of his commentators. But irony is not darkness.

Miraculously they thrived, each self-inspired, mostly, each day lived without visible signs of despair. I have come to believe that they knew of the infernos of the modern world, hell-bound outside of them, but they would not admit these into their souls. Their trust in transcendence and immanence stopped them at the brink of any faithless questions about final meaninglessness. Sometimes I feel chastened by this trust (which I have not always had). But I know that a reading of them which evades their spiritual imperatives will be severely limited. They appeared to fend off calamities with the agility of nimble souls. Their horror of darkness led them to keep stoking the fires of illumination in the furnaces of learning.

The wisest thing an inspirational teacher can do is turn the searcher, the pilgrim of longing, back to signs and paths. There are the signs in Toronto that say Northrop Frye Hall and Marshall McLuhan Way. But the keys and codes to the visionary are in your hands. They were from the start. The true teachers of inspiration will likely say it is the receptivity that matters. That is why we need them and then must learn to do without them.

The road and the hall on the university grounds preserve the memory of their nearness to one another. I have tried to show how McLuhan and Frye were contrary figures but not as antithetical as they appeared, even at times to their obstreperous selves. Their styles of writing and working were radically different, of course. Yet they scolded and provoked one another. One felt the electric surround, apprehending its currents; one gazed into the disarray of printed texts, comprehending their unity. They are primary reconfiguring presences and influences in the Canadian cultural landscape. Each knew this was true of the other. But when I read them closely – mustering all my attention – I found harmonies. Each carried a portion of the whole and communicated their inspirations and disagreements with vitality and style. They taught the discontent of joy.

It has not been, however, the point of my book to read their contest in terms of envy or fear. You could do so. Their combativeness could have been the result of the acute recognition of the other's stature and breakthroughs. Envy can be crippling; academia is, like literary circles, often rife with jealousies and cliques of personal animosity and territorial antagonism. These can be clandestine and blatant. Why one intellectual or theorist succeeds and another does not compels conjecture. Envy is a bruise that can become a festering wound. Another subtextual reading of the McLuhan-Frye clash from the mid-1950s to the early 1970s could stress a corrosion of invidious feeling between them. Wrenching envy can lock two figures into a war of wills where both lose something of themselves. The devastation may leave psychological ruins. Peter Shaffer's impressive play *Amadeus* (1979) is a parable of this battle of envy and bewilderment. The conflict between Salieri and Mozart is taken, of course, to a murderous end. However, few stories or discourses known to me have explored the inspirational aspect of envy.

We know of the mark left by teachers on their students. What masters have survived or transcended their fellow masters? Envy can be a prompt. Moreover, envy may be tempered by the disciplines of faith or spiritual exercise, or by collegial concern, or by a cultural temper that supports contrariness, or by the subtle ethical recognition that the other is indispensable. Frye says in *Fearful Symmetry* that what we learn from poetics is "self-sacrifice, kindliness and endurance" (47). They were sufficiently large enough in their souls to acknowledge that a fellow figure was of importance not only to literature and to their epics of insight but to their own getting of wisdom.

※

Frye pledged himself to absorbing everything he read into the Great Text – the alphabetic code of rising and falling, the book of awareness – and to turn us into revisionaries who could emerge from sheltered solitudes dreaming of a better world drawn back from the shadow of death.

McLuhan confronted shadows all his life – he called them the subliminal and invisible influences of images and screens – and yet sought to shift us into awareness of how natural and spiritual energies move over and through our inventions and their phantasmagoria.

※

In the beginning of my book I described how Genesis 32 tells the story of how Jacob wrestled with the mysterious angel. Arguably, it is also a parable of forces wrestling with the power of the other. Perhaps it is an image of two sides of oneself, arguing out the conflict of utopian dream and existential anxiety. From the struggle between angel and person comes new life: difference. And there comes the blessing: I think this is best articulated in Numbers 11:29, a biblical passage much favoured by both McLuhan and Frye: "Would God that all the Lord's people were prophets, and that the Lord would put his spirit upon them." Moreover, I have emphasized all along, they knew the importance of the other's pursuits. Practically speaking, they had research opportunities – and tenure – granted to them by the administrators of the University of Toronto. They had student audiences. Still the presence of a fellow apocalyptic was inevitably a spur – to necessary irritation and inspiration. Frye's conciliatory tonality in the essays he wrote after McLuhan's death evokes a sense of absence, surprisingly of a missed opportunity. "I wish I had known Marshall better," he said to Corinne McLuhan.[1]

It is impossible for any writer or intellectual in Canada to evade their ambitions. Our boldest visionaries, they thrive at the crux of our culture. In the inventive recesses of their missionary hunger, they were hunting for the contours of cosmos, where the overlooked or the gnomic (TV, a literary genre) became alchemical mirrors of the greater processes of cognition and identity. They were telling us, and they are still informing us: read the ciphers, the forms, the types, the words, and we will soon find infinite correspondence, the surplus of our pact with meaning. Quickened by their inspirations, we move along carrying their percepts and concepts, sometimes letting their voices possess us, their injunctions whispering in our ears. They are still saying, "make it new, be a torch in the maze." There is a golden thread leading through the labyrinth; steady yourself in the storm; if you find the right word *(verbum significatum)*, the magic that has been waiting for us, then your time will open, and there could be the opening of hearts and minds.

We may evade them, but truly there is no avoiding them: we go on absorbing their traces even when we do not know we are doing so. They repay us through the enhanced sense of the power of the imagination, in the skills we may develop to perceive invisible energies. The two together: from them we get the story of purpose and the environment (natural, electronic) trembling, transiting.

Their nearness to one another is now part of the Canadian communiqué. Their current standing in intellectual theoretical circles is respectful but in partial eclipse I believe because of their dissenting spiritual originality. This abiding concern is manifested on most pages of their work. "I'm a Blakean, a visionary disciple," Frye acknowledges in his notebooks.[2] McLuhan repeatedly said, "I am a metaphysician."

Although their exchanges in *The Listener* debate were sharp, their goals were a plenitude of responses, to keep clear, to keep lively, the forms of experience and our imaginative-perceptual being. Their disagreements were over more than pedagogical and literary merit: I have argued that the disputes were over myths by which to live. Without their conflict and their harmonies, Canada would be less interesting; though there is more to the McLuhan-Frye matrix than the merely interesting. The Canadian cultural event would have less negotiation with intellectual range and textual insight, with destiny and apogees. McLuhan and Frye created voices, in prose, in aphorisms, and their rhythms and tones compose cultural tonalities: Frye's voice, eloquent and subdued, pressing us with heresies; McLuhan's voice, quixotically incendiary, impressing us with conundrums.

They were each other's horizons. Theirs is an authentic indigenous re-creative seer matrix which we can, if we are to take our cultural difference seriously, reject and elude, revisit, revise, extend, and amplify. In one of our last vestiges of the colonialist mindset we often look to other theoretical protocols for authority and justified fascinations. The apocalyptics of McLuhan and Frye show that what metamorphosed in the vortex of their *paideuma* is a synergy of percept and concept, of environmental awareness and the reading of the essential story. Education is upward metamorphosis to find and maintain energy without the downward spiral of despair. "It is always good to have the avant-garde behind you," McLuhan said in response to a question about how he stood in terms of the new theorists.[3] I find in them a revival and a deepening continuation of the Romantic-Modernist line of poet-seers and prophetic intellectuals. They emerged from that lineage into our concerns with rebellious excentricities in the hyper-communications of the global theatre. Frye says in *Fables of Identity: Studies in Poetic Mythology*, "The Romantic movement in English literature seems to me now to be a small part of one of the most decisive changes in the history of culture, so decisive as to make everything that has been written since post-Romantic, including, of course, everything that is regarded by its producers as anti-Romantic."[4]

Their passions have sent us on our way.

The way is surely this: they held in common visions of a communicating cosmos. Nature and super-Nature speak; on the pages of printed books the voices of time awaken every time we open them; when we open our senses – the *sensus communis* – to cosmos, the intimations of wind and wires become available. I find this a beautiful conceit. I ponder it, and it brings me solace.

Between sunrise and sunset (and after sunset and before sunrise), there is an epic tale unfolding. This tale mirrors the rise and fall, the fall and rise, that we each sense in our souls, and that we will meet in our engagement with our inventions and in the waking dream that we engage in the pages of literature. I contemplate this, and it also comforts and inspires me.

Like Frye's Great Code story, McLuhan's aphorism, "the medium is the message," illuminates realms of constant communication. The point is that the texts of the world – elemental, written, oral, hieroglyphic, and electronic – never stop communicating. Even silence is another articulation. Open the senses, open the texts: the McLuhan-Frye revisionary struggle is to re-construe symmetries out of a broken world.

Frye chided McLuhan for pandering to the corrupting influence of big media; McLuhan mocked Frye for being a POV person whose narrow perspective excluded the multiple perspectives of audiovisual fields. But McLuhan was a "literal man" too. He recognized that the advent – the religious overtone of the word is important – of electronic media changed our milieu and our sense of self. His probes often imply that the speed and imagery of the electronic media suppress imagination. Our senses are wholly affected before interpretations occur; hence the need for new metaphors. McLuhan might have said the Great Code offers a vision of what we would like to be but does not engage media's spectacular energies. Nevertheless, McLuhan would not have denied the power of the allegoric principle because it underwrites the spiritual movement of his own perceptions.

They shared the sense of destiny that they were to be great readers. "Read, read again, and you will find" is an alchemical maxim. McLuhan wrote in *The Classical Trivium*, "The doctrine of names is, of course, the doctrine of essence ... The great grammarians are ... also alchemists" (16–17). McLuhan said he found his name in a book whose pages are full of voices and sounds: "Orion of the orgiasts, Meereschal MacMuhun, the Ipse dadden, product of the extremes." He read this in the *Wake* (254) years before he became famous.[5] In a late-night contemplation Frye said in his notebooks, "Note to cheer myself up with: I'm not a great 17th c. poet like Milton, or a great 18th–19th c. visionary like Blake, but I am a great 20th c. reader, and this is the age of the reader."[6] Later that same night he wrote a note that allowed his moment of humility to leap again into the boast of his readings: "It doesn't matter how often I'm mentioned by other critics: *I form the subtext of every critic worth reading*" (205; emphasis mine).

I know that for all the possibilities of synergies in their thought, there remains between them profound differences of sensibility and character, of intellectual preference and stylistic concern. McLuhan's aphorisms state a limit for language. We participate in the phenomenal world, but the spiritual realm, like electricity, can be known only through effects. An aphorism is a provocative exempla of a compressed philosophy. It suggests the limitations of language through its brevity. Kafka, a fellow aphorist, is useful here: "For everything outside the phenomenal world, language can only be used allusively, but never ever approximately in a comparative way, since, corresponding as it does to the phenomenal world it is concerned only with property and its relations."[7] Describing our world through an aphorism pays homage to what created the world and yet is beyond it. Frye is the patient re-reader of the singular human book; but what is the point of the concentrated gaze of the contemplative eye? Kafka helps again: "It was because of impatience that they were expelled from Paradise; it is because of indolence that they do not return."[8] Nothing is more reminiscent of Kafka than Frye's proposition that we are already in the heaven and hell of innocence and experience; our minds make it so. Rereading McLuhan and Frye replenishes a sense of wholeness in an understanding of the electronic saga and our indispensable books. This whole vision is a Canadian dynamism.

I said at the start that they were my teachers. What were the lessons? The Great Code is the personal legend. Your story has to be lived truly and then told. Inspiration has its shadows, but to be influenced is to be in the current of enthusiasm (*en-theos* means to be breathed into by the Spirit). The shadows do not have to become a permanent darkness. (It is one thing to spend time in Gethsemane, the thorny garden of grave doubt; it is quite another to take up permanent residence there.) What is the theme of the code? You, always you. This does not mean narcissistic self-obsession but that through you the cosmos flows. Each person is a medium. What are the codes or laws of the cosmos? Motion, transformation, the movement towards warmth, deeper connectedness. What are the laws at work? These are what was called the two truths of the wisdom tradition: everything has two sides, which can be called the double vision and figure/ground, innocence and experience together, the visible and invisible always in vibrations of influence. Imaginative, soulful intention transforms the elements. The complementary vision turns to fours when we recall the structure of the tetrad: with every invention, with every idea, something new is added to the cosmos, something is taken away, something reverses into its unexpected opposite, and something very old returns.

There is the lesson that says do without your elders. You must abandon them to move on, living deeply. The path must be yours. I have learned this teaching slowly. But I have found the trust that you can come back – someday – fresh from frontiers, in a changed form, to meet your mentors again. Then other new and vital lessons can begin.

Notes

Prologue

1 Harold Bloom, "Foreword to *Anatomy of Criticism: Northrop Frye in Retrospect*," in Northrop Frye, *Anatomy of Criticism: Four Essays*, 15th ed. (Princeton: Princeton University Press, 2000), ix.
2 Marshall McLuhan, *The Medium and the Light: Reflections on Religion*, ed. Eric McLuhan and Jacek Szklarek (Toronto: Stoddart, 1999), 59.
3 Virginia Woolf, *A Room of One's Own* (London: Penguin, 1945), 7–8.
4 Quoted in Douglas Coupland's *Marshall McLuhan* (Toronto: Penguin, 2009), 8. I am indebted to Coupland's latest description of McLuhan's life. His narrative is, so far, the most novelistic I will be quietly disagreeing with some of his conjectures about McLuhan's illness being the prompt for his inspirations throughout my book. But Coupland's work makes the life of the media guru very vivid and accessible; for this, we are all in his debt.
5 Northrop Frye, *Late Notebooks, 1982–1990: Architecture of the Spiritual World*, ed. Robert D. Denham, vol. 5–6 of *Collected Works* (Toronto: University of Toronto Press, 2000), 6:725.
6 Marshall McLuhan, *Letters of Marshall McLuhan*, ed. Matie Molinaro, Corinne McLuhan, and William Toye (Toronto: Oxford University Press, 1987), 83–4.
7 T.S. Eliot, "What the Thunder Said," in *Selected Poems* (London: Faber & Faber, 1971), 67.
8 I'm indebted (again) to Coupland's biography for his descriptions of McLuhan's legacies. I think he accurately catches the eerily prophetic quality of many of McLuhan's utterances. And I share with Coupland a sense of the uncanny quality of McLuhan's foresight. The conservative Catholic would

have found much to dislike about the World Wide Web. Nevertheless, he saw ahead.
9 McLuhan, *The Book of Probes*, ed. Eric McLuhan, David Carson, and William Kuhns (Corte Madera, CA: Gingko Press, 2003), 372.
10 Frye, *Notebooks and Lectures on the Bible and Other Religious Texts*, ed. Robert D. Denham, vol. 13 of *Collected Works* (Toronto: University of Toronto Press, 2003), 97.
11 McLuhan, "The Marfleet Lectures," in *Understanding Me: Lectures and Interviews*, ed. Stephanie McLuhan and David Staines (Toronto: McClelland and Stewart, 2003), 112.
12 Frye, *Who Was Marshall McLuhan*, ed. Maurice McLuhan and Barrington Nevitt (Toronto: Comprehensivist Press, 1994), 126.
13 Frye, interview in David Cayley, *Northrop Frye in Conversation* (Toronto: Anansi, 1992), 123–4.
14 George Steiner said this in conversation with me at the Living Literacies Conference, 16 November 2002, York University, Toronto, Canada.

1 Intentions and Overview: Apocalypse and Alchemy in McLuhan and Frye

1 William Blake, *The Marriage of Heaven and Hell*, in *Complete Writings, with Variant Readings*, ed. Geoffrey Keynes (London: Oxford University Press, 1972), 149.
2 Northrop Frye, *Anatomy of Criticism: Four Essays*, 15 ed. (Princeton: Princeton University Press, 2000), 187.
3 Marshall McLuhan, *The Medium and the Light: Reflections on Religion*, eds. Eric McLuhan and Jacek Szklarek (Toronto: Stoddart, 1999), 59.
4 Marshall McLuhan, *Report on Project in Understanding New Media* ([Washington, D.C.]: National Association of Educational Broadcasters, US Department of Health, Education and Welfare, 1960); hereafter *ROPUNM*. McLuhan says, "the medium becomes the message" (19). He asks, "Is the medium the message?" (41). In part 2 of the report, on page 3 of the section called "Recommendations," he says, "The medium is the message."
5 McLuhan and Carson, *The Book of Probes*, 18–19.
6 Marshall McLuhan and Bruce R. Powers, *The Global Village: Transformations in World Life and Media in the 21st Century* (New York: Oxford University Press, 1989), xi.
7 Janine Marchessault, *Marshall McLuhan: Cosmic Media* (London: Sage Publications, 2005), xiv.

8 *Kerygma* has many references and sources in Northrop Frye's writings. He first uses it in *The Great Code: The Bible and Literature* (Toronto: Academic Press, 1982), see 29–30, 231. It is used in these contexts to indicate the rhetoric of prophecy and annunciation. Though he uses the word only on those three occasions in the book, it is an idea that underwrites his entire exploration of *The Great Code*.
9 Frye, *Late Notebooks, 1982–1990*, 515.
10 A.C. Hamilton, *Northrop Frye: Anatomy of His Criticism* (Toronto: University of Toronto Press, 1990), 205–6.
11 Friedrich Nietzsche, "On the Gift Giving Virtue," section 3 of *Thus Spoke Zarathustra: First Part*, in *The Portable Nietzsche*, ed. and trans. Walter Kaufmann (New York: Penguin/Viking Portable Library, 1976), 90.
12 The Authorized or King James Version of 1611 is the version that McLuhan and Frye would have consulted. However, Frye would also have looked at the Revised Standard Edition for purposes of comparison. My edition of the King James Bible: Racine, WI: Whitman Publishing Company, 1937.
13 The four parts are outlined and expanded upon in "The Theory of Symbols" essay in *Anatomy of Criticism*, 73–128. They are introduced again in *Great Code*, 222–3. Northrop Frye, *Words with Power: Being a Second Study of the Bible and Literature* (Toronto: Penguin Books, 2007), begins the chapter "Sequence and Mode" with reflections on the "polysemous," another word for the four levels working in harmony (17). The entire chapter is pertinent to Frye's awareness of how the synchronic structure works (18–39). He often employs vertical-horizontal terminology throughout his text.
14 Frye, *Great Code*, 223.
15 Blake, "Auguries of Innocence," in *Complete Writings*, 431.
16 Ernst Robert Curtius, *European Literature and the Latin Middle Ages*, trans. Willard R. Trask (New York: Harper & Row, 1963). The text serves as an introduction to the sources for the trope of the Book of Nature. See Curtius's chapters on "Rhetoric," 62–79; "Topics," 79–105; "Metaphorics," 128–44; and most apposite to this book, "The Book as Symbol," 302–47. The "Excursus" chapter on "The Poet's Divine Frenzy," 474–5, applies very well to my argument put forward on the analogical furor in Frye's late books and in his notebooks in chapter 3 of this book. The chapters "Poetry as Entertainment," 478–9, and "Poetry and Scholasticism," 480–4, are relevant to McLuhan's polemical-celebrational relationship with electronic media.
17 Marshall McLuhan, "James Joyce: Trivial and Quadrivial," in *The Interior Landscape: The Literary Criticism of Marshall McLuhan, 1943–1962*, ed. Eugene McNamara (New York: McGraw-Hill, 1969), 23.

18 Marshall McLuhan, *Understanding Media: The Extensions of Man* (New York: McGraw-Hill, 1964), 64. The line attributed to Yeats in fact appears in Arthur Symons's introduction to *The Symbolist Movement in Literature* (New York: Dutton, 1958), 2–3. There are no footnotes in McLuhan's 1964 edition; he shared with Frye a reluctance to annotate his writings in detail. Symons's statement is not quoted or rephrased anywhere in Yeats's writings. It should come as no surprise to see that the reference in Symons's line is to literature and not to media. McLuhan's perceptions are often, if not mostly, literary in source.

19 Bloom's agon proposal is found primarily in *The Anxiety of Influence: A Theory of Poetry* (New York: Oxford University Press, 1973). The books listed in his "Overview" and bibliography are variations on the argument proposed in that work. "I come out of Frye," Bloom says in his "An Interview with Harold Bloom," by Irme Salusinzky, *Scripsi* 4 (July 1986): 87. Bloom helps to define and redefine my interpretation of agon. Bloom's early works of criticism are indebted to Frye. In the 1986 interview, he says, "He is certainly the largest and most crucial literary critic in the English language since the divine Walter and the divine Oscar." For Bloom to place Frye in such company is to elevate Frye's and Bloom's lineage to the highest literary degree. In *The Visionary Company: A Reading of English Romantic Poetry* (1961; repr., Ithaca, NY: Cornell University Press, 1971) and in its sequel, *Blake's Apocalypse: A Study in Poetic Argument* (New York: Doubleday, 1963), Bloom pays homage to his mentor. He acknowledges his debt in the early pages of *Blake's Apocalypse*: "by reading him I learned to read Blake" (x). In *The Anxiety of Influence*, where Bloom leaps into his theoretical protocol, he turns from Frye. This note cannot deal with the entire argument but can make allusions to it, to identify their concerns. Here is Frye's response:

> Bloom's *Anxiety of Influence*: an embarrassing book to me, because it's about him & not about its subject, & I'm one of the influences he's anxious about. I think the fear of death ... is *the* anxiety, is really just the centre of a much larger anxiety of metamorphosis ... The anxiety of continuity is salvaged from this.
> (Frye, *Northrop Frye Unbuttoned: Wit and Wisdom from the Notebooks and Diaries.* Ed. Robert D. Denham. Toronto: Anansi, 2004, p. 13)

Creating and criticizing literature are about necessary influence: books come out of other books. The continuity Frye speaks of in his entry refers to this confluence. Behind his remark is spiritual grounding. The conflicts of imaginative energies to make the new are harmonized by transcendental faith. This may be a construct, but it is the window through which he sees. To echo Blake, the critic-seer learns to see beyond the window.

What was Frye reacting to in Bloom's book? He had noticed Frye's missionary bias. To Bloom, Frye steps away from the demonic independent inventiveness of Blakean aesthetics into harmonious conjunctions. Instead of a sect of one, we get an apologist for ethical concern. Bloom comments on Milton's Satan, illuminating the decline of the oppositional mind, not only in Frye but in other readers of *Paradise Lost*:

> It is sad to observe most modern critics observing Satan, because they never do observe him. The catalogue of unseeing could hardly be more distinguished, from Eliot who speaks of "Milton's curly haired Byronic hero" (one wants to reply, looking from side to side: "Who?") to the astonishing backsliding of Northrop Frye, who invokes, in urbane ridicule, a Wagnerian context (one wants to lament: "A true critic, and of God's party without knowing it").
>
> (Bloom, *Anxiety of Influence*, 23)

Bloom's objection is to the conciliatory tones often evident in Frye's books. If criticism is prophecy, then the heir to the Blakean tradition should sound like a true prophet and less like a serene lecturer at an urbane Canadian university. Frye hides his prophetic fire in a bush garden. Frye turns his library into a chapel, his classrooms into congregations. Bloom would have liked to hear more Milton in Frye, and less Matthew Arnold or John Henry Cardinal Newman.

Bloom's critique is an American counter-charge to the Canadian lightness of spirit. Perhaps he has not looked closely enough at the Canadian agon with the American emphasis on the majestically ambiguous "self-reliance." Frye's teaching-writing goals were missionary, spiritual, peacefully democratic, and hopeful. Rather than antithetic, Frye's work is inspirational.

But Bloom does not stop his critique in *Anxiety*. We see his most passionate uprising in this assembly of quotations from *A Map of Misreading* (London: Oxford University Press, 1975). My italics highlight the key contrary points:

Frye, who increasingly looks like the Proclus or Iamblichus of our day, has *Platonized the dialectics of tradition, its relation to fresh creation, into what he calls the Myth of concern, which turns out to be low Church of T.S. Eliot's Anglo-Catholic Myth of Tradition and the Individual Talent. In Frye's reduction, the student discovers that he becomes something, and thus he uncovers or demystifies himself, by first being persuaded that tradition is inclusive rather than exclusive, and so makes a place for him.* The student is a cultural assimilator who *thinks* because he has joined a larger body of thought ... This fiction is a *noble idealization, and as lie against time* will go the way of every noble idealization.

(Bloom, *A Map of Misreading*, 23)

We recognize the Nietzschean tone: Frye's critical conciliation is the heroic construct against the outrage of death. Idealization denies the agonistic exploration of language and image through the cultivated inward eye. Students may look over a poet's shoulder with the guidance of a critic, but nothing else. Bloom's reference to Iamblichus raises his suspicion that Frye's mission is part of a reborn mystery cult. It is a droll piece of Bloomian wit. In any agon there is goading. Frye will thunder back, we shall see. There is more from Bloom:

[E]ven the strong Romantic imagination is not capable of power over things as they are ... Criticism is in danger of being over-spiritualized by the heirs of [Eric] Auerbach and by Northrop Frye ... Frye idealizes more powerfully than even Blake does.

(ibid., 66, 79, 199)

He raises important points about Frye's idealizations. Will reality roll back in the wake of imaginative force? Is poetry a force against oppression, or merely a lone individual's sectarian triumph against mortality? A poet's authority for Bloom comes from his or her ability with images and tropes. Prophetic authority comes from religious conviction. These qualities can be combined in one person; they are in Blake. If Frye speaks from a spiritual source, then we could wonder why he does he not do so with Blakean vigour. Frye's answer to Bloom comes in "Expanding Eyes" in *Spiritus Mundi: Essays on Literature, Myth, and Society* (Toronto: Fitzhenry & Whiteside, 1976):

When one finds that very perceptive people are describing one as the exact opposite of what one is, one may feel that one has hit a fairly central area of social resistance. And when I, who have fought the iniquity of mystery in criticism all my life, am called a neo-Gnostic and a successor of Proclus and Iamblichus, both of them pagans, initiates of mystery-cults, and very cloudy writers. (117)

There is wounded pride and outrage in this. Bloom has succeeded in his goading. The next sentences show Frye in passionate flight:

Even granting the human tendency to look in every direction but the right one, it seems strange to overlook the possibility that the arts, including literature, might just conceivably be what they have always been taken to be, possible techniques of meditation ... ways of cultivating, focusing and ordering one's mental processes, on a basis of symbol rather than concept. Certainly that was what Blake thought they were: his own art was a product of his power of meditation, and he addresses his readers in terms which indicate that he was presenting his illuminated works to them also, not as icons, but as mandalas. (ibid.)

There are many tones in this: the annoyance at Bloom mingling with enunciations of his identification with Blake and his techniques of meditation. Mandalas become entry points for contemplating the imaginative cosmos. Frye resists the identification with the pagan mystery schools – a tinge of the United Church preacher speaks there – then reinvents ritual processes of focusing "one's mental processes" on his own defiant terms.

In *The Book of J* (New York: Grove Weidenfeld, 1990) and *Jesus and Yahweh: The Names Divine* (New York: Riverhead Books, 2005), Bloom states how "Frye ... sinks" in the face of theological speculation (*Jesus and Yahweh*, 11). They are Bloom's rejoinders to the reconciling "categorizing vision" of *The Great Code* and *Words with Power*. To counter Frye's literary-mystical ministry, he laments (in "Middle Twentieth-Century Criticism: Kenneth Burke and Northrop Frye," in *The Art of the Critic: Literary Theory and Criticism from the Greeks to the Present*, vol. 10, *Contemporary* [New York and Philadelphia: Chelsea House, 1990]) how "the uncanny originality of J [the original redacted text on which the early books of the Hebrew Bible are based] is melted down in the visionary flames of Toronto" (xiv). He sees Frye as too busy erecting an original edifice to notice uniqueness of voice. This striving surely qualifies as an act of critical genius. Yet in *Genius: A Mosaic of One Hundred Exemplary Critical Minds* (New York: Warner Books, 2002), Bloom barely mentions Frye. Bloom gives ample space to critics and philosophers, but not to the critic he revered. Perhaps the absence presumes Bloom's swerve into his own theoretical architecture, one slivered by struggle and death. In the 1986 interview with Salusinzky Bloom explains his stance towards Frye. He says, "[Frye is] for all my complaints about his idealization and his authentic Platonism and his authentic Christianity – a kind of Miltonic figure." Notice how Bloom calls Frye "Miltonic," not Blakean. Frye made his name with *Fearful Symmetry*. Although his writings on Milton are formidable, they do not overshadow his Blake studies. The irony is obvious.

Neither Frye nor Bloom disputed the centrality of the printed word. They are students of literature's content. Thus we may see why Bloom never discusses McLuhan. McLuhan would have been an obvious selection for his pantheon of geniuses: McLuhan offered authentic divinations; his insights, often involuntary, possessed the future. But Bloom, like Frye at times, likely considered McLuhan an apologist for the triumph of screens and images.

The Frye-Bloom agon shares another feature. Their books are comprehensible to readers outside the university. McLuhan's aphorisms belong to this public intellectual stream too. While Bloom denounces most postmodernist theorizing for being opaque, he neglects to see the ground for the rhetorical strategies of its avatars. McLuhan would have pointed out, if the book is no longer the cultural centre, what remains are conversations among the mandarin guardians of the alphabetic mind. In conditions alienated from a broad public, a new hybrid of wordplay and collage, typographic innovation and calligraphy, graphic art and found texts, will emerge in an experimental shorthand. Marjorie Perloff's book *Radical Artifice: Writing Poetry in the Age of Media* (Chicago: University of Chicago Press, 1991) examines alternative takes in poetics. To the question, "Why can't they write like Kafka?" she replies that Kafka came before TV (xi–xii). Her exploration of the idea continues through the preface (xi–xiv) and "Avant-Garde in Endgame" (1–28).

20 The four primary biographies: Philip Marchand, *Marshall McLuhan: The Medium and the Messenger* (Toronto: Random House, 1989); W. Terrence Gordon, *Marshall McLuhan: Escape into Understanding* (Toronto: Stoddart, 1997); Douglas Coupland, *Marshall McLuhan*; John Ayre, *Northrop Frye: A Biography* (Toronto: Random House, 1989). My book refers to the passages on the agon in subsequent chapters. Also of use for biographical information, see the following: Joseph Adamson, *Northrop Frye: A Visionary Life* (Toronto: ECW Press, 1993), and Paul Benedetti and Nancy DeHart, eds., *Forward Through the Rearview Mirror: Reflections on and by Marshall McLuhan* (Toronto: Prentice-Hall, 1996). See Marchessault's *Marshall McLuhan: Cosmic Media* for a tracing of biographical detail and intellectual formations; her research has been very useful here and in subsequent chapters.

21 Northrop Frye, archival material, from Robert D. Denham (Roanoke College, supplied in 2007–8), 1–2. These are excerpts and pieces taken from unpublished and published material by Northrop Frye on his relationship with Marshall McLuhan. They were gathered for this book by Professor Denham. I am in his debt for guidance through the Frye Archives. Henceforth I will be referring to this material as "Frye Archives." I am also indebted to Professor Denham's studies of Frye, especially to his book *Northrop Frye: Religious Visionary and Architect of the Spiritual World* (Charlottesville: University of Virginia Press, 2004) and to the book he edited with Thomas Willard, *Visionary Poetics: Essays on Northrop Frye's Criticism* (New York: Peter Lang, 1991).

22 Frye, *Late Notebooks, 1982–1990*, 626.
23 Marshall McLuhan, *Culture Is Our Business* (Toronto: McGraw-Hill, 1970), 70. Variations on the fish in water theme can be found in McLuhan and Carson, *The Book of Probes*, 268.
24 These are paraphrases from the following three books by Marshall McLuhan: *Culture Is Our Business*; with Wilfred Watson, *From Cliché to Archetype* (New York: Viking Press, 1970); and with Barrington Nevitt, *Take Today: The Executive as Dropout* (New York: Harcourt Brace Jovanovich, 1972).
25 Marshall McLuhan, *The Mechanical Bride: Folklore of Industrial Man* (Corte Madera, CA: Gingko Press, 2002), v.
26 Northrop Frye, *The "Third Book" Notebooks of Northrop Frye, 1964–1972: The Critical Comedy*, ed. Michael Dolzani, vol. 9 of *Collected Works* (Toronto: University of Toronto Press, 2002), 232.
27 A bias is a twist on perception or an angle on experience. Harold A. Innis's title essay in *The Bias of Communications* (Toronto: University of Toronto Press, 1991) alludes to the impact of communications' technologies from hieroglyph to print on the way we organize the flow of information – or in Innis's case to socio-economic history. See 33–60. Innis's impact on McLuhan is well documented, though the influence that he exerted on McLuhan is exaggerated by critics who wish to see an ideological-theoretical base to his observations. McLuhan's training on literature precluded such a base. Moreover, McLuhan was aware of the effects of media before he read Innis – the evidence is in his literary essays and in the drafts for *The Mechanical Bride*. However, his encounter with Innis's work bolstered his faith in his observations and developing techniques.
28 Frances A. Yates, *The Art of Memory* (Chicago: University of Chicago Press, 1966). Yates's entire book is of relevance to this study of the interpenetrations of McLuhan and Frye. Both acknowledged the impact of reading her book. It was not a source at the time of their readings (1966–7) but a confirmation of their explorations and speculations. McLuhan's reference to Yates's work can be found in a 1966 letter to William Jovanovich, in *Letters of Marshall McLuhan*, 339. Frye's reference and acknowledgment can be found in David Cayley's *Northrop Frye in Conversation*, 62–3. The Cayley conversation with Frye will be one of my primary sources throughout this book. McLuhan and Frye converged in their thought and perception on Yates's recognitions of the role of memory theatres and memory systems in Renaissance thought.
29 I observed the sign on the wall in 1978 at the University of Toronto, at McLuhan's Centre for Culture and Technology. The precise wording is confirmed in *The Book of Probes* (424). I have traced the quotation to

a likely source in Proverbs 4:7. However, the passage in Proverbs refers to wisdom: "Wisdom *is* the principal thing; *therefore* get wisdom; with all thy getting get understanding." The Latin source uses the word *principium*, and this can have various translations. It is possible it was one of McLuhan's revisions. The passage by Frye comes from the sermons collected by Robert D. Denham in Frye, *Reading the World: Selected Writings, 1935–1976*, ed. Robert D. Denham (New York: Peter Lang, 1990), 253.

30 We find the mandala discussion in Frye's essay, "Expanding Eyes," in *Spiritus Mundi*, 117.
31 Friedrich Nietzsche's profound observation, typically incisive, can be found in Aphorism 38 of "The Free Spirit," in *Beyond Good and Evil*, in Walter Kaufmann, trans. and ed., *Basic Writings of Nietzsche* (New York: Modern Library, 2000), 239.
32 Roberto Calasso, *K.*, trans. Geoffrey Brock (New York: Knopf, 2005), 49–50.
33 McLuhan and Nevitt, *Take Today*, 3. The pun is a variation on "Hush! Caution! Echoland!" (HCE), from James Joyce's *Finnegans Wake* (London: Penguin, 1992), 13.
34 McLuhan and Nevitt, *Take Today*, 96.
35 Denham, *Northrop Frye: Religious Visionary and Architect of the Spiritual World*, 52. Research for this book has often been informed by Denham's work. The following are two quotes useful to my argument. The first: "the goal of Frye's quest [is] the Everlasting Gospel, Milton's Word of God in the heart, the interpenetration of Word and Spirit" (28). Second, "Frye's quest has to do more with seeing than with knowing: hence the centrality of light and sight, of recognition and vision and illumination" (28).
36 Frye, *Notebooks and Lectures on the Bible and Other Religious Texts*, 109.
37 Frye, *Late Notebooks, 1982–1990*, 414.
38 Northrop Frye and Helen Kemp, *A Glorious and Terrible Life with You: Selected Correspondence of Northrop Frye and Helen Kemp, 1932–1939*, ed. Margaret Burgess (Toronto: University of Toronto Press, 2007), 212–13.
39 Frye, *Notebooks and Lectures on the Bible and Other Religious Texts*, 215. The entire entry on reversals is of considerable interest and relevance.
40 Linda Hutcheon, "Introduction: The Field Notes of a Public Critic," in *The Bush Garden: Essays on the Canadian Imagination*, by Northrop Frye, 2nd ed. (repr., 1995; Toronto: House of Anansi, 1971), xix.
41 Ronald Bates, "Onamuttony Legture," in *Northrop Frye* (Toronto: McClelland and Stewart, 1971), 19–28; David Cook, *Northrop Frye: A Vision of the New World* (Montreal: New World Perspectives, 1985), 6, 16, 105, 110.
42 Glenn Willmott, *McLuhan, or Modernism in Reverse* (Toronto: University of Toronto Press, 1996), 180.

43 See Richard Cavell, "Borderlines," in *McLuhan in Space: A Cultural Geography* (Toronto: University of Toronto Press, 2002), 197–222. Cavell examines John Fekete's responses too. I am indebted to Cavell's analyses; his chapter is a pioneering piece of research.
44 Ibid., 206.
45 Francesco Guardiani, "The Common Ground of McLuhan and Frye," *McLuhan Studies: Premiere Issue* (1996): 1–14. (McLuhan's unpublished essay "Have with You to Madison Avenue or The Flush-Profile of Literature" is included as an appendix.) Guardiani opens ground in this short essay. He begins his essay with a citation of my first writings on the McLuhan and Frye agon in *A Climate Charged* (Oakville: Mosaic Press, 1984), and uses my polemic to trigger and bolster his responses. My three essays in that book had sought to set up an "either/or" tension between McLuhan and Frye. At that time, in the early 1980s, McLuhan's reputation was low and Frye's was high among the Canadian literati. I sharpened being and mind through opposition. I welcomed Frye, a crucial enemy; McLuhan, a pivotal master. Frye's reputation went into the doldrums in the 1990s. Then I found myself reversing my position on Frye when asked to review the publication of his notebooks by the University of Toronto Press by *The Globe and Mail*. My subsequent essay was published in that newspaper on July 26, 2003. In the essay I reversed my antagonism, articulated in the essay "Fear of Fryeing," and confessed to having misread Frye's intentions and aspirations. The notebooks returned me to *Fearful Symmetry, The Educated Imagination, The Great Code,* and *The Double Vision*. I began teaching courses on McLuhan and Frye in the English department at York University in 2003.

I was an auditor in Frye's graduate class. I had made a commitment to finish my master's thesis and so could not formally enroll. Nevertheless, I attended every class, read and annotated all the books on the reading list, engaged in the classroom discussions, and met with him on occasion to talk about authors. I wrote papers that I never submitted; but I absorbed the ideas of those papers into later writings. After Frye's class, every week I ventured out with my fellow students to local pubs to debate his vivid premises. I was formally enrolled in McLuhan's small seminar. At the end of the winter term I received an "A" from him for my work.
46 McLuhan and Powers, *Global Village*, 56.
47 Frye, *Late Notebooks, 1982–1990*, 127.
48 iLiteracy is a term passed on by Michael Barnes, a student in English 3700 in the Department of English, York University, 2007. It appears to have been his invention. This book acknowledges Mr Barnes's originality.

49 "The Making of Typographic Man" is the subtitle to Marshall McLuhan, *The Gutenberg Galaxy* (Toronto: University of Toronto Press, 1962).
50 Northrop Frye, *The Double Vision: Language and Meaning in Religion* (Toronto: University of Toronto Press, 1991), 55.
51 Marshall McLuhan, *Marshall McLuhan Unbound*, ed. W. Terrence Gordon (Corte Madera, CA: Gingko Press, 2006), 18.

2 Presences and Signatures: These Figures in Their Ground

1 Frye, *Words with Power*, 148, 282–3. In *Fearful Symmetry: A Study of William Blake* (Princeton: Princeton University Press, 1969), Frye addresses the idea of the inner Jerusalem in "The City of God" chapter.
2 Cayley, *Northrop Frye in Conversation*, 154.
3 Marshall McLuhan, in Maurice McLuhan and Barrington Nevitt, *Who Was Marshall McLuhan? Exploring a Mosaic of Impressions* (Toronto: Comprehensivist Publications, 1994), 235–6.
4 Donald Theall, professor of English at Trent University, Peterborough, Ontario, author and scholar. These comments come from a telephone interview conducted with Theall on 6 December 2007. In *The Virtual Marshall McLuhan* (Montreal: McGill-Queen's University Press, 2001), Theall calls Frye McLuhan's "alter ego" (49). Theall's study of McLuhan's poetics in his 2001 examination is seminal, and strangely bypassed by scholars and critics. His book delves deeper, arguably, than most critics tend to do into the literary McLuhan. This book owes much to his scholarship and to his conversation. He confirmed in my dialogue with him that McLuhan and Frye belong together in a Canadian prophetic matrix of interaction. I will be referring to Theall's insights into his time working with McLuhan in my agon chapter. Professor Theall died in May 2008.
5 Eric McLuhan interviewed in conversations on 20–21 April 2005.
  Mrs Corinne McLuhan, in interviews conducted on those same dates, also called Frye and McLuhan "twin geniuses." Pierre Elliott Trudeau called them "the Northern Lights," in a conversation with me in Montreal 1992.
6 Edith Sitwell's review of *Fearful Symmetry* appeared in 1947 in *The Spectator*. The passage alluded to is quoted in Ayre's *Northrop Frye: A Biography*, 205.
7 Tom Wolfe, "What If He Is Right?" in *The Pump House Gang* (New York: Farrar, Straus & Giroux, 1968), 138.
8 Fredric Jameson's responses in *The Political Unconscious: Narrative as a Socially Symbolic Act* (Ithaca, NY: Cornell University Press, 1981) will be examined later in this book. The phrase "meteoric theoretical ascendancy" is Edward Said's. Said's strongest responses – respectful, attentive, critical, and

absorbing – can be found in *The World, the Text, and the Critic* (Cambridge, MA: Harvard University Press, 1983). See the references in the following essays from that book: "Secular Criticism" (22); "The World, The Text, and the Critic" (50); "On Originality" (131); "Roads Taken and Not Taken" (147); "American 'Left' Literary Criticism," which is where Said's phrase appears, on 165. McLuhan and Frye are criticized for their religious-based criticism in his "Conclusion" (290–2).

9 George Steiner, *Language and Silence* (New York: Atheneum, 1976); see also *Grammars of Creation* (New Haven, CT: Yale University Press, 2001). See Camille Paglia's essay collections, *Sex, Art and American Culture: Essays* (New York: Vintage, 1992) and *Vamps and Tramps* (New York: Vintage, 1991); these books do not mention McLuhan directly in terms of her own essaying, but the McLuhan mark is clearly there. See Sven Birkerts's *The Gutenberg Elegies: The Fate of Reading in an Electronic Age* (New York: Fawcett Columbine, 1994) and William Irwin Thompson, *Coming into Being: Artifacts and Texts in the Evolution of Consciousness* (New York: St Martin's Press, 1996); see also Thompson's *Imaginary Landscape: Making Worlds as Myth and Science* (New York: St Martin's Press, 1989).

10 "The Three A's" appear throughout Frye's notebooks. One citation, useful here, can be found in *Northrop Frye Unbuttoned*, 286.

11 Quoted in A.C. Hamilton's preface to *Anatomy of His Criticism*, xi. Hamilton outlines in the preface and chapter 1, "Introduction to Frye's Poetics," how we can see the praise and the controversies that accompanied Frye's soaring reputation in the 1950s and 1960s; Hamilton also looks at some aspects of the eclipse of that reputation in the 1970s and 1980s. See 3–8 for a highly detailed recital of the boom and bust aspect of Frye's career. Frank Lentricchia's *After the New Criticism* (Chicago: University of Chicago Press, 1980) also recites, in the first chapters of his book, the homages and the impressive controversies that accompanied Frye. His intentions are to move on from Frye's methodologies; but to do so he must begin with an overview of Frye's centrality.

12 The acknowledgments can be found in *Northrop Frye in Modern Criticism: Selected Papers from the English Institute*, ed. Murray Krieger (New York: Columbia University Press, 1966). With some moderate exceptions, the encomia throughout Krieger's text are strong indeed. These essays show Frye's reputation at its height.

13 Northrop Frye, "Installation Address," *Acta Victoriana* (Victoria College Union) 74.1, ed. Katherine Lehmann (1959): 15.

14 The reference to "voyaging on strange seas" appears earlier in the address (ibid., 17).

15 The "Installation Address," virtually a manifesto, was published in a campus magazine edited by students: one was Peter Such, a future novelist; another was M.E. Atwood. She contributed a powerful poem called "Confessional."
16 Stéphane Mallarmé, *Le Livre, Instrument Spirituel*, in *Mallarmé: Selections*, trans. Anthony Hartley (London: Penguin, 1970), 189. I have re-translated, embedded, and enlarged lines from Mallarmé's speculations (197, 205).
17 The entry appears in *Late Notebooks, 1982–1990*, 247.
18 George Grant, "Review of The Great Code: The Bible and Literature," *The Globe and Mail*, 27 February 1982, E17.
19 Frye, *Late Notebooks, 1982–1990*, 424–5. It is worth noting that Frye follows up "The text is the presence" with the terse and sublimely ironic recognition, "I know this sounds a little like 'the medium is the message.'"
20 Lyotard's implications can be found in *The Post-Modern Condition: A Report on Knowledge*, trans. Geoff Bennington and Brian Massumi (Minneapolis: University of Minnesota Press, 1984), xxiv–xxv, 65, 67, 82.
21 Terry Eagleton, *Literary Theory: An Introduction* (Minneapolis: University of Minneapolis Press, 1983), 93. The entire chapter, "Structuralism and Semiotics" (91–126), is apposite.
22 Frye, *Double Vision*, 7, 85.
23 Marchand and Gordon do so in a rare moment of biographical unanimity. See especially 11–13, 50, 62, and 89 of Marchand's *The Medium and the Messenger*; see also 19–24 and 38–49 of Gordon's *Escape into Understanding*. McLuhan's letters to his mother show her dramatic influence. Several of these most distinctive letters will be quoted shortly.
24 Marjorie Perloff, *Wittgenstein's Ladder: Poetic Language and the Strangeness of the Ordinary* (Chicago: University of Chicago Press, 1996), 9. Perloff cites a reference to F.R. Leavis's essay "Memories of Wittgenstein," in the book *Recollections of Wittgenstein*, ed. Rush Rees (Oxford: Oxford University Press, 1984), as her primary source. The meetings with Leavis on Sunday afternoons at Cambridge were confirmed to me in conversation with Eric McLuhan on May 2009 in a telephone interview. In Perloff's *Wittgenstein's Ladder*, we find analogies between Wittgenstein's poetic stimulations in the *Tractatus Logico-Philosophicus* (English translation: 1922) and McLuhan's techniques of probe, poetics, discontinuity, aphorism, and mosaic. There is in both a resistance to the belief that any theory will be comprehensive enough to encompass all aspects of being and perception. Textual consistency appears limited in the face of facts and things. Parataxis, parable, process, practice, poetics, perceptions, and aphorisms leave gaps, or "ladders," for the gestures towards the inexpressible. Theory is one thing, but the world of things is another. This is from Wittgenstein, Propositions 6:54 and 7,

Tractatus Logico-Philosophicus, trans. D.F. Pears and B.F. McGuiness (London: Routledge & Kegan Paul, 1974), 74:

> My propositions serve as elucidations in the following way: anyone who understands me eventually recognizes them as nonsensical, when he has used them – as steps – to climb up beyond them. He must, so to speak, throw away the ladder after he has climbed up it ... He must transcend these propositions, and then he will see the world aright. What we cannot speak about we must ponder over in silence.

Blake says in his "Proverbs of Hell," "A fool sees not the same tree that a wise man sees" (*Complete Writings*, 151). According to Frye, this means states of mind govern perception. Persist in the folly of your visionary pursuit: eventually the natural tree yields to angels singing on light-struck leaf-tips. The imagination resists the actual tree, turning perception towards the inner eye.

But in the Wittgensteinian formulations of the limits of language, another possible reading of Blake's maxim emerges. We say many things, perhaps even an infinite number of things, about the tree. Yet the fact of the tree remains at the edge of words. This "manifest" is what Wittgenstein calls in Proposition 6:52 "the mystical" (73).

His propositions announce the "nonsensical" nature of most philosophical systems and theoretical undertakings (74). This sets off associations with McLuhan's methods, his aphorisms in particular. How many critics have said over the years that McLuhan's thinking is (was) "nonsense"? The title of Sidney Finkelstein's book, *Sense and Nonsense of McLuhan* (New York: International Publishers, 1968) alludes to that judgment. To Finkelstein, McLuhan's writings compose "history into a fantastically jumbled form." In Finkelstein's eyes McLuhan's dubious achievement is "the brilliant feat of writing a book *[Understanding Media]* which raises the discussion of technology ... to the level of a TV commercial" (8, 14).

We can hypothesize that McLuhan listened to Wittgenstein's lectures in Cambridge. He must have heard about his ideas from F.R. Leavis during his Sunday teas. We have already explored how McLuhan attended seminars by Richards. He was looking at the effects of poems on readers, probing outside the contents of the page, into minds and sensibilities, the conditionings and the contexts of readership. Q.D. Leavis's *Fiction and the Reading Public* – Queenie Leavis was Frank Leavis's wife – also had a seminal impact on McLuhan's developing mind. Q.D. Leavis's book probed the surround of print, the milieu of public taste and publishing agendas. When McLuhan listened to Wittgenstein, or absorbed his ideas through Leavis's conversation, he may have been moved to see there are spaces and silences beyond verbal description.

McLuhan must have taken away with him a sense of how philosophy can be a form of poetics. "Media Poetics," he called his work in the last chapter of McLuhan and Eric McLuhan, *Laws of Media: The New Science* (Toronto: University of Toronto Press, 1988), 215. His refusal to systematize his thinking and his willingness to offer gaps, apothegms, images, jokes, misquotations, and allusions to painting, movies, commercials, ads, and cartoons were in part a fulfilment of Wittgenstein's dictum that theory ends in "nonsense." Poetics point to process, the crisis of the inexpressible, what can be known only through evocation and practice and the humility of letting silence speak through concepts. McLuhan said he was interested in description, not explanation.

Wittgenstein proposes that to perceive, one must "throw away the ladder after he has climbed up it." The *Tractatus* proposition suggests there can be no followers. Words limit, falter. Myriad realities glance from the tip of every proposition or aphorism. Wittgenstein's presence at Cambridge helps to give us a glimpse into McLuhan's thought. He made the leap from typographic text into what cannot be absorbed by print. Wittgenstein may also have introduced McLuhan to the idea of de-familiarization: to see a ground we must stand to one side of it, so much as that is possible.

Wittgenstein must have planted some of these seeds in McLuhan's mind. I have asked Philip Marchand and Eric McLuhan about the possible influence. They tended to see the *Tractatus* in terms of Bertrand Russell–like logical positivism. This philosophical line did not much interest McLuhan. Wittgenstein denied any involvement in the movement. This research comes from conversations with Eric McLuhan in April and August 2008. The telephone interview with Marchand took place 10 December 2007.

Wittgenstein's propositions were part of the campus air of ideas in the 1930s. Air is the charging atmosphere, the imprint of a milieu, the environment's pressures, the aura of a time and place. A tone or tenor is nothing you can see. But a hearer always listens, feeling the press. Life is breathed into you. The acoustic-tactile cosmos inhales and exhales. McLuhan was breathing that air. Environments are echolands. Echoing is reverberation and resonance. "Hush! Caution! Echoland!" Joyce's "echoland" (and HCE) reference is found in *Finnegans Wake*, 13. The "echoland" metaphor sometimes becomes "Eco-land" for McLuhan: ecological reverberations, the auditory mind and sensibility of the global villager or voyager, the Magnetic City citizen. Echoing is resonance, an association and not a direct connection – a key McLuhan percept. "Eco-land" can be found in McLuhan and Watson's *From Cliché to Archetype*, 38; and in many expressions throughout McLuhan and Nevitt's *Take Today*, 119, 231–3, 295, 297. The "Eco-land" pattern dominates McLuhan's last works. "Eco" is meant to resonate with the Latin "ecco," which means "here." "Ecco!" is a Latin phrase that means "Here you are!"

A medium is an atmosphere surrounding the obvious figure. McLuhan was a figure in the Cambridge milieu; and that milieu was informed and stirred by F.R. and Q.D. Leavis, Richards, and Wittgenstein. Environments are part of the life of the forms. Atmospheres and forms are mutable. Ideas, like words, pulse over the air, through conversation, lectures, readings, arguments, and radio waves.

25 Marshall McLuhan, Foreword to *The Interior Landscape*, xiii–xiv.
26 Lionel Elvin as quoted in Marchand, *Marshall McLuhan: The Medium and the Messenger*, 41.
27 This is the title of McLuhan's essay on Gerard Manley Hopkins, in *The Interior Landscape*, 63–73. The entire essay is relevant here.
28 One of his students at Saint Louis was Walter Ong, who extended McLuhan's explorations into orality and literacy. It is often said, incorrectly, that McLuhan was a student of Ong's.
29 The two issues of *Blast* can be found in their republished versions: P. Wyndham Lewis, *Blast 1* and *Blast 2* (Santa Barbara, CA: Black Sparrow Press, 1981). The manifesto styles and typographical formats of these works deeply influenced McLuhan, especially in *Explorations*. Lewis's mark extends beyond *Blast*. McLuhan took the Magnetic City phrase from Lewis's *The Human Age* trilogy – *The Childermass* (1928), *Monstre Gai* (1928), and *Malign Fiesta* (1928). The afterlife mixture of heaven and hell, where angels coexist with devils, is called Magnetic City; it is always capitalized in Lewis's texts. We note McLuhan's mental metamorphoses in his noosphere views, from the recognition to the global village, to the global theatre, to circuit city, to information megalopolis, to the Magnetic City, which is part Ciba4 – the name of the dystopia in William Gibson's *Neuromancer* (New York: Ace Books, 1984) – and part Jerusalem. McLuhan thought these states unsteady, always available to instantaneous reversal.
30 Marshall McLuhan and Harley Parker, *Counterblast* (Toronto: McClelland and Stewart, 1969), 4–5.
31 See Cayley's *Northrop Frye in Conversation*, 123–41.
32 Northrop Frye, letter to Richard Kostelanetz, Frye Archives, 30.
33 "The once respectable literary scholar" was said by Andrew Ross, in *No Respect: Intellectuals and Popular Culture* (New York: Routledge, 1989), in his damning chapter, "Media Shepherd, King of Popthink," 114. See Judith Stamps's twists and turns of thought, and her attempt to enroll McLuhan in the Frankfurt School, in *Unthinking Modernity: Innis, McLuhan, and the*

Frankfurt School (Montreal and Kingston: McGill-Queen's University Press, 1995). It is an intriguing exercise in theoretical reconception. Whether McLuhan's work is reconcilable with Marxism, however, is dubious, given his dismissive probes into Marx that are concentrated in the aphorisms we find in *Counterblast*, 56; McLuhan and Quentin Fiore, *War and Peace in the Global Village* (Toronto: Penguin, 2003), 35; and *Take Today*, 60–78.

34 Jonathan Miller, *Marshall McLuhan* (New York: Viking Press, 1971), 124.
35 Steiner made this acid observation to me at the Living Literacies Conference at York University in 2002. I did not dispute it with him at what was a social occasion, held after his formidable lecture. I dispute it here.
36 Described in Marchand's biography, *Marshall McLuhan: The Medium and the Messenger*, 117. The debate amounted to little. It is difficult to know if the outspoken Edmund Carpenter was on that occasion a mouthpiece for McLuhan. Frye himself dismissed the occasion in his Diaries, saying, "Nobody got hurt, and we put on a fair show." Frye Archives, 5.
37 McLuhan speaking at the Coach House in November 1978 at the University of Toronto. Reported and confirmed by Eric McLuhan in a telephone interview, 20 May 2009.
38 Michael Ignatieff, "Medium-Rare Message," *London Observer*, 6 March 1988, 42.
39 McLuhan and McLuhan, *Laws of Media*, 88–9; McLuhan and Powers, *Global Village*, 78–9.
40 Arthur Siegel, "Northrop Frye and the Toronto School of Communication Theory," in *The Toronto School of Communication Theory: Interpretations, Extensions, Applications*, ed. Rita Watson and Menahem Blondheim (Toronto: University of Toronto Press, 2007; Jerusalem: Hebrew University Magnes Press, 2007), 114–15.
41 John Fekete, *The Critical Twilight: Explorations in the Ideology of Anglo-American Literary Theory from Eliot to McLuhan* (London: Routledge and Kegan Paul, 1977), 107.
42 John Fekete, "Massage in the Mass Age: Remembering the McLuhan Matrix," *Canadian Journal of Political and Social Theory* 6.3 (Autumn 1982): 50–67.
43 The reference to Frye's narrative code is on page 53.
44 Theall's letter is quoted in Gordon's *Escape into Understanding* (253–4).
45 Marshall McLuhan and Harley Parker, *Through the Vanishing Point: Space in Poetry and Painting* (New York: Harper Colophon, 1968), 63, 87.
46 McLuhan, quoted in Gordon, *Escape into Understanding*, 164. It is archival material, probably written in 1955, but not published anywhere except for Gordon's book.

47 "Ecstatic metaphor" is a phrase that recurs in Frye's *Words with Power*. See 85–9 especially. I will save my discussion of this phrase for chapter 4.
48 In Frye, *Late Notebooks, 1982–1990*, "The gate of horn" (228) and "the place of beginning" (281).
49 Quoted in S. Krishnamoorthy Aithal, ed., *The Importance of Northrop Frye* (New York: Columbia University Press, 1966), 6–7.
50 Northrop Frye, *The Return of Eden: Five Essays on Milton's Epics* (Toronto: University of Toronto Press, 1965), 143.
51 Quoted in Aithal, *Importance of Northrop Frye*, viii.
52 Northrop Frye, "Blake's Bible," in *Myth and Metaphor: Selected Essays, 1974–1988*, ed. Robert D. Denham (Charlottesville: University of Virginia Press, 1990), 286.

3 The Critical Conflict between McLuhan and Frye

1 Marshall McLuhan, "Inside Blake and Hollywood," in *Marshall McLuhan Unbound*, ed. W. Terrence Gordon (Corte Madera, CA: Gingko Press, 2006), 8.
2 McLuhan's literary essays explore these points, as we would see in *The Interior Landscape*.
3 "Have with You to Madison Avenue or The Flush-Profile of Literature." Unpublished review of Northrop Frye's *Anatomy of Criticism*, 1957. McLuhan Archives, in the possession of Eric McLuhan. The pages are unnumbered.
4 McLuhan said this. It was noted and recorded by Eric McLuhan. The comment was made in 1978. Confirmed by Eric McLuhan in telephone interview, May 2009.
5 McLuhan's early explanations of "Light On/Light Through" are articulated in *ROPUNM* (11, 25–8). McLuhan's letter to *The Listener*, August 1971, on Miller's book, explains aspects of the probe; this can be found in *Letters of Marshall McLuhan*, 435–8. One could argue that all of *Through the Vanishing Point* is devoted to exploring the suggestions of the "On/Through" dynamics.
6 McLuhan, *Letters*, 256. This appears before the direct critique of Frye in the letter to Watson, 256–7. The cited passage also appears in *ROPUNM*, 9.
7 The letters were written in 1977.
8 *Medium and the Light*, 47.
9 "Playboy Interview," in *Essential McLuhan*, ed. Eric McLuhan and Frank Zingrone (Toronto: Anansi, 1995), 268–9.
10 McLuhan and Watson, *From Cliché to Archetype*, 10.
11 Confirmed by Eric McLuhan in telephone interview, 20 May 2009.
12 The letter to Wilfrid Watson is quoted in Richard Cavell's *McLuhan in Space* (214).

13 Frye, letter to Walter J. Ong, 28 March 1973, Frye Archives, 30.
14 Frye Archives, 7.
15 Northrop Frye, "The Dialectics of Belief and Vision," in *Myth and Metaphor*, 94–5.
16 Northrop Frye, *The Modern Century*, in *Northrop Frye on Modern Culture*, ed. Jan Gorak, vol. 11 of *Collected Works* (Toronto: University of Toronto Press, 2003), 20.
17 Jonathan Hart, Introduction to *City of the End of Things: Lectures on Civilization and Empire*, Northrop Frye, J. Robert Oppenheimer, Edward Togo Salmon (Toronto: Oxford University Press, 2009), 20.
18 Frye, "The Expanding World of Metaphor," in *Myth and Metaphor*, 121.
19 Frye, "The Quality of Life in the '70s," in *Northrop Frye on Modern Culture*, 290.
20 Frye, *Northrop Frye Unbuttoned*, 249.
21 See the bibliographic references to Steiner and Thompson cited earlier in these notes. Two respected books by Neil Postman that engage and acknowledge McLuhan are *Amusing Ourselves to Death: Public Discourse in the Age of Show Business* (London: Penguin, 1986) and *The End of Education: Redefining the Value of School* (New York: Knopf, 1995).
22 Frye Archives, 15.
23 Robert D. Denham, email to author, 11 October 2008.
24 Confirmed by Eric McLuhan in telephone interview, 20 May 2009.
25 Northrop Frye, "L'Anti-McLuhan," interview with Naïm Kattan, *Le Devoir*, 23 November 1968, 74–8. The reference to McLuhan appears on (76–7).
26 Frye, "The View from Here," in *Myth and Metaphor*, 77–8.
27 Northrop Frye, "Communications," *The Listener*, 84.2154 (9 July 1970): 33.
28 Marshall McLuhan, "Views," *The Listener*, 84.2167 (8 October 1970): 475–6.
29 Reported to me by Eric McLuhan and Frank Zingrone, in interviews conducted in 2004, 2007, and 2008.
30 Northrop Frye, *The Critical Path: An Essay on the Social Context of Literary Criticism* (Bloomington: Indiana University Press, 1971), 13.
31 Confirmed by Eric McLuhan in telephone conversation, 20 May 2009.
32 Cayley, *Northrop Frye in Conversation*, 184.
33 McLuhan, "The Analogical Mirrors," in *The Interior Landscape*, 65.
34 James Joyce, *Ulysses*, ed. Hans Walter Gabler (London: Penguin Books, 1986), 32.
35 Frye, *Northrop Frye Unbuttoned*, 47; *Late Notebooks, 1982–1990*, 717.
36 Frye, *Notebooks and Lectures on the Bible and Other Religious Texts*, 342.
37 Frye, *Late Notebooks, 1982–1990*, 110.
38 Frye, *Words with Power*, 6.
39 Frye, *Northrop Frye Unbuttoned*, 19.
40 McLuhan, *Letters*, 244. The entire letter reflects McLuhan's dispute with Frye's Gnosticism.

41 Frank Zingrone, *The Media Symplex: At the Edge of Meaning in the Age of Chaos* (Toronto: Stoddart, 2001), 256.
42 Pierre Teilhard de Chardin expanded his ideas in his two most influential books, *The Phenomenon of Man*, trans. Bernard Wall (New York: Harper Torchbooks, 1961), and *The Future of Man*, trans. Norman Denny (London: Collins, Fontana Books, 1970). These two works of speculative evolutionary thought were published in France in 1955 and 1959. Teilhard de Chardin died in 1955. His works caused considerable controversy in the Catholic hierarchy. Though Teilhard himself was a Jesuit priest and a highly regarded paleontologist and teacher, his ideas gave offense to Catholic doctrine; his books were placed under edict by the Church. The offense was thought to be in the ideas of the Omega point in time – that the Christos was in all humanity and that we are evolving towards the achievement of this high spiritual condition. The noosphere idea suggested that the planet's atmosphere itself was an externalization of thought. He was also deeply receptive to other religious modes of thought and did not see Catholicism as the one supreme faith. In spite of the edict on his books, his ideas had been circulating for many years in mimeographed forms. One of his first major interpreters – and advocates – was Walter J. Ong. Teilhard's ideas are infused through Ong's works. McLuhan's close ties with Father Ong, also a Jesuit, would have led him to many encounters with Teilhard's ideas.

The word "hominisation" appears in several McLuhan aphorisms; for example, from *Counterblast* (mimeograph, 1954, McLuhan Archives), 34: "Extensions of man are the hominization of the world." He often amends the word to read "super-hominisation." It is a Teilhard neologism, appearing in *The Phenomenon of Man* for the first time (164). McLuhan would have also been familiar with Teilhard's ideas of emergence (consciousness rising, consciousness is the great event of the cosmos) and of convergence: everything that rises must converge. The latter idea is pertinent to my argument that indeed McLuhan and Frye converge. This association with Teilhard's ideas places McLuhan in the "Practical Mystic" camp. Teilhard's mysticism was not obscurantism; nor was it otherworldly, formed and experienced in monastic retreat. It was shaped by everyday experience and by his research and excavations. The evolutionary nature of consciousness, its biogenetic event in history, was proof to Teilhard of uniqueness and of a narrative destiny, perhaps a version of the Great Code.

There is an interesting, enigmatic adaptation of Teilhard's ideas in the last passages of the McLuhan and Fiore collaboration *War and Peace in the Global Village*; see 177–90.

43 McLuhan, "An Ancient Quarrel in Modern America," in *The Interior Landscape*, 225.
44 Richard A. Lanham, *The Electronic Word: Democracy, Technology, and the Arts* (Chicago: University of Chicago Press, 1995), xii.
45 McLuhan, *Letters*, 410.
46 McLuhan, "G.K. Chesterton: A Practical Mystic," in *Marshall McLuhan Unbound*, 4–5.

4 The Harmonies in Two Seers: Orchestrations and Complementarities

1 Fritjof Capra, *The Tao of Physics: An Exploration of the Parallels between Modern Physics and Eastern Mysticism*, 2nd ed. (Boston: Shambhala, 1985), 160, 217.
2 Frye, "The Double Mirror," in *On Religion*, ed. Alvin A. Lee and Jean O'Grady, vol. 4 of *Collected Works* (Toronto: University of Toronto Press, 2000), 90.
3 The *DEW-line* was the name McLuhan gave to his late 1960s newsletter. There is no publishing data on its pages. Frye's metaphor of "the garrison mentality" was outlined in his "Conclusion to a *Literary History of Canada*." See this chapter in *The Bush Garden: Essays on the Canadian Imagination*, 2nd ed. (repr., 1995; Toronto: Anansi, 1971).
4 McLuhan and Powers, *Global Village*, 165. The reference to *Finnegans Wake* is a McLuhanesque gloss on "The book of Doublends Jined."
5 Frye, *Northrop Frye Unbuttoned*, 31.
6 James Joyce, *A Portrait of the Artist as a Young Man* (New York: Viking Press, 1964), 253.
7 Northrop Frye, "Across the River and out of the Trees," in *On Canada*, ed. Jean O'Grady and David Staines, vol. 12 of *Collected Works* (Toronto: University of Toronto Press, 2003), 559.
8 Denis Saurat, *Blake and Milton* (New York: Russell & Russell, 1965), 13, 15, 16.
9 Frye, *Notebooks and Lectures on the Bible and Other Religious Texts*, 153.
10 McLuhan, *Letters*, 205–6.
11 Eric McLuhan's observations are taken from a telephone interview, 20 May 2009.
12 William Blake, "Jerusalem," in *Complete Writings*, 716.
13 McLuhan and Nevitt, *Take Today*. My variation; the original appears on page 282.
14 Quotation confirmed by Eric McLuhan in telephone conversation, 20 May 2009. It was said in the Centre for Culture and Technology in 1978.
15 Frye, *Northrop Frye Unbuttoned*, 159.

16 Frye, "Preface," in *Spiritus Mundi*, viii–ix.
17 McLuhan, quoted in Lance Strate and Edward Wachtel, eds., *The Legacy of McLuhan* (Cresskill, NJ: Hampton Press, 2005), 84.
18 McLuhan, *Understanding Media*, 80.
19 Dennis Duffy, *Marshall McLuhan* (Toronto: McLelland and Stewart, 1969), 32.
20 Erik Davis, *Techgnosis: Myth, Magic and Mysticism in the Age of Information* (New York: Harmony Books, 1998), 18.
21 George Steiner, "On Reading Marshall McLuhan," in *Language and Silence*, 257.
22 McLuhan and Fiore, *War and Peace in the Global Village*, 1.
23 Frye, *Late Notebooks, 1992–1990*, 549.
24 A.N. Whitehead, *Science and the Modern World* (New York: Macmillan, 1925), 133.
25 Frye, *Double Vision*, vi. The letter to Butts was sent by Blake on 22 November 1802.
26 Northrop Frye, *Divisions on a Ground: Essays on Canadian Culture*, ed. James Polk (Toronto: Anansi, 1982), 47, 95–6.
27 Northrop Frye, "Conclusion to the Second Edition of *Literary History of Canada*," in *On Canada*, 460–2.
28 Tom Harpur, *The Pagan Christ: Recovering the Lost Light* (Toronto: Thomas Allen, 2004), 1–2, 12.
29 Frye, *Late Notebooks, 1982–1990*, 426.
30 Harpur's fate with Christian Evangelicals or Fundamentalists was told to me by his editor, Patrick Crean, at Thomas Allen Publishers, in Toronto. The date of the conversation was 21 April 2006.
31 Frye, *Northrop Frye Unbuttoned*, 109–10.
32 Frye, "Sermons," in *Reading the World*, 267–8.
33 G.K. Chesterton, *Heretics* (London: The Bodley Head, 1905), 129.
34 G.K. Chesterton, *Orthodoxy* (London: The Bodley Head, 1909), 136–7.
35 T.S. Eliot, "East Coker," in *Four Quartets* (London: Faber and Faber, 1963), 22.
36 Confirmed by Eric McLuhan in telephone interview, 20 May 2009.
37 Joyce, *Finnegans Wake*, "Outer nocense," 378.
38 McLuhan and Fiore, *War and Peace in the Global Village*, 22.
39 Frye, "Cycle and Apocalypse in *Finnegans Wake*," in *Myth and Metaphor*, 372–4.
40 Gilles Deleuze and Félix Guattari, *Anti-Oedipus: Capitalism and Schizophrenia*, trans. Robert Hurley, Mark Seem, and Helen R. Lane (Minneapolis: University of Minnesota Press, 1983), 240–1.
41 Frye, *Northrop Frye Unbuttoned*, 51.
42 Frye Archives, 31.
43 Eric McLuhan and Frank Zingrone, "Introduction," in Marshall McLuhan, *Essential McLuhan*, 3.

44 Frye, *Northrop Frye Unbuttoned*, 69.
45 The two theorists sometimes resisted the idea that they had a theory. They evaded the implication that they possessed theories in which everything they encountered could be fit. Why the unease? Theory gives new eyes; it lends intensity and strength to the gaze and the grasp. It beats a lineal pathway, giving order to the array of obstreperous facts. But at turning points in the journey-quest, explanation may not suffice. Something comes to unsettle, if not unseat, the clarity that theoretical initiative gave. The following excerpt shows McLuhan in full denial; it is from an unpublished, unpaginated essay by Eric McLuhan (2005), called "Marshall McLuhan's Theory of Communication: The Yegg." Notice how McLuhan Sr. swerves and bends; McLuhan Jr. then proceeds to paraphrase and amplify, bending and swerving himself:

> Whenever provoked, Marshall McLuhan would declare, "Look I don't have a theory of communication. I don't use theories. I just watch what people do, what you do." ... He insisted regularly ... that he didn't use theories in his work ... if you begin with a theory, then one way or another your research winds up geared to making the case for or against the truth of the theory ... When McLuhan insisted that he didn't use theories, he meant that he didn't use them in the way that people expect theories to be used. "I don't have a Theory of Communication" means "I don't work in the way of Natural Science. I don't start with a theory to prove or disprove to submit to the torturers ..."

> We can sample stages from Frye's thought on theory. They are excerpts from his notebooks, and they span decades. The entries begin around the time of the publication of *Anatomy* and extend to the time when he was writing *The Great Code* and *Words with Power*, and then on to the time of *The Double Vision*. In the last three books he does not, in his introductory outlines of argument, use the word "theory" to evoke what is about to unfold. He uses the word "principles" instead. In these notebook entries he veers from defensive to reflective:

> A theory that explains a lot of facts is a good theory ... literary facts can only be explained by a literary theory ... This is so obvious & elementary that I simply can't communicate with anybody who questions it, or thinks he's questioning it ... There are two kinds of theory. There are the dialectically organized theories, which lead to interminable argument & create innumerable schools, schisms, sects ... there are theories that lead to theories, to a synoptic view of the subject ... if I go to the top of the Empire State building for a view of Manhattan and see the Chrysler building, what I say is "there's the Chrysler building." I do not say "there's where the Chrysler building fits in ..."

... in my view of the Bible as a model of kerygmatic criticism, which I think of as getting past the imaginative creation for its own sake without going back to the old ideological dialectics, I think I'm passing beyond "deconstruction" into a reconstruction no longer structural.

(*Northrop Frye Unbuttoned*, 284–5)

[E]very member of a humanities department ... is supposed to be a productive scholar, & no reasonable person will deny that a tremendous amount of overproduction, repetition and straw-thrashing results. Hence one of the causes of the proliferating of critical theories is to provide inexhaustible fields of critical enterprise. The struggle for a unified perspective on the whole subject seems to pose the threat of exhaustion. But there is little danger of that: whenever a subject approaches such a point it goes into a metamorphosis.

(*Late Notebooks, 1982–1990*, 310)

Literary criticism moved in the 1970s through the 1990s towards deconstruction. It is useful to consider why McLuhan and Frye dissented from those movements. There is an edge to theory: it is the new. The edge is the unknown at the rim of things, the place where the ladders start. Doubt is not the opposite of faith; doubt drives faith. The opposite of faith is nothingness, thinking or perceiving nothing.

Perhaps instead of the word "beyond" that shadows Frye in his last books, and the words "breakdown" and "breakthrough" that shadow McLuhan in his late books, I could suggest the word "more."

Frye, after the death of his wife Helen in 1986, made plan after plan for more books. She had fallen into the incomprehension of dementia during her illness. The verbal furore of *Words with Power*, the quiet meditations of *The Double Vision*, and the ambitious outlines for future work ("the great doodle" leading him on to the plans for "The Ogdoad," the eight-volume study of analogy) we find in the *Late Notebooks* showed him preparing for more words. "It may be nonsense for a man of 75 to talk about a 'new life,' but all I want is a new book. With God all things are possible," he wrote; in 1990, he dreamed, "'next time' ... putting my spiritual case more forcefully yet, and addressed to still more readers." (Frye's talk of new books occurs throughout the pages of his *Late Notebooks, 1982–1990*. See pages 272, 417, and 153. "The Ogdoad" is the epic undertaking of his last notebooks; it was Frye's plan for an eight-volume study of analogy, images, and symbols. See pages 49 and 50 for his outline.)

McLuhan, bruised by illness and thrown off by the crash of his reputation in the mid- and late 1970s, rallied to start over. There were to be more probes, more controversies. He enlisted colleagues and students to help. They assembled notes and files. Even in his near-silence after his stroke, he gestured towards writing a book with his son Eric on the art of discovery. There was to be a book on the future of the book and on libraries. If he could not speak, then his surrogates and his children could do the job for him. Visitors to 3 Wychwood Park were encouraged to read to him. His preference was for anything by James Joyce.

All theory, even anti-theory, promises a beginning. Theory is a calling out for company during the quest. If it is big enough to compel world attention, then one brings many into the fold. A theory is a memory device like an aphorism, or a mandala, that says to those who encounter it, "remember this." Everything else, the processes of response, approval, critique, dissent, dismissal, revision, extension, forgetting, and rediscovery are the broken pieces of a half-glimpsed symbol. The thinkers stopped, thought continues.

Joyce helps us again to see McLuhan and Frye in this light. *Ulysses* offers guidance. The episode is from chapter 9, in what is called "Scylla and Charybdis." It is, perhaps, fitting that we go with Joyce into a room full of books and conversations. At 2 p.m., the Dublin National Library, 16 June 1904: Stephen Dedalus is spinning a theoretical web on the life and work of Shakespeare. Joyce is, arguably, speaking through his character here. Still Joyce gives his Stephen the liberty to unsheathe his dagger definitions. Stephen conjures Hamlet and the ghost. The aspiring poet, with the quixotic last name that echoes the name of the Cretan labyrinth-builder, juggles stories and ideas, enthralling listeners, annoying his antagonists.

"-You are a delusion, said roundly John Eglinton to Stephen. You have brought us all this way to show us a French triangle. Do you believe your own theory?

-No, Stephen said promptly." (175)

46 McLuhan, quoted in Gerald E. Stearn, ed., *McLuhan: Hot & Cool: A Critical Symposium* (New York: Dial Press, 1967), 335.
47 See Finklestein, *Sense and Nonsense of McLuhan*; Miller, *Marshall McLuhan*; and S.D. Neill, *Clarifying McLuhan: An Assessment of Process and Product* (Westport, CT: Greenwood Press, 1993).
48 The *Penseroso* subject is addressed by Frances Yates in *The Occult Philosophy in the Elizabethan Age* (London: Routledge Classics, 1979). See the chapter "Agrippa and Elizabethan Melancholy: George Chapman's Shadow of Night," 157–71, and "Shakespearean Fairies, Witches, Melancholy: King Lear and the Demons," 172–85. Her chapter on Prospero is of great relevance here. I also direct the reader towards Yates's studies in *The Rosicrucian Enlightenment* (London: Routledge Classics, 1972) for further reflections on

alchemy and the mingling of Renaissance science, art, literature, culture, and technology. Frye was clearly drawn to the occult aspects of Yates's studies; McLuhan, more to the identification of the structure of memory theatres in *The Art of Memory*.
49 Frye, "Expanding Eyes," in *Spiritus Mundi*, 99–100.
50 Frye, *T.S. Eliot: An Introduction* (Chicago: University of Chicago Press, 1981), 77.
51 Interview with Corinne McLuhan, April 2005, at 3 Wychwood Park, Toronto.

5 Alchemy: Synergy in the Thinking of McLuhan and Frye

1 Confirmed by Eric McLuhan in telephone interview, 20 May 2009.
2 Frye, *Great Code*, xv.
3 Frye, *Late Notebooks, 1982–1990*, 329–30.
4 T.S. Eliot, "Little Gidding," in *Four Quartets*, 44.
5 Frye, *Northrop Frye Unbuttoned*, 113.
6 Frye, *Late Notebooks, 1982–1990*, 471.
7 McLuhan and Carson, *The Book of Probes*, 316–17.
8 McLuhan and Fiore, *War and Peace in the Global Village*, 46, 48.
9 Eric McLuhan, *The Role of Thunder in Finnegans Wake* (Toronto: University of Toronto Press, 1997).
10 Marshall McLuhan, "James Joyce: Trivial and Quadrivial," in *The Interior Landscape*, 37. I have yet to find this line in the *Wake*; but McLuhan frequently appropriates and then revises Joyce.
11 McLuhan, "G.K. Chesterton: Practical Mystic," in *McLuhan Unbound*, 15.
12 My paraphrase of Jameson's arguments; his analyses appear on 70–4.
13 Umberto Eco, "Towards a Semiological Guerrilla Warfare," in *Travels in Hyperreality*, trans. William Weaver (New York: Harcourt, 1986), 136–9.
14 Jean Baudrillard, *Paroxysms: Interviews with Philippe Petit*, trans. Chris Turner (London: Verso, 1998), 2.
15 See especially Arthur Kroker's incisive and perceptive *Technology and the Canadian Mind: Innis/McLuhan/Grant* (Montreal: New World Perspectives, 1984). It remains a landmark inquiry into the Canadian intellectual traditions. Also of interest are the collaborations between Arthur and MariLouise Kroker. See the Works Cited of Secondary Sources for exact coordinates for their books.
16 McLuhan and Parker, *Counterblast*, 135.
17 Northrop Frye, *The Double Vision: Language and Meaning in Religion*. (Toronto: University of Toronto Press, 1991), 84.
18 Yates, *The Art of Memory*. See the following chapters for details and references, "Renaissance Memory: The Memory Theatre of Giulio Camillo,"

129–59; "Camillo's Theatre and the Venetian Renaissance," 160–72; "Fludd's Memory Theatre and the Globe Theatre," 342–67. These are of particular relevance to this book. Throughout her book Yates examines how images, symbols, signs, tokens, and talismans operate to trigger memory and to reinforce the analogical mirroring of mind and cosmos.
19 Gayatri Chakravorty Spivak, *Death of a Discipline* (New York: Columbia University Press, 2003), 4, 13.
20 McLuhan and Powers, *Global Village*, 98.
21 McLuhan and Nevitt, *Take Today*, 291.
22 Jacob Boehme, quoted in Henry Miller's *The Time of the Assassins: A Study of Rimbaud* (New York: New Directions, 1962), 101.
23 Email forward to me, from Eric McLuhan, 9 February 2010.
24 Richard Tarnas, *The Passion of the Western Mind: Understanding the Ideas that Have Shaped Our World View* (New York: Ballantine Books, 1991), 440.

6 The Lessons of Two Teachers: Guidance and Signs

1 Corinne McLuhan interview, 21 April 2005. Confirmed by Eric McLuhan, also present during that conversation in 2005, in telephone interview, 20 May 2009.
2 Frye, *Northrop Frye Unbuttoned*, 9.
3 McLuhan speaking off the cuff in a lecture given at the Centre for Culture and Technology in 1978. Confirmed by Eric McLuhan in telephone interview, 20 May 2009.
4 Northrop Frye, *Fables of Identity: Studies in Poetic Mythology* (New York: Harcourt, Brace, & World, 1963), 3.
5 Bob Dobbs, a McLuhan archival website manager, and George Thompson, former office manager of McLuhan's Centre for Culture and Technology, drew my attention to this Joycean passage in telephone conversations conducted in April 2008.
6 Frye, *Late Notebooks, 1982–1990*, 203.
7 Franz Kafka, *The Blue Octavo Notebooks*, ed. Max Brod, trans. Ernst Kaiser and Eithne Wilkins (Cambridge: Schocken Books, 1991), Aphorism 57, p. 92.
8 Ibid., Aphorism 3, p. 87.

Bibliography

Adamson, Joseph. *Northrop Frye: A Visionary Life*. Toronto: ECW Press, 1993.
Aithal, S. Krishnamoorthy, ed. *The Importance of Northrop Frye*. New York: Columbia University Press, 1966.
Alighieri, Dante. *The Divine Comedy: Inferno, Purgatorio, Paradiso*. Trans. Allen Mandelbaum. New York: Bantam, 1983.
–. *La Vita Nuova*. Trans. Barbara Reynolds. London: Penguin Books, 1969.
Altizer, Thomas J.J. *The New Apocalypse: The Radical Christian Vision of William Blake*. East Lansing: Michigan State University Press, 1967.
Aquinas, Thomas. *Basic Writings of Thomas Aquinas*. Trans. A.C. Pegis. New York: Random House, 1945.
Armstrong, Karen. *A Short History of Myth*. Toronto: Knopf, 2005.
Arnold, Matthew. *Selected Poetry and Prose*. Ed. Frederick L. Mulhauser. New York: Holt, Rinehart, and Winston, 1967.
Artaud, Antonin. *The Theatre and Its Double*. Trans. Mary Caroline Richards. New York: Grove Press, 1958.
Ayre, John. *Northrop Frye: A Biography*. Toronto: Random House, 1989.
Bachelard, Gaston. *On Poetic Imagination and Reverie*. Trans. Colette Gaudin. Dallas: Spring Publications, 1987.
Baigent, Michael. *From the Omens of Babylon: Astrology and Ancient Mesopotamia*. London: Arkana, 1994.
Baigent, Michael, and Richard Leigh. *The Elixir and the Stone: A History of Magic and Alchemy*. London: Penguin, 1998.
Ballard, J.G. *Crash*. New York: Vintage, 1985.
Barfield, Owen. *Saving the Appearances: A Study in Idolatry*. New York: Harcourt Brace Jovanovich, 1965.
Barnstone, Willis, ed. *The Other Bible: Jewish Pseudepigrapha, Christian Apocrypha, Gnostic Scriptures, Kabbalah, Dead Sea Scrolls*. New York: Harper Collins, 2005.

Barthes, Roland. *A Barthes Reader.* Ed. Susan Sontag. New York: Hill and Wang, 1982.
–. *Mythologies.* Trans. Annette Lavers. New York: Hill and Wang, 1972.
Bates, Ronald. *Northrop Frye.* Toronto: McClelland and Stewart, 1971.
Baudelaire, Charles. *Selected Poetry.* Trans. Joanna Richardson. London: Penguin, 1975.
–. *Selected Writings on Art and Artists.* Trans. P.E. Charret. London: Penguin, 1972.
Baudrillard, Jean. *Paroxysm: Interviews with Phillippe Petit.* Trans. Chris Turner. London: Verso, 1998.
–. *Simulacra and Simulation.* Trans. Sheila Faria Glaser. Ann Arbor: University of Michigan Press, 1994.
–. *The Spirit of Terrorism and Requiem for the Twin Towers.* Trans. Chris Turner. London: Verso, 2002.
–. *The Uncollected Baudrillard.* Ed. Gary Genosko. Thousand Oaks, CA: Sage Publications, 2001.
Becker, Robert O., and Gary Selden. *The Body Electric: Electromagnetism and the Foundation of Life.* New York: William Morrow, 1985.
Benedetti, Paul, and Nancy DeHart, eds. *Forward Through the Rearview Mirror: Reflections on and by Marshall McLuhan.* Toronto: Prentice-Hall, 1996.
Benjamin, Walter. "One-Way Street," "Paris, Capitol of the Nineteenth Century," and "The Destructive Character." In *Reflections,* ed. Peter Demetz. Trans. Edmund Jephcott. New York: Schocken, 1986.
–. "Unpacking My Library," "On Some Motifs in Baudelaire," and "The Work of Art in the Age of Mechanical Reproduction." In *Illuminations,* ed. Hannah Arendt. Trans. Hurry Zohn. New York: Schocken, 1969.
Bergson, Henri. *Creative Evolution.* Trans. Arthur Mitchell. Lanham, MD: University Press of America, 1983.
Berman, Morris. *The Re-enchantment of the World.* Ithaca, NY: Cornell University Press, 1981.
Birkerts, Sven. *The Gutenberg Elegies: The Fate of Reading in an Electronic Age.* New York: Fawcett Columbine, 1995.
Blake, William. *Complete Writings, with Variant Readings.* Ed. Geoffrey Keynes. London: Oxford University Press, 1972.
–. *A Grain of Sand: Selected Poems.* Ed. Rosemary Manning. London: The Bodley Head, 1967.
–. *The Marriage of Heaven and Hell.* Ed. Geoffrey Keynes. London: Oxford University Press, 1975.
Blavatsky, Helena P. *Isis Unveiled.* Ed. Michael Gomes. Wheaton: Quest Books, 1997.

Bloom, Harold. *Agon: Towards a Theory of Revisionism*. Oxford: Oxford University Press, 1982.
—. *The Anxiety of Influence: A Theory of Poetry*. New York: Oxford University Press, 1973.
—. *Blake's Apocalypse: A Study in Poetic Argument*. New York: Doubleday, 1963.
—. *The Book of J*. New York: Grove Weidenfeld, 1990.
—. *The Breaking of the Vessels*. Chicago: University of Chicago Press, 1982.
—. "Foreword to *Anatomy of Criticism: Northrop Frye in Retrospect*." In *Anatomy of Criticism: Four Essays*, 15th ed., by Northrop Frye. Princeton: Princeton University Press, 2000.
—. *Genius: A Mosaic of One Hundred Exemplary Creative Minds*. New York: Warner Books, 2002.
—. "An Interview with Harold Bloom," by Irme Salusinzky. *Scripsi* 4 (July 1986): 69–88.
—. *Jesus and Yahweh: The Names Divine*. New York: Riverhead Books, 2005.
—. *Kabbalah and Criticism*. New York: Seabury Press, 1975.
—. *A Map of Misreading*. London: Oxford University Press, 1975.
—. "Middle Twentieth-Century Criticism: Kenneth Burke and Northrop Frye." In *The Art of the Critic: Literary Theory and Criticism from the Greeks to the Present*, vol. 10, *Contemporary*. New York and Philadelphia: Chelsea House, 1990.
—. "Northrop Frye Exalting the Designs of Romance." Review of *The Secular Scripture*. *New York Times*, 18 April 1976, 179.
—. *The Visionary Company: A Reading of English Romantic Poetry*. Ithaca, NY: Cornell University Press, 1971.
—. *Where Shall Wisdom Be Found?* New York: Riverhead Books, 2004.
Bodanis, David. *Electric Universe: How Electricity Switched on the Modern World*. New York: Three Rivers Press, 2005.
Bodkin, Maud. *Studies of Type-Images in Poetry, Religion, and Philosophy*. London: Oxford University Press, 1951.
Borges, Jorge Luis. *Labyrinths: Selected Stories & Other Writings*. Ed. Donald A. Yates and James E. Irby. New York: New Directions, 1964.
—. *Selected Non Fictions*. Ed. Eliot Weinberger. Trans. Esther Allen, Suzanne Jill Levine, and Eliot Weinberger. London: Penguin, 2000.
Boyd, David, and Imre Salusinszky, eds. *Re-reading Frye: The Published and Unpublished Works*. Toronto: University of Toronto Press, 1999.
Brand, Stewart. *The Media Lab: Inventing the Future at MIT*. New York: Viking, 1987.
Brown, Norman O. *Closing Time*. New York: Vintage, 1974.

–. *Hermes the Thief: The Evolution of a Myth*. New York: Vintage, 1969.
–. *Life Against Death: The Psychoanalytical Meaning of History*. Middletown, CT: Wesleyan University Press, 1959.
–. *Love's Body*. Berkeley: University of California Press, 1966.
Bucke, Richard Maurice. *Cosmic Consciousness: A Study in the Evolution of the Human Mind*. New York: E.P. Dutton, 1901.
Burckhardt, Titus. *Alchemy: Science of the Cosmos, Science of the Soul*. Trans. William Stoddart. Baltimore: Penguin Books, 1972.
Burke, Kenneth. "Medium as 'Message.'" In *McLuhan: Pro and Con*, ed. Raymond Rosenthal. New York: Funk and Wagnalls, 1968.
Burkert, Walter. *Ancient Mystery Cults*. Cambridge, MA: Harvard University Press, 1987.
Burroughs, William. *Naked Lunch*. New York: Grove Press, 1959.
Cage, John. *Silence: Lectures and Writings*. Hanover: Wesleyan University Press, 1973.
Calasso, Roberto. *K*. Trans. Geoffrey Brock. New York: Knopf, 2005.
–. *Literature and the Gods*. Trans. Tim Parks. New York: Vintage Books, 2001.
Campbell, Joseph. *The Hero with a Thousand Faces*. Princeton: Bollingen-Princeton University Press, 1972.
–. *The Mythic Image*. Princeton: Bollinger-Princeton University Press, 1974.
–. *Myths to Live By*. New York: Viking, 1972.
Canetti, Elias. *The Agony of Flies: Notes and Notations*. Trans. H.F. Broch Rothermann. New York: Farrar, Straus, and Giroux, 1994.
Capra, Fritjof. *The Tao of Physics: An Exploration of the Parallels between Modern Physics and Eastern Mysticism*. 2nd ed. Boston: Shambhala, 1985.
Carey, James W. "Harold Adams Innis and Marshall McLuhan." In *McLuhan: Pro and Con*, ed. Raymond Rosenthal. New York: Funk and Wagnalls, 1968.
Cargill, S.T. *The Philosophy of Analogy and Symbolism*. London: Rider and Company, 1950.
Cavafy, C.P. *Selected Poems*. Trans. Avi Sharon. London: Penguin Books, 2008.
Cavell, Richard. *McLuhan in Space: A Cultural Geography*. Toronto: University of Toronto Press, 2002.
Cayley, David. *Northrop Frye in Conversation*. Toronto: Anansi, 1992.
Chesterton, G.K. *Heretics*. London: The Bodley Head, 1905.
–. *Orthodoxy*. London: The Bodley Head, 1909.
Churton, Tobias. *The Gnostics*. London: Weidenfeld and Nicolson, 1990.
Coleridge, Samuel Taylor. *Poetical Works*. Ed. Ernest Hartley Coleridge. London: Oxford University Press, 1969.
–. *The Portable Coleridge*. Ed. I.A. Richards. New York: Viking Press, 1967.

Cook, David. *Northrop Frye: A Vision of the New World.* Montreal: New World Perspective, 1985.
Copenhaver, Brian P. *Hermetica.* Cambridge: Cambridge University Press, 1992.
Corbishley, Thomas. *The Spirituality of Teilhard de Chardin.* London: Collins, 1971.
Cotrupi, Caterina Nella. *Northrop Frye and the Poetics of Process.* Toronto: University of Toronto Press, 2000.
Coupland, Douglas. *Marshall McLuhan.* Toronto: Penguin, 2009.
Crean, Patrick. Personal interview. 21 April 2006, Toronto.
Culkin, John M. "A Schoolman's Guide to Marshall McLuhan." In *McLuhan: Pro and Con,* ed. Raymond Rosenthal. New York: Funk and Wagnalls, 1968.
Curtius, Ernst Robert. *European Literature and the Latin Middle Ages.* Trans. Willard R. Trask. New York: Harper & Row, 1953.
Davis, Erik. *Techgnosis: Myth, Magic and Mysticism in the Age of Information.* New York: Harmony Books, 1998.
De Kerckhove, Derrick. *Connected Intelligence: The Arrival of the Web Society.* Toronto: Somerville House, 1997.
–. "Understanding McLuhan." *The Canadian Forum* 5 (May 1981): 10–12.
Debord, Guy. *Society of the Spectacle.* Detroit: Black and Red, 1983.
Deleuze, Gilles, and Félix Guattari. *Anti-Oedipus: Capitalism and Schizophrenia.* Trans. Robert Hurley, Mark Seem, and Helen R. Lane. Minneapolis: University of Minnesota Press, 1983.
–. *A Thousand Plateaus: Capitalism and Schizophrenia.* Trans. Brian Massumi. Minneapolis: University of Minneapolis Press, 2007.
DeLillo, Don. *Libra.* Toronto: Lester & Orpen Dennys Limited, 1988.
–. *Mao II.* New York: Viking, 1991.
Denham, Robert D. *Northrop Frye: A Bibliography of His Published Writings, 1931–2004.* Emory, VA: Iron Mountain Press, 2004.
–. *Northrop Frye: Religious Visionary and Architect of the Spiritual World.* Charlottesville: University of Virginia Press, 2004.
–. "Questions for You on McLuhan and Frye." Message to B.W. Powe. 11 October 2008. Email.
–. *A World in a Grain of Sand: Twenty-Two Interviews with Northrop Frye.* New York: Peter Lang, 1991.
Denham, Robert D., and Thomas Willard, eds. *Visionary Poetics: Essays on Northrop Frye's Criticism.* New York: Peter Lang, 1991.
Dennet, Daniel. *Consciousness Explained.* Boston: Back Bay Books, 1991.
Dickinson, Emily. *The Poems of Emily Dickinson.* Ed. R.W. Franklin. Cambridge, MA: Belknap Press, 1999.
Dorsch, T.S. *Classical Literary Criticism.* London: Penguin Books, 1974.

Dowling, William. *Jameson, Althusser, Marx: An Introduction to The Political Unconscious*. Ithaca, NY: Cornell University Press, 1984.
Duffy, Dennis. *Marshall McLuhan*. Toronto: McClelland and Stewart, 1969.
Eagleton, Terry. *Literary Theory: An Introduction*. Minneapolis: University of Minneapolis Press, 1983.
Eco, Umberto. *Travels in Hyperreality: Essays*. Trans. William Weaver. New York: Harcourt, 1986.
Eliade, Mircea. *A History of Religious Ideas: From the Stone Age to the Eleusinian Mysteries*. Trans. Willard R. Trask. Vol. 1. Chicago: University of Chicago Press, 1978.
–. *Myths, Dreams and Mysteries: The Encounter between Contemporary Faiths and Archaic Realities*. Trans. Philip Mairet. New York: Harper and Row, 1960.
–. *The Myth of the Eternal Return*. Trans. Willard R. Trask. New York: Pantheon, 1954.
–. *The Quest: History and Meaning in Religion*. Chicago: University of Chicago Press, 1969.
–. *The Sacred and the Profane: The Nature of Religion*. Trans. Willard R. Trask. New York: Harcourt, Brace & World, 1959.
Eliot, T.S. *Four Quartets*. London: Faber and Faber, 1963.
–. *The Sacred Wood: Essays on Poetry and Criticism*. London: Methuen & Company, 1974.
–. *Selected Poems*. London: Faber and Faber, 1971.
–. *The Waste Land*. Ed. Valerie Eliot. New York: Harcourt Brace Jovanovich, 1971.
Ellul, Jacques. *Propaganda: The Formation of Men's Attitudes*. Trans. Konrad Kellen and Jean Lerner. New York: Vintage, 1973.
Ellwood, Robert S. *The Sixties Spiritual Awakening: American Religion Moving from Modern to Postmodern*. New Brunswick, NJ: Rutgers University Press, 1994.
Emerson, Ralph Waldo. *The Portable Emerson*. Ed. Carl Bode. New York: Penguin, 1983.
Entralgo, Lain Pedro. *The Therapy of the Word in Classical Antiquity*. Trans. L.J. Rather and John M. Sharp. New Haven, CT: Yale University Press, 1970.
Farrer, Austin. *A Rebirth of Images*. Boston: Beacon Press, 1949.
Fekete, John. *The Critical Twilight: Explorations in the Ideology of Anglo-American Literary Theory from Eliot to McLuhan*. London: Routledge and Kegan Paul, 1977.
–. "Massage in the Mass Age: Remembering the McLuhan Matrix." *Canadian Journal of Political and Social Theory* 6.3 (Autumn 1982): 50–67.
Finkelstein, Sidney. *Sense and Nonsense of McLuhan*. New York: International Publishers, 1968.
Fitzgerald, Judith. *Marshall McLuhan: Wise Guy*. Montreal: XYZ, 2001.

Fletcher, Angus. *Allegory: The Theory of a Symbolic Mode.* Ithaca, NY: Cornell University Press, 1964.

–. "Utopian History and the *Anatomy of Criticism.*" In *Northrop Frye in Modern Criticism: Selected Papers from the English Institute,* ed. Murray Krieger. New York: Columbia University Press, 1966.

Ford, Russell. *Northrop Frye on Myth.* New York: Garland Publishing, 1998.

Franklin, Ursula M. *The Real World of Technology.* Rev. ed. Toronto: Anansi, 1999.

Fraser, P.M. *Ptolemaic Alexandria.* 2 vols. Oxford: Clarendon Press, 1972.

Frazer, Sir James George. *The Golden Bough, a Study in Magic and Religion.* London: Macmillan, 1974.

Freke, Timothy, and Peter Gandy. *The Hermetica: The Lost Wisdom of the Pharaohs.* London: Piatkus, 1997.

–. *The Wisdom of the Pagan Philosophers.* Boston: Journey Editions, 1998.

Freud, Sigmund. *The Basic Writings of Sigmund Freud.* Trans. A.A. Brill. New York: Modern Library, 1938.

–. *Civilization and Its Discontents.* Trans. Joan Riviere. London: Hogarth Press, 1972.

–. *On Dreams.* Trans. James Strachey. London: Hogarth Press, 1972.

Frye, Northrop. *Anatomy of Criticism: Four Essays.* 15th ed. Princeton: Princeton University Press, 2000.

–. Archival material, unpublished notes. Frye Archives. From Robert D. Denham, Roanoke College, supplied in 2007–8, 1–32.

–. *The Bush Garden: Essays on the Canadian Imagination.* 2nd ed. Repr., 1995; Toronto: Anansi, 1971.

–. "Communications." *The Listener* 84.2154 (9 July 1970): 33–7.

–. *Creation and Recreation.* Toronto: University of Toronto Press, 1980.

–. *The Critical Path: An Essay on the Social Context of Literary Criticism.* Bloomington: Indiana University Press, 1971.

–. *Divisions on a Ground: Essays on Canadian Culture.* Ed. James Polk. Toronto: Anansi, 1982.

–. *The Double Vision: Language and Meaning in Religion.* Toronto: University of Toronto Press, 1991.

–. *The Educated Imagination.* Toronto: House of Anansi, 2002.

–. *The Eternal Act of Creation: Essays, 1979–1990.* Ed. Robert D. Denham. Bloomington and Indianapolis: Indiana University Press, 1993.

–. *Fables of Identity: Studies in Poetic Mythology.* New York: Harcourt, Brace & World, 1963.

–. *Fearful Symmetry: A Study of William Blake.* Princeton: Princeton University Press, 1969.

–. *Fools of Time: Studies in Shakespearean Tragedy.* Toronto: University of Toronto Press, 1967.

–. *The Great Code: The Bible and Literature.* Toronto: Academic Press, 1982.
–. "Installation Address." *Acta Victoriana* (Victoria College Union) 74.1, ed. Katherine Lehmann (1959): 14–24.
–. "L'Anti-McLuhan." Interview with Naïm Kattan. *Le Devoir,* 23 November 1968, 74–8.
–. *Late Notebooks, 1982–1990: Architecture of the Spiritual World.* Ed. Robert D. Denham. Vols. 5–6 of *Collected Works.* Toronto: University of Toronto Press, 2000.
–. *The Modern Century.* In *On Modern Culture.* Ed. Jan Gorak. Vol. 11 of *Collected Works.* Toronto: University of Toronto Press, 2003.
–. *Myth and Metaphor: Selected Essays, 1974–1988.* Ed. Robert D. Denham. Charlottesville: University of Virginia Press, 1990.
–. *Northrop Frye Unbuttoned: Wit and Wisdom from the Notebooks and Diaries.* Ed. Robert D. Denham. Toronto: Anansi, 2004.
–. *Notebooks and Lectures on the Bible and Other Religious Texts.* Ed. Robert D. Denham. Vol. 13 of *Collected Works.* Toronto: University of Toronto Press, 2003.
–. *On Canada.* Ed. Jean O'Grady and David Staines. Vol. 12 of *Collected Works.* Toronto: University of Toronto Press, 2003.
–. *On Literature and Society, 1936–1989: Unpublished Papers.* Ed. Robert D. Denham. Vol. 10 of *Collected Works.* Toronto: University of Toronto Press, 2002.
–. *On Modern Culture.* Ed. Jan Gorak. Vol. 11 of *Collected Works.* Toronto: University of Toronto Press, 2003.
–. *On Religion.* Ed. Alvin A. Lee and Jean O'Grady. Vol. 4 of *Collected Works.* Toronto: University of Toronto Press, 2000.
–. *Reading the World: Selected Writings, 1935–1976.* Ed. Robert D. Denham. New York: Peter Lang, 1990.
–. *The Return of Eden: Five Essays on Milton's Epics.* Toronto: University of Toronto Press, 1965.
–. *The Secular Scripture: A Study of the Structure of Romance.* Cambridge, MA: Harvard University Press, 1976.
–. *Spiritus Mundi: Essays on Literature, Myth, and Society.* Toronto: Fitzhenry & Whiteside, 1976.
–. *The Stubborn Structure: Essays on Criticism and Society.* Ithaca, NY: Cornell University Press, 1970.
–. *A Study of English Romanticism.* New York: Random House, 1968.
–. *The "Third Book" Notebooks of Northrop Frye, 1964–1972: The Critical Comedy.* Ed. Michael Dolzani. Vol. 9 of *Collected Works.* Toronto: University of Toronto Press, 2002.
–. *T.S. Eliot: An Introduction.* Chicago: University of Chicago Press, 1981.

–. *The Well-Tempered Critic.* Bloomington: Indiana University Press, 1963.
–. *Words with Power: Being a Second Study of the Bible and Literature.* Toronto: Penguin Books, 2007.
Frye, Northrop, and Helen Kemp. *A Glorious and Terrible Life with You: Selected Correspondence of Northrop Frye and Helen Kemp, 1932–1939.* Ed. Margaret Burgess. Toronto: University of Toronto Press, 2007.
Gebser, Jean. *The Ever-Present Origin.* Trans. Noel Barstad and Algis Mickunas. Athens: Ohio University Press, 1985.
Genosko, Gary, ed. *Marshall McLuhan: Critical Evaluations in Cultural Theory.* London: Routledge, 2005.
–. *McLuhan and Baudrillard: The Masters of Implosion.* London: Routledge, 1999.
Gibson, William. *Neuromancer.* New York: Ace Books, 1984.
Giedion, Sigfried. *The Eternal Present: A Contribution to Constancy and Change.* 2 vols. New York: Bollingen, 1962.
Gill, Glen Robert. *Northrop Frye and the Phenomenology of Myth.* Toronto: University of Toronto Press, 2006.
Gleick, James. *What Just Happened: A Chronicle from the Information Frontier.* New York: Pantheon, 2002.
Godwin, Joscelyn. *Mystery Religions in the Ancient World.* London: Thames and Hudson, 1981.
Gombrich, E.H. *Art and Illusion: A Study in the Psychology of Pictorial Representation.* Princeton: Princeton University Press, 1972.
Gordon, W. Terrence. *Marshall McLuhan: Escape into Understanding.* Toronto: Stoddart, 1997.
Graham, Gordon. *The Internet: A Philosophical Inquiry.* London: Routledge, 1999.
Grant, George. "Review of The Great Code: The Bible and Literature." *The Globe and Mail,* 27 February 1982, E17.
Graves, Robert. *The White Goddess.* New York: Farrar, Straus, and Giroux, 1974.
Grosswiler, Paul. *Method Is the Message: Rethinking McLuhan through Cultural Theory.* Montreal: Black Rose Press, 1988.
Guardiani, Francesco. "The Common Ground of McLuhan and Frye." *McLuhan Studies: Premiere Issue* (1996): 1–14. Available online at http://projects.chass.utoronto.ca/mcluhan-studies/v1_iss1/1_1art12.htm.
Hall, Manly P. *Secret Teachings of All Ages: An Encyclopedic Outline of Masonic, Hermetic, Qabbalistic and Rosicrucian Symbolical Philosophy.* Los Angeles: Philosophical Research Society, 1988.
Hamilton, A.C. *Northrop Frye: Anatomy of His Criticism.* Toronto: University of Toronto Press, 1990.

Harpur, Tom. *The Pagan Christ: Recovering the Lost Light*. Toronto: Thomas Allen, 2004.
Hart, Jonathan. Introduction to *City of the End of Things: Lectures on Civilization and Empire, Northrop Frye, J. Robert Oppenheimer, Edward Togo Salmon*. Toronto: Oxford University Press, 2009.
–. *Northrop Frye: The Theoretical Imagination*. London: Routledge, 1994.
Hartman, Geoffrey H. *Beyond Formalism: Literary Essays 1958–1970*. New Haven, CT: Yale University Press, 1970.
–. *Criticism in the Wilderness: The Study of Literature Today*. New Haven, CT: Yale University Press, 1980.
–. "Ghostlier Demarcations." In *Northrop Frye in Modern Criticism: Selected Papers from the English Institute*, ed. Murray Krieger. New York: Columbia University Press, 1966.
–. *The Unmediated Vision: An Interpretation of Wordsworth, Hopkins, Rilke, and Valéry*. New York: Harcourt, Brace & World, 1966.
Havelock, Eric A. *Origins of Western Literacy*. Toronto: Ontario Institute for Studies in Education, 1976.
–. *Preface to Plato*. Cambridge, MA: Harvard University Press, 1963.
Heidegger, Martin. *Poetry, Language, Thought*. Trans. Albert Hofstadter. New York: Harper Colophon Books, 1971.
–. *The Question Concerning Technology, and Other Essays*. Trans. William Lovitt. New York: Harper & Row, 1977.
Heim, Michael. *Electric Language: A Philosophical Study of Word Processing*. New Haven, CT: Yale University Press, 1987.
Heraclitus. *The Cosmic Fragments*. Ed. G.S. Kirk. Cambridge: Cambridge University Press, 1962.
Hesse, Hermann. *Magister Ludi or The Glass Bead Game*. Trans. Richard and Clara Winston. New York: Holt, 1978.
Hildegard von Bingen. *Selected Writings*. Trans. Mark Atherton. London: Penguin, 2001.
Hillman, James. *Emotion: A Comprehensive Phenomenology of Theories and Their Meanings for Therapy*. Evanston, IL: Northwestern University Press, 1992.
Holmyard, E.J. *Alchemy*. Middlesex: Penguin Books, 1968.
Homer. *The Odyssey*. Trans. Robert Fitzgerald. New York: Vintage Books, 1990.
Horn, Stacy. *Cyberville: Clicks, Culture, and the Creation of an Online Town*. New York: Warner, 1998.
Horrocks, Christopher. *Marshall McLuhan and Virtuality*. Cambridge: Icon, 2000.
Hutcheon, Linda. *The Canadian Postmodern: A Study of Contemporary English-Canadian Fiction*. Toronto: Oxford University Press, 1988.

–. "Introduction: The Field Notes of a Public Critic." In *The Bush Garden: Essays on the Canadian Imagination*, by Northrop Frye. 2nd ed. Repr., 1995; Toronto: Anansi, 1971.
Idel, Moshe. *Kabbalah: New Perspectives.* New Haven, CT: Yale University Press, 1988.
–. *Studies in Ecstatic Kabbalah.* Albany: State University of New York Press, 1988.
Ignatieff, Michael. "Medium-Rare Message." *London Observer,* 6 March 1988, 42.
Innis, Harold A. *The Bias of Communication.* Toronto: University of Toronto Press, 1991.
James, William. *The Varieties of Religious Experience.* New York: Triumph Books, 1991.
Jameson, Fredric. *Marxism and Form.* Princeton: Princeton University Press, 1971.
–. *The Political Unconscious: Narrative as a Socially Symbolic Act.* Ithaca, NY: Cornell University Press, 1981.
–. *Postmodernism or, the Cultural Logic of Late Capitalism.* Durham, NC: Duke University Press, 1991.
–. *The Prison-House of Language.* Princeton: Princeton University Press, 1972.
Jaynes, Julian. *The Origin of Consciousness in the Breakdown of the Bicameral Mind.* Toronto: University of Toronto Press, 1976.
Jonas, Hans. *The Gnostic Religion.* Boston: Beacon Press, 1963.
–. *Philosophical Essays: From Ancient Creed to Technological Man.* Englewood Cliffs, NJ: Prentice-Hall, 1974.
Joyce, James. *Finnegans Wake.* London: Penguin, 1992.
–. *A Portrait of the Artist as a Young Man.* New York: Viking Press, 1964.
–. *Ulysses.* Ed. Hans Walter Gabler. London: Penguin, 1986.
Jung, Carl G. *Man and His Symbols.* New York: Anchor-Doubleday, 1964.
–. *Mysterium Coniunctionis.* Trans. R.F.C. Hull. Princeton: Princeton University Press, 1977.
–. *On Alchemy.* Princeton: Princeton University Press, 1995.
Kafka, Franz. *The Blue Octavo Notebooks.* Ed. Max Brod. Trans. Ernst Kaiser and Eithne Wilkins. Cambridge: Schocken Books, 1991.
–. *Parables and Paradoxes.* New York: Schocken Books, 1961.
–. *The Trial.* Trans. Willa and Edwin Muir. New York: Schocken Books, 1984.
Kaufmann, Walter, trans. and ed. *Basic Writings of Nietzsche.* New York: Modern Library, 2000.
–. *Nietzsche: Philosopher, Psychologist, Antichrist.* Princeton: Princeton University Press, 1974.

–, trans. and ed. *The Portable Nietzsche.* New York: Penguin/Viking Portable Library, 1976.
Kennedy, H.A.A. *St. Paul and the Mystery Religions.* London: Hodden and Stoughton, 1914.
Kenner, Hugh. *The Pound Era.* Berkeley: University of California Press, 1971.
–. "Understanding McLuhan." In *McLuhan: Pro and Con,* ed. Raymond Rosenthal. New York: Funk and Wagnalls, 1968.
Kingsley, Peter. *Ancient Philosophy, Mystery, and Magic: Empedocles and Pythagorean Tradition.* Oxford: Clarendon Press, 1995.
Kogan, Pauline. *Northrop Frye: The High Priest of Clerical Obscurantism.* Montreal: Progressive Books and Periodicals, 1969.
Krieger, Murray, ed. *Northrop Frye in Modern Criticism: Selected Papers from the English Institute.* New York: Columbia University Press, 1966.
Kroker, Arthur. *Panic Encyclopedia: The Definitive Guide to the Postmodern Scene.* Montreal: New World Perspectives, 1989.
–. *Spasm: Virtual Reality, Android Music and Electric Flesh.* New York: St Martin's Press, 1993.
–. *Technology and the Canadian Mind: Innis/McLuhan/Grant.* Montreal: New World Perspectives, 1984.
–. *The Will to Technology and the Culture of Nihilism: Heidegger, Nietzsche, and Marx.* Toronto: University of Toronto Press, 2004.
Kroker, Arthur, and MariLouise Kroker. *Hacking the Future: Stories for the Flesh-Eating 90's.* New York: St Martin's Press, 1996.
Kroker, Arthur, and Michael A. Weinstein. *Data Trash: The Theory of the Virtual Class.* Montreal: New World Perspective, 1994.
Kuhns, Thomas S. *The Structure of Scientific Revolutions.* Chicago: University of Chicago Press, 1970.
Kurzweil, Ray. *The Age of Spiritual Machines.* New York: Viking, 1999.
–. *The Singularity Is Near: When Humans Transcend Biology.* New York: Viking, 2005.
Lamberti, Elena. *Marshall McLuhan's Mosaic: Probing the Literary Origins of Media Studies.* Toronto: University of Toronto Press, 2012.
Languirand, Jacques. *De McLuhan a Pythagore.* Montreal: Les Editions de Mortagne, 1982.
Lanham, Richard A. *The Electronic Word: Democracy, Technology, and the Arts.* Chicago: University of Chicago Press, 1995.
Layton, Bentley. *The Gnostic Scriptures.* Toronto: Doubleday, 1995.
Leavis, F.R., with Denys Thompson. *Culture and Environment: The Training of Cultural Awareness.* London: Chatto & Windus, 1933.
Leavis, Q.D. *Fiction and the Reading Public.* London: Penguin, 1979.

Lee, Alvin A. Introduction to *Words with Power: Being a Second Study of the Bible and Literature*, by Northrop Frye. Toronto: Penguin, 2007.
Lee, Alvin A., and Robert D. Denham, eds. *The Legacy of Northrop Frye*. Toronto: University of Toronto Press, 1994.
Lentricchia, Frank. *After the New Criticism*. Chicago: University of Chicago Press, 1980.
Levinson, Paul. *Digital McLuhan: A Guide to the Information Millennium*. London: Routledge, 1999.
Lewis, P. Wyndham. *Blast 1*. Santa Barbara, CA: Black Sparrow Press, 1981.
–. *Blast 2*. Santa Barbara, CA: Black Sparrow Press, 1981.
–. *Malign Fiesta*. London: Calder and Boyars, 1966.
–. *Men Without Art*. Ed. Seamus Cooney. Santa Rosa, CA: Black Sparrow Press, 1987.
–. *Monstre Gai*. London: John Calder, 1965.
–. *Self-Condemned*. Santa Barbara, CA: Black Sparrow Press, 1983.
Logan, Robert K. "McLuhan and Frye." Message to B.W. Powe. 17 September 2007. Email.
Lyotard, Jean-Francois. *The Post-Modern Condition: A Report on Knowledge*. Trans. Geoff Bennington and Brian Massumi. Minneapolis: University of Minnesota Press, 1984.
Mallarmé, Stéphane. *Mallarmé: Selections*. Trans. Anthony Hartley. London: Penguin, 1970.
Mandel, Eli. Introduction to *Contexts of Canadian Criticism*, ed. Eli Mandel. Toronto: University of Toronto Press, 1977.
Marchand, Philip. *Marshall McLuhan: The Medium and the Messenger*. Toronto: Random House, 1989.
–. Telephone interview. 10 December 2007.
Marchessault, Janine. *Marshall McLuhan: Cosmic Media*. London: Sage Publications, 2005.
Massey, Gerald. *Ancient Egypt, the Light of the World: A Work of Reclamation and Restitution*. 2 vols. London: Stuart & Watkins, 1970.
–. *A Book of the Beginnings*. 2 vols. Secaucus, NJ: University Books, 1974.
–. *The Natural Genesis*. 2 vols. New York: Samuel Weiser, 1974.
McLuhan, Corinne. Personal interviews. 20–21 April 2005, Toronto.
McLuhan, Eric. *Electric Language: Understanding the Present*. Toronto: Stoddart, 1998.
–. "Marshall McLuhan's Theory of Communication: The Yegg." Unpublished essay, 2005.
–, ed. *McLuhan Studies: Explorations in Culture and Communication*. Vol. 1. Toronto: University of Toronto Press, 1991.

–. *The Role of Thunder in Finnegans Wake.* Toronto: University of Toronto Press, 1997.
–. Telephone interviews. 2005, 2006, 2008, 2009.
McLuhan, Marshall. Archival material, unpublished essays, "Cyborg" (1965) and "Varieties of Psychedelic Experience" (1966), supplied 2005–8. McLuhan Archives, in the possession of Eric McLuhan, 1–100.
–. *The Classical Trivium: The Place of Thomas Nashe in the Learning of His Time.* Ed. W. Terrence Gordon. Corte Madera, CA: Gingko Press, 2006.
–. *Counterblast.* Mimeograph, 1954. McLuhan Archives.
–. *Culture Is Our Business.* Toronto: McGraw-Hill, 1970.
–. *Essential McLuhan.* Ed. Eric McLuhan and Frank Zingrone. Toronto: Anansi, 1995.
–. *Explorations: Studies in Culture and Communications.* Ed. Edmund Carpenter and Marshall McLuhan. Toronto: University of Toronto, 1957.
–. *The Gutenberg Galaxy: The Making of Typographic Man.* Toronto: University of Toronto Press, 1962.
–. "Have With You to Madison Avenue or The Flush-Profile of Literature." Unpublished review of Northrop Frye's *Anatomy of Criticism*, 1957. McLuhan Archives.
–. "Inside Blake and Hollywood." In *Marshall McLuhan Unbound*, ed. W. Terrence Gordon. Corte Madera, CA: Gingko Press, 2006.
–. *The Interior Landscape: The Literary Criticism of Marshall McLuhan, 1943–1962.* Ed. Eugene McNamara. New York: McGraw-Hill, 1969.
–. *Letters of Marshall McLuhan.* Ed. Matie Molinaro, Corinne McLuhan, and William Toye. Toronto: Oxford University Press, 1987.
–. *Marshall McLuhan Unbound.* Ed. W. Terrence Gordon. Corte Madera, CA: Gingko Press, 2006.
–. *The McLuhan DEW-line* 1, no. 11 (May 1969).
–. *The Mechanical Bride: Folklore of Industrial Man.* Corte Madera, CA: Gingko Press, 2002.
–. *Media Research: Technology, Art, Communication: Marshall McLuhan Essays.* Ed. Michel A. Moos. Amsterdam: G&B Arts International, 1997.
–. *The Medium and the Light: Reflections on Religion.* Ed. Eric McLuhan and Jacek Szklarek. Toronto: Stoddart, 1999.
–. "Pound, Eliot, and the Rhetoric of The Waste Land." *New Literary History* 10 (Spring 1979): 557–80.
–. *Report on Project in Understanding New Media (ROPUNM).* [Washington, D.C.]: National Association of Educational Broadcasters, US Department of Health, Education and Welfare, 1960. McLuhan Archives.
–. *Understanding Media: The Extensions of Man.* New York: McGraw-Hill, 1964.

–. *Understanding Me: Lectures and Interviews.* Ed. Stephanie McLuhan and David Staines. Toronto: McClelland and Stewart, 2003.
–. "Views." *The Listener* 84.2167 (8 October 1970): 475–6.
McLuhan, Marshall, and David Carson. *The Book of Probes.* Ed. Eric McLuhan and William Kuhns. Corte Madera, CA: Gingko Press, 2003.
McLuhan, Marshall, and Quentin Fiore. Coordinated by Jerome Agel. *The Medium is the Massage: An Inventory of Effects.* Corte Madera, CA: Gingko Press, 2001.
–. *War and Peace in the Global Village.* Toronto: Penguin, 2003.
McLuhan, Marshall, and Eric McLuhan. *Laws of Media: The New Science.* Toronto: University of Toronto Press, 1988.
McLuhan, Marshall, and Eric McLuhan, with Kathryn Hutchon. *City as Classroom: Understanding Language and Media.* Agincourt, ON: The Book Society of Canada, 1977.
McLuhan, Marshall, and Barrington Nevitt. *Take Today: The Executive as Dropout.* New York: Harcourt Brace Jovanovich, 1972.
McLuhan, Marshall, and Harley Parker. *Counterblast.* Toronto: McClelland and Stewart, 1969.
–. *Through the Vanishing Point: Space in Poetry and Painting.* New York: Harper Colophon, 1968.
McLuhan, Marshall, and Bruce R. Powers. *The Global Village: Transformations in World Life and Media in the 21st Century.* New York: Oxford University Press, 1989.
McLuhan, Marshall, and Richard J. Schoeck. *Voices of Literature.* 2 vols. New York: Holt, 1965–6.
McLuhan, Marshall, and Wilfred Watson. *From Cliché to Archetype.* New York: Viking Press, 1970.
McLuhan, Maurice, and Barrington Nevitt. *Who Was Marshall McLuhan? Exploring a Mosaic of Impressions.* Toronto: Comprehensivist Publications, 1994.
McLuhan, T.C. *The Way of the Earth: Encounters with Nature in Ancient and Contemporary Thought.* New York: Simon & Schuster, 1994.
Mendelson, Alan, and Jeffrey Donaldson. *Frye and the Word: Religious Contexts in the Criticism of Northrop Frye.* Toronto: University of Toronto Press, 2004.
Meyer, Martin W., ed. *The Ancient Mysteries: A Sourcebook.* San Francisco: Harper and Row, 1987.
Middleton, John, ed. *Myth and Cosmos: Readings in Mythology and Symbolism.* New York: Natural History Press, 1967.
Miller, Henry. *The Time of the Assassins: A Study of Arthur Rimbaud.* New York: New Directions, 1962.
Miller, Jonathan. *Marshall McLuhan.* New York: Viking Press, 1971.

Mitchell, William J. *City of Bits: Space, Place, and the Infobahn*. Cambridge, MA: MIT Press, 1995.
Mosco, Vincent. *The Digital Sublime: Myth, Power, and Cyberspace*. Cambridge, MA: The MIT Press, 2004.
Moulthrop, Stuart. "You Say You Want a Revolution? Hypertext and the Laws of Medium." In *The Norton Anthology of Theory and Criticism*, ed. Vincent B. Leitch. New York: W.W. Norton and Company, 2001.
Mumford, Lewis. *Technics and Civilization*. New York: Harcourt, Brace & World, 1963.
Mylonas, George E. *Eleusis and the Eleusinian Mysteries*. Princeton: Princeton University Press, 1969.
Neill, S.D. *Clarifying McLuhan: An Assessment of Process and Product*. Westport, CT: Greenwood Press, 1993.
Neumann, Erich. *The Great Mother: An Analysis of the Archetype*. Trans. Ralph Manheim. Princeton: Princeton University Press, 1974.
Nietzsche, Friedrich. *Beyond Good and Evil: Prelude to a Philosophy of the Future*. Trans. R.J. Hollingdale. London: Penguin, 1973.
–. *Birth of Tragedy, and the Genealogy of Morals*. Trans. Francis Golffing. New York: Anchor Books, 1956.
–. *The Dawn of Day*. Trans. J.M. Kennedy. Mineola, NY: Dover Publications, 2007.
–. *Thus Spoke Zarathustra: A Book for Everyone and No One*. Trans. R.J. Hollingdale. London: Penguin, 1971.
–. *Twilight of the Idols, and The Anti-Christ*. Trans. R.J. Hollingdale. London: Penguin, 1974.
–. *The Will to Power*. Trans. Walter Kaufmann and R.J. Hollingdale. New York: Vintage, 1968.
O'Grady, Jean, and Wang Ning, eds. *Northrop Frye: Eastern and Western Perspectives*. Toronto: University of Toronto Press, 2003.
Ong, Walter J. *Orality and Literacy: The Technologizing of the Word*. London: Routledge, 2002.
Otto, Rudolph. *The Idea of the Holy*. Trans. John W. Harvey. London: Oxford University Press, 1982.
Pagels, Elaine. *Beyond Belief: The Secret Gospel of Thomas*. New York: Random House, 2003.
–. *The Gnostic Gospels*. New York: Vintage, 1989.
Pagels, Heinz R. *The Cosmic Code: Quantum Physics as the Language of Nature*. New York: Simon and Schuster, 1982.
Paglia, Camille. "Cults and Cosmic Consciousness: Religious Vision in the American 1960's." *Arion* 10.3 (2003): 57–111.

–. *Sex, Art and American Culture: Essays.* New York: Vintage, 1992.
–. *Vamps and Tramps.* New York: Vintage, 1991.
Pascal, Blaise. *Pensées.* Trans. A.J. Krailsheimer. London: Penguin, 1966.
Pearsall, Ronald. *The Alchemists.* London: Weidenfeld and Nicolson, 1986.
Perloff, Marjorie. *Radical Artifice: Writing Poetry in the Age of Media.* Chicago: University of Chicago Press, 1991.
–. *21st-Century Modernism: The "New" Poetics.* Oxford: Blackwell Publishers, 2002.
–. *Wittgenstein's Ladder: Poetic Language and the Strangeness of the Ordinary.* Chicago: University of Chicago Press, 1996.
Plato. *Plato's Cosmology: The Timaeus of Plato.* Trans. Francis MacDonald Cornford. New York: Bobbs-Merrill, 1980.
Plotinus. *The Enneads.* Abridged. Trans. Stephen Mackenna. London: Penguin, 1991.
Postman, Neil. *Amusing Ourselves to Death: Public Discourse in the Age of Show Business.* London: Penguin, 1985.
–. *Conscientious Objections: Stirring Up Trouble about Language, Technology, and Education.* New York: Knopf, 1988.
–. *The End of Education: Redefining the Value of School.* New York: Knopf, 1995.
Pound, Ezra. *The Cantos.* New York: New Directions, 1975.
Pynchon, Thomas. *The Crying of Lot 49.* New York: Harper Perennial, 1999.
–. *Gravity's Rainbow.* New York: Viking Press, 1973.
Redgrove, H. Stanley. *Alchemy: Ancient and Modern.* Chicago: Ares, 1980.
Reitzenstein, Richard. *Hellenistic Mystery-Religions: Their Basic Ideas and Significance.* Trans. John E. Steely. Pittsburgh: Pickwick Press, 1978.
Richards, I.A. *Practical Criticism: A Study of Literary Judgment.* New York: Harcourt, Brace & World, 1929.
Ricks, Christopher. "McLuhanism." In *McLuhan: Pro and Con,* ed. Raymond Rosenthal. New York: Funk and Wagnalls, 1968.
Rimbaud, Arthur. *Complete Works.* Trans. Paul Schmidt. New York: Harper Perennial, 2008.
–. *Illuminations, and Other Prose Poems.* Trans. Louise Varèse. New York: New Directions, 1957.
–. *Season in Hell and The Drunken Boat.* Trans. Louise Varèse. New York: New Directions, 1961.
Rivano, Juan. *The Ideas of Marshall McLuhan.* Trans. Ivan Jaksic. Amherst, NY: SUNY Press, 1979.
Ronell, Avita. *The Telephone Book: Technology, Schizophrenia, Electric Speech.* Lincoln: University of Nebraska Press, 1989.

Rosen, Jonathan. *The Talmud and the Internet: A Journey between Worlds.* New York: Picador, 2000.
Rosenthal, Raymond, ed. *McLuhan: Pro and Con.* New York: Funk and Wagnalls, 1968.
Ross, Andrew. *No Respect: Intellectuals and Popular Culture.* London: Routledge, 1989.
Ross, Malcolm, ed. *Our Sense of Identity: A Book of Canadian Essays.* Toronto: Ryerson Press, 1954.
Rudolph, Kurt. *Gnosis: The Nature and History of Gnosticism.* Trans. and ed. Robert McLachlan Wilson. San Francisco: Harper and Row, 1987.
Rushkoff, Douglas. *Media Virus! Hidden Agendas in Popular Culture.* New York: Ballantine Books, 1994.
Russell, Ford. *Northrop Frye on Myth.* New York: Garland Publishing, 1998.
Said, Edward W. *The World, the Text, and the Critic.* Cambridge, MA: Harvard University Press, 1983.
Sanders, Barry, and Ivan Illich. *ABC, The Alphabetization of the Popular Mind.* New York: Vintage, 1989.
Saurat, Denis. *Blake and Milton.* New York: Russell & Russell, 1965.
–. *Blake and Modern Thought.* New York: Russell & Russell, 1964.
–. *Literature and Occult Tradition: Studies in Philosophical Poetry.* London: G. Bell, 1930.
Scholem, Gershom. *Kabbalah.* New York: Meridian, 1978.
–. *On the Kabbalah and Its Symbolism.* Trans. Ralph Manheim. New York: Schocken Books, 1969.
–. *Origins of the Kabbalah.* Trans. Allan Arkush. Princeton: Princeton University Press, 1987.
Schwartz, Arturo. *Kabbalah and Alchemy: An Essay on Common Archetypes.* Northvale, NJ: Jason Aronson, 2000.
Sewell, Elizabeth. *The Orphic Voice: Poetry and Natural History.* London: Routledge & Kegan Paul, 1961.
Shaffer, Peter. *Amadeus: A Play.* London: Penguin Books, 1993.
Shakespeare, William. *The Yale Shakespeare: Poems, Sonnets, and Plays.* Ed. Wilbur Cross and Tucker Brooke. New Haven, CT: Yale University Press, 1957.
Siegel, Arthur. "Northrop Frye and the Toronto School of Communication Theory." In *The Toronto School of Communication Theory: Interpretations, Extensions, Applications,* edited by Rita Watson and Menahem Blondheim, 114–145. Toronto: University of Toronto Press; Jerusalem: Hebrew University Magnes Press, 2007.
Spengler, Oswald. *Decline of the West.* 2 vols. Trans. Charles Francis Atkinson. New York: Knopf, 1980.

Spivak, Gayatri Chakravorty. *Death of a Discipline*. New York: Columbia University Press, 2003.
Stamps, Judith. *Unthinking Modernity: Innis, McLuhan, and the Frankfurt School.* Montreal and Kingston: McGill-Queen's University Press, 1995.
Stearn, Gerald E., ed. *McLuhan: Hot & Cool: A Critical Symposium.* New York: Dial Press, 1967.
Steiner, George. *After Babel: Aspects of Language and Translation.* London: Oxford University Press, 1977.
–. *Grammars of Creation.* New Haven, CT: Yale University Press, 2001.
–. *Language and Silence.* New York: Atheneum, 1976.
–. *Real Presences.* Chicago: University of Chicago Press, 1989.
–. Personal interview. 16 November 2002, Toronto.
Stevens, Wallace. *The Collected Poems of Wallace Stevens.* New York: Knopf, 1977.
–. *Opus Posthumous.* New York: Knopf, 1989.
Still, Colin. *Shakespeare's Mystery Play: A Study of "The Tempest."* London: C. Palmer, 1921.
Strate, Lance, and Edward Wachtel, eds. *The Legacy of McLuhan.* Cresskill, NJ: Hampton Press, 2005.
Surette, Leon. *A Light from Eleusis.* Oxford: Clarendon Press, 1979.
Symons, Arthur. *The Symbolist Movement in Literature.* New York: Dutton, 1958.
Tarnas, Richard. *Cosmos and Psyche: Intimations of a New World View.* New York: Viking, 2006.
–. *The Passion of the Western Mind: Understanding the Ideas that Have Shaped Our World View.* New York: Ballantine Books, 1991.
Taylor, Charles. *Varieties of Religion Today: William James Revisited.* Cambridge, MA: Harvard University Press, 2002.
Taylor, Thomas. *Selected Writings.* Ed. Kathleen Raine and George Mills Harper. Princeton: Princeton University Press, 1969.
Teilhard de Chardin, Pierre. *The Divine Milieu.* Trans. Bernard Wall. New York: Torchbooks, 1960.
–. *The Future of Man.* Trans. Norman Denny. London: Collins, Fontana Books, 1970.
–. *The Phenomenon of Man.* Trans. Bernard Wall. New York: Harper Torchbooks, 1961.
Theall, Donald F. *The Medium Is the Rear View Mirror: Understanding McLuhan.* Montreal: McGill-Queen's University Press, 1971.
–. Telephone interview. 6 November 2007.
–. *The Virtual Marshall McLuhan.* Montreal: McGill-Queen's University Press, 2001.

Thompson, William Irwin. *Coming into Being: Artifacts and Texts in the Evolution of Consciousness.* New York: St Martin's Press, 1996.
–. *Imaginary Landscape: Making Worlds as Myth and Science.* New York: St Martin's Press, 1989.
Turkle, Sherry. *Life on the Screen: Identity in the Age of the Internet.* New York: Touchstone Press, 1997.
Underhill, Evelyn. *The Essentials of Mysticism, and Other Essays.* Oxford: Oneworld Publications, 2000.
Vico, Giambattista. "The New Science." In *Theories of History: Readings from Classical and Contemporary Sources,* ed. Patrick Gardiner. New York: Free Press, 1959.
Virlio, Paul. *Desert Storm: War at the Speed of Light.* Trans. Michael Degener. London: Continuum, 2002.
–. *Open Sky.* Trans. Julie Rose. New York: Verso, 1997.
Walker, D.P. *The Ancient Theology: Studies in Christian Platonism from the Fifteenth to the Eighteenth Century.* London: Duckworth, 1972.
Wasson, R. Gordon, Albert Hoffmann, and Carl A.P. Ruck. *The Road to Eleusis: Unveiling the Secret of the Mysteries.* New York: Harcourt Brace Jovanovich, 1978.
Weiss, Irving J. "Sensual Reality in the Mass Media." In *McLuhan: Pro and Con,* ed. Raymond Rosenthal. New York: Funk and Wagnalls, 1968.
Weston, Jessie L. *From Ritual to Romance.* Garden City, NY: Doubleday Anchor, 1957.
Whitehead, A.N. *Science and the Modern World.* New York: Macmillan, 1925.
Whitman, Walt. *Leaves of Grass.* New York: The Modern Library, 1985.
–. *Leaves of Grass: The 1855 Edition.* New York: Penguin, 2005.
Wilber, Ken, ed. *Quantum Questions: Mystical Writings of the World's Great Physicists.* Boston: Shambhala, 1985.
Wilde, Oscar. *Complete Works.* Ed. Vyvyan Holland. London and Glasgow: Collins, 1973.
Willmott, Glenn. *McLuhan, or Modernism in Reverse.* Toronto: University of Toronto Press, 1996.
Wimsatt, W.K. Jr. "Criticism as Myth." In *Northrop Frye in Modern Criticism: Selected Papers from the English Institute,* ed. Murray Krieger. New York: Columbia University Press, 1966.
–. *Hateful Contraries.* Studies in Literature and Criticism. Lexington: University of Kentucky Press, 1965.
Wimsatt, W.K. Jr., and Cleanth Brooks. "Myth and Archetype" and "On Northrop Frye." In *Literary Criticism: A Short History.* New York: Knopf, 1965.
Wittgenstein, Ludwig. *Tractatus Logico-Philosophicus.* Trans. D.F. Pears and B.F. McGuinness. London: Routledge and Kegan Paul, 1974.

Wolfe, Tom. "What If He Is Right?" In *The Pump House Gang*. New York: Farrar, Straus & Giroux, 1968.
Woolf, Virginia. *A Room of One's Own*. London: Penguin, 1945.
Wurman, Richard Saul, Loring Leifer, and David Sume. *Information Anxiety 2*. Ed. Karen Whitehouse. New York: Random House, 2002.
Xie, Shaobo. "History and Utopian Desire: Fredric Jameson's Dialectical Tribute to Northrop Frye." *Cultural Critique* 34 (Autumn 1996): 115–42.
Yates, Frances A. *The Art of Memory*. Chicago: University of Chicago Press, 1966.
–. *Giordano Bruno and the Hermetic Tradition*. Chicago: University of Chicago Press, 1964.
–. *The Occult Philosophy in the Elizabethan Age*. London: Routledge Classics, 1979.
–. *The Rosicrucian Enlightenment*. London: Routledge Classics, 1972.
–. *Theatre of the World*. London: Routledge and Kegan Paul, 1969.
Yeats, W.B. *Essays and Introductions*. New York: Collier, 1968.
–. *Selected Poetry*. Ed. A. Norman Jeffares. London: Macmillan, 1972.
–. *A Vision*. London: Macmillan, 1969.
Zingrone, Frank. *The Media Symplex: At the Edge of Meaning in the Age of Chaos*. Toronto: Stoddart, 2001.
Žižek, Slavoj. *Welcome to the Desert of the Real: Five Essays on September 11 and Related Dates*. London: Verso, 2002.

Index

Abrams, M.H., 71
"Across the River and out of the Trees" (Frye, H.N.), 179–80
Acta Victoriana magazine, 71
Acts: 2:1–26, 28; 2:17–18, 34
A.E.I.O.U. (Art Education I Owe You), 226
afflatus (inspiration), 276
agon: Bloom on, 35–6, 290n19; definition of, 13–15. *See also* McLuhan-Frye conflict
Agon: Towards a Theory of Revisionism (Bloom), 36
Albertus Magnus, 29, 157
alchemy, 43, 234, 262. *See also* McLuhan-Frye alchemy
Alexandrian *museion*, 263–4
allegory: of Mental Traveller, 32; political-historical dimension in, 253; role of, 31, 231, 240
alphabetic text: multidimensional meanings of, 33; role of, 7–8, 39, 117–18
Amadeus (Shaffer), 280
American Academy of Arts and Sciences, 171
Amusing Ourselves to Death: Public Discourse in the Age of Show Business (Postman), 134
analogical mirrors, 84, 111, 149
Anatomy of Criticism (Frye, H.N.): conclusion of, 39, 209–10, 221; as encyclopedic satire, 45; first page of, 108; foreword to, 77, 166, 224; four essays in, 220, 226; four levels of exegesis in, 29, 289n13; passages from, 208; "Polemical Introduction" to, 23, 127; possible title for, 44; publication of, 66, 71; reviews of, 113–16, 123, 125, 127, 268; structure of, 28; theories outline in, 42; "Theory of Myths" essay of, 14–15; views on, 146, 148, 149, 155
The Anatomy of Melancholy (Burton), 45, 220
"An Ancient Quarrel in Modern America (Sophists vs. Grammarians)" (McLuhan, H.), 162
Ant Farm, 67
"L'Anti-McLuhan," 127
Anti-Oedipus (Deleuze and Guattari), 206–7

The Anxiety of Influence (Bloom), 36, 134, 290n19
aphorisms: *in The Book of Probes*, 17, 119, 211–12, 233–4; Frye, H.N., and, 12, 144–6; McLuhan, H., and, 6, 12, 17, 29, 34, 40–1, 46, 52, 95, 144–6, 185, 191–2, 249, 259, 294n19; in *Notebooks and Lectures on the Bible and Other Religious Texts*, 12. *See also specific aphorisms*
apocalypse: practical, 16–24, 33, 149–53; Suzuki on, 245; views on, 4, 12, 16–17, 19–21, 23, 269, 273. *See also kerygma*; visionary-apocalyptic tradition
apocalyptic, as term, 27
Aquinas, Thomas, 29
archetypes, 8, 106, 120–3, 245
Architecture of the Spiritual World (Frye, H.N.), 228
Arnold, Matthew, 164
Art Education I Owe You (A.E.I.O.U.), 226
The Art of Memory (Yates), 41, 265, 295n28, 314n18
Atwood, Margaret, 66, 173, 179, 248
audile-tactile work, 43, 136, 213
"Auguries of Innocence" (Blake), 32
Ayre, John, 80; biography by, 127, 181, 190; *Northrop Frye: A Biography*, 37

Babin, Pierre, 118, 249–50
Bacon, 143
Balfour, Ian, 173
Ballard, J.G., 67, 241
Barnes, Michael, 297n48
Barthes, Roland, 93
Bates, Ronald, 47; *Northrop Frye*, 66
Baudelaire, Charles, 23

Baudrillard, Jean, 187, 214, 252, 256–60
Beatles, 251
Bezos, Jeff, 274
Bible: Authorized or King James, 289n12; Frye, H.N., on, 29, 72–6, 102, 151, 196–8; influence of, 31, 189, 248. *See also* Great Code; *The Great Code: The Bible and Literature*; specific books
Birkerts, Sven, 67; *The Gutenberg Elegies*, 134
Bissell, Claude, 89, 172–3
Blake, William: "Auguries of Innocence," 32; Frye, H.N., and, 3, 7, 14, 32, 44–6, 69–74, 78, 150–1, 184, 292n19; influence of, 4, 48, 94, 100, 167, 189, 192–3, 224, 225, 248; "Jerusalem," 70; letter to Butts, 14, 28, 191; McLuhan, H., and, 14, 81, 153; *The Marriage of Heaven and Hell*, 14, 45, 78, 116, 150; on Orc cycle of revolution and reaction, 22; "Proverbs of Hell," 70, 301n24
Blake and Milton (Saurat), 181
Blake and Modern Thought (Saurat), 68, 181
"Blake's Bible" (Frye, H.N.), 108
Blast, 84, 303n29
Blondheim, Menahem, 97–8
Bloom, Harold, 71; on agon, 35–6, 290n19; *Agon: Towards a Theory of Revisionism*, 36; *Anatomy of Criticism* foreword by, 77, 166, 224; *The Anxiety of Influence*, 36, 134, 290n19; *The Breaking of the Vessels*, 36; *Genius*, 157, 293n19; *A Map of Misreading*, 291n19; *The Western Canon*, 72
Blunden, Edmund, 4, 69, 80
Boehme, Jacob, 273

Bohm, David, 170
Bohr, Niels, 169
Bonaventure, 29
Book of Nature, 7, 43, 92, 119
The Book of Disquiet (Pessoa), 202
The Book of Probes (McLuhan, H.), 8; aphorisms in, 17, 119, 211–12, 233–4; passages from, 105, 188, 226, 231, 276–7
Borges, Jorge Luis, 99
Bradbrook, Muriel C., 4, 56, 81
brain, hemispheres of, 58, 124
Braque, Georges, 62
breakdown-breakthrough method, 14, 184–5, 231, 267, 275, 311n45
breaking, 274
The Breaking of the Vessels (Bloom), 36
Brooks, Cleanth, 117
Browning, 189
Bucke, Richard Maurice, 187
Buddhism, 224
Burroughs, William, 84, 129, 190
Burton, Robert, 45, 220
The Bush Garden: Essays on the Canadian Imagination (Frye, H.N.), 46, 174–6
Butts, Thomas, 14, 28, 191

Cage, John, 67, 214
Calasso, Roberto, 42
Cambridge University, 4, 29, 56, 80, 81–2, 84, 301n24
Cameron, James, 67
Campbell, Joseph, 65
Canada, 24; during centennial year, 129; writings about, 61, 172–80
Canadian communiqué, 173–80, 281
Canadian difference, 62, 176–7
Canadian Forum, 179
Canadian identity, 35, 100, 272–3
Canadian sublime, 12

Canetti, Elias, 144
Cantos (Pound, E.), 202
Capra, Fritjof, 169–70
Carpenter, Edmund, 87, 92, 304n36
Carson, David, 234
Carter, Jimmy, 157
Catholicism, 142; McLuhan, H., and, 3, 46, 82–4, 91, 97, 154–5, 157, 159–60, 195, 200
Cavafy, C.P., 1
Cavell, Richard, 48
Cayley, David: Frye, H.N., interview with, 9, 61, 91, 96, 143, 148, 232, 295n28; *Northrop Frye in Conversation*, 57, 78–9, 151
CBC Radio's *Sunday Morning* interview, 134–5
Celan, Paul, 202, 207
Centre for Culture and Technology, University of Toronto, 93, 117; closing of, 96; establishment of, 89; role of, 135; sign on wall of, 41, 295n29
charismatic personalities, 180–4, 264
Chesterton, G.K.: essay on, 150, 168, 250; *Heretics*, 199; influence of, 79, 82, 83; *Orthodoxy*, 199
Christianity, 3, 46, 60, 67–8, 72, 195, 199, 225. *See also specific denominations*
"The Circus Animals' Desertion" (Yeats), 59
City as Classroom: Understanding Language and Media (McLuhan, H., McLuhan, E., and Hutchon), 56, 92
City of the End of Things (Hart), 132
The Classical Journal, 110
The Classical Trivium: The Place of Thomas Nashe in the Learning of Time (McLuhan, H.), 29, 33, 43, 56, 283

classrooms, 56, 62–5, 193
CN Tower, Toronto, 57–9, 98, 172
Cohen, Leonard, 62
coincidentia oppositorum (coinciding of opposites), 266
Coleridge, Samuel Taylor, 39
Collected Works series, 179
Colombo, John Robert, 62; in *Who Was Marshall McLuhan?*, 59–60
Colossians 2:9, 20
"The Common Ground of McLuhan and Frye" (Guardiani), 49
communication: communion and, 22, 52, 167, 193, 230, 232–3; role of, 231–2; theatre of global communications, 18
communion: communication and, 22, 52, 167, 193, 230, 232–3; liturgy of, 265
complementarity, 10, 169–70, 172, 201, 210, 233
"Conclusion to a Literary History of Canada" (Frye, H.N.), 176, 194–5
confession, 278
Conrad, Joseph, 251
Conscientious Objections (Postman), 134
conspiracy, 88, 130; Masonic conspiracy theory, 114, 155–8, 160, 200
Contexts of Canadian Criticism (Mandel), 48
continuity, discontinuity versus, 40–1, 96, 132, 143–5, 147, 248
Cook, David, 47
Coppola, Francis Ford, 251
Cosmic Consciousness (Bucke), 187
cosmological code, theory of, 74
Counterblast (McLuhan, H.), 84–5, 154, 175, 269

Coupland, Douglas: biography by, 99, 287n4, 287n8; *Marshall McLuhan*, 37
Creation and Recreation (Frye, H.N.), 96
The Critical Path: An Essay on the Social Context of Literary Criticism (Frye, H.N.), 127, 142–3, 216
Critical Twilight: Explorations in the Ideology of Anglo-American Literary Theory from Eliot to McLuhan (Fekete), 99–103
critic-seer, 148, 190, 208, 228, 245
Cromwell, Oliver, 4, 45, 80
crucial time (*kairos*), 53
cruciform, 225–6
The Crying of Lot 49 (Pynchon), 155
Culture and Anarchy (Arnold), 164
Culture and Environment: The Training of Critical Awareness (Leavis, F.R.), 80
Culture Is Our Business (McLuhan, H.), 92, 191–2, 213
Curtius, Ernst Robert, 33, 141
"Cycle and Apocalypse in *Finnegans Wake*" (Frye, H.N.), 204

Dalhousie Review, 110, 150
Dante: *The Divine Comedy*, 119; influence of, 16, 17, 248; numerology and, 29; *Vita Nuova*, 16
Davis, Erik, 187
Death of a Discipline (Spivak), 266–9
"Death of the Author" (Barthes), 93
de Beauvoir, Simone, 101
de Broglie, Louis, 169
de Chirico, Giorgio, 222
Decline of the West (Spengler), 68
A Defence of Poetry (Shelley), 73–4
De Kerckhove, Derrick, 173
Deleuze, Gilles, 206–7

Index 341

DeLillo, Don, 155
Denham, Robert D., 173; interview with, 136; on Masonic conspiracy theory, 160; *Northrop Frye Unbuttoned* and, 77; observations by, 37, 38; *Religious Visionary and Architect of the Spiritual World*, 43–4, 195
Department of Health, Education and Welfare, US, 17
Derrida, Jacques, 75
"A Descent into the Maelstrom," (Poe), 38–9, 245
Le Devoir's "L'Anti-McLuhan" interview, 127, 138
DEW-line, 175–6
"The Dialectic of Belief and Vision" (Frye, H.N.), 128
Dickens, Charles, 101
Dickinson, Emily, 62, 151, 189, 207, 248
discontinuity: continuity versus, 40–1, 96, 132, 143–5, 147, 248; role of, 60
discovery: prospects of, 235; quests of, 5
divine comedy of criticism, 232, 249
The Divine Comedy (Dante), 119
Divisions on a Ground: Essays on Canadian Culture (Frye, H.N.), 174, 193–4
Dolzani, Michael, 44
Dostoyevsky, Fyodor, 101
The Double Vision (Frye, H.N.): eloquence of, 53; last sentences of, 228; observations in, 19, 44, 171, 197, 211, 277; publication of, 14, 76, 191, 228
dream-time of literature, 20, 107, 245
Dudek, Louis, 47, 62
Duffy, Dennis, 187
Dylan, Bob, 32

Eagleton, Terry, 75, 76
"East Coker" poems (Eliot), 200, 223
Easterbrook, W.T., 87
echoland, 265, 302n24
Eckhart, Meister, 1, 262
Eco, Umberto, 252, 254–6, 260
ecstatic metaphor, 107, 109, 137, 273, 305n47
educated imagination, 12, 56, 172, 228
The Educated Imagination (Frye, H.N.): observations on, 20, 146, 148, 211, 240; passages from, 183, 235; publication of, 72
education, theory on, 262–4
egg and chicken, 259
ego, 116
electronica, 16, 17, 22, 52
The Electronic Word: Democracy, Technology, and the Arts (Lanham), 164–5
Eliot, T.S.: "East Coker" poems, 200, 223; *Four Quartets*, 29, 151, 200, 215, 223, 225; influence of, 62, 84, 149, 189; "The Waste Land," 6, 121, 151; "What the Thunder Said," 232, 247
Elvin, Lionel, 82
Emerson, Ralph Waldo, 62, 144
emotions, quartet of, 28
epiphanies, 5–6, 13, 16, 27, 185
2 Esdras 14:25, 224
Essential McLuhan (McLuhan, E., and Zingrone), 213
Euripides, 31
European Literature and the Latin Middle Ages (Curtius), 33, 141
"Expanding Eyes" (Frye, H.N.), 222, 262–3, 292n19

Explorations project, 85, 87–8, 273
Extraterritorial (Steiner), 134

Fables of Identity (Frye, H.N.), 72, 282
Fearful Symmetry (Frye, H.N.), 14; coda of, 168; conclusion of, 39; as manifesto, 45; narrative structure in, 231; passages from, 148, 192, 280; publication of, 3, 66, 123; review of, 20, 86–7, 110–13, 117; utopian inner city of imagination in, 57; views on, 44, 146; writing of, 7, 69
Feigen, Gerald, 90
Fekete, John, 47, 48, 193, 252; *The Critical Twilight*, 99–103; "Massage in the Mass Age: Remembering the McLuhan Matrix," 103
fictions, 31
Finnegans Wake (Joyce): allusion to, 178; influence of, 8, 101, 151, 178, 183, 201–11, 242, 249, 262, 283; publication of, 82; thunder in, 202, 215, 247
First Corinthians: 12:31, 13:4–7, 13:13, 38; 15: 51, 34–5
First Nations' peoples, 23, 219
"A fish is never aware of water," 38
Fishwick, Marshall, 219
Fitzgerald, F. Scott, 62
Flahiff, Frederick, 115, 127
Fletcher, Angus, 71
"Flush-Profile" essay. *See* "Have with You to Madison Avenue or The Flush-Profile of Literature"
Foucault, Michel, 63
four levels of exegesis, 29–34, 289n13; allegoric level, 29, 31, 33; anagogic level, 29, 31–2; literal level, 29, 30–1, 33; moral level, 29, 30–1

Four Quartets (Eliot), 29, 151, 215, 225; "East Coker" poems in, 200, 223
fours, role of, 27–33, 224–7
Freud, Sigmund: critics of, 30; Frye, H.N., and, 252–3; influence of, 36, 111, 121
From Cliché to Archetype (McLuhan, H., and Watson, W.), 48, 92, 120–3, 158, 213, 232, 238
frontiers, 9, 54
Frye, Helen (wife): death of, 75, 278, 311n45; letter to, 45–6; role of, 6, 68
Frye, H. Northrop: "Across the River and out of the Trees," 179–80; aphorisms and, 12, 144–6; *Architecture of the Spiritual World*, 228; background of, 3–6, 55; backstory of, 65–7; on Bible, 29, 72–6, 102, 151, 196–8; biography of, 64, 67–79; Blake and, 3, 7, 14, 32, 44–6, 69–74, 78, 150–1, 184, 292n19; "Blake's Bible," 108; *The Bush Garden*, 46, 174–6; Cayley interview with, 9, 61, 91, 96, 143, 148, 232, 295n28; CBC Radio's *Sunday Morning* interview of, 134–5; centenary of, 161; "Conclusion to a Literary History of Canada," 176, 194–5; *Creation and Recreation*, 96; *The Critical Path*, 127, 142–3, 216; "Cycle and Apocalypse in *Finnegans Wake*," 204; death of, 10, 76; *Le Devoir's* "L'Anti-McLuhan" interview of, 127, 138; "The Dialectic of Belief and Vision," 128; diaries of, 127; *Divisions on a Ground*, 174, 193–4; *The Double Vision*, 14, 19, 44, 53, 76, 171, 191, 197, 211, 228, 277;

dualism of, 47; *The Educated Imagination*, 20, 72, 146, 148, 183, 211, 235, 240; "Expanding Eyes," 222, 262–3, 292n19; *Fables of Identity*, 72, 282; family of, 63, 67, 68, 76, 223; Freud and, 252–3; *A Glorious and Terrible Life with You*, 68; Governor General's Award for, 37, 75; installation address by, 71–2; journal of, 5; "The Language of Poetry," 87; lecture by, 171; meteoric theoretical ascendancy of, 66; motto of, 149; *Myth and Metaphor: Selected Essays*, 108, 128, 132–3, 204; *Northrop Frye on Shakespeare*, 75; *Northrop Frye Unbuttoned*, 77, 144, 189–91, 203; notebooks of, 40, 46, 48, 73, 77; *On Canada*, 179; at Oxford University, 4, 69, 80, 181; prodigiousness of, 39; Protestantism and, 46, 67, 92, 154, 196–7; *Reading the World: Selected Writings*, 199; reputation of, 75, 79, 161, 297n45, 299nn11–12; *The Secular Scripture*, 74; *Spiritus Mundi*, 222, 262–3, 292n19; *The Stubborn Structure*, 74; summary of, 106–9; "Third Book" Notebooks, 1964–1972, 77, 133, 137, 146, 185, 212–13, 235–6, 246; *T.S. Eliot*, 72, 225, 231, 244; as United Church minister, 9, 60, 68, 73, 118, 157, 194, 228, 293; at University of Toronto, 3–5, 8–9, 24, 35, 37, 41, 69–72; "The View from Here," 138–9; *The Well-Tempered Critic*, 72; *Who Was Marshall McLuhan?* and, 143; wrestling with, 24–7, 277. *See also Anatomy of Criticism; Fearful Symmetry; The Great Code: The Bible and Literature; Late Notebooks, 1982–1990*; McLuhan-Frye alchemy; McLuhan-Frye association; McLuhan-Frye conflict; *The Modern Century; Notebooks; Words with Power*
Fuller, Buckminster, 269

Garabedian, John, 126
Garden of Gethsemane, 50–1, 284
garrison mentality, 174–6
Genesis 28, 57
Genesis 32: allusions to, 272; Jacob in, 25–6, 54, 247, 280
genius, 78
Genius: A Mosaic of One Hundred Exemplary Critical Minds (Bloom), 157, 293n19
Gershwin, George, 251
Gibson, William, 67
Ginsberg, Allen, 251
Giovanelli, Felix, 86
"G.K. Chesterton: A Practical Mystic" (McLuhan, H.), 168, 214
globalization, 159, 259
global theatre, 10; borderless, 269; change in, 118; impacts of, 174, 228, 257, 266, 282; ramping up of, 58
The Global Village: Transformations in World Life and Media in the 21st Century (McLuhan, H., and Powers): accusations in, 124; finishing of, 96; four levels of exegesis in, 29; hearer and seer in, 50; observations in, 62, 65, 175, 178, 213; passages from, 18, 158, 271–2; publication of, 97
global village, 129, 259
The Globe and Mail, 74, 297n45
A Glorious and Terrible Life with You (Frye, H.N., and Kemp), 68

Gnosticism, 112, 153–4, 156–7
gold, 265
Gordon, W. Terrence, 234; *Marshall McLuhan: Escape into Understanding*, 37, 89, 109; on reviews, 87
Gossage, Howard Luck, 90
Governor General's Award, 37, 75
Grant, George, 74, 194; *Lament for a Nation*, 131
Graves, Robert, 87
Gravity's Rainbow (Pynchon), 59, 74
Great Code: aspects of, 102, 248; identity and, 7, 16, 40, 231, 237–8; meaning of, 42; "medium is the message" and, 41, 185, 230, 237, 248, 275; story, 20, 231, 239–46, 284; views on, 73, 269
great Spirit of creation, 7
The Great Code: The Bible and Literature (Frye, H.N.): final pages of, 273; four levels of exegesis in, 29, 289n13; influence of, 196; *kerygma* in, 19; preparation of, 96; publication of, 211, 228; review of, 74; title of, 239; views on, 19, 146
Guardiani, Francesco, 49
Guattari, Félix, 206–7
The Gutenberg Elegies: The Fate of Reading in an Electronic Age (Birkerts), 134
The Gutenberg Galaxy (McLuhan, H.): Governor General's Award for, 37; observations in, 48, 191, 202; original title for, 88; publication of, 18, 66–7, 96, 99; review of, 88, 128

Hacktivism, 256
Hall, Edward, 195
Hamilton, A.C.: insights of, 216–17; *Northrop Frye: Anatomy of His Criticism*, 21, 74, 227

Harpur, Tom, 196, 198–9
Hart, Jonathan, 132
Hart House debate, 92
"Have with You to Madison Avenue or The Flush-Profile of Literature" (McLuhan, H.), 113–16, 158
hearer and seer, 50–1, 138, 229
Hebrews 12–1, 14
Hemingway, Ernest, 62, 180
Heretics (Chesterton), 199
"Hermetic Melancholy" (De Chirico), 222
Hesse, Hermann, 190
Hildegard von Bingen, 69, 116, 262
Holzer, Jenny, 214
Homer: *The Iliad*, 31; influence of, 31, 51, 189, 248; *The Odyssey*, 31, 33–4
Hopkins, Gerard Manley, 81, 110, 149
Hoskins, Hubert, 196
hubris, 15, 38, 116, 190
Hulme, T.E., 62
humanism, 13, 102, 199; goal of, 16, 262; intentions, 23; restoring, 266–75; traditions, 48
"The Humanities in The Electronic Age" (McLuhan, H.), 53–4
Hutcheon, Linda, 46–7, 175
Hutchon, Kathryn, 56, 92
Huxley, Aldous, 58, 220
hybrid energy, 21, 251

I Ching, 137
iconoclasm, 12, 43, 89, 156, 185, 206
identity: Canadian, 35, 100, 272–3; Great Code and, 7, 16, 40, 231, 237–8; online, 274; search for, 7, 14–15, 39, 56; views on, 65–6
identity code, 185

Ignatieff, Michael, 97
The Iliad (Homer), 31
iLiteracy, 51–4, 93; announcement of, 114; dawning, 232; new ground of, 164; nihilistic aspects of, 257; as term, 297n48
imagination: Coleridge on, 39; educated, 12, 56, 172, 228; literature and, 5, 7, 13, 268; utopian inner city of, 57
Innis, Harold: influence of, 40, 87, 180, 295n27; Toronto School of Communication Theory and, 9, 232
"Inside Blake and Hollywood" (McLuhan, H.), 110–13
inspiration, 8, 276
intellectual-spiritual centre (*omphalos*), 3
intensified consciousness: conditions of, 5; edge of, 11–13
The Interior Landscape: The Literary Criticism of Marshall McLuhan, 1943–1962 (McLuhan, H.), 81
International Northrop Frye Festival, 67
"Introduction: The Field Notes of a Public Critic" (Hutcheon), 46–7, 175
invisible school, 98, 173, 217
De Italorum Sapientia (Vico), 209

Jackson, Stonewall, 180, 252–4
Jacob (fictional character): in Genesis 28, 57; in Genesis 32, 25–6, 54, 247, 280
James, William, 278
"James Joyce: Trivial and Quadrivial" (McLuhan, H.), 33
Jameson, Fredric, 66, 75, 252–4, 260, 262

Janus (god), 60–1
Jeffrey, Liss, 173
"Jerusalem" (Blake), 70
Jesus, 198
jokes, 6, 8
Joyce, James: influence of, 4, 17, 62, 189, 248; *A Portrait of the Artist as a Young Man*, 16–17, 178, 206; puns of, 33; *Ulysses*, 150, 151, 202, 208, 312n45. See also *Finnegans Wake*
Jung, Carl G., 121, 123

K. (Calasso), 42
Kabbalah, 26, 30
Kafka, Franz, 42, 144, 242, 284
kairos (crucial time), 53
Kelly, Kevin, 97
Kemp, Helen, 45, 68. See also Frye, Helen
Kenner, Hugh, 171
The Kenyon Review, 110
Keogh, J.G., 200
kerygma (apocalyptic proclamation): example of, 130, 190; references to, 19, 20, 98, 184, 228, 265, 289n8
Kierkegaard, Sören, 23, 144
Kostelanetz, Richard, 126
Krieger, Murray, 71
Kroker, Arthur, 173, 214, 260
Kroker, MariLouise, 173, 214, 260
Kuhns, William, 218

Lacan, Jacques, 75
Lamberti, Elena, 173; *Marshall McLuhans Mosaic*, 188
Lament for a Nation (Grant), 131
Lampman, Archibald, 129
Language and Silence (Steiner), 134
"The Language of Poetry" (Frye, H.N.), 87

Lanham, Richard A., 164–5
Late Notebooks, 1982–1990 (Frye, H.N.): coda to volume 2 of, 77; passages from, 20, 38, 44, 136, 145, 151, 170, 194–5, 236–7, 242, 311n45; on reviews, 74–5; subjects in, 104, 106
Laugh-In (TV show), 8
Laws of Media: The New Science (McLuhan, H.), 29; accusations of, 124; finishing of, 96, 143; McLuhan, E., and, 93, 97, 124, 143; overview of, 92–3, 105, 213; passages from, 247–8; "Proteus Unbound" chapter of, 58; subtitle for, 97, 143, 209
Layton, Irving, 62, 179
Leaves of Grass (Whitman), 30, 119, 170, 189
Leavis, F.R.: *Culture and Environment*, 80; influence of, 79–80, 300n24
Leavis, Queenie, 301n24
Lee, Alvin, 37, 38, 44
Lee, Dennis, 66, 179
Lee, Stan, 251
Lennon, John, 146
Letters of Marshall McLuhan (McLuhan, H.), 96–7, 149
Lewis, Corinne. *See* McLuhan, Corinne
Lewis, C.S., 80
Lewis, Percy Wyndham: background of, 179; influence of, 62, 84–5, 89, 189, 303n29; *Men Without Art*, 123; *Self-Condemned*, 84
Libra (DeLillo), 155
Life of Apollonius of Tyana (Philostratus), 1
"Like a Rolling Stone" (Dylan), 32
The Listener debate, 48, 124, 127, 139, 142, 281

literacy, 275. *See also* iLiteracy
literal man, 123, 125, 166, 188, 191, 200, 232, 283
literary studies: future of, 51–2, 182; impact on, 221; specialization in, 8, 66, 89, 118, 263
literature: dream-time of, 20, 107, 245; goal of, 29; imagination and, 5, 7, 13, 268; unity of, 69
Le Livre, Instrument Spirituel (Mallarmé), 73–4, 189
Logan, Robert K., 117, 173
London Observer, 97
Luke 13–24, 14
Lyotard, Jean-Francois, 75–6

Macdonald, Dwight, 62
McCarthy, Mary, 62
McLuhan, Corinne (wife): death of, 85; interviews with, 228–9, 298n5; letters and marriage to, 84; role of, 6
McLuhan, Elsie (mother): influence of, 79; letters to, 5, 86, 300n23
McLuhan, Eric (son), 173, 234; *City as Classroom*, 56, 92; *Essential McLuhan*, 213; *Laws of Media* and, 93, 97, 124, 143; on Lennon and Ono's visit, 146; "Marshall McLuhan's Theory of Communication: The Yegg," 310n45; observations of, 113, 182; *The Role of Thunder in Finnegans Wake*, 247
McLuhan, H. Marshall: "An Ancient Quarrel in Modern America (Sophists vs. Grammarians)," 162; aphorisms and, 6, 12, 17, 29, 34, 40–1, 46, 52, 95, 144–6, 185, 191–2, 249, 259, 294n19; Babin interview with, 118, 249–50; background of,

3–6; backstory of, 65–7; biography of, 36–7, 64, 79–99; Blake and, 14, 81, 153; *The Book of Probes*, 8, 17, 105, 119, 188, 211–12, 226, 231, 233–4, 276–7; at Cambridge University, 4, 29, 56, 80, 81–2, 84, 301n24; Catholicism and, 3, 46, 82–4, 91, 97, 154–5, 157, 159–60, 195, 200; as celebrity, 12, 35, 113, 127, 134, 165, 220, 232, 261; centenary of, 161; *City as Classroom*, 56, 92; *The Classical Trivium*, 29, 33, 43, 56, 283; *From Cliché to Archetype*, 48, 92, 120–3, 158, 213, 232, 238; *Counterblast*, 84–5, 154, 175, 269; *Culture Is Our Business*, 92, 191–2, 213; death of, 9, 10, 76, 90, 96, 134, 199, 281; electronica and, 16, 17, 22, 52; family of, 63, 79, 85, 88, 96, 223; "G.K. Chesterton: A Practical Mystic," 168, 214; *The Gutenberg Galaxy*, 18, 37, 48, 66–7, 88, 96, 99, 128, 202; as half-thinker, 91–2, 93, 143; "Have with You to Madison Avenue or The Flush-Profile of Literature," 113–16, 158; home of, 85, 229; "The Humanities in The Electronic Age," 53–4; illnesses of, 91, 95, 96, 179, 216, 278, 311n45; "Inside Blake and Hollywood," 110–13; *The Interior Landscape*, 81; Internet cliché about, 274; "James Joyce: Trivial and Quadrivial," 33; *Letters of Marshall McLuhan*, 96–7, 149; Marfleet Lectures by, 9; *Marshall McLuhan Unbound*, 110; as media guru, 8, 18; *The Medium and the Light*, 200–1, 210; *The Medium is the Massage*, 90, 147, 194, 237, 273; motto of, 149; *Playboy* interview of, 118; "Pound, Eliot, and the Rhetoric of *The Waste Land* ," 29; prodigiousness of, 39; reputation of, 91, 96, 110, 153, 179, 297n45; ROPUNM, 17, 18–19, 88, 99, 117; Saint Louis University and, 3, 84, 303n28; summary of, 104–6; *Take Today*, 92, 147, 213–14, 228, 233–4, 238; on typographic man, 52, 88, 114; at University of Toronto, 3–5, 8–9, 24, 35, 37, 41, 85–7, 89, 97–8; *Through the Vanishing Point*, 105, 154, 183, 192, 213; *War and Peace in the Global Village*, 189, 202, 247; wrestling with, 24–7, 277. *See also The Global Village*; *Laws of Media*; *The Mechanical Bride*; *Understanding Media*

McLuhan, Maurice (brother), 79; *Who Was Marshall McLuhan?*, 57, 59–60, 143

McLuhan, or Modernism in Reverse (Willmott), 47–8, 88, 176, 187

McLuhan, T.C., 173

McLuhanacy, 131

McLuhanesque, 134, 147, 164–5

McLuhan-Frye alchemy, 11, 24, 27, 233, 236, 251, 257

McLuhan-Frye association: call to restore wonder and, 184–201; charismatic personalities and, 180–4, 264; comparisons and, 3–10, 35–43, 53–4; dynamics of, 169–73; meetings and, 3–5, 8, 35, 171; no followers and, 217–24; numerology and, 27–33, 224–9; references to, 46, 97; studies of, 46–9, 99–104; styles and, 26, 211–17, 279; synergy and, 35, 41, 230–75, 284; theories and, 218, 310n45

McLuhan-Frye conflict, 110–68; as ancient quarrel, 161–8; continuation of, 142–4; crux of, 110–13; direction of thought and, 149–53; Frye's counterblast, 125–39; McLuhan's blast, 113–25; observations on, 13–16, 37–8, 90; orator and theorist in, 144–9; paranoia and, 153–61; subtextual reading of, 279–80
McLuhan: Hot & Cool, 90, 218
McLuhan in Space: A Cultural Geography (Cavell), 48
McLuhanism, 37, 90, 131, 139, 260
McLuhanisme, 219
McLuhan: Pro and Con, 90
McLuhan Studies, 49
maelstrom, 33; metaphor, 45
Magic and Myth of the Movies (Tyler), 110, 113
Magister Ludi (Hesse), 190
Magnetic City, 303n29; data overload in, 149; references to, 120, 184, 186, 232–3, 238, 247–8, 267, 273; Toronto as, 11
Mailer, Norman, 62
Mallarmé, Stéphane, 75, 227; *Le Livre, Instrument Spirituel*, 73–4, 189
Malraux, Ándre, 101
mandala, 42
Mandel, Eli, 48
Manichaeism, 111, 112, 133, 153
The Man Without Qualities (Musil), 202
A Map of Misreading (Bloom), 291n19
Marchand, Philip: biography by, 80, 82, 92, 97, 116, 127, 156, 187; *Marshall McLuhan: The Medium and the Messenger*, 36, 115
Marchessault, Janine, 19, 83, 88, 188, 226–7

Marfleet Lectures, 9
Maritain, Jacques, 118
The Marriage of Heaven and Hell (Blake), 14, 45, 78, 116, 150
Marshall McLuhan (Coupland), 37
Marshall McLuhan (Duffy), 187
Marshall McLuhan: Cosmic Media (Marchessault), 19, 83, 88, 188, 226–7
Marshall McLuhan: Escape into Understanding (Gordon), 37, 89, 109
Marshall McLuhans Mosaic: Probing the Literary Origins of Media Studies (Lamberti), 188
"Marshall McLuhan's Theory of Communication: The Yegg" (McLuhan, E.), 310n45
Marshall McLuhan: The Medium and the Messenger (Marchand), 36, 115
Marshall McLuhan Unbound (McLuhan, H.), 110
Marshall McLuhan Way, 10, 55–6, 97, 279
Marxism, 30, 91, 100, 104, 304n33
Masonic conspiracy theory, 114, 155–8, 160, 200
"Massage in the Mass Age: Remembering the McLuhan Matrix" (Fekete), 103
maze, 33; sealed maze metaphor, 45
The Mechanical Bride: The Folklore of Industrial Man (McLuhan, H.): drafts for, 295n27; original title of, 35; passage from, 170–1; preface to, 38; publication of, 3, 87
"Media Burn" (Ant Farm), 67
media echology, 213
media ecology, 188, 211, 229, 234
The Media Symplex: At the Edge of Meaning in the Age of Chaos (Zingrone), 157–8

Medium Cool, 67
"medium is the message," 6; Great Code and, 41, 185, 230, 237, 248, 275; meaning of, 104–5, 158, 255, 258, 283; "user is content" and, 191, 219; views on, 11, 17, 41–3, 128, 131
The Medium and the Light: Reflections on Religion (McLuhan, H.), 200–1, 210
The Medium is the Massage (McLuhan, H.), 90, 147, 194, 237, 273
Melville, Herman, 62
Mental Traveller, 32, 58, 78, 261
Men Without Art (Lewis, P.), 123
meta-narratives, 31
metaphor: of Book of Nature, 119; ecstatic, 107, 109, 137, 273, 305n47; gold as, 265; maelstrom, 45; role of, 148, 171; sealed maze, 45; use of, 106, 108, 128, 130, 198, 217
metaphysical drama, 109–10
Miale, Walter, 126
Miller, Henry, 62
Miller, Jonathan, 91
Milton, John: influence of, 150, 189, 248; *Paradise Lost*, 140, 151, 243, 291n19
misquotations, 95, 146, 147, 218
mnemonic devices, 41–2
The Modern Century (Frye, H.N.): commentary in, 48, 126–7, 129, 135, 136, 139; conclusion to, 173–4, 178; introduction to, 132; oracular mode in, 215; publication in French, 138
monism, 111
Montaigne, 22
Moore, George, 199
Morrison, Toni, 189

Muggeridge, Malcolm, 96
Muller-Thym, Bernard, 261
Musil, Robert, 202
Myth and Metaphor: Selected Essays (Frye, H.N.), 108, 128, 132–3, 204

Naked Lunch (Burroughs), 190
narcissism, 130
Nashe, Thomas, 56, 92, 161, 209
National Association of Educational Broadcasters, 17
Nevitt, Barrington: *Take Today*, 92, 147, 213, 228, 233–4, 238; *Who Was Marshall McLuhan?*, 57, 59–60, 143
New Literary History, 29
Nietzsche, Friedrich: influence of, 23, 36, 42, 64, 144; *Thus Spoke Zarathustra*, 25
Nin, Anais, 62
noosphere, 159, 172, 187, 264, 267, 307n42
"Norrie Frye – what a guy," 8
Northrop Frye (Bates), 66
Northrop Frye: A Biography (Ayre), 37
Northrop Frye: Anatomy of His Criticism (Hamilton), 21, 74, 227
"Northrop Frye and the Toronto School of Communication Theory" (Siegel), 98
Northrop Frye Hall, 10, 55, 56, 97, 279
Northrop Frye in Conversation (Cayley), 57, 78–9, 151
Northrop Frye on Shakespeare (Frye, H.N.), 75
Northrop Frye Unbuttoned (Frye, H.N.), 77, 144, 189–91, 203
Notebooks and Lectures on the Bible and Other Religious Texts (Frye, H.N.), 238; aphorisms in, 12; genius in, 78; last sections of, 196; passages

from, 8, 44, 133, 136, 137, 177, 185, 249–50, 270–1; publication of, 197
Numbers 11:29, 280
numerology, 27–33, 224–9. *See also* fours, role of; tetrads

Occupy Wall Street movement (2011), 256
The Odyssey (Homer), 31, 33–4
O'Grady, Jean, 179
omphalos (intellectual-spiritual centre), 3
On Canada (Frye, H.N.), 179
O'Neill, John, 99
Ong, Walter: letters to, 112, 126, 153, 154, 210; relationship with, 303n28, 307n42
online identity, 274
Ono, Yoko, 146
opinions, 30
oracular criticism, 215
orators: theorist and, 144–9; writers and, 161–8, 211
Orc cycle of revolution and reaction, 22
Orthodoxy (Chesterton), 199
otherness, 267
Ovid, 31, 189, 248
Oxford University, 4, 69, 80, 181

The Pagan Christ: Recovering the Lost Light (Harpur), 196
Paglia, Camille, 67, 214
paideuma (vortex of prophetic knowledge), 10, 98, 282
parabola, 244
Paradise Lost (Milton), 140, 151, 243, 291n19
paranoia, 153–61
Parker, Harley, 85

Paroxysm (Petit), 256
participation mystique, 158
Pascal, Blaise, 22
The Passion of the Western Mind (Tarnas), 275
Pater, Walter, 224
Pelham, Edgar, 68
Penseroso mood, 221
Pentecostal, as term, 27, 34
Pentecostal dove, 29
Pentecostal gift, 28–9
Perloff, Marjorie, 79–80, 300n24
Pessoa, Fernando, 202
Petit, Phillippe, 256
Philostratus, 1
Picasso, Pablo, 62, 154, 251, 272
planetarity, 266–8
Plato, 23
Playboy interview, 118
Poe, Edgar Allen, 38–9, 245
poetry: quotations of, 6; role of, 30, 33, 54, 80–2
Polanyi, John, 145
polemos, meanings for, 121, 138
The Political Unconscious: Narrative as a Socially Symbolic Act (Jameson), 252–4
Pollock, Jackson, 251
polysemous, 28, 289n13
A Portrait of the Artist as a Young Man (Joyce), 16–17, 178, 206
Postman, Neil, 134
postmodernism, 31, 75
The Post-Modernist Condition: A Report on Knowledge (Lyotard), 75–6
Pound, Dorothy Shakespear, 182
Pound, Ezra: *Cantos*, 202; influence of, 62, 70, 90; letters to, 87, 155
"Pound, Eliot, and the Rhetoric of *The Waste Land*" (McLuhan, H.), 29
Powers, Bruce R. *See The Global Village*

Practical Criticism (Richards), 80
Pratt, E.J., 179
probe, as term, 137, 144
prophecy, 270–2
Protestantism, 46, 67, 92, 154, 196–7
Proust, Marcel, 62, 171
Proverbs: 4:7, 296n29; 9:13, 224
"Proverbs of Hell" (Blake), 70, 301n24
puns and witticism, 6, 33, 65
Pynchon, Thomas, 189; *The Crying of Lot 49*, 155; *Gravity's Rainbow*, 59, 74

quest-conflict structure, 14–16

radical illumination, 41, 67–8
ratios of sacred learning, 224
reading: impacts of, 41, 69, 107, 151; role of, 7–8, 16, 22, 107, 198, 227, 245; on screen, 273–4; subtextual, of McLuhan-Frye conflict, 279–80; yogic importance of, 185
Reading the World: Selected Writings (Frye, H.N.), 199
Rebel Art Centre, London, 89
Religious Visionary and Architect of the Spiritual World (Denham), 43–4, 195
Report on Project in Understanding New Media (ROPUNM) (McLuhan, H.), 17, 18–19, 88, 99, 117
Revelation (Bible), 21
revolution, 146. *See also* Orc cycle of revolution and reaction
Richards, I.A., 79–80
ricorso, 206–8, 254
Rimbaud, Arthur, 23, 30, 94, 149, 241
The Role of Thunder in Finnegans Wake (McLuhan, E.), 247
Rolling Stone magazine, 32

romance-quest: meanings of, 66, 268; structure of, 34, 231; views of, 14–15, 20, 225, 254, 263, 270, 275
Romantics, 41, 45, 81–2
A Room of One's Own (Woolf), 267
ROPUNM. *See Report on Project in Understanding New Media*

sacred geometry, 28
Said, Edward, 66, 298n8
"Sailing to Byzantium" (Yeats), 56, 264
Saint Clair Illumination, 73–4
Saint Louis University, 3, 84, 303n28
Saint Michael's College, 55, 60, 85, 194
Salusinzky, Irme, 293n19
Sartre, Jean-Paul, 101
satire, 45, 218–20, 222–3
Saurat, Denis: *Blake and Milton*, 181; *Blake and Modern Thought*, 68, 181
Schafer, R. Murray, 67
Schick, Dan, 228
Schrödinger, Erwin, 169
Science and the Modern World (Whitehead), 191
The Secular Scripture (Frye, H.N.), 74
seer: hearer and, 50–1, 138, 229; intentions of, 15; mode of, 21; as term, 27; tradition, 48. *See also* critic-seer; visionary-seer tradition
Self-Condemned (Lewis, P.), 84
September 11, 2001, 121
Sewanee Review, 86
Shaffer, Peter, 280
Shakespeare, William: five-part structure of plays by, 226; influence of, 151, 189, 248; round theatre for, 265; *The Tempest*, 107, 136, 151, 182, 208
shamans, 23

Shelley, Percy Bysshe, 73–4, 100, 189
Siegel, Arthur, 98
Simulations (Baudrillard), 256
singing school, 56, 98, 264
Sitwell, Edith, 66
solipsism, 111, 118, 245
Sontag, Susan, 62
Sophocles, 31
soul: revision of, 7; views on, 49, 116; in wisdom tradition, 28
Spengler, Oswald, 68
Spiritus Mundi: Essays on Literature, Myth, and Society (Frye, H.N.), 222, 262–3, 292n19
Spivak, Gayatri Chakravorty, 266–9
Staines, David, 179, 228–9
Stamps, Judith, 91
Stein, Gertrude, 62, 80
Steiner, George: *Extraterritorial*, 134; *Language and Silence*, 134; observations by, 9, 67, 92, 187, 304n35
Stewart, Margaret, 93
Stowe, Harriet Beecher, 62
The Stubborn Structure (Frye, H.N.), 74
styles, McLuhan-Frye, 26, 211–17, 279
summas, 23, 104–9, 221–2
super-Nature: electronic, 5, 6, 33, 150, 189; Hyper-Text of, 7
Suzuki, D.T., 245
synchronicity, 234, 250
syncretism, 235, 263, 264
synergy, McLuhan-Frye, 35, 41, 230–75, 284

Take Today: The Executive as Dropout (McLuhan, H., and Nevitt), 92, 147, 213, 228, 233–4, 238
Tarnas, Richard, 275
Taylor, Charles, 62

Techgnosis: Myth, Magic and Mysticism in the Age of Information (Davis), 187
technologies: high-definition and low-definition, 105; impacts of, 6, 8, 43, 52
Teilhard de Chardin, Pierre, 159, 187, 264, 267, 307n42
television, 18; content of, 128; effects of, 93, 258; rejection of, 133–4; sensory grounding of, 89
The Tempest (Shakespeare), 107, 136, 151, 182, 208
Teresa of Avila, 116
tetrads, 28, 92–3, 209, 226
Theall, Donald, 66, 103, 156, 298n4
"Third Book" Notebooks, 1964–1972 (Frye, H.N.): mission in, 146; passages from, 77, 133, 137, 185, 212–13, 235–6, 246
Thomism, 56, 104, 142, 158
Thompson, William Irwin, 67
Thoreau, Henry, 62
three A's (anxiety, alienation, and absurdity), 106, 172
Through the Vanishing Point (McLuhan, H.), 105, 154, 183, 192, 213
thunder, 202, 215, 247
Thus Spoke Zarathustra (Nietzsche), 25
Times Square, New York City, 258
Tiresias, 33, 51
Torah, 225
Toronto: CN Tower in, 57–9, 98, 172; as Magnetic City, 11; as *omphalos*, 3; recognitions in, 55–62
Toronto School of Communication Theory, 162, 265; critics of, 261; Innis and, 9, 232; philosophers of, 252; promotion of, 217
The Toronto School of Communication Theory: Interpretations, Extensions,

Applications (Watson, R., and Blondheim), 97–8
"Towards a Semiological Guerrilla Warfare" (Eco), 254–6
Tractatus Logico-Philosophicus (Wittgenstein), 300n24
transcendentalism, 62, 100
Trudeau, Pierre Elliott: interviews with, 298n5; letters to, 43, 177, 179, 200; supporter of, 157
"The Truth shall Make You Frye" placard, 79
T.S. Eliot (Frye, H.N.), 72, 225, 231, 244
Tyler, Parker, 110, 113
typographic man, 52, 88, 114
Tyrwhitt, Jacqueline, 87

Ulysses (Joyce), 151; end of, 202; "Proteus" episode of, 150; "Scylla and Charybdis" episode of, 312n45
Understanding Media: The Extensions of Man (McLuhan, H.), 37; critics of, 102, 186; "Hybrid Energy" chapter of, 236; narcissism in, 130; passages from, 34, 186–9, 191, 196; publication of, 18, 66–7, 89, 99; "Spoken Word" section of, 159, 186–7
United Church, 3, 60, 68, 73, 118, 157, 194, 228, 293
University of Being and Becoming, 172, 261–6
University of Toronto, 266; Centre for Culture and Technology at, 41, 89, 93, 96, 117, 135, 295n29; Frye, H.N., at, 3–5, 8–9, 24, 35, 37, 41, 69–72; McLuhan, H., at, 3–5, 8–9, 24, 35, 37, 41, 85–7, 89, 97–8; Saint Michael's College at, 55, 60, 85, 194; Victoria College at, 3, 8, 9, 41, 68, 71–2, 158, 196

University of Toronto Quarterly, 110, 179
The University of Toronto Graduate, 135
"user is content," 190–1, 205, 268; "medium is the message" and, 191, 219

verum factum principle, 109, 178, 198, 209–10, 221, 233
Vico, Giambattista, 108, 111, 202, 215, 227; *De Italorum Sapientia*, 209
Victoria College, 3, 8, 9, 41, 68, 71–2, 158, 196
"The View from Here" (Frye, H.N.), 138–9
Virgil, 31, 56, 152, 189
visionary: conditions for, 27; as term, 27, 43
visionary-apocalyptic tradition, 11, 40, 273
visionary-prophetic tradition, 35, 161, 237, 269
visionary-seer tradition, 230
Vita Nuova (Dante), 16
vortex of prophetic knowledge (*paideuma*), 10, 98, 282

War and Peace in the Global Village (McLuhan, H.), 189, 202, 247
"The Waste Land" (Eliot), 6, 121, 151
Watson, Rita, 97–8
Watson, Sheila, 97
Watson, Wilfred: *From Cliché to Archetype*, 48, 92, 120–3, 158, 213, 232, 238; letter to, 117, 124–5
The Waves (Woolf), 202
"The Way," 225
Weil, Simone, 144
The Well-Tempered Critic (Frye, H.N.), 72
The Western Canon (Bloom), 72
What Is Literature? (Sartre), 101

"What the Thunder Said" (Eliot), 232, 247
Whidden Lectures, McMaster University, 129, 133, 135
Whitehead, A.N., 191, 238
white spaces, 40, 51, 205–7, 210, 217, 273
Whitman, Walt, 62, 78; *Leaves of Grass*, 30, 119, 170, 189
Who Was Marshall McLuhan? (McLuhan, M. and Nevitt): Colombo in, 59–60; Frye, H.N., and, 143; passage from, 57
Wilde, Oscar, 144, 164
wild pitch, 238–9, 277
Williams, Carl, 87
Willmott, Glenn, 47–8, 88, 176, 187
Wimsatt, W.K., 123
Wired magazine, 97, 125
wisdom tradition, 12; lesson of, 30; references to, 42, 58; soul in, 28; two truths of, 284
Wittgenstein, Ludwig, 79–80, 300n24
Wittgenstein's Ladder: Poetic Language and the Strangeness of the Ordinary (Perloff), 79–80, 300n24
witticism. *See* puns and witticism

Wolfe, Tom, 90, 99, 140
Woolf, Virginia, 4, 62; *A Room of One's Own*, 267; *The Waves*, 202
Words with Power: Being a Second Study of "The Bible and Literature" (Frye, H.N.), 126; fourfold chaptering in, 226; four levels of exegesis in, 29; "Fourth Variation: The Furnace" chapter of, 236; influence of, 196; notebook entry written during, 216, 245–6; observations in, 19, 57, 198, 217, 254; passages from, 152, 203; publication of, 74, 211, 228; "Spirit and Symbol" chapter of, 215

Yates, Frances A., 41, 265, 295n28, 314n18
Yeats, William Butler: "The Circus Animals' Desertion," 59; influence of, 34, 225; "Sailing to Byzantium," 56, 264

Zarathustra, 219, 222
Zingrone, Frank: *Essential McLuhan*, 213; *The Media Symplex*, 157–8
Zola, Émile, 101

www.ingramcontent.com/pod-product-compliance
Lightning Source LLC
Chambersburg PA
CBHW030301080526
44584CB00012B/399